3rd
EDITION

ASSET BUILDING
& COMMUNITY
DEVELOPMENT

26 in 26
Neighborhood Resource Centers
26 Neighborhood Strategies in a 26 month time frame
A Grant Funded by the LSTA
(Library Services & Technology Act)

Riverside Public Library

3rd
EDITION

ASSET BUILDING
& COMMUNITY
DEVELOPMENT

Gary Paul Green
University of Wisconsin–Madison

Anna Haines
University of Wisconsin–Stevens Point

Los Angeles | London | New Delhi
Singapore | Washington DC

Los Angeles | London | New Delhi
Singapore | Washington DC

FOR INFORMATION:

SAGE Publications, Inc.
2455 Teller Road
Thousand Oaks, California 91320
E-mail: order@sagepub.com

SAGE Publications Ltd.
1 Oliver's Yard
55 City Road
London EC1Y 1SP
United Kingdom

SAGE Publications India Pvt. Ltd.
B 1/I 1 Mohan Cooperative
Industrial Area
Mathura Road, New Delhi 110 044
India

SAGE Publications Asia-Pacific Pte. Ltd.
33 Pekin Street #02-01
Far East Square
Singapore 048763

Acquisitions Editor: Lisa Cuevas Shaw
Editorial Assistant: MaryAnn Vail
Production Editor: Astrid Virding
Copy Editor: Gillian Dickens
Permissions Editor: Karen Ehrmann
Typesetter: C&M Digitals (P) Ltd.
Proofreader: Ellen Birk
Indexer: Gloria Tierney
Cover Designer: Gail Buschman
Marketing Manager: Helen Salmon

Copyright © 2012 by SAGE Publications, Inc.

Printed in the United States of America

Library of Congress Cataloging-in-Publication Data

Green, Gary P.

[Asset building & community development]
Asset building and community development / Gary Paul Green, Anna Haines. — 3rd ed.

p. cm.
Includes bibliographical references and index.

ISBN 978-1-4129-8223-8 (pbk. : acid-free paper)

1. Community development—United States.
2. Community development corporations.
3. Community development. I. Haines, Anna.
II. Title.

HN90.C6G724 2012 307.1′4—dc22 2010039810

This book is printed on acid-free paper.

11 12 13 14 15 10 9 8 7 6 5 4 3 2 1

Contents _____

Preface _____

Can community residents work together to improve their quality of life? There are numerous examples of residents collaborating to provide affordable housing, job training, and credit for local businesses. Yet there continues to be skepticism about the ability of communities to overcome problems of concentrated poverty in the inner city, underdevelopment in rural areas (especially in Appalachia and on Native American reservations), and social isolation in so many of our communities today. In this book, we examine the promise and limits of community development.

We define community development as a planned effort to build assets that increase the capacity of residents to improve their quality of life. These assets may include several forms of community capital: physical, human, social, financial, environmental, political, and cultural. For each type of community capital, we examine the role of community-based organizations in mobilizing these assets, the strategies communities use to improve their quality of life, and the institutions and organizations involved in the community development process. We contend that these assets will not generate as many local benefits if communities rely on either markets or governments to guide their development. Development that is controlled by community-based organizations provides a better match between the assets and the needs of the communities, whether we are talking about job skills, housing, or financial capital.

We should note that we define community development in fairly broad terms. Many people today limit the definition of community development to the activities of community development corporations (CDCs). Although CDCs certainly have become key actors in the affordable housing and economic development arenas, there are many other organizations and institutions actively involved in promoting locality development. Although we discuss the role of CDCs, we also explore other organizations outside the "industry." In particular, we discuss local economic development organizations, neighborhood associations, and faith-based organizations. There are many other informal organizations, such as neighborhood watches, building-level tenant associations, block clubs, and volunteer youth groups doing community service, that serve as the foundation for community development work. We also consider the role of specialized organizations, such as micro-enterprise loan funds, land trusts, and training consortia.

Most people use the term *community* to refer to residents of a specific geographical area. Our book is directed primarily at "communities of place," although the material is relevant for "communities of interest," such as organizations and associations, as well. We also discuss many innovative regional programs that go beyond traditional place-based community development efforts. Although most of the literature on community development focuses on urban issues, we address rural communities and their concerns, too. Discussions of community development also are limited frequently to low-income neighborhoods. Again, we take a broader perspective and examine how middle-class communities are relying increasingly on community-based organizations to address problems associated with urban sprawl and the environment. Many of the lessons learned about working in low-income neighborhoods can be applied to a variety of settings.

We do not intend this book to be a cookbook on how to mobilize communities. There are several excellent books and manuals that readers could turn to for these strategies. We discuss some different approaches to community organizing, but our focus is much more on the outcomes of these processes. Instead, we provide students and practitioners with several elements of community development: (a) the basic concepts and theories; (b) a map of the institutions, organizations, and actors involved in various arenas of community development; (c) common strategies and tactics used by communities; (d) case studies of successful (and unsuccessful) communities; and (e) resources available on various topics related to community development.

In Chapter 1, we discuss the major concepts, issues, and theories used in the field of community development. Although community development draws from a variety of disciplines, a growing number of concepts and theories help define community development in theory and in practice. In Chapter 2, we present a brief overview of the history of community development in the United States. We begin with a discussion of early attempts at community development with the rise of settlement houses through the New Deal and the War on Poverty to contemporary efforts of CDCs, community development finance institutions (CDFIs), and comprehensive community initiatives (CCIs). A critical assessment of the history of the movement helps to identify the strengths and weaknesses of contemporary community development efforts.

In Chapter 3, we introduce the concept of community sustainability. Originally a concept from ecology, sustainability has been given many definitions. Essentially, the term *sustainability* refers to the ability of a system to sustain itself without outside intervention. We evaluate how communities are attempting to incorporate sustainability in their development strategies and the types of indicators communities are using to assess their progress toward the goal of achieving sustainability. The concept of sustainability is not considered a separate topic, but it is woven through our entire discussion of community development throughout this text.

Chapter 4 focuses on four stages of the community development process: community organizing, visioning, planning, and implementation/evaluation.

Many academics and practitioners have debated the importance of process (development *of* community) versus outcomes (development *in* the community). Most community development programs today involve both elements. In this chapter, we focus on various strategies for developing a process that will engage residents in the strategic decisions affecting their localities. We also discuss alternative approaches to community planning and public participation.

CDCs are the most visible organizations engaged in community and neighborhood development. There continues to be a debate over the effectiveness of CDCs. Critics charge that CDCs have lost their capacity to mobilize communities and have become primarily technical assistance providers. We examine these debates and assess the future of CDCs. In Chapter 5, we describe the structure of CDCs and review some of their strengths and weaknesses. We examine some of the constraints and limitations CDCs face in promoting neighborhood development. We also look at other community-based organizations, such as local development organizations, neighborhood organizations, faith-based organizations, and youth organizations. The larger issue for this discussion is whether organizational dynamics contribute to the loss of local control and bureaucratization of these entities.

We next examine seven forms of community capital: human, social, physical, financial, environmental, political, and cultural. We refer to these attributes as capital because investments in these resources yield greater returns in the quality of community life. In many cases, these forms of capital are public goods that require collective action, rather than individual investments, to grow. Each chapter follows a similar structure: limits to individual or government solutions to these problems, history of community development efforts in these areas, the theoretical basis for community intervention, key actors and institutions, and strategies.

Human capital theory focuses on the relationship between a worker's education, skills, and experience and the individual's labor market experiences. According to the theory, workers with lower level skills tend to be less productive and therefore are rewarded less in the labor market. A major focus of many community-based development organizations is training, which is assumed to increase the level of human capital and ultimately the quality of life in the community. In the chapter on human capital (Chapter 6), we focus on workforce development and the role of community-based organizations in providing training and linking workers to jobs. We discuss how federal and state efforts are placing increasing emphasis on comprehensive approaches to workforce development that rely on community-based organizations. These workforce development strategies help overcome some of the obstacles workers face in obtaining training and the barriers employers encounter in providing job training.

Social capital is defined as the norms, shared understandings, trust, and other factors that make collective action feasible and productive. Social capital enables members of a neighborhood or social network to help one another, especially in terms of economic opportunity and social mobility. In the chapter on social capital (Chapter 7), we concentrate on community networks (both individual and organizational) that influence local development. These social ties and networks can serve as both resources and constraints in a community's effort to promote collective action. In many ways, social capital is at the center of asset building for all the forms of community capital we discuss. It is an essential feature of community action.

Physical capital refers to buildings, tools, and infrastructure. In Chapter 8, we discuss housing, primarily affordability issues. The federal government has had a huge role in physical capital since the Great Depression, evidenced by the variety of programs for housing and other areas of physical capital, such as roads and other infrastructure. Due to federal devolution to lower levels of government and others, communities have an opportunity to pursue innovative affordable housing solutions. In this chapter, we examine the variety of ways in which communities can address affordable housing problems. We also assess why community-based organizations are at the forefront of the efforts to build more affordable housing options.

Poor and minority communities frequently lack access to financial capital. Capital markets typically do not solve these problems. Many communities are building local financial institutions, such as revolving loan funds, micro-enterprise loan funds, and community development banks, to address their credit problems. Chapter 9 explores various strategies for addressing credit problems in communities. Most of the emerging community-based models emphasize the importance of social as well as economic objectives.

In Chapter 10, we discuss environmental capital. Many communities are beginning to recognize that wisely managed natural resources, a community's environmental capital, play a major role in community satisfaction, quality of life, and economic development. Community-based organizations can offer an alternative to public sector zoning and regulations that aim to protect a community's environmental capital, especially in places that do not have the broad support necessary for protecting key environmental resources. To demonstrate the role of community-based organizations in preserving natural resources, we look carefully at the role of land trusts in addressing environmental problems.

Power is central to the community development process. Before engaging in a community development project, it is essential to understand the local power structure. It is equally important to know how to organize residents to build community power. In Chapter 11, we discuss different ways of measuring and analyzing the local power structure. We discuss different strategies that organizations use to build political capital.

Cultural capital, the subject of Chapter 12, is seen increasingly as an important factor in community development. Unfortunately, cultural resources are often viewed as something consumed by the rich and having little to do with middle-class and working-class residents. This view of culture and its potential contribution to the community is very limited.

The next two chapters illustrate how the asset-based development approach can be applied to food, energy, and natural disasters. In Chapter 13, we examine how community assets interact to promote local self-reliance through the development of community food systems and renewable energy systems. The growing criticism of our global food system has spawned a wide variety of community initiatives that promote local food systems. Similarly, the challenges we face in the area of energy policy have sparked a movement to promote new renewable sources of energy at the local level. These examples illustrate how local initiatives can build on community assets to promote greater sustainability. Similarly, in Chapter 14, we explore how the asset-based development approach can promote local responses to global climate change and natural disasters. While these local strategies are not a solution to these larger problems, they do represent some ways in which communities can become less vulnerable.

Globalization and technological change are presenting new challenges and obstacles to community development and to the organizations that pursue it. As financial capital becomes more mobile, it may be increasingly difficult to establish bonds among other forms of capital to create a sense of place in a community. In Chapter 15, we consider how technological changes are presenting new obstacles, and possibly new opportunities, to the field of community development.

Acknowledgments_____

Several people contributed to this third edition of our book. Pat Walsh and Dave Sprehn provided support early on in the project. They convinced us of the need for basic materials for community development practitioners. Steve Halebsky helped us identify community visioning efforts across the United States and made important contributions to the chapter on community development processes. Many colleagues reviewed individual chapters for us, including Elaine Andrews, Bo Beaulieu, Terry Besser, Calvin Brutus, Tim Carlisle, Steve Deller, Dan Diaz, Steve Malpezzi, Dave Marcouiller, John Merrill, Dave Neueundorf, Jeff Sharp, Daniel Sullivan, Greg Wise, and Ann Ziebarth. The manuscript has benefited immensely from all of their comments and suggestions. In addition, we appreciate all of the reviewer comments from Mary Emery, Iowa State University; M. E. Swisher, University of Florida; Jeff Courtright, Illinois State University; Takashi Tsukamoto, University of North Carolina at Greensboro; and Desna L. Wallin, University of Georgia. Valeria Galetto was an outstanding research assistant and helped us take care of all of the loose ends. Jill Lucht assisted with much of the library work. Michael Dougherty helped with the revisions in the second edition, and Jennifer Skolaski contributed to the third edition.

It has been a joy to work with the staff from Sage Publications again. We would especially like to thank Lisa Cuevas Shaw and MaryAnn Vail for their support and enthusiasm for this project.

Finally, we would like to thank the students and practitioners we have worked with over the years. Community development is an exciting field, partly because it can bring together academics and practitioners. Not only have we learned from our interaction with students and practitioners, but also we continue to be influenced by their enthusiasm for the potential of community development.

—*Gary Paul Green and Anna Haines*

1

The Role of Assets in Community-Based Development

Community development has its roots in several academic disciplines, including sociology, economics, political science, planning, social work, and even architecture. The interdisciplinary approach of community development has many advantages, but it also presents analytical problems. It lacks a common language, a conceptual framework, or a set of agreed-upon issues and problems. Community development is frequently driven more by practice than by theory. There also is considerable debate among practitioners whether community development is primarily a process or an outcome.

Community development has always had a diverse set of objectives: solving local problems (e.g., unemployment and poverty), addressing inequalities of wealth and power, promoting democracy, and building a sense of community (Rubin & Rubin, 1992). As a result, it has been defined in a variety of ways, including local economic development, political empowerment, service provision, housing programs, comprehensive planning, and job training. In this book, we do not overcome this ambiguity, but we define some of the major concepts and issues for which there is considerable agreement in the community development field today. We believe the asset approach offers the best potential for providing a common conceptual basis for community development theory and for practitioners. We begin with one of the most slippery terms—*community*.

BOX 1.1 COMMUNITY DEVELOPMENT FACTS

- The share of the metropolitan population in extreme-poverty neighborhoods (census tracts with poverty rates of 40% or more) was 12% in 2000.
- The share of high-poverty neighborhoods in the suburbs is increasing, but central cities still have the highest proportion.
- The share of high-poverty neighborhoods with predominately African American populations has declined markedly since 1980, whereas those that are predominately Hispanic increased during this period.

SOURCE: Pettit and Kingsley (2003).

Whither Community?

Community is one of the central concepts in the social sciences, yet it frequently lacks a precise definition. In a review of the community literature many years ago, Hillery (1955) found more than 94 separate definitions. The term *community* also has been used interchangeably with *neighborhood*. In this section, we provide working definitions of *community* and *neighborhood* and discuss some of the implications of these definitions for the field of community development.

Following Wilkinson (1991), we define *community* as including three elements: (1) territory or place, (2) social organizations or institutions that provide regular interaction among residents, and (3) social interaction on matters concerning a common interest. This definition excludes communities of interest, such as professional organizations or religious groups. Although many people have broadened the concept of community to include interaction solely on interest, we focus on communities of place in this book. As we will discuss in more detail later, our approach is somewhat problematic because people are becoming less attached to specific places and increasingly linked to communities of interest. Growth of the Internet, for example, provides new opportunities for individuals to connect with other people who have similar interests and concerns. Individuals have become more strongly linked to national and international organizations and institutions. Many issues that affect residents, however, remain place based, such as schools, housing, and environmental quality. So, though we recognize that there are social and economic forces changing the nature of community, place-based issues continue to influence the quality of life of most people. Communities of place can vary considerably in terms of size and density. Areas with very low population densities present some obstacles to community development. Low density may reduce the opportunities for social interaction, which may ultimately make it more difficult to develop a sense of community.

We also consider the existence of local institutions, such as a school or even a restaurant, as an important factor in facilitating the development of a sense of community. Local organizations and institutions are important for a couple of reasons. They provide residents with opportunities for interaction and frequently represent the common interests of those in the area, such as a school district. Many local institutions today, however, are actually controlled by national and international organizations. This situation may influence the relationship of the institution to the locality. We will discuss in the later chapters how community-based organizations and institutions are more likely to benefit local residents and contribute to a sense of community. One of the central goals of the asset-based development approach is to provide stronger ties between institutions and the residents in a locality.

Finally, this definition suggests that community is a contingent phenomenon, dependent on a number of conditions to achieve social interactions in pursuit of mutual interests. Simply living in the same place does not create community. Action promoting a common interest is not necessarily a result of objective conditions, participation in local organizations and institutions, or even the realization that individual well-being is linked to the quality of life in the community. We discuss some of the factors that can contribute to community later in the book. This argument suggests, however, that community development is often more of an art than a science. It is not just about helping people realize their own interests. It is about identifying assets that can help, developing the leadership to mobilize residents, and building the capacity to act in the future.

We need to make one more qualifying remark about this definition of community. Some critics charge that the concept of community implies a consensus or common values. Communities of place are often sharply divided by class and race. Other divisions, such as gender or length of residence, may also create conflicts. We do not believe the process of community development assumes homogeneity of values or consensus. In fact, much of the discussion in this book focuses on conflict and power relations within communities. There are numerous case studies, however, that illustrate how diverse communities have been able to identify common interests that provide the basis for local action. Of course, there will always be those instances of structural conflict, say between developers and environmentalists, where it is more difficult to find common ground. Conflict is not inherently bad. It may help to resolve some of the underlying tensions that communities face.

Next we turn to distinguishing between the concepts of **community** and **neighborhood**. Probably the easiest way to distinguish between the two is to use the latter to refer exclusively to a specific geography and the former as social interaction on matters concerning a common interest. Based on this distinction, a community may or may not be place based. Community can be defined, for example, as a group of residents acting on a common interest, such as a school or road issue. Or community may be defined as a group sharing a common interest that is not necessarily place based, such as religious beliefs, professions, or ethnicity. In most cases, the development of a sense of community involves the existence of social institutions or organizations that provide the opportunity for regular social interaction among members. For our purposes, we limit our discussion to place-based communities. Neighborhoods usually refer to a specific geography, such as residential areas demarcated by major streets or other physical barriers. This does not assume, however, that there is any social interaction or effort to address common needs in the area, as is the case in the definition of community.

This simple distinction between neighborhood and community does not resolve some of the conceptual problems that exist in using these concepts. One of the perennial problems is that individuals in neighborhoods and communities of place, especially those people who live in metropolitan areas, do not limit their social relationships to people in the same locality. Studies have consistently shown that most individuals have extensive social ties with other people outside their neighborhood (Gans, 1962; Suttles, 1972). Thus, the boundaries of the neighborhood or community are difficult to define. Many researchers use official areas, such as census tracts (Jargowsky, 1997) or counties (Lobao, 1990), to define neighborhoods or communities. These designations, however, do not necessarily correspond to bounded areas of social relationships, although the Census Bureau considers things such as natural barriers in its process of defining census tracts. One result of the growing tendency to maintain contacts outside one's neighborhood is that it may be increasingly difficult to develop a sense of common interest.

This problem of defining the boundaries of neighborhoods and communities, however, does not mean that individuals do not maintain social relationships and ties with their neighbors. There is ample evidence that neighborhood ties and relationships continue to be important sources of support for many people (Campbell & Lee, 1992). Communities of place, therefore, should not be considered bounded entities that contain the bulk of social ties and relationships that residents hold. As individuals now tend to work, live, and consume in different places, it is more likely they will develop social relationships in these different settings. The liberation of community ties may make the development of community of place more difficult to achieve in some settings, but not impossible. Although local crises, such as a plant closing or an environmental threat, may lead to short-term actions based on common interest, these actions may not be sustained long term.

Growth Versus Development

Growth and development are often considered synonymous. Community residents see the two concepts increasingly in negative terms, especially by those who assume that growth and development automatically lead to more people, traffic, congestion, and environmental degradation. There are some important differences, however, between the two concepts. *Growth* refers to increased quantities of specific phenomena, such as jobs, population, and income. It also could be used to refer to changes in quality, such as better jobs or more secure sources of income. *Development* involves structural change in the community, especially in how resources are used, the functioning of institutions, and the distribution of resources in the community. One of the primary goals of community development is to reduce vulnerability to shifts in production technology and in the market environment. Many people suggest that there is actually a great deal of overlap between the concepts of development and sustainability. Perhaps a more precise definition would focus on community resiliency.

Community development is often equated with economic development. Many practitioners, however, consider community development as a set of activities that must precede economic development. Communities need to provide a good infrastructure, including housing and schools, in order to generate jobs and income. Some community development activities, however, are more directly related to economic development, such as job training and business management. The concept of community development, then, is broader than economic development and may include many activities that are directly economic in nature.

Amartya Sen, the Nobel Prize winner economist, defined development as freedom (Sen, 1999). From his perspective, high levels of social and economic inequality present obstacles to development because the poor do not have the same opportunities to develop their capacity. Sen argued that development should encompass five different types of freedom: (1) political freedoms, (2) economic facilities, (3) social opportunities, (4) transparency guarantees, and (5) protective security. Political freedoms refer primarily to civil liberties. Economic facilities are the resources that families hold to produce, consume, or exchange in the marketplace. Social opportunities are the societal arrangements for the conditions to improve quality of life, such as education, health care, and so on. Transparency guarantees can be defined as the level of trust that exists among individuals and between individuals and their government. Finally, protective security includes institutional arrangements that "provide a social safety net for preventing the affected population from being reduced to abject misery, and in some cases even starvation and death" (Sen, 1999, p. 40). Although Sen's analysis focuses on national and global development, many of these elements can be applied to the local level as well. The main point, however, is that development cannot simply be reduced to growth in income or jobs. Instead, it should be viewed as a much broader process that improves the opportunities and quality of life for individuals. Many economists assume that economic growth will automatically improve quality of life. Sen's analysis suggests the relationship is much more complex.

Based on this discussion, we can see that growth may or may not lead to development. A few examples may help to further illustrate this difference. If a community experiences an increase in wealth, but most of it is held by a few families, this change would be considered growth and not development. Similarly, if a community is able to attract a new employer that provides 100 new jobs, but 90 of the jobs are taken by people outside the community (and those 90 workers do not purchase goods and services locally), this too may be considered an example of growth and not development. Another example might be if a fast-food chain establishes a restaurant in a community but most of the profits from the operation are drained from the local area. This is an example of growth rather than development. Finally, if a forest-dependent community is able to attract a paper mill that exploits the natural resources of the area in an unsustainable manner, this case would be considered growth, not development. If the resources for future economic activity are destroyed, it cannot lead to additional development.

Development may lead to a more efficient use of resources, reduce a community's dependency on external resources and decision making, and create a better system of managing markets (financial, housing, labor, etc.) to satisfy local (societal) needs. A key element of the process is the allocation of development decisions to the local level, where relationships between economic development, the environment, and social needs are most visible.

People Versus Place

One of the continuing debates in the field of community development is whether policies and programs should emphasize place or people. Supporters of people-based policies contend that there is no evidence that place-based programs really work (Lemann, 1994). These critics point out that it is very difficult to attract established businesses to poor communities or to help new businesses start there. There also is a tendency for workers to leave the community if the community programs are successful. The dilemma for most communities is that increasing the skills and education of their existing workforce may not have any payoff if workers cannot find jobs in the area. Lemann (1994, p. 30) argued, however, that there are several reasons that place-based policies are attractive. First, politicians represent geographic areas, so they see logical benefits in promoting the welfare of places. If they can provide benefits to residents, they are more likely to get reelected. Foundations invest in place-based development because they can have a greater impact at that smaller scale. It is more difficult for them to reform large-scale systems, such as an educational or health care system. Finally, the business sector often supports place-based approaches to development because it eschews big government approaches. Community development often receives support from those who would like to see the federal and state governments downsized and services shifted to the private sector or to nonprofit organizations.

Place-based approaches have been at the core of community development efforts for more than 50 years. Advocates of place-based programs argue that an emphasis on people rather than places ultimately leads to more problems because those who are successful leave their community. As a result, these programs contribute to concentrated poverty and social problems. Placed-based strategies assume that community still matters. Advocates of place-base strategies recognize the social and economic costs of promoting community disintegration. In many cities, for example, local policies promote growth on the suburban fringe and decline in the inner city. This pattern has enormous costs that are not often considered. Building new schools and providing new infrastructure to the suburbs adds to the fiscal pressures for most cities. Abandonment of old buildings and declining enrollment in inner-city schools adds to the problems of poor neighborhoods. A more appropriate strategy is to emphasize place-based development in existing neighborhoods that reduces the social, economic, and environmental costs.

There is a variety of place-based strategies. For example, communities may choose to attract outside capital through tax and financial incentives. The Clinton administration established the Empowerment Zones (EZs) and

Enterprise Communities (ECs) in several poor communities in the United States in an effort to promote development. These communities offer a variety of incentives for businesses locating in these areas.

Other place-based approaches focus less on outside investments and more on ways of increasing the quality of life by establishing new institutions, improving the physical infrastructure, or building on existing resources in the community. The New Urbanism movement emphasizes the benefits of higher density development and in-fill of existing properties as a key to promote place-based development. The assumption behind New Urbanism is that the existing institutional structure undermines the viability of most poor and minority communities. Institutional change is required to improve the quality of life and to capture the resources leaving the community. Most of these efforts attempt to leverage local resources to promote local ownership and control of resources (i.e., land, labor, capital). In other words, community-based strategies frequently generate demand among extralocal actors that produces benefits and returns the created surplus to the community (Gunn & Gunn, 1991).

Finally, place-based approaches recognize the contribution and value of community sentiment and support to residents. Many would argue that building strong social relationships is essential to both human and community development. In addition, places become the shared arena in which the disenfranchised can obtain political power. Many of the policies we discuss in later chapters focus on helping the poor become more spatially mobile. Although research suggests this may have some individual benefits for families, there are still questions about the impacts of such policies on community activism.

Community Sustainability

There is a growing interest in promoting social, economic, and environmental sustainability at the community level. This concept is taken from the environmental literature but has much broader meaning in the context of community development. Efforts to promote **community sustainability** focus on local practices and policies and evaluate whether they contribute to the long-term survival of the social, economic, and environmental base of the locality. Sustainability is often considered an outcome of community development, but we view it as a guiding principle to the process of community development practice. This approach forces us to examine the interconnections between local economic, social, and environmental issues. Practices that promote economic development, for example, need to ensure the sustainability of the environment and provide opportunities for marginalized residents in the community.

What is the relationship between community sustainability and asset-based development? First of all, we must recognize that sustainability strategies must focus on finding new methods of connecting local resources in a way that reduces environmental problems and increases economic opportunities. In a later chapter, we will explore how community development practitioners are working on sustainability efforts through local food systems and renewable energy projects. The success of these sustainability programs will depend largely on identifying the key assets or resources that are available at the local level.

Similarly, we need to understand that many of the assets that exist in communities are multifunctional in nature. By this we mean that the resources can serve a variety of functions or purposes. Natural resources, for example, can serve both production and consumption functions. They can be the inputs into an extractive production process or amenities to support tourism-related activities. Community development efforts need to work at the local level to find the most appropriate strategy that provides social, economic, and environmental benefits to residents.

The Challenge of Regionalism

Aside from the criticism that it is too difficult to create development in poor neighborhoods and communities, two other critiques frequently are made of place-based community development efforts. The first critique is that the focus on community and neighborhoods ignores the regional nature of development, especially in metropolitan areas. For example, Myron Orfield (1997) has argued for a regional approach to addressing the problems of concentrated poverty in the central city. Orfield contended that racial segregation of housing, the lack of resources in ghettos, and incentives for migration to the suburbs make traditional community development efforts inadequate unless they address these social and economic forces. Among Orfield's policy recommendations are property tax base sharing across cities and suburbs, deconcentration of affordable housing across suburban areas, and land use policies that discourage sprawl. Other regionalists such as David Rusk (1993) have emphasized the importance of cities' ability to expand their boundaries to capture the benefits of the movement of people and jobs to the suburbs.

A second critique is that the community development literature creates a false choice between people and place. One example is the so-called mobility strategy (Hughes, 1991), which attempts to help city residents commute to suburban jobs, rather than try to bring employers to the city or move workers to where the jobs are. This approach has the advantage of solving the labor market and income problems of the poor, while still keeping them in their neighborhoods. This strategy could be addressed in a few different ways. The most common tactic is to develop transportation systems that assist workers in finding and obtaining jobs in other parts of the region. Many cities are now providing transportation from the inner city to jobs in the suburbs. Another approach, however, might be to bring work (rather than the entire business) from employers in the suburbs into the inner city. This tactic helps develop the experience of the workforce in the inner city and often provides employers with some confidence that these workers have the needed skills.

These regional strategies are not necessarily an alternative to traditional place-based community development strategies. Instead, they build on existing links between communities and their regions. Recommendations for the mobility strategy are still based on the assumption that it is important to build the community or neighborhood. The challenge for regional development strategies is to remain connected to community-based organizations and local efforts to mobilize residents. Without these connections, regionalism can take a "top-down" approach and lose grassroots support.

Asset Building

Community development is a planned effort to build assets that increase the capacity of residents to improve their quality of life. We now turn to a more detailed discussion about community assets. Kretzmann and McKnight (1993) defined assets as the "gifts, skills and capacities" of "individuals, associations and institutions" within a community (p. 25). Melvin Oliver (2001), the former vice president of the Ford Foundation, further elaborated on the importance of asset building:

> An "asset" in this paradigm is a special kind of resource that an individual, organization, or entire community can use to reduce or prevent poverty and injustice. An asset is usually a "stock" that can be drawn upon, built upon, or developed, as well as a resource that can be shared or transferred across generations. . . . As the poor gain access to assets, they are more likely to take control of important aspects of their lives, to plan for their future and deal with economic uncertainty, to support their children's educational achievements, and to work to ensure that the lives of the next generations are better than their own. (p. xii)

This focus on community assets, rather than the needs, represents a significant shift in how community development practitioners have approached their work in recent years. In the past, community development practitioners began their efforts by conducting a needs assessment that examined the problems and weaknesses of the community (Johnson, Meiller, Miller, & Summers, 1987). One of the advantages of needs assessment is that problem identification can help mobilize communities to address local issues. The tendency, however, is for residents to look to others outside the community, especially to professionals, for help. By relying on professionals and others, communities become more dependent on outside resources and often lose control over the development process. In response to these tendencies, Kretzmann and McKnight (1993) emphasized the importance of looking to community assets as a way to identify strengths and resources that can contribute to a strategic planning process.

As McKnight (1995) suggests, it is in the interests of professionals and technical-assistance providers to promote dependency. Communities frequently turn to outside assistance because they believe the issues or problems are too complex for local residents. This type of assistance does very little to help build community capacity. It is possible, however, for professionals and technical-assistance providers to empower local residents. This might mean helping residents develop the research skills, substantive knowledge, or both, to address community issues.

The distinction between needs and assets does not mean that practitioners have to make a decision to use one approach or another. In many cases, it may make sense to begin by identifying a community's assets and then assess its needs. A discussion of the needs and problems is almost inevitable in community processes and often serves to mobilize residents to act on an issue. The concern with an exclusive focus on needs is that a community often jumps immediately to problem solving rather than identifying its goals and strengths.

CASE STUDY 1.1 THE DUDLEY STREET NEIGHBORHOOD INITIATIVE

Probably one of the most widely acclaimed success stories in the community development field in recent years is the Dudley Street Neighborhood Initiative (DSNI). The philosophy behind DSNI was to build on the local assets rather than to focus on the needs of residents. Dudley Street is located in Boston's Roxbury District, one of the poorest areas in Massachusetts. Approximately 35% of the families in the area live below the poverty line, and the neighborhood contained many abandoned buildings, a large number of vacant lots (20% of the lots), and a persistent drug problem.

The DSNI began in 1984 when the Riley Foundation, a Boston-area community foundation, decided to make an investment in the neighborhood. Local residents challenged the plan presented by the Riley Foundation because it was not "their" plan. In response to this initiative, residents established DSNI, which had a 31-member board of directors, with the majority consisting of local residents. There are more than 2,500 voting members of DSNI and the organization employs approximately 16 full-time staff.

The organization launched several projects that were immediately successful, including removal of illegal dumps on Dudley Street and even provision of affordable housing for residents. Part of DSNI's success was due to its combining the role of developer of low-income housing and provider of social services with the role of community organizer. The most controversial project of the DSNI was their program to take eminent domain of 30 acres of vacant land and develop it as a land trust. The DSNI had strong support from the city government for this project.

The DSNI took control of more than 1,300 abandoned parcels of land in the neighborhood, converting them into parks, gardens, and other public spaces as well as 400 single-family and cooperative homes for low- and middle-income residents. DSNI organized a youth committee to address young people's concerns, such as recreation and educational opportunities. The DSNI, which has been especially concerned about recognizing the various cultures in the neighborhood, sponsored several multicultural festivals. The organization also has moved into the area of economic development but has had less success with these efforts.

For more information on DSNI, see Medoff and Sklar (1994).
The video *Holding Ground: The Rebirth of Dudley Street*
(Lipman & Mahan, 1996) documents the efforts of DSNI as well.

CASE STUDY 1.2 ASSET BUILDING IN INDIAN COUNTRY

The First Nations Institute was founded in 1980 to assist Native American people in building the capacity of tribal communities. The institute has used asset-building strategies to promote culturally compatible stewardship of the assets they own, including land, cultural heritage, and natural resources, to develop tribal communities. They consider several types of assets in their approach, including financial, physical, natural, institutional, human, cultural, social, and political assets. The institute emphasizes strategies that enable Native American communities to control, retain, increase, use, leverage, and create assets. Some examples of asset-building strategies include starting a Community Development Financial Institution (CDFI), using Individual Development Accounts (IDAs), and establishing a fitness program for tribal youth. For a good discussion of their approach and model, see http://www.firstnations.org/publications/AssetBuildinginNative CommunitiesJanuary262004.pdf.

It is difficult to identify a single theory or conceptual basis for the asset-based community development approach. Asset-based development is more a method than it is a theory of community social change. It clearly has some intellectual ties to Wilkinson's (1991) interactional theory of communities, which rejects the view of communities as independent social structures. Instead, through interaction in a locality, an awareness of common interests emerges. In this process, people learn to identify, manage, and leverage local resources to the benefit of their locality (Wilkinson, 1991). Much of this is dependent on developing social ties and relationships that enhance the ability of residents to act collectively to address local concerns.

Asset building has some interesting similarities to social capital theory as well (Putnam, 2000). Participation in local organizations and associations builds social relationships and trust that are so essential in mobilizing community residents. Social capital becomes the basis for building other community assets, such as human and financial capital.

There are a variety of other theoretical ties to asset-based development. Dependency theory, which is often applied to nation-states, points to the exploitive relationships that develop through international trade and investment. Its focus on the development of dependency is very similar to the critique of needs-based approaches that McKnight (1995) criticizes. Finally, there are some parallels to theories about social movements, such as resource mobilization theory. The success of social movements depends largely on the ability to mobilize people and to acquire resources that enable them to achieve their goals.

The bottom line is that asset-based development has a variety of intellectual ties and roots to other social and political theories. The strength of this approach is that the connection between theory and practice is much stronger than most social or political theories. Asset mapping is a process of learning about the resources that are available in a community. The following items include examples of assets mapping:

- The identification of economic development opportunities through the mapping of available skills and work experience
- The documentation of natural resource assets that may promote economic development through tourism or increased home values
- The assessment of consumer spending practices to identify the potential for new businesses in the neighborhood
- The development of a community resources inventory to identify the expediencies of residents in providing services, such as child care, to identify the potential for more providers in the community

In this book, we expand the definition of community assets to include seven forms of **assets:** physical, human, social, financial, environmental, political, and cultural. There are other assets that we might consider, but most community development activities focus on these seven forms of **community capital.** We use the term *community assets* for a couple of reasons. First, this concept suggests that there are underused resources available in the community (Kretzmann & McKnight, 1993). Individuals may have jobs skills or experiences that do not match the local demand. Individuals and families may have savings that are being invested outside the community. The community may have natural resources that could potentially be of value as an amenity. The goal of asset-based community development is to identify these resources and mobilize residents to make use of them to meet the needs of residents.

We refer to these forms of assets as community capital. *Capital* is used here in a very broad sense. Most of the time capital is defined as wealth that is used to create more wealth. This concept, however, can be applied to other resources as well. Investments in education and training (human capital) produce additional benefits for workers. Similarly, investments in social relationships (social capital) generate social resources that can be used later. When communities make the right investments in the resources they have, it creates future benefits in the quality of life for residents.

The asset approach also implies that the community development effort is directed toward the locality or place. Rather than providing training for jobs that workers must take elsewhere, there is an attempt to match training efforts to jobs that can be created locally. Similarly, if an absentee-owned firm processes natural resources, many of the benefits will flow outside the community. The same thing may occur if families place their savings in banks and other financial institutions that invest these resources in other localities.

Finally, the asset-based approach assumes that there are many institutional obstacles to the development of places that cannot be overcome through individual action but instead must be addressed through the activities of community-based organizations (CBOs). Community-based organizations can overcome many of the collective-action and economies-of-scale problems associated with community development. For example, though individual employers in a community may lack skilled workers, and though they all have an interest in having a skilled workforce, individual businesses may be reluctant to invest in training because they may lose these trained workers. Community development offers collective solutions to these problems by building on the existing resources within the community. In his analysis of community-based development organizations (CBDOs), Rubin (2000) found that asset building is the real objective of these organizations:

> It matters less what is built than that projects introduce assets, both material and social, for those in neighborhoods of deprivation. These assets create an economic stake in society, for both recipients and the CBDO, as well as a set of obligations—paying rent, maintaining property, concern with the quality of the neighborhood—that is socially empowering. (p. 162)

Kretzmann and McKnight (1993) identified several steps in mobilizing community assets. The first step is to identify the capacities of residents, organizations, and institutions. The idea that all individuals have the capacity to contribute to their community is fundamental to this approach. Also often overlooked are the potential contributions of youth, seniors, and people with disabilities. In addition to standard labor market skills and experiences, communities need to know about volunteering activities, hobbies, care-giving experiences, and so on. This information is often captured through surveys, conducted either face to face or through the mail. An excellent resource for measuring individual capacities is a workbook by Kretzmann, McKnight, and Sheehan (1997).

Associations and organizations can facilitate mobilization. Asset-based development efforts usually attempt to map both formal and informal organizations in the community. Formal organizations are usually visible, and there are directories to help identify them. Informal organizations, such as block clubs, neighborhood watches, and garden clubs, however, usually do not appear on formal lists because they are not incorporated or they do not have paid staff. Probably the most efficient way to collect this information is to conduct a survey of individuals that asks them to identify all of their memberships. These data can help identify the organizations to be contacted. It is helpful to compile a list of board members, leaders, and resources available in the organization.

Community institutions, such as schools, hospitals, and libraries, are potentially important resources for community development. Institutions purchase goods and services that could contribute to the local economy. They have facilities that can be used for community events. They also employ workers, which affects the local economy. Mapping these institutions involves assessing the institutional assets with the goal of identifying resources that could contribute to community building. For example, farm-to-school programs have developed across the country in recent years. These programs identify ways of improving markets for regional farmers and improving the quality of food in school. By purchasing local produce, schools are a powerful asset of the local economy.

After mapping these community assets, practitioners build relationships across the community that will help implement the goals and vision of the project. Mobilizing assets requires broad-based support. The asset-based development approach relies on leveraging local resources to gain outside support. Although it is important to build from local resources, it is also important to tap into existing resources that will enhance those assets.

The asset-building approach is not without its critics. Proponents of asset-based development have often been accused of ignoring power relations within communities. The needs assessments approach, however, establishes power relationships between professionals and citizens. By identifying problems and needs, communities often become dependent on **technical assistance** and experts to help address these issues. Asset building attempts to address these power relationships by building on existing resources and strengths to guide the community planning effort. This approach does not rely solely on local resources but focuses on innovative ways of leveraging these resources.

Asset-based development tends to be less conflict oriented than many other community organizing approaches. It emphasizes common interests and can serve as an excellent basis for mobilizing residents to address the critical issues facing their communities. In this regard, it has much in common with the techniques and strategies employed by the Industrial Areas Foundation, which is discussed in a later chapter. There is nothing inherent in the approach that avoids conflict with the power elite. Nor does the emphasis on common interests ignore conflict. The approach seeks to overcome racial, gender, and class differences that frequently constrain community development projects.

Public Participation

Community development requires the involvement and participation of local residents in identifying the strategies they wish to use to improve their quality of life. Most people use the term citizen participation to characterize this process. We prefer to use the concept of public participation. Langton (1978) defined *citizen participation* as "purposeful activities in which citizens take part in relation to government" (p. 17). This concept is too restrictive for a couple of reasons. First, this definition is limited to citizens (i.e., legal residents). By using the term *public*, we also include people who do not have all of the rights and obligations of citizenship. Given the high rates of immigration in many American cities, and rural areas as well, and the disproportionate number of poor communities with a large number of immigrants, this restriction does not make sense today. Second, citizen participation includes only activities related to the government. Public participation refers to activities in any public institution of society or the government, which includes organizations and institutions other than government. Although many community development activities either collaborate with or are directed at governments (e.g., improving social service provision or transportation systems), many more activities do not involve government at any level.

Having differentiated between citizen and public participation, we should comment that much of the public's participation in the past has been in relation to local, state, and federal governments. It is useful to distinguish between two types of participation here. First, there is community action resulting from activities initiated and controlled by CBOs that is frequently directed at changing government services and policies. Second, there is community action that can be referred to as public involvement, which is initiated and controlled by the government.

There has been rapid growth in the number of programs initiated by the government to promote public involvement. Increasingly, the public has been directly involved in decisions (Roberts, 2004). Almost all federal and state programs contain some element of public participation. Some examples are federal requirements for public participation in the Coastal Zone Management Act, the Federal Water Pollution Control Act, the Airport and Airways Development Act, and, more recently, the Intermodal Surface Transportation Efficiency Act (ISTEA). The primary purpose of these programs is to gain support for decisions, programs, and services. Of course, many of these programs have been criticized for not allowing the public to make these decisions but simply to have an opportunity to comment on decisions that have already been made. We examine these issues in more detail later when we discuss the community development process (in Chapter 4).

Why is there so much emphasis on public participation in community development? Participation is seen as developmental, educative, and integrative and as a means of protecting freedom (Roberts, 2004). One of the key assumptions of participation is that local residents will be more supportive of the project, and therefore increase the likelihood of its success, if residents have input in the decision-making process. Also, local residents probably have much better knowledge about the assets and needs of the community. Finally, public participation is considered the centerpiece of the democratic process. Local officials, however, have not always accepted this emphasis on public participation. As we discuss in Chapter 2, public participation among the poor during the 1960s was an especially controversial topic.

The Role of Community-Based Organizations

One of the distinguishing characteristics of community development is that it involves the creation of local organizations to help build assets. Throughout this text, we place a great deal of emphasis on the role of CBOs. These organizations offer several advantages, compared with nonlocal organizations, for carrying out place-based programs. CBOs are rooted in place and have extensive contacts and information about the neighborhood. Their primary mission is aimed at the community; they emphasize the importance of place over other goals. Also, in ideal situations, CBOs are controlled by local residents. Typically, control is characterized by representation on the board and input into the organization's policies and programs.

One of the principal vehicles for carrying out community development activities in the United States today is the community development corporation (CDC). Because these organizations are so important to the community development movement, we devote almost an entire chapter to discussing their activities (see Chapter 5). Community development, however, can occur in a variety of other CBOs. For example, we also examine local development corporations, which are responsible for coordinating economic development activities in many communities and regions. Neighborhood associations address issues such as real estate development and social service provision. Faith-based organizations are increasingly called on to provide social services to the needy. Religious organizations have played an increasingly important role in providing services to the poor and are more involved in job training and housing issues than they were in the past, largely due to welfare reform. A large number of nonreligious nonprofit organizations, such as homeless shelters, neighborhood clinics, and child care centers, serve a more specialized function in communities. And nongovernmental organizations are major actors in international development. Community foundations are nonprofit organizations that provide long-term funds for organizations and activities in a defined geographic area. Currently, more than 400 community foundations exist, with their total assets exceeding $8 billion (Mayer, 1994). Throughout this book, we discuss other specialized community-based organizations, such as loan funds and training organizations.

The organizations discussed previously tend to have paid staff. There are many nonprofit organizations without staff that play a critical role in community development. Examples of these organizations are parent-teacher organizations, tenant associations, block clubs, recreational clubs, and other smaller organizations. These organizations receive very little attention in the literature.

—————————— Models of Community Development

Although there are some common issues and problems in the field of community development, there is still wide variation in how practitioners approach their work. One of the ways of conceptualizing these differences is the typology developed by Christenson (1989). Christenson identified three different community development themes or models: self-help, technical assistance, and conflict. Although many community development efforts do not fall neatly into one of these three models, the typology is useful for understanding some of the different ways practitioners may approach their work.

Self-Help

At the heart of the **self-help** approach is the belief that community development is primarily about helping people to learn how to help themselves. Practitioners who adopt this model tend to define their role as a facilitator, helping communities identify goals and increasing capacity to participate in the solution of collective problems. The facilitator adopts a neutral position in the change process and is primarily concerned about the process of community development rather than the specific outcomes (e.g., jobs, houses, services). The self-help approach assumes that increasing the capacity of residents to address their problems will ultimately result in long-term improvements in quality of life.

The self-help approach requires several conditions to be effective: Individuals must have the necessary democratic skills, participants must have a reasonable expectation that their efforts will have some impact, and they also must identify their shared interests to develop a common set of goals. When these conditions do not exist, it may be necessary to build the capacity of the community prior to taking on development projects. This may involve building leadership skills, resolving conflict, or simply bringing residents together to identify common concerns. Community development efforts using the self-help approach tend to have more long-lasting effects than do some of the other approaches because residents have greater ownership in the process.

Facilitators are always faced with the dilemma of how to balance the need for information and technical assistance with the facilitation process. We will discuss this issue in more detail in the chapter on the community development process. It is important that facilitators clearly identify the goals and expected outcomes before the community moves to "solutions." In addition, there are strategies facilitators can use to help ensure that the community maintains control of the process while seeking information and technical assistance.

Technical Assistance

Practitioners who adopt the technical assistance model assume that the most important obstacle communities face concerns information. This model is firmly rooted in the rational planning approach to development. Thus, the appropriate role for the community development practitioner is one of a consultant. Those who advocate the technical assistance model are much more concerned with the eventual outcome of the community development effort than they are with the capacity of residents. Technical assistance also can be provided in a variety of ways, from ongoing local assistance to short-term consulting.

A variety of issues should be considered when taking the technical assistance approach to community development: Whose values are being served by the assistance? How have the goals been established? Should other alternatives be considered? Will the assistance help residents address community problems in the future?

Technical assistance can be provided through several different institutional arrangements: a centralized location, a regional provider, or local assistance. Technical assistance offered through a centralized location is the most cost efficient but often lacks the follow-up that is frequently necessary. The consultant may deliver a product or advise and leave it to the community to decide whether or how to use the information. An alternative is to provide technical assistance through local or regional providers. This approach has several advantages. The consultant usually has much more knowledge about local or regional conditions and also is available for follow-up consultation once the project has been initiated. Of course, this type of technical assistance is usually much more costly than the traditional consultant model.

Conflict

Probably one of the most established traditions in community development is the conflict approach, which is most often identified with Saul Alinsky (1969). The practitioner's approach in this model is one of organizer or advocate. Practitioners who adopt this approach assume that the fundamental source of most community problems is the lack of power. And this approach is most often used in places where residents have been marginalized or lack the ability to shape decisions that are affecting their quality of life. Neighborhoods generally lack power because they are not well organized. This approach often begins with an assessment of the local power structure. We discuss several methods of analyzing local power structures in a later chapter.

According to Alinsky (1969), the community organizer then needs to choose a problem to address and organize the community around this problem. The conflict should be small and winnable. The goal is to demonstrate to residents that they can be successful. Alinsky's approach is based on the assumption that community organizations should not directly confront the power structure. Instead, they should use a variety of tactics to embarrass local political leaders and to demonstrate the value of power to residents. Although this approach has proven to be successful in low-income neighborhoods, it is unclear how successful these tactics would be in middle-class neighborhoods. This approach also may have difficulty in cross-racial, ethnic, and class lines in a neighborhood. Finally, community organizers using this approach frequently have difficulty maintaining momentum in the community development process once residents have achieved some success.

To address some of these weaknesses, Alinsky (1969) argued that it was important to work through existing organizations in the neighborhood. These organizations can provide resources, contacts, and legitimacy in the neighborhood. His strategy was to identify common concerns and issues that are identified by leaders of these organizations and work toward a consensus on addressing the problem.

These three models represent very broad approaches to community development. It is important for practitioners to understand how the context may influence their decisions about which model is most appropriate for a particular situation. Similarly, it may be necessary to shift models in the process as the community develops capacity or encounters obstacles in its path.

Summary and Conclusions

Community development defies many of the standard assumptions we make about community and development in America today. Its emphasis on community-based organizations rather than the power of markets or government programs challenges the policy prescriptions of both political conservatives and liberals. The requirement that residents participate in the solutions to common problems contradicts the accepted view today that community no longer exists. Emphasis on place rather than people also puts community development squarely in opposition with the individualistic nature of our culture and society.

Yet community development is consistent with some of the ideals we hold, regardless of our political views, to be extremely important, such as democratic control and local autonomy. The political system may be driven by financial interests and individuals may have little control over bureaucratic institutions (e.g., corporations, educational systems, the government), but the community offers a place for people to learn the value of cooperation and civic virtue. Participation, like any other skill, must be learned through experience. The promise of community development is that these skills can be transferred to other walks of life.

KEY CONCEPTS

Asset-based development

Assets

Citizen participation

Community

Community capital

Community sustainability

Conflicts

Development

Growth

Neighborhood

Public involvement

Public participation

Regionalism

Self-help

Technical assistance

QUESTIONS

1. Compare and contrast the three models of community development described by Christenson.

2. What are the three necessary elements in the definition of community? Why is community such a difficult concept to define?

3. What is the difference between growth and development? Provide some examples.

4. Identify three key differences between the assets approach and the needs assessments approach to community development.

5. What are the basic strengths and weaknesses of place- versus people-oriented approaches to development?

EXERCISES

1. Ask several of your neighbors to draw a map of your community or neighborhood. How much agreement is there in these maps and how do they differ? How many neighbors do they know in this area? How often do they have contact with these people? Do they belong to any clubs, organizations, or associations in this neighborhood?

2. Identify all of the CBOs (both nonprofit and profit) in your neighborhood or community. Build a directory that identifies the services that each provides and a contact person for each organization. Assess the overlap in their missions and the networks that exist between these organizations.

3. Identify a community-based organization and evaluate its efforts to promote public participation. How does the organization engage the public? To what extent is the board representative of the community? How does the organization solicit input from residents? How could the organization improve its efforts to promote public participation?

REFERENCES

Alinsky, S. D. (1969). *Reveille for radicals.* New York: Random House.

Campbell, K., & Lee, B. (1992). Sources of personal neighbor networks: Social integration, need, or time? *Social Forces, 70,* 1077–1100.

Christenson, J. A. (1989). Themes in community development. In J. A. Christenson & J. Robinson (Eds.), *Community development in perspective* (pp. 26–47). Ames: Iowa State University Press.

Gans, H. J. (1962). *The urban villagers: Group and class in the life of Italian-Americans.* New York: Free Press of Glencoe.

Gunn, C., & Gunn, H. (1991). *Reclaiming capital: Democratic initiatives and community development.* Ithaca, NY: Cornell University Press.

Hillery, G. A., Jr. (1955). Definitions of community: Areas of agreement. *Rural Sociology, 20,* 111–123.

Hughes, M. (1991). Employment decentralization and accessibility: A strategy for stimulating regional mobility. *Journal of the American Planning Association, 57,* 288–298.

Jargowsky, P. A. (1997). *Poverty and place: Ghettos, barrios, and the American city.* New York: Russell Sage Foundation.

Johnson, D. E., Meiller, L. R., Miller, L. C., & Summers, G. F. (Eds.). (1987). *Needs assessment: Theory and methods.* Ames: Iowa State University Press.

Kretzmann, J., & McKnight, J. (1993). *Building communities from the inside out: A path toward finding and mobilizing a community's assets.* Evanston, IL: Center for Urban Affairs and Policy Research, Northwestern University.

Kretzmann, J. P., McKnight, J. L., & Sheehan, G. (1997). *A guide to capacity inventories: Mobilizing the community skills of local residents.* Chicago: ACTA Publications.

Langton, S. (Ed.). (1978). *Citizen participation in America.* Lexington, MA: Lexington Books.

Lemann, N. (1994, January 9). The myth of community development. *New York Times Magazine,* pp. 27–31.

Lipman, M., & Mahan, L. (Producers & Directors). (1996). *Holding ground: The rebirth of Dudley Street* [Video]. (Available from New Day Films, 22nd Hollywood Avenue, Ho-Ho-Kus, NJ 07423)

Lobao, L. M. (1990). *Locality and inequality: Farm and industry structure and socioeconomic conditions.* Albany: State University of New York Press.

Mayer, S. E. (1994). *Building community capacity: The potential of community foundations.* Minneapolis, MN: Rainbow Research.

McKnight, J. (1995). *The careless society: Community and its counterfeits.* New York: Basic Books.

Medoff, P., & Sklar, H. (1994). *Streets of hope: The fall and rise of an urban neighborhood.* Boston: South End Press.

Oliver, M. (2001). Foreword. In T. M. Shapiro & E. N. Wolff (Eds.), *Assets for the poor: The benefits of spreading asset ownership.* New York: Russell Sage Foundation.

Orfield, M. (1997). *Metropolitics: A regional agenda for community and stability.* Washington, DC: Brookings Institution Press.

Pettit, K. L. S., & Kingsley, G. T. (2003). *Concentrated poverty: A change in course.* Washington, DC: Urban Institute.

Putnam, R. (2000). *Bowing alone: The collapse and revival of American community.* New York: Simon & Schuster.

Roberts, N. (2004). Public deliberation in an age of direct citizen participation. *American Review of Public Administration, 34,* 315–353.

Rubin, H. J. (2000). *Renewing hope within neighborhoods of despair: The community-based development model.* Albany: State University of New York Press.

Rubin, H. J., & Rubin, I. S. (1992). *Community organizing and development* (2nd ed.). Boston: Allyn & Bacon.

Rusk, D. (1993). *Cities without suburbs.* Washington, DC: Woodrow Wilson Center Press.

Sen, A. (1999). *Development as freedom.* New York: Anchor Books.

Suttles, G. D. (1972). *The social construction of communities.* Chicago: University of Chicago Press.

Wilkinson, K. P. (1991). *The community in rural America.* New York: Greenwood Press.

ADDITIONAL READINGS AND RESOURCES

Readings

Bebbington, A. (1999). *Capitals and capabilities: A framework for analyzing peasant viability, rural livelihoods, and poverty in the Andes.* London: International Institute for Environment and Development.

Boyte, H. C. (1984). *Community is possible: Repairing America's roots.* New York: Harper & Row.

Brophy, P. C., & Shabecoff, A. (2000). *A guide to careers in community development.* Washington, DC: Island Press.

Bruyn, S., & Meehan, J. (Eds.). (1987). *Beyond the market and the state: New directions in community development.* Philadelphia: Temple University Press.

Chaskin, R. J., Brown, P., Venkatesh, S., & Vidal, A. (2001). *Building community capacity.* New York: Aldine de Gruyter.

Downs, A. (1994). *New visions for metropolitan America.* Washington, DC: Brookings Institution Press.

Ferguson, R. F., & Dickens, W. T. (Eds.). (1999). *Urban problems and community development.* Washington, DC: Brookings Institution Press.

Fisher, D. (2003). *Assets in action: A handbook for making communities better places to grow up.* Minneapolis, MN: Search Institute.

Gottlieb, P. D. (1997). Neighborhood development in the metropolitan economy: A policy review. *Journal of Urban Affairs, 19,* 163–182.

Green, G. P., & Goetting, A. (Eds.). (2010). *Mobilizing communities: Asset building as a community development strategy.* Philadelphia: Temple University Press.

Jacobs, J. (1961). *The death and life of Great American cities.* New York: Random House.

Mattessich, P., & Monsey, B. (1997). *Community building: What makes it work, a review of factors influencing successful community building.* Saint Paul, MN: Fieldstone Alliance.

McKibben, B. (2007). *Deep economy: The wealth of communities and the durable future.* New York: Times Books.

Murphy, P. W., & Cunningham, J. V. (2003). *Organizing for community controlled development: Renewing civil society.* Thousand Oaks, CA: Sage.

Peterman, W. (2000). *Neighborhood planning and community-based development: The potential and limits of grassroots action.* Thousand Oaks, CA: Sage.

Plastik, P. (n.d.). *Asset building for social change: Pathways to large scale change.* New York: Ford Foundation. Retrieved June 8, 2010, from http://www.fordfound.org/pdfs/impact/assets_pathways.pdf

Philips, R., & Pittman, R. H. (2008). *An introduction to community development.* New York: Routledge.

Robinson, J., & Green, G. P. (Eds.). (2010). *Introduction to community development: Theory, practice, & service-learning.* Thousand Oaks, CA: Sage.

Shaw, M. (2008). Community development and the politics of community. *Community Development Journal, 43,* 24–36.

Sherraden, M. (1991). *Assets and the poor: A new American welfare policy.* New York: M. E. Sharpe.

Shuman, M. H. (2000). *Going local: Creating self-reliant communities in a global age.* New York: Routledge.

Sirianni, C., & Friedland, L. (2001). *Civic innovation in America: Community empowerment, public policy, and the movement for civic renewal.* Berkeley: University of California Press.

Smock, K. (2003). *Democracy in action: Community organizing and urban change.* New York: Columbia University Press.

Summers, G., & Branch, K. (1984). Economic development and community social change. *Annual Review of Sociology, 10,* 141–166.

Websites

ABCD Training Group—http://www.abcdtraininggroup.org/. This website provides information on training in the principles, concepts, and application of asset-based community development.

Asset Building Community Development Institute—www.northwestern.edu/ipr/abcd.html. This program at Northwestern University provides resources, publications, and training on capacity-building approaches to community development.

Comm-Org: The On-line Conference on Community Organizing and Development—http://comm-org .wisc.edu/index.html. This site has a wealth of information on references, data, syllabi, and other resources on community organizing and development.

Community Development Society—www.comm-dev.org. The international Community Development Society is a professional association of community development practitioners. The society represents a variety of fields, including health care, social services, economic development, and education.

Ford Foundation Asset Building and Community Development Program—http://www.fordfound.org/ program/asset_main.cfm

International Association for Community Development—http://www.iacdglobal.org/. This organization aims to develop a global network of practitioners involved in community development. On the website, there are several publications and case studies of asset-based development.

NeighborWorks—http://www.nw.org/network/training/training.asp. This nonprofit organization provides financial support, technical assistance, and training for community-based revitalization efforts.

Search Institute—http://www.search-institute.org/. This nonprofit organization focuses on asset building, with a focus on youth and communities. The institute provides several tools for asset building and has a wonderful set of case studies.

Videos

Mobilizing Community Assets, by John Kretzmann and John McKnight. This video training program is for *Building Communities From the Inside Out.* Produced by Civic Network Television. Distributed by ACTA Publications, 4848 N. Clark South, Chicago, IL 60640; phone: (800) 397–2282.

Inviting Neighbors to Participate in Community Development. This video provides a nice summary of how to engage local citizens in a community development process. http://www.youtube.com/ watch?v=g4b56ky6118&feature=related

Other Resources

Community Development Council. This nonprofit organization was established to promote the accreditation of community development educational programs, professional certification, and the development of community volunteer leaders. It offers training and certification programs in several different locations of the United States.

Community Development Digest. This publication provides an excellent summary of pending legislation on community development issues.

A Guide to Careers in Community Development, by Paul C. Brophy & Alice Shabecoff (2000). Washington, DC: Island Press. This book is an excellent reference for anyone considering working in the community development field. The authors include information on jobs, universities and colleges offering community development curricula, training programs, and other resources on community development.

Shelterforce (http://www.shelterforce.org/). This is a valuable source of information on housing and community development. This online magazine is published by the National Housing Institute and covers a wide variety of community development topics, including housing, community organizing, economic development, sustainability, and policy issues.

The Urban Research Monitor. A useful reference tool developed by HUD USER. The publication makes it easy for researchers, policy makers, academicians, and other professionals to keep up with the literature on housing and community development. Each issues contains a listing of recent books, articles, reports, dissertations, and other publications related to housing and community development.

2

A History of Community Development in America

Community development matured in the United States in the 1960s with the rise of place-based policies (mostly antipoverty programs), professional training programs and degrees, and formal organizations with community development as their primary mission. Many of the ideas behind community self-reliance, however, have their roots in earlier intellectual sources, such as those of John Dewey (1916). Some of the first intentional efforts at promoting community development occurred at the turn of the century.

In this chapter, we trace the evolution of community development in America. We begin our analysis at the turn of the century, with the **Progressive Era** and some of the efforts to construct community programs to address poverty and other social problems. We examine the programs of the New Deal and the Great Society, which placed the federal government in a central role in community development. Finally, we discuss current efforts to promote development in poor and minority neighborhoods.

In this brief history, we point out several tensions and contradictions in the community development movement. One of the most critical tensions is the role of public participation in place-based development efforts. On one hand, it has been difficult to obtain public participation in local decision making. Residents have few experiences with and face numerous obstacles to participation. On the other hand, governmental officials and professionals often are threatened by public participation when it is successful. The result is a great deal of rhetoric about the importance of participation, which is seldom achieved in practice. Federal programs also have been contradictory. Although the federal government developed several programs to address the problems of localities, it has provided incentives through tax breaks and infrastructure to encourage suburban development. In doing so, the government has undermined many of the place-based policies that were established.

The Evolution of Community Development ————————

Although there continues to be much debate about the best approach to promote community development, the public generally supports the ideas of local control and the importance of community in social life. The idea of community development has evolved considerably during this century. In this brief review, we identify the main currents of thought in the community development field in the past century.

The Progressive Era

The origins of community development can be traced to the Progressive Era, especially to the ideas of social scientists and reformers at the turn of the century. The most distinguishing characteristic of the Progressives was their resistance to individualistic explanations for poverty and social disorganization (e.g., juvenile delinquency, crime, and the breakup of the family). Instead, they explained poverty and deviant behavior as results of social conditions in communities, as products of the subcultures of these neighborhoods. Progressives considered these subcultures to be obstacles to integration into the larger society. They argued that to improve local conditions, social intervention should have three important characteristics (O'Connor, 1999). First, social intervention should be comprehensive, focusing on the integration of education, social services, jobs, and physical conditions in a locality. Second, intervention should promote collaboration between experts and citizens in addressing local problems. The growth of comprehensive city planning during the period is one example of this model. Finally, Progressives placed a great deal of emphasis on citizen participation. As we discuss in this chapter, in the 1960s, this element of the community development program was highly controversial, especially during the War on Poverty.

One of the most visible efforts to promote community development in urban areas at the turn of the century was the **settlement house** movement. The objective of the settlement house movement was to help immigrants adjust to their new environment. The programs of the movement provided adult education (especially English language lessons), day care centers, libraries, recreational facilities, and other social services to help integrate residents into the larger society. Jane Addams and Ellen Gates Starr established probably the most famous of the settlement houses, Hull House, in Chicago. The clear intention was to reduce the impact of immigrants' native culture and introduce them to American society.

Whereas the focus of concern in urban America at the time was on poverty and social disorganization, the problems in rural areas were different: the lack of technical information on agricultural conditions, poor educational opportunities, monopolization of forest land, inadequate roads, poor health services, soil depletion, and the limited role of women. The major impetus to improving rural life at the time was President Theodore Roosevelt's 1908 Country Life Commission. One of the outcomes of this movement was the Cooperative Extension Service, established by the Smith-Lever Act of 1914. The Cooperative Extension Service provided an educator in each agricultural county who was responsible for programs related to the social, economic, and financial well-being of rural residents. The system had the same emphasis as the Progressive movement in urban reforms on collaboration between experts and citizens in solving local problems. The Cooperative Extension Service was able to draw on the research and expertise of the land grant system and build its program based on the involvement of local residents in identifying community needs. In many states, it also focused on comprehensive solutions that acknowledged the importance of recreation and social activities.

The Chicago School of Sociology, and especially Robert Park's (1915) theory of urban development, provided much of the intellectual foundation for intervention in urban neighborhoods. These academics provided a stronger intellectual basis for community organizing than did the proponents of the settlement houses. Park insisted that the problems of cities, such as juvenile delinquency and crime, rather than being the result of social disorganization, reflected the gradual assimilation of immigrants into the mainstream society. Park claimed that there was more social order in these settings than observers recognized. Neighborhood disorganization was necessary because it meant that immigrants were shedding their cultural influences. Park argued that this process was necessary for immigrants to eventually be integrated into the social life of cities. It was important, however, to provide stability at the neighborhood level—for example, through the provision of social services—to facilitate social integration.

Community development during the Progressive Era focused on community-level intervention that was intended to integrate residents into the larger society. The philosophy behind the movement was that professional expertise could be linked with participation by the poor in solving these problems. The goal was to help residents become full citizens by either improving the services available to them or providing them with the scientific information they would need to improve their quality of life. There was very little concern at the time with the potential for dependency relations developing between the public and experts. In both rural and urban areas, there was an interest in helping residents develop their own organizations to more adequately serve their needs.

The New Deal

President Franklin Roosevelt's New Deal programs constructed a new approach to the problems of depressed communities. Initiated in the 1930s, these programs dealt with a wide array of problems, including job creation, land ownership, housing, physical infrastructure, and social welfare. They provided federal support for community intervention and became the foundation for community development programs for the next 40 years. One of the chief characteristics of community development efforts during this period was the strong role of the federal government in helping communities address their needs.

Probably the most influential piece of legislation directly affecting depressed communities during the New Deal was the Housing Act of 1937. The Housing Act provided the basis for public housing. Like many of the other New Deal programs, the Housing Act of 1937 established a decentralized system of market subsidies and local control. Local authorities were responsible for issuing bonds, purchasing land, and contracting with local builders (O'Connor, 1999). The housing programs were used primarily for slum clearance, which was beneficial to the many real estate developers involved in opening up efforts to revitalize downtown areas. Local control also meant that almost all public housing built at the time was concentrated in central cities.

Many of the New Deal programs had objectives that worked against the goal of reducing urban poverty. The primary objective of the New Deal housing programs was to promote home ownership. There are several elements to these programs, but some of the most important are the home mortgage loans that were made available to middle- and working-class residents and the loan guarantees to private lenders. These programs provided incentives for people to move to the suburbs, leaving the central cities with a higher rate of unemployment, poverty, and social problems. The federal programs of the 1950s that built interstate highways also exacerbated many of these problems.

One of the most visible programs of the New Deal was the Works Progress Administration (WPA), which was established in 1935. The WPA provided jobs for the large number of unemployed workers during the Depression. The program provided more than $11 billion, mostly for public projects such as highways, streets, utilities, libraries, bridges, dams, and recreation facilities. Workers were paid the prevailing wage in the region, and many localities benefited immensely from the development of their infrastructure. The program offered on-the-job training and courses through adult education, which gave many workers concrete skills and experience.

The New Deal programs made some important strides in helping distressed communities. The programs, however, also faced other basic problems that have plagued community development programs over the years. In particular, the programs that might have benefited tenant farmers and African Americans in the South were bitterly fought by Southern legislators and businesses. Many of the social assistance programs were administered through local welfare offices, where the local elite could influence access to and levels of support for the poor (Piven & Cloward, 1971). This was the trade-off that President Roosevelt made for getting the support of Southern Democrats for the New Deal. This tension between local control and federal support continued through several decades of programs related to community development. The New Deal, however, did represent a major shift in the role of the federal government in attempting to address the problems of poor communities.

Urban Renewal and Area Redevelopment

During the 1940s and 1950s, population and employment decentralization contributed to the growth of suburbs and the rise in poverty and blight in central cities. The federal government's response to these problems was the Housing Act of 1949, which came to be known as **urban renewal**. The primary objective of urban renewal was to clear the slums in efforts to revitalize downtowns and attract middle-class residents back to cities. The Housing Act permitted local redevelopment authorities to use eminent domain to reclaim land for commercial purposes. Urban renewal came to be known as "Negro removal" and was criticized for bulldozing low-income neighborhoods.

The Area Redevelopment Act (ARA) of 1961 focused on a different set of issues at the time—joblessness in areas affected by economic modernization. The program provided low-interest loans to businesses willing to locate or expand in the designated depressed areas. The ARA was eliminated after a relatively brief period (4 years). Among the major criticisms were that the ARA was recruiting nonunion businesses and that it was largely ineffective. The program was transformed into the Economic Development Administration (EDA) and focused on rural infrastructure and regional planning.

The War on Poverty

Three programs during the mid-1960s provided the foundation for President Lyndon Johnson's **War on Poverty**: the **Community Action Program (CAP)**, **Model Cities**, and the **Special Impact Program (SIP)**. These programs were qualitatively different from the New Deal programs.

CAP became one of the most controversial programs of the War on Poverty (Moynihan, 1969). In Title II-A, Section 202 (a)(3) of the Economic Opportunity Act of 1964, CAPs were authorized to be "developed, conducted and administered with the maximum feasible participation of residents of the areas and members of the groups served." There was considerable disagreement among activists, bureaucrats, and policy makers about the involvement of the poor in CAP policy making and program development. Some people thought of this requirement as simply involvement, not decision-making responsibility. Others interpreted it as requiring some form of social action among the poor.

The most serious criticisms of the program were (1) that it contributed to the conflict and violence in the inner city during the 1960s, (2) the government adopted this idea without any understanding of community participation, (3) bureaucrats had perverted congressional intent of the program, and (4) the poor were not ready to assume power in their communities. Daniel Moynihan's (1969) principal concern was that the program led to rising expectations on which it could not deliver. This, he argued, was the central reason for the riots in the major cities during this period.

The requirement for citizen participation was a threat to many local politicians. City mayors were accustomed to working with established neighborhood organizations and leaders representing minority groups and the poor, not the emerging coalitions in these cities. CAPs were demanding changes in services and resources allocated to poor neighborhoods. In reality, however, most CAPs were never very representative of the poor. The boards did not have many poor people on them, and the CAPs were required to work through the system to achieve any results.

There is a consensus that most of the citizen participation programs of the 1960s were not effective. Several factors worked against the efforts. The federal and local governments never really trusted the CAPs. As a result, many local government officials were able to minimize the level of real community control in the organizations. Resources for the War on Poverty were insufficient for dealing with the magnitude of the problems. The Vietnam War siphoned off money that could have been devoted to the poverty programs. Thus, it is not clear whether the CAP was a failed idea, because it was never given the chance to demonstrate how effective it could have been.

The second major program directed at concentrations of poor and minority households was the Model Cities program. This program was established through the Demonstration and Metropolitan Development Act (1966). The act provided grants to city agencies to improve housing, the physical environment, and social services in low-income neighborhoods. In many respects, it was a diluted version of the CAP because it placed less emphasis on citizen participation. The major difference was that CAPs worked around local government officials, whereas Model Cities worked with them.

The third major program initiated during this period was the SIP. This program provided funds to community development corporations (CDCs) to finance comprehensive development strategies. SIP was an outcome of Senator Robert Kennedy's visit to Brooklyn's Bedford-Stuyvesant neighborhood in 1965, which formed the nation's first CDC.

One of the most controversial issues of this era, and one that continues today, is the role of eminent domain in urban renewal. Eminent domain refers to the government condemnation of private property for public purposes. During the 1960s, the federal government condemned a large number of parcels and tore down buildings, leaving property vacant for development. In many cities, however, this property remained vacant or was sold to private developers. The concept of eminent domain remains controversial today, especially after the recent *Kelo v. New London* (2005) decision by the Supreme Court. This case supported the right of government to take private property for public use.

The community development programs of the 1960s placed considerably more emphasis on local control than had any previous attempts to address the problems of poor communities. Most assessments of the programs have concluded that these efforts to increase the level of participation by the poor in decision making were relatively unsuccessful. These programs also emphasized the need for neighborhood organizations to address local problems. The continued growth of CDCs today suggests that this may have been one of the most successful long-term elements of these programs.

Retrenchment in the Nixon and Reagan Administrations

The Nixon administration's New Federalism restructured the role of the federal government in community development. The administration attempted to dismantle many of the programs that were created in the 1960s by giving states and localities more authority in influencing how public funds were spent. Probably the best example of this shift was the creation of **Community Development Block Grants (CDBGs)** in 1974, which replaced many (seven) of the categorical grants to localities for specific purposes to address poverty. The Nixon administration replaced these categorical grants with a form of revenue sharing that gave localities much more autonomy in their decisions in how to spend these dollars. The CDBGs fall in between these two extremes.

The CDBGs have three major objectives: (1) to benefit low- and moderate-income families (defined as families earning no more than 80% of the area median income), (2) to eliminate or prevent slums, and (3) to meet urgent community needs. Communities must use at least 70% of the CDBG funds to benefit principally low- and moderate-income persons. The CDBG program is one of the largest of the federal grant programs. Over the past 30 years, the federal government has allocated almost $100 billion to CDBGs.

Communities receiving funds directly from the federal government today are referred to as entitlement communities. These metropolitan cities and urban counties (842 cities and 147 counties) receive direct grants that can be used to revitalize neighborhoods, expand affordable housing and economic development efforts, and improve community facilities and services. A separate CDBG program allocates funds to the states. States in turn provide grants to localities not covered under the entitlement funds, referred to as nonentitlement communities.

To receive its CDBG entitlement grant, a community must have a plan approved that describes how it will use its funds. Throughout most of the 1980s and 1990s, housing was the most important use of CDBGs in localities. There has been a gradual shift in priorities, however, toward other objectives, such as economic development activities. Jobs created through CDBG-funded programs must meet several tests for quality. A study by the Urban Institute, funded through the U.S. Department of Housing and Urban Development (HUD, 1995), found that 96% of the jobs created through CDBG funds were full-time jobs, 89% of the jobs remained after 4 years, 90% paid more than minimum wage, and 32% were held by the businesses' neighborhood residents. CDBG funds are supposed to be targeted to needy communities through a formula allocation system that considers population size, poverty, overcrowded housing, and age of housing.

How do communities use their CDBG funds? Communities may acquire real property for public purposes, such as abandoned houses purchased for rehabilitation. Many localities have used the funds to build public facilities, such as streets, sidewalks, water and sewer systems, and recreational facilities. Increasingly, communities are using CDBG funds to help for-profit businesses by establishing revolving loan funds, assembling land for new industry, or helping existing businesses expand to hire low-income workers. In 1998, entitlement communities spent the largest share of their funding for housing and public facilities and improvements.

CASE STUDY 2.1 CDBG FUNDS: DIRECT ASSISTANCE TO LOW- AND MODERATE-INCOME HOMEBUYERS, WAUKESHA COUNTY, WISCONSIN

Waukesha County is located in the suburbs of Milwaukee and is one of the fastest growing areas in Wisconsin. Rapid growth and a high median family income mean that housing costs are out of range for most low- and moderate-income families, with only a few homes for sale under $100,000. To respond to these needs, the county used CDBG funds to underwrite low- and moderate-income buyers in three new subdivisions to promote home ownership through innovative methods. The county is also using $350,000 "float loan" financing for buyers' land write-downs in another development.

SOURCE: Gunther (2000).

The Reagan administration changed the CDBG program to allow states to administer the grants to small cities. Governors maintained that they could direct the resources better to distressed communities than could the federal government. The evidence suggests that states and localities vary considerably in their capacity and will to target these funds to the most distressed communities (Rich, 1993). When states target the funds, they tend to distribute the funds to a broader set of communities and are less likely to target the most distressed communities.

Local officials like CDBG funds because they are a predictable source of funding for community development. In addition, the funds are relatively flexible, although there has been some controversy over the years regarding how flexible these funds should be. The funds also can be used to leverage private funds (and other public funds) for community projects.

Probably the most lasting impact of the Reagan administration on community development was the federal budget cuts throughout the 1980s. Most of the federal programs that supported community development programs, especially those through HUD, were cut severely. Ironically, these cuts may have strengthened many community-based organizations (CBOs), such as CDCs, which were forced to find new sources of funding, primarily through foundations and other private sources.

The Clinton Years

The Clinton administration's efforts at community development focused primarily on the Empowerment Zone/Enterprise Community (EZ/EC) initiative. The objective of this program was to stimulate economic opportunity in America's distressed communities. The program provided tax incentives and performance grants and loans to create jobs and business opportunities. It also focused on activities to support people looking for work, such as job training, child care, and transportation.

Employers in the EZ are eligible for wage tax credits, worth $3,000, for every employee hired who lives in the EZ. EZ businesses also may write off the expense of the cost of depreciable, tangible property they purchase up to $37,000. All of the communities are eligible to receive tax-exempt bond financing that offers lower rates than conventional financing to finance business property and land, renovations, or expansion.

To receive funds, communities are required to submit strategic plans developed with the active participation of low-income community residents, and only communities with high rates of poverty are eligible. In the first round, rural EZs received grants of $40 million and rural ECs received about $3 million from the Social Services Block Grant program. Urban EZs received $100 million; urban ECs received the same amount as rural ECs. The first round of empowerment zones included Atlanta, Baltimore, Chicago, Cleveland, Detroit, Los Angeles, New York, Philadelphia, Kentucky Highlands, Mid-Delta Mississippi, and the Rio Grande Valley in Texas. There were 95 enterprise communities.

The effectiveness of these programs has been hotly debated. HUD reports that by 1998, almost 10,000 jobs were created or saved, 14,000 workers were trained, 25,000 youth were served, and 102 water or waste treatment systems were under construction. Most of the businesses would have located or stayed in these communities without the tax incentives, and these programs have had only a very limited impact on poverty in these areas. EZ/EC communities also face some of the same opposition by local government officials that the CAPs faced in the 1960s.

By the late 1990s, most states passed their own enterprise-zone legislation. States vary widely in what they offer businesses to locate in these zones, including tax incentives (e.g., property tax abatements, investment tax credits, employer and employee tax credits, and lender and investment deductions), financial assistance (e.g., low-interest loans and bond financing), and regulatory changes (e.g., environmental regulations, building permits).

The other major Clinton administration initiative was overhaul of the welfare system. In 1996, Congress passed the Personal Responsibility and Work Opportunity Reconciliation Act (PRWOR), which ended the program known as Aid to Families with Dependent Children (AFDC). This act had important implications for states and localities because CBOs became more involved in providing services to welfare recipients and designing programs that would facilitate their entrance into the labor force. These programs relied heavily on CBOs to coordinate many of the services and training programs that were available to workers.

The Workforce Investment Act of 1998, one of the most ambitious and comprehensive workforce education and training programs ever passed by the U.S. Congress, emphasizes community building to meet local workforce needs. This program requires local partnerships in designing training programs. The act also mandates participation of local businesses, government officials, and other local organizations in the program and policy development of workforce development boards. The Clinton administration benefited from the longest period of economic expansion since World War II. This economic growth meant that many regions suffered from labor shortages. As a result, there were many job openings for welfare recipients, and the tight labor market began to increase the wages for the lowest-paid workers. Although many jobs were created, most former welfare recipients have not moved out of poverty. Additional training and support programs are needed to provide them with economic and social mobility.

Overall, the Clinton administration did not rebuild the federal support for community development programs that existed in the 1960s. Instead, the administration continued the trend begun by the Nixon and Reagan administrations to cut back the role of the federal government. It also continued to decentralize much of the decision making, giving the responsibility to local officials. Probably the best illustration of this trend has been the legislation that reformed the federal government's role in welfare programs. Foundations, such as the Ford Foundation and the Kellogg Foundation, have picked up some of the slack that was left from the declining financial support for community development programs.

The Bush Administration

The Bush administration had planned to cut many of the community development programs in the federal government but had little success. For example, in 2005, the administration proposed to eliminate HUD's CDBG program. The program, however, is highly valued in Congress and brings much-needed resources to many communities.

The major effort affecting community development under the Bush administration has been its faith-based initiative, which is discussed in more detail in Chapter 5. This initiative established a White House office to help faith-based organizations address problems of homelessness and drug abuse. Opposition to the initiative has focused on its potential to erode the separation between church and state. The administration defended its program by arguing that it is putting faith-based organizations on a level playing field with other CBOs and is simply recognizing the critical role faith-based organizations play in addressing social needs.

The Bush administration's general approach toward community development was to emphasize the importance of private rather than public institutions as the appropriate mechanism to promote development. The administration's tendency has been to focus on community issues as individual rather than social problems. Of course, the larger culture tends to reinforce public policy. For example, a growing number of gated suburban communities have been established in response to urban poverty and crime (Blakely & Snyder, 1997). Combined with growing income inequality, restrictive land policies, and racial and economic segregation, these suburban migration patterns make it more difficult to address broader social problems.

Community development, however, stands on firmer ground than it did 30 years ago. The number of CBOs and nonprofit organizations working in the area of poverty has increased. Although many of these organizations continue to struggle for financial support, they have developed many relatively successful programs. Similarly, the concept of public participation has become more institutionalized in federal and state programs. Elements of public participation are now included in environmental, health, transportation, housing, and economic development programs. Public participation is now considered an important element of good policy making.

Obama's Challenges

President Barrack Obama came to office with considerable experience in community organizing. He worked in the mid-1980s as a community organizer with the Developing Communities Project (DCP), a church-based community organization on the South Side of Chicago. He worked with the Gamaliel Foundation as a consultant as well. These community roots provided President Obama with a rich understanding of the obstacles and challenges low-income residents faced in their neighborhoods.

The most immediate concern of the Obama administration in 2009 was the recession. The financial and housing bubbles led to tightening of the credit system and the highest unemployment rates in more than 25 years. The American Recovery and Reinvestment Act (ARRA) of 2009 provided aid to cities and states in an attempt to provide a stimulus to the economy. There were several components to the act that focused on community development initiatives. ARRA provided $1.5 billion to fund regional transportation projects and $8 billion to initiate high-speed rail systems in several states. In addition to the support for infrastructure projects, the act provided funds for a clean energy project and injected capital for low-cost loans to banks that focus on funding development in lower-income communities. Clean energy projects focused on sustainability efforts and financing for retrofitting old residences and businesses. Funds were also directed at low-income neighborhoods that suffered high foreclosure rates as a result of the housing crisis.

Key features of the Obama administration's metropolitan policy are its emphasis on regionalism and sustainability. Many of these programs will be coordinated by the new White House Office of Urban Affairs. The 2010 budget contained several new initiatives. The Sustainable Communities Initiative provides grants to metropolitan areas where several municipalities come together to coordinate transportation, housing, and land use decisions. The Choice Neighborhoods Initiative focuses on neighborhoods where rental housing is currently clustered. This program provides funding for housing redevelopment and other forms of neighborhood revitalization. The Choice Neighborhoods Initiative will replace HOPE VI, which was designed to replace public housing projects in concentrated neighborhoods. The Promise Zone Initiative is modeled after a program in Harlem that provides a wide range of services that focus on the well-being of children.

Community Organizing

This discussion of the history of community development emphasizes the institutional evolution of the field, but it says little about the impact of organized labor and social unrest resulting from the New Deal and other social movements (civil rights, farm workers, and even environmental movements) on community development. Many of the programs we discussed were in response to social unrest or pressure from various civil society organizations. In their book *Regulating the Poor,* Frances Fox Piven and Richard Cloward (1971) documented how public assistance programs are linked to economic conditions and labor unrest. Their argument was that welfare programs function to regulate labor. Public assistance expands in times of high unemployment and social unrest and contracts when order is restored and the economy improves. Community development programs, especially the War on Poverty programs, were a part of this response. Piven and Cloward concluded that these programs would not have emerged if the poor had been placid. They suggest, however, that many of the programs were symbolic and were rolled back once the unrest subsided.

Other social movements shaped the nature of community development in the 1960s and 1970s. In the mid-1960s, Cesar Chavez played a critical role in his unionization efforts of the National Farm Workers Association (NFWA) and the United Farm Workers (UFW). Prior to his work with the NFWA, Chavez worked for a decade at a community service organization (CSO) in California that had an affiliation with Saul Alinsky's Industrial Areas Foundation (discussed in Chapter 10). The goal of the CSO was to improve services, especially those provided to Chicano communities. Chavez's experience with the organization led to his interest in organizing farm workers. Chavez's unique contribution was that he organized farm workers using community-based strategies he learned from the CSO, rather than labor union tactics, which were used normally. He relied on some of the techniques used by the Industrial Areas Foundation, such as conducting house meetings with farm workers to understand their concerns and issues. Chavez also was successful in linking his movement to the civil rights movement and the poor people's movement of the 1960s.

Another key development in the 1970s was the community reinvestment movement. Using Alinsky-style tactics in Chicago, Gale Cincotta led a national collation of neighborhood groups to challenge the disinvestment activities of financial institutions in urban areas. This movement led to the Community Reinvestment Act (discussed in Chapter 9), which has successfully directed more than a billion dollars into depressed communities in the past few decades.

Social movements have played a critical role in shaping the community development field. Although some of the responses have been symbolic and short term, community development has become institutionalized in policies and programs today. One of the lessons learned, however, is that the responsiveness of government officials to local needs is driven by the level of community organization. Recent attempts to eliminate some of the basic programs, such as the CDBG program, have not been successful. Politicians from a broad political spectrum can ideologically support community development, evidenced by political conservatives' opposition to cuts in basic programs. Even local elites view community development programs as legitimate and will defend them to the federal government.

——————— Recurring Issues in Community Development

Throughout the history of the United States, several tensions and issues have plagued community development efforts. Among the most important are the role of participation and the importance of gender and race in shaping development efforts in poor communities.

Participation

Public participation in programs directed at low- and middle-income neighborhoods has been institutionalized since the 1960s. There continues to be debate over how effective this participation has been. At its worst, public participation has been used to simply legitimate the decisions of government officials. At its best, public participation has brought CBOs to the table in some cities, though it probably has not resulted in community control in most cases.

Unfortunately, most government programs look more like pseudo- rather than full participation (Pateman, 1970). That is, they provide residents with an opportunity to participate but really have no power to make decisions. Government agencies frequently are required to include some form of public participation, but are unwilling to leave the decision-making process to local residents. Instead, officials use the opportunity to gain legitimacy for their decisions. Similarly, efforts by the federal government to promote public participation have been fought by local government officials, who see these efforts as reducing their political patronage or support.

Decentralization of federal programs does not mean that poor residents will have more control over programs because, as is evident with many community development programs, decentralization leads to greater control by the local elite. Centralization of the programs, however, usually ensures that the poor will have very little control over programs.

One of the central issues in the debates over public participation is how much information and knowledge residents need to be effective. On one hand, advocates of public participation contend that residents hold the most relevant information about their community and that they should be the ones making decisions about issues affecting their locality. On the other hand, many of the issues affecting communities today are highly technical, and residents should rely on experts to help them make decisions or should be educated on the issues. There probably is no resolution to this problem, but in recent years the community development field has emphasized the importance of the local knowledge of residents and the significance of their participation, even in highly technical decisions.

As the field of community development has matured, practitioners and community advocates have often viewed the issue of participation as secondary to the substantive issues facing communities. In many cases, the public participation element is simply a part of the process. Even among many CBOs, the concept of direct participation is seen as unwieldy and messy.

Race

Another critique of community development programs is that they are race neutral, ignoring the role of racial discrimination in generating high poverty rates in minority communities (Jennings, 2004). The high poverty rate among minorities, especially among African Americans, has been assumed to be a result of low levels of human capital, high rates of crime in poor neighborhoods (which deter businesses from locating there), and high levels of unemployment in metropolitan areas. Although these issues are certainly a constraint to place-based policies, other factors that more directly focus on racial discrimination are seldom considered.

Racial discrimination is defined as involving actions that serve to limit the social, political, or economic opportunities of particular groups (Fredrickson & Knobel, 1982). Racial discrimination may take a variety of forms. Redlining by lending institutions and insurance companies may be directed at minority neighborhoods. Similarly, employer discrimination may focus on workers from specific neighborhoods or schools (Kirschenman & Neckerman, 1991).

Quadagno (1994) argued that racial discrimination played an important role in undermining the War on Poverty in the 1960s. She provided several examples where community development programs failed because of White opposition and the unwillingness or inability of the federal government to overcome this opposition. When the CAPs were formed, many were quickly taken over by civil rights activists, who challenged many big-city mayors and political organizations. The Office of Economic Opportunity (OEO) was sensitive to the criticism by local government officials that the CAPs had provided the spark for the urban riots of the 1960s. In 1973, President Nixon abolished the OEO.

Training programs devised during the War on Poverty also suffered some of the same problems. The goal of many of these programs was to increase the skills of workers from poor neighborhoods. Unions, which attempted to restrict the supply of labor to maintain a high level of demand, were opposed to these programs. In addition, the unions were unwilling to change their recruiting practices, which often discriminated against minorities. Eventually, training programs focused less on low-income and minority workers and became more acceptable to the larger public. Quadagno (1994) showed how attempts by the federal government to deal with racial segregation also created a backlash by local governments, developers, and others. Because most of the housing programs focused on rental subsidies for minorities, local governments frequently challenged them.

These three cases illustrate how race has played a critical role in affecting the success of community development programs. There continue to be debates over whether community development programs should directly confront the issue of racial discrimination. Critics of race-specific policies suggest that these programs need broad support and targeting race-based policies will cause programs to fail. In her analysis of the War on Poverty, Margaret Weir (1988) argued that "the racial targeting of the War on Poverty helped to create the conditions for a powerful backlash that would severely damage prospects for meaningful cooperation between blacks and labor in support of employment programs" (p. 184). A better solution, according to Weir, would have been to develop strategies that would press for broader solutions, such as full employment.

Wilson (1978, 1987) probably has been the strongest critic of race-specific programs to address the problems of concentrated poverty. Wilson contended that concentrated poverty is the result of the decline of manufacturing jobs in cities (which paid good wages), the suburbanization of employment, and the rise of low-wage service-sector jobs, which has reduced employment opportunities in most central cities. As a result, the number of communities with high levels of poverty (greater than 40%) has increased rapidly since the 1960s (though the number actually declined somewhat during the 1990s). Wilson argued that programs like affirmative action have benefited minorities with higher levels of education and training but that they have not helped the underclass. Like Weir, Wilson believes that creating tight labor markets is, in the long run, the best way to address the problems of concentrated poverty.

Critics, such as Massey and Denton (1993), claim that racial discrimination, primarily in the area of housing, continues to be the root cause of urban poverty. Massey and Denton argued that housing segregation results in higher concentrations of poverty and the deterioration of social and economic conditions in Black communities and that it ultimately leads to attitudes and behaviors that make it difficult for residents to obtain employment outside poor neighborhoods. They focus on better enforcement of the **Fair Housing Act of 1968** and other race-specific policies directed toward poor neighborhoods.

Race has been an underlying issue throughout the history of community development. Advocates continue their efforts for projects that focus on the importance of race, such as those that address lending, housing, and employment discrimination. Although most community development practitioners recognize the importance of these issues, they continue to debate the effects of these programs in helping the poor and gaining assistance from the larger society.

Gender

Women dominate most neighborhood and community organizations, but this fact is largely ignored in much of the literature on community development. Haeberle (1989) found that gender was the strongest predictor of community activists' perceptions of their neighborhood organization's success. Men and women approach their neighborhood organizations differently. Men are much more likely to define their neighborhoods in material terms, whereas women focus more on the social relationships and bonds. There also are gender differences in whether residents emphasize the process or outcomes of community development. Men tend to favor community development projects that focus on physical improvement projects, such as new or better roads and recreational facilities. Women tend to emphasize the importance of organizational participation in the community development process.

There is very little literature on the role of women in community organizing and development. An exception is Naples's (1998a) longitudinal study of women community workers hired in the CAPs during the War on Poverty and her edited book on community activism and feminist politics (Naples, 1998b). Naples found that the War on Poverty provided opportunities for women to receive pay for the work they performed on the behalf of communities. Although many of these women were pulled into other jobs, especially into professionalized social service agencies, they continued to work on behalf of their communities.

Like the debates over race-specific policies, there is a growing recognition that women, especially minority women, may have been disadvantaged by the structural changes in the economy over the past 30 years.

In particular, there may be fewer job opportunities for women in central cities that provide a living wage. Thus, strategies for creating jobs in these poor neighborhoods need to recognize the special constraints that women face in the labor market (especially child care) and the role that gender segregation plays in the labor market.

Summary and Conclusions

Community development efforts during the past four decades have shared two key aspects. First, efforts have been place based, with a special emphasis on minority and low-income neighborhoods and communities. Second, community development programs have emphasized public participation and community control. Both of these elements continue to be controversial. Critics suggest that these programs do not address the larger structural forces affecting poor neighborhoods. Looking at the evidence, we would have to agree that the outcomes of these programs have been limited. Many of the problems, however, are not due to the theory or practice of community development but to opposition by local officials or federal programs that undermined community development efforts.

This brief review of the evolution of community development also highlights the difficult role the federal government plays in promoting development in poor and minority neighborhoods. It is clear that the federal government can play an important role in funneling resources to local organizations. It is less clear, however, whether the federal government can actually build neighborhood organizations or create public participation. As we discuss in the chapter on CBOs, the federal government may not be able to overcome the many institutional obstacles that exist. Thus, the real hope for community development may rely on grassroots efforts initiated at the local level.

KEY CONCEPTS

Community Action Program (CAP)

Community Development
  Block Grants (CDBGs)

Cooperative Extension Service

Country Life Commission

Empowerment Zone/Enterprise
  Community (EZ/EC)

Fair Housing Act of 1968

Model Cities

Progressive Era

Racial discrimination

Settlement house

Special Impact Program (SIP)

Urban renewal

War on Poverty

QUESTIONS

1. Describe the history of community development in America. What do you consider the most important trends in how community development has been approached in the United States?

2. Why was the Community Action Program so controversial? How did these controversies affect poverty programs in the late 1960s?

3. What have been the long-term effects of New Federalism on community development programs?

4. Discuss some of the strengths and weaknesses of the EZ/EC program.

5. What are the arguments for and against race-based programs in community development?

EXERCISES

1. Interview a local government official in your community and assess how community development programs have affected residents in your area. How many people receive rent subsidies? How is the CDBG program used in your community? Try to obtain some historical information on how your community participated in previous programs to help poor neighborhoods. How has community development changed in the past 30 years in your community?

2. Contact a Fair Housing Association in your community. Meet with representatives of the organization to discuss their recent activities. In what types of projects is the organization involved? What is the primary source of complaints regarding fair housing in your community?

3. Identify a local agency responsible for community and/or economic development. Interview some of the officials in this agency about their efforts to promote public participation in their programs. Have these programs successfully created opportunities for minorities and women to participate in community development efforts? How could these programs be improved?

REFERENCES

Blakely, E. J., & Snyder, M. G. (1997). *Fortress America: Gated communities in the United States.* Washington, DC: Brookings Institution Press.

Dewey, J. (1916). *Democracy and education: An introduction to the philosophy of education.* New York: Macmillan.

Fredrickson, G. M., & Knobel, D. T. (1982). A history of discrimination. In S. Thernstrom, A. Orlov, & O. Handlin (Eds.), *Prejudice: Dimensions of ethnicity* (pp. 30–87). Cambridge, MA: Harvard University Press.

Gunther, J. J. (2000). *Blue ribbon practices in community development.* Washington, DC: U.S. Department of Housing and Urban Development.

Haeberle, S. H. (1989). *Planting the grassroots: Structuring citizen participation.* New York: Praeger.

Jennings, J. (2004). Race, politics, and community development in U.S. cities. *The Annals of the American Academy of Political and Social Science, 594,* 1–11.

Kelo v. City of New London, 545 U.S. 469 (2005).

Kirschenman, J., & Neckerman, K. M. (1991). We'd love to hire them, but . . . : The meaning of race for employers. In C. Jencks & P. Peterson (Eds.), *The urban underclass* (pp. 201–235). Washington, DC: Brookings Institution Press.

Massey, D. S., & Denton, N. A. (1993). *American apartheid: Segregation and the making of the underclass*. Cambridge, MA: Harvard University Press.

Moynihan, D. P. (1969). *Maximum feasible misunderstanding: Community action in the war on poverty*. New York: Free Press.

Naples, N. A. (1998a). *Grassroots warriors: Activist mothering, community work, and the war on poverty*. New York: Routledge.

Naples, N. A. (Ed.). (1998b). *Community activism and feminist politics: Organizing across race, class and gender*. New York: Routledge.

O'Connor, A. (1999). Swimming against the tide: A brief history of federal policy in poor communities. In R. F. Ferguson & W. T. Dickens (Eds.), *Urban problems and community development* (pp. 77–137). Washington, DC: Brookings Institution Press.

Park, R. E. (1915). The city: Suggestions for the investigation of human behavior in the city. *American Journal of Sociology, 20*, 577–612.

Pateman, C. (1970). *Participation and democratic theory*. Cambridge, UK: Cambridge University Press.

Piven, F., & Cloward, R. A. (1971). *Regulating the poor: The functions of public welfare*. New York: Vintage Books.

Quadagno, J. (1994). *The color of welfare: How racism undermined the war on poverty*. New York: Oxford University Press.

Rich, M. J. (1993). *Federal policymaking and the poor: National goals, local choices, and distributional outcomes*. Princeton, NJ: Princeton University Press.

U.S. Department of Housing and Urban Development. (1995). *Federal funds, local choices: An evaluation of the Community Development Block Grant Program*. Washington, DC: Author.

Weir, M. (1988). The federal government and unemployment: The frustration of policy innovation from the New Deal to the Great Society. In M. Weir, A. S. Orloff, & T. Skocpol (Eds.), *The politics of social policy in the United States* (pp. 149–197). Princeton, NJ: Princeton University Press.

Wilson, W. J. (1978). *The declining significance of race: Blacks and changing American institutions*. Chicago: University of Chicago Press.

Wilson, W. J. (1987). *The truly disadvantaged: The inner city, the underclass, and public policy*. Chicago: University of Chicago Press.

ADDITIONAL READINGS AND RESOURCES

Readings

Berry, J. M., Portney, K. E., & Thomson, K. (1993). *The rebirth of urban democracy*. Washington, DC: Brookings Institution Press.

Lemann, N. (1994, January 9). The myth of community development. *New York Times Magazine*, pp. 27–31.

Levitan, S. A. (1969). *The Great Society's poor law: A new approach to poverty*. Baltimore: Johns Hopkins University Press.

Websites

Department of Housing and Urban Development (HUD)—www.hud.gov. This website provides information on HUD programs, especially related to housing.

Department of Housing and Urban Development (HUD)—www.hud.gov/cpd/cpdalloc.html. This website provides data on the CDBG allocations—how much each entitlement community has received.

3

Community Sustainability

Sustainability is a critical feature of the community development process. One of the many goals of community development is to sustain places and people using all forms of community capital. In this chapter, we argue that sustainability should play an explicit role in the practice of community development. By making this argument, we believe it is necessary to define community sustainability, discuss its history, and explain approaches or frameworks for practicing community sustainable development. Sustainable community development relies heavily on a systems approach that recognizes the interconnections between the economy, environment, and social basis of the community. For example, if a community-based organization (CBO) is planning an affordable housing project, should energy efficiency be made a part of that type of project? Without getting into details, the simple answer is yes. If community development practitioners take a systems approach, they will not only think about the short-term shelter issue but the long-term financial issue of paying for utility costs. If housing is energy efficient and can reduce or eliminate utility bills for heating and cooling, for example, a portion of that person's/family's income can go to food, health care, and other goods and services they may need. Energy efficiency also has an environmental impact by reducing fossil fuel use and greenhouse gases. With one decision, social, economic, and environmental concerns are addressed.

In this chapter, we define key concepts and debates that pertain to community sustainability, examine the idea's origins and its use, and introduce two approaches to community sustainability. This discussion is relevant to our larger framework on different forms of community capital and asset-based development. The tendency in most communities is to emphasize one form of capital over others. The concept of sustainability helps us understand and appreciate the important links and relationships between these different assets. Some of the most obvious links are between physical and natural forms of capital. Expansion of physical capital often comes at the expense of natural capital. There are interrelationships as well, such as between social, cultural, financial, and political capital.

What Is Community Sustainability?

Sustainability can be viewed as a concept, a method, or even a way of life. It allows communities to sort through development options and arrive at a strategy that takes into consideration the full range of economic, environmental, and social characteristics of a community (Beatley & Manning, 1997; Maser, 1997; Roelofs, 1996; Roseland, 1994; Sargent, Lusk, Rivera, & Varela, 1991; Van der Ryn & Calthorpe, 1986). The drive toward sustainable communities results from a host of problems, such as rapid global population growth, global warming, species extinction, ozone depletion, widespread hunger, and deforestation. At a local level in the United States, the loss of farmland and open space, solid waste crises, crime, and widening income disparities are other problems feeding the community sustainability movement.

It has been a challenge to provide a concrete definition of sustainability. It seems that each organization and individual wants to define it anew. Thus, there are many definitions for sustainability. Box 3.1 provides several definitions. There are three common themes among these definitions: (1) a focus on current behavior to benefit the future, (2) the link between economy with ecology, and (3) a general dissatisfaction with current human lifestyles and behavior.

BOX 3.1 DEFINITIONS OF SUSTAINABILITY

- "Sustainable development is development that meets the needs of the present without compromising the ability of future generations to meet their own needs" (Brundtland, 1987, p. 24).
- "We stand for environmental justice which means a decent environment for all without using more than our fair share of the world's resources. We aim to make the right to a decent environment available to everyone in Scotland and around the globe" (Friends of the Earth Scotland, 2006).
- "The practice of sustainability is about creating new ways to live and prosper while ensuring an equitable, healthy future for all people and the planet" (The Natural Step, 2006).
- "A stable and sustainable society cannot be achieved when high levels of extreme poverty prevail" (World Business Council on Sustainable Development, 2006).
- "A sustainable community continues to thrive from generation to generation because it has:
  - A healthy and diverse ecological system that continually performs life sustaining functions and provides resources for humans and other species
  - A social foundation that provides for the health of all community members, respects cultural diversity, is equitable in its actions, and considers the needs of future generations
  - A healthy and diverse economy that adapts to change, provides long-term security to residents, and recognizes social and ecological limits" (Sustainable Community Roundtable Report, 2006).

Three important dimensions, referred to as the three Es in the literature, underlie sustainability: economics, environment, and equity (or social justice). Each of these dimensions needs to be in balance with the others for sustainability to be achieved. For example, if the economic dimension is too strong, it can create disparities in income or overuse of a particular animal or plant (e.g., overfishing the cod in New England). From a systems perspective, these three dimensions operate in complex ways and call for cooperative relationships among individuals, communities, and institutions. As with any system that involves humans and a political process, there are compromises to be made. Advocates of sustainability believe that choices should be made to ensure that the three dimensions remain balanced (Berke & Kartez, 1995). Conceptual thinking about sustainability has evolved from a view that each silo—economy, ecology, and equity (or society)—is linked to a systems view where ecology or natural resources is the base on which the economy and society exist (see Figure 3.1). The concentric ring image emphasizes not only that there are links or relationships between silos but also that a healthy and functioning economy cannot exist without a healthy and functioning society and ecosystem.

Another key concept is resilience, which originally comes from ecology. Resilience means the ability of a system to respond to and adapt to disturbance or change. This concept can be applied to communities, regions, and states. Think about Hurricane Katrina and the devastation it wrought to New Orleans. Katrina struck in 2005 and New Orleans has still not fully recovered and many neighborhoods remain devastated. The Lower Ninth Ward, for example, has yet to recover fully, and many of its original inhabitants have not returned. Think about other natural disasters as well and how communities responded to that disturbance, such as the Asian tsunami in 2004, the Haiti earthquake and devastation to Port au Prince in 2010, and the Chilean earthquake and its effect on Concepción in 2010. These natural disasters were widespread, but some places are able to recovery more quickly in part because the initial capacity or its existing assets were already strong and could withstand a shock. It is clear as these countries and the world respond to these devastating natural disasters that some communities are more resilient than others.

Another catalyst that tests a community's resilience is an economic crisis. The "Great Recession" that started in late 2007 has had unequal effects across communities. Some communities, such as Flint, Michigan, and Elkhart, Michigan, which suffered from manufacturing shutdowns in the past, were hit hard again by this recession. From these examples, we can see that the scale of a disturbance is important, as well as the underlying assets of a community.

To understand community sustainability and resilience more thoroughly, we need to discuss the concept of scale. The now familiar adage "Think globally, act locally" addresses the idea of scale. Sustainability is relevant at the local level for several reasons. First, the local level is where people and

FIGURE 3.1   Conceptual Evolution of Community Sustainability

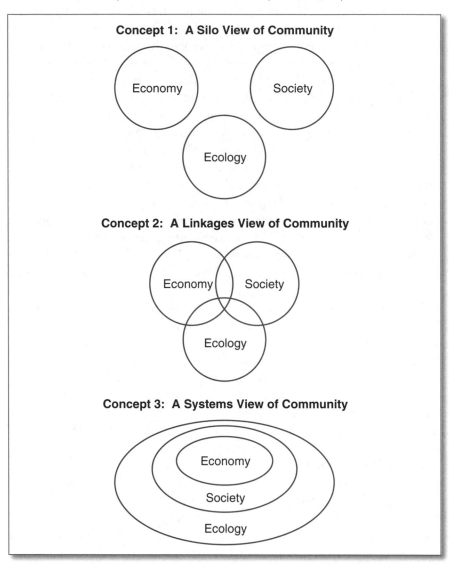

SOURCE: From *Guide to Sustainable Community Indicators* by Maureen Hart (1999). West Hartford, Connecticut: Sustainable Measures. http://www.sustainablemeasures.com. Reprinted with permission.

the natural environmental interact most often and directly. Second, local actions and strategies are frequently the most effective at addressing environmental, economic, and social problems. Third, individuals live their lives in a particular place and can have an impact by altering how they consume and what they consume. To have an impact, people must act locally while being aware of how their actions can be felt at a broader scale, even globally. For example, many individual households recycle glass, plastics, and paper products. These individual actions over time (and originally with lots of encouragement and incentives) spawned a recycling industry that in the Northeast alone was valued at $7 billion (Touart, 1998). The e-waste industry was valued at $5.7 billion in 2009 (ABI Research, 2010). There are many other industries linked to the economy that also have an environmental impact. Acting at the local level has cumulative impacts whether people think about reducing their carbon footprint, recycling and reusing more, or using less water. Linking individual responsibility to local sustainable development, however, does not preclude collective actions at the local level (Maser, 1997). Case Study 3.1 tells the brief story of a small rural region collectively taking action.

CASE STUDY 3.1 CHEQUAMEGON BAY

In Wisconsin, along the shores of Lake Superior in an area known as the Chequamegon Bay, the cities, reservations, and many organizations are moving forward with a sustainability plan for the region. The Chequamegon (pronounced *che-wa-megon*) Bay Area of Ashland and Bayfield counties includes the cities of Ashland, Bayfield, and Washburn and the Bad River and Red Cliff Bands of Chippewa. The population of this area is about 32,000. The City of Washburn was the first city in the United States to pass a resolution declaring it an ecomunicipality based on the Swedish model using the Natural Step Framework. The City of Ashland soon followed. The City of Bayfield is currently considering adoption of a similar ecomunicipality resolution. These communities have most recently received state funding to create an energy plan for the area.

However, these actions didn't suddenly occur in the Chequamegon Bay region. The Alliance for Sustainability for many years has sponsored a variety of educational forums of which "Pie and Politics," held at Big Top Chautauqua (a summer entertainment venue), is a prominent example. In addition, the Alliance coordinated numerous study circles over 8 years or so reaching about 200 people. In addition, the Alliance organized "Green Teams" so that like organizations could discuss actions, opportunities, challenges, and barriers to sustainable development. These learning forums helped many individuals realize that it may indeed be possible to have a sustainable city and inspired them to finally take action in the community.

SOURCE: Haines (2006).

The concept of intergenerational equity is an integral part of community sustainability. It means acting in a way so that the next generations are inheriting a healthy economy, environment, and society. Mazmanian and Kraft (1999) distinguished between strong and weak sustainability. Weak sustainability refers to passing on to future generations an average capital stock. This means that the present and future generations should not further deplete resources. This type of sustainability is weak because many resources have been depleted far enough to be considered unsustainable and need to regain vitality. Under this view, it is assumed that technological and other innovations can maintain sustainability. The United States has taken measures, for example, to control cod fishing in the ocean off New England after fishermen had depleted the cod fishery to such an extent that the cod could not reproduce in large enough numbers to maintain a healthy population and be fished for human consumption.

In contrast, **strong sustainability** refers to restoring certain critical ecological resources to higher levels rather than simply maintaining them at a current state of depletion. In this approach, critical ecological resources should not be averaged over future generations. Such natural resources as the ozone layer are too important to treat the same as others. Each asset must be evaluated, and technological and other innovations should not be relied on to achieve sustainability.

Another way to discuss sustainability is to focus on energy. Activities are sustainable when they use material in continuous cycles and use reliable energy sources. Conversely, activities are not sustainable when they require continuous inputs of non-renewable resources, cause cumulative degradation of the environment, and lead to the extinction of other life forms. Table 3.1 provides a series of indicators of unsustainability at the global, national, and local levels. At the global scale, the indicators address issues such as species extinction, soil degradation, and decline in fisheries. At a local scale, unsustainability is marked by sprawl, racial and economic segregation, and the depletion and degradation of natural resources, to name a few. In contrast, sustainability should be unsustainability's opposite. The next section discusses the why of sustainability and many of the facts will underscore unsustainable practices.

TABLE 3.1 Indicators of Unsustainability

Global	Local
Global warming	Suburban sprawl
Soil degradation	Segregation/unequal opportunity
Deforestation	Loss of agricultural land and open space
Species extinction	Depletion and degradation of groundwater resources
Declining fisheries	Traffic congestion and smog
Economic inequity	Disproportionate exposure to environmental hazards

SOURCE: James, Power, and Forrest (2000).

Why Sustainability?

So far in this chapter, we have defined sustainability, but we have not explained why communities, local governments, and community-based organizations are adopting community sustainability approaches. People who live and work within communities are talking about and taking action toward a more sustainable future for a variety of reasons. From a scientific perspective, there are several trends that are driving the sustainability conversation.

- Human populations have increased from 2.52 billion people in 1950 to 4.06 billion in 1975 to 6.11 billion in 2000 and 6.91 billion in 2010. By 2050, the United Nations estimates that the human population could be from 8.0 billion to 10.5 billion (United Nations, 2008).

- More land was converted to cropland in the 30 years after 1950 than in the 150 years between 1700 and 1850. Cultivated systems (areas where at least 30% of the landscape is in croplands, shifting cultivation, confined livestock production, or freshwater aquaculture) now cover one quarter of the earth's terrestrial surface.

- Approximately 20% of the world's coral reefs were lost and an additional 20% degraded in the last several decades of the 20th century, and approximately 35% of mangrove areas were lost during this time (in countries for which sufficient data exist, which encompass about half of the area of mangroves).

- The amount of water impounded behind dams has quadrupled since 1960. Water withdrawals from rivers and lakes have doubled since 1960; most water use (70% worldwide) is for agriculture.

- The early 1990s collapse of the Newfoundland cod fishery due to overfishing resulted in the loss of tens of thousands of jobs and cost at least $2 billion in income support and retraining.

- In 2001, 1.1 billion people survived on less than $1 per day of income, with roughly 70% of them in rural areas where they are highly dependent on agriculture, grazing, and hunting for subsistence.

- Despite the growth in per capita food production in the past four decades, an estimated 852 million people were undernourished in 2000–2002, up 37 million from the period 1997–1999. Some 1.1 billion people still lack access to improved water supply, and more than 2.6 billion people lack access to improved sanitation.

- Water scarcity affects roughly 1–2 billion people worldwide. Since 1960, the ratio of water use to accessible supply has grown by 20% per decade.

- Since 1750, the atmospheric concentration of carbon dioxide has increased by about 32% (from about 280 to 376 parts per million in 2003), primarily due to the combustion of fossil fuels and land use changes. Approximately 60% of that increase (60 parts per million) has taken place since 1959.

SOURCE: Millennium Ecosystem Assessment (2005).

These statistics underpin the need for sustainability with a sense of urgency. The next section discusses the history of sustainability.

The History of Sustainability

What is the source of the idea of community sustainability? Some claim that the Iroquois Nation believed in sustainability because of their law that required consideration of the impact of every decision over the next seven generations (Krizek & Power, 1996, p. 8). Lamont Hempel (1999) traced the sources of the sustainable communities' movement to several major and a few minor sources in the last 100 years. Box 3.2 provides an evolutionary picture of the major intellectual threads that have influenced community sustainability.

BOX 3.2 MAJOR SOURCES INFLUENCING COMMUNITY SUSTAINABILITY

- Garden City movement, led by Ebenezer Howard
- Bioregional planning and design insights of Patrick Geddes, Ian McHarg, and the Regional Association of America
- American New Towns movement (e.g., Reston, Virginia; Radburn, New Jersey; Columbia, Maryland) that began in the 1920s
- Grassroots communitarian movements of the late 1940s
- Great Society urban program of Lyndon Johnson in the 1960s
- The decline of faith in technological progress as a solution to urban problems
- Spaceship Earth idea
- "Limits to growth" arguments of the late 1960s and early 1970s
- Studies of the resilience of ecological communities
- Local self-reliance and appropriate technology movement of the 1970s and early 1980s
- Urban ecology and eco-city movements
- The strategic coupling of environment and development interests in the 1980s (e.g., the Brundtland Commission of 1987) and the 1990s (e.g., the Earth Summit of 1992 and Habitat II of 1996)
- The new urbanism, neotraditional towns, and healthy cities

- Social capital debate of the 1990s led by Robert Putnam and Amitai Etzioni
- Application of industrial ecology concepts, environmental audits, and sustainability indicators in the early 1990s by struggling communities attempting to recover from economic downturns and urban decay (e.g., Sustainable Chattanooga)

SOURCE: From "Conceptual and Analytical Challenges in Building Sustainable Communities," by L. C. Hempel, in *Toward Sustainable Communities: Transition and Transformations in Environmental Policy*, edited by D. A. Mazmanian & M. E. Kraft, 1999 (pp. 43–74). Cambridge, MA: MIT Press. Copyright 1999 by MIT Press. Reprinted with permission.

One of the earliest sources dates to the late 19th century with the work of Ebenezer Howard and his Garden City movement in England. Howard's idea was to create cities with prominent greenbelts around them connected by rail. He was reacting to the growth of cities, particularly London, and their inability to provide adequate housing, physical infrastructure, and amenities for the people who migrated there during the period of industrialization.

Other architects and planners were influenced similarly. In 1915, Patrick Geddes, an architect and planner, stressed that urban design needed to integrate the natural world with how society was organized. Only a decade or so later, Lewis Mumford founded and led the Regional Planning Association of America in the 1920s. Mumford believed in the unity of city and countryside and that regional planning, which for him emphasized an educative, grassroots process, was essential (Hempel, 1999). These early sources have influenced the community sustainability movement by emphasizing comprehensiveness, creating a link with the region, and stressing public participation.

Before the term *sustainability* was coined, steady-state economics was pursued as an opposing paradigm to the dominant neoclassical economics paradigm. Steady-state economics, and its best-known advocate, Herman Daly, proposed the idea that "enough is best" rather than "growth is best." In his work, Daly (1996) maintained that "population growth and production growth must not push us beyond the sustainable environmental capacities of resource regeneration and waste absorption. Once that point is reached, production and reproduction should be for replacement only. Physical growth should cease, while qualitative improvement continues" (p. 3).

The idea of sustainability began to gain ground and become part of mainstream thought beginning in the 1980s. But it was not until 1987, when the Brundtland Commission report, *Our Common Future,* was published that sustainability entered the lexicon. The report focused on defining and operationalizing the idea of sustainable development (Krizek & Power, 1996, p. 10). It defined sustainable development as the ability to "meet the needs of the present without sacrificing the ability of the future to meet its needs" (Daly, 1996, p. 1). The Brundtland Commission examined two central questions: (a) Is it possible to increase the basic standard of living of the world's expanding population without depleting our natural resources and further degrading the environment on which all people depend? and (b) Can humanity collectively step back from the brink of environmental collapse and, at the same time, lift its poorest members up to the level of basic human health and dignity? This report was the first international policy document to address sustainability in a manner that linked the natural world with the human/economic world (Krizek & Power, 1996, p. 10).

Several years later, at Earth Summit 1992, Agenda 21 focused on both local and national sustainable development strategies. Part of this shift was due to the problems of addressing environmental problems at a global or national scale. Agenda 21 was a plan to achieve global sustainability. The plan's goal was "to halt and reverse the environmental damage to our planet and to promote environmentally sound and sustainable development in all countries on earth" (Krizek & Power, 1996, p. 11). It focused on six themes—quality of life on Earth, efficient use of the earth's natural resources, the protection of our global commons (air and water resources), the management of human settlements, chemicals and the management of waste, and sustainable economic growth—and proposed many ways for their implementation.

Following the Earth Summit in 1992, Habitat II was convened in 1996 in Istanbul. Habitat II aimed to make the world's cities, towns, and villages healthy, safe, equitable, and sustainable (Krizek & Power, 1996). Six thousand delegates attended, with 2,400 from nongovernmental organizations (NGOs). In 2010, the 5th World Urban Forum took place in Brazil. Discussions focused on rapid urbanization and its impact on communities, cities, economies, climate change, and policies. Other United Nations initiatives have focused on climate change. In December 2009, the United Nations Climate Change Conference took place in Denmark. One result of that meeting was the Copenhagen Accord, where representatives of many countries agreed that climate change was an enormous challenge, that greenhouse gas emissions need to be reduced, and that adaptation will need to be addressed.

Other movements, such as smart growth and new urbanism, have recently gained momentum. Smart growth focuses on making land use planning and decisions more attune with regional efficiency, environmental protection, and fiscal responsibility (Hempel, 1999, p. 52). New urbanism focuses on renewing city centers, creating new centers in sprawling suburbs, and protecting the environment. Both of these movements can be considered elements of community sustainability, but they do not go far enough to achieve sustainability goals.

The U.S. government started to pursue a sustainability agenda under President Clinton. The Environmental Protection Agency (EPA), the Department of Energy, and the President's Council on Sustainable Development were three key players. The EPA established the Office of Sustainable Ecosystems and Communities (OSEC) in 1995 but closed its doors in 1999. Many of the programs under that office moved elsewhere within the EPA. One initiative started under OSEC is called Community-Based Environmental Protection (CBEP). Under this program, the EPA encouraged local groups to address their own environmental concerns. CBEP operated under a silo-based approach by focusing on environmental issues exclusively. By 2001 or so, the sustainability agenda was lost or dismantled. The Sustainable Development Challenge Grant Program (SDCG) is another program that granted federal funds to communities to leverage private and other public funds to integrate programs of economic development, environmental protection, and social well-being through community partnerships, educational efforts, and voluntary action (Mazmanian & Kraft, 1999, p. 28). It funded 123 projects from 1996 to 1999. Rather than the federal government providing leadership in the area of sustainability, that role has now turned to local governments and CBOs.

Approaches to Sustainability

There are a number of approaches to community sustainability. Two of the most common approaches are described below. A critical point is that these approaches are not mutually exclusive and, in fact, can be used simultaneously to think through community sustainability. Each approach can be integrated within a community development framework.

The Natural Step (TNS) is a systems-based approach. Begun in Sweden by an oncologist, TNS has spread internationally. Dr. Karl Henrik Robert worked with scientists and others from around the world and arrived at four scientific principles that, if followed, would allow both organizations and communities to move toward a sustainable world (James & Lahti, 2004). In Sweden, about 70 municipalities follow TNS principles. In the United States, cities that use the TNS framework include Pittsburgh, Pennsylvania; Madison, Wisconsin; and Santa Monica, California. In addition, several smaller rural communities are using TNS. Box 3.3 provides the four guiding principles and example practices that communities can or have taken. The TNS framework encourages efficiency and ultimately profitability and is regularly used by corporations. Nike, Interface, Electrolux, and Ikea among many more businesses have used TNS to transform the way they do business.

Like corporations, many communities find TNS to provide a useful framework for thinking about sustainability, which moves them to the next steps of process and actions. Communities and organizations moving toward sustainability are in search of an approach that is not prescriptive but makes sense to its locally elected officials, employees, and public. Many communities and businesses are adopting either TNS or natural capitalism or some other approach and using an indicators framework, discussed in the next section, to move toward a sustainable future.

The TNS has many similarities to strategic planning processes used by community development practitioners (Hembd & Silberstein, 2010). One of the central differences is that strategic planners often rely on "forecasting" to identify actions that should be taken. Based on current trends, communities can identify issues and concerns. TNS relies more on "backcasting," which is a method of envisioning successful outcomes and identifying specific actions that should be taken to achieve those outcomes. In many ways, it is similar to the process of visioning, which will be discussed in more detail in the next chapter. TNS relies on a process it calls "ABCD." "A" is awareness building, "B" is establishing a baseline (collecting data and establishing indicators), "C" is creating a vision and a plan, and "D" is the implementation phase. Backcasting takes place during the "C" step.

BOX 3.3 THE NATURAL STEP SYSTEM CONDITIONS AND PRACTICES

Guiding Objective	Types of Practices
1. Eliminate our community's contribution to fossil fuel dependence and to wasteful use of scarce metals and minerals.	Transit and pedestrian-oriented development; development heated and powered by renewable energy; alternatively fueled municipal fleets; incentives for organic agriculture that minimize phosphorus and petrochemical fertilizers and herbicides.
2. Eliminate our community's contribution to dependence on persistent chemical and wasteful use of synthetic substances.	Healthy building design and construction that reduces or eliminates use of toxic building materials; landscape design and park maintenance that uses alternatives to chemical pesticides and herbicides; municipal purchasing guidelines that encourage low- or nonchemical product use.
3. Eliminate our community's contribution to encroachment on nature (e.g., land, water, wildlife, forest, soil, ecosystems).	Redevelopment of existing sites and buildings before building new ones; open space, forest, and habitat preservation; reduced water use and recycling of wash water.
4. Meet human needs fairly and efficiently.	Affordable housing for a diversity of residents; locally based business and food production; use of waste as a resource; ecoindustrial development, participatory community planning, and decision making.

SOURCE: James and Lahti (2004).

Another approach to community sustainability is the Transition Towns movement. It started in the United Kingdom and is focused on building community resilience to deal with the impacts of peak oil and climate change. The founders of the Transition Towns movement believe that communities need to transition from a dependence on oil and its by-products to a new paradigm independent of fossil fuels, particularly oil.

The following list of principles and assumptions underpins Transition Towns.

- Peak oil, climate change, and the economic crisis require urgent action.
- Adaptation to a world with less oil is inevitable.
- It is better to plan and be prepared than be taken by surprise.
- Industrial society has lost the resilience to be able to cope with shocks to its systems.
- We have to act together and we have to act now.
- We must negotiate our way down from the "peak" using all our skill, ingenuity, and intelligence.
- Using our creativity and cooperation to unleash the collective genius within our local communities will lead to a more abundant, connected, and healthier future for all.

SOURCE: Transition United States. (n.d.). *Why Transition.* Retrieved March 10, 2010, from http://www.transitionus.org/why-transition

A primary focus of Transition is on organizing and process (see Box 3.4). Its website provides many "how-to" guides and webinars. The last step in the process is the Energy Descent Action Plan. This planning process is similar to The Natural Step process and includes a visioning and backcasting. Transition initiatives occur through a grassroots effort. People in a community with this common interest begin to discuss sustainability issues. Over time, some of these groups become more formal and in their own right should be considered community-based organizations.

BOX 3.4 TRANSITION'S 12 STEPS

1. Set up a steering group and design its demise from the outset.
2. Raise awareness.
3. Lay the foundations (networking).
4. Organize a Great Unleashing (first big event).
5. Form groups.
6. Use open space (public participation).
7. Develop visible, practical manifestations of the project.
8. Facilitate the great reskilling (workshops and courses).
9. Build a bridge to local government.
10. Honor the elders (learn from the past).
11. Let it go where it wants to go.
12. Create an Energy Descent Action Plan.

Both of these approaches fit in with a community development process. In addition, an asset-based framework can include the general principles from either of these two sustainable community approaches.

Summary and Conclusions

It is important to understand the concept of sustainability because it has become and will continue to be important, in all aspects of political, social, and economic life. At the same time, it is important to recognize that there are formidable challenges in making the sustainability concept operational. This chapter defined sustainability, provided some history as to its origins, and introduced a couple of community sustainability approaches that many communities are using in the United States and elsewhere.

The term *sustainability* and the strategies and actions to achieve a sustainable community still seem vague and unrealizable. Without support from the local political structure, the business community, and local residents, it is hard to imagine that one will see sustainable communities in the near future. The processes and approaches toward community development discussed in the other chapters will provide a framework for moving toward community sustainability.

Communities and CBOs of many kinds have an opportunity to continue with their primary focus but to adjust their strategies and actions to include sustainability. Sustainability in many respects represents a new way to live, work, and recreate. Sustainability ideas need to be integrated into the work that communities and CBOs do. Sustainability should not and cannot be separated from the everyday work of communities and organizations. For example, a CDC that focuses on housing could begin to construct affordable housing using green building techniques. The same CDC might work on economic development and could focus on bringing green industries into a neighborhood industrial area or assist in developing an ecoindustrial park. The possibilities are as diverse and broad as the society in which we live. CBOs and the communities with which they work need to be creative and thoughtful about how they can fully integrate sustainability into their everyday operations.

Given the motivation of sustainability advocates, the extent of the literature on the topic, and the increasing number of community organizations and local governments involved in sustainability projects, it is a certainty that more communities will attempt to adopt a sustainability agenda. Throughout the rest of this book, particularly in the chapters focused on the different forms of capital, we weave in examples and case studies that highlight both the asset-based idea and sustainability principles.

KEY CONCEPTS

Garden City movement

Habitat II

Intergenerational equity

The Natural Step

New urbanism

Resilience

Smart growth

Steady-state economics

Strong sustainability

Three Es

Weak sustainability

QUESTIONS

1. What is your definition of community sustainability?

2. Why is sustainability important at the local level?

3. Compare and contrast weak and strong sustainability.

4. Name three people or movements that influenced the current sustainability movement and discuss how they did so.

5. Describe the findings of the Brundtland Commission report and discuss the implications of this view of sustainability for communities.

6. Compare and contrast the different approaches to community sustainability.

EXERCISES

1. Identify a community development project in your community. The project can be a private development effort, an existing government program, or any project that is being considered by the local government. Evaluate how well this project meets sustainability goals. In particular, assess how well this project balances environmental, social, and economic goals. What specific actions could the community take to improve the sustainability of this project?

2. A central feature of sustainability is the importance of looking at issues from a systems view. Looking at your own community, how are different forms of community capital related to one another? Try to make connections between each of the different forms of community capital discussed in this book.

3. Conduct a search on the Internet to find innovative green practices among universities and colleges. For example, identify institutions that are using renewable sources of energy, green design in buildings, or strategies for reducing electrical usage. Summarize these initiatives and evaluate how these practices could be implemented at your institution.

REFERENCES

ABI Research. (2010). *E-waste recovery and recycling.* Retrieved May 24, 2010, from http://www.abiresearch.com/research/1004501

Beatley, T., & Manning, K. (1997). *The ecology of place: Planning for environment, economy, and community.* Washington, DC: Island Press.

Berke, P. R., & Kartez, J. (1995). *Sustainable development as a guide to community land use.* Cambridge, MA: Lincoln Institute of Land Policy.

Brundtland, G. H. (1987). *Our common future: Report of the World Commission on Environment and Development.* New York: United Nations, General Assembly.

Daly, H. (1996). *Beyond growth: The economics of sustainable development.* Boston: Beacon Press.

Friends of the Earth Scotland. (2006). *About FoE.* Retrieved March 25, 2007, from www.foe-scotland.org.uk/about/about_foes.htm

Haines, A. (2006, Summer). Sustainable communities and Wisconsin: Lessons from Sweden and Wisconsin. *Wisconsin American Planning Association Newsletter,* pp. 1, 3–6.

Hart, M. (1999). *Guide to sustainable community indicators.* West Hartford, CT: Sustainable Measures.

Hembd, J., & Silberstein, J. (2010). Sustainable communities: Sustainability and community development. In J. Robinson & G. P. Green (Eds.), *Introduction to community development: Theory, practice, and service-learning* (pp. 261–278). Thousand Oaks, CA: Sage.

Hempel, L. C. (1999). Conceptual and analytical challenges in building sustainable communities. In D. A. Mazmanian & M. E. Kraft (Eds.), *Toward sustainable communities: Transition and transformations in environmental policy* (pp. 43–74). Cambridge, MA: MIT Press.

James, S., & Lahti, T. (2004). *The natural step for communities: How cities and towns can change to sustainable practices.* British Columbia, Canada: New Society Publisher.

Krizek, K. J., & Power, J. (1996). *A planners guide to sustainable development.* Chicago: American Planning Association.

Maser, C. (1997). *Sustainable community development: Principles and concepts.* Boca Raton, FL: St. Lucie Press.

Mazmanian, D. A., & Kraft, M. E. (1999). The three epochs of the environmental movement. In D. A. Mazmanian & M. E. Kraft (Eds.), *Toward sustainable communities: Transition and transformations in environmental policy* (pp. 3–41). Cambridge, MA: MIT Press.

Millennium Ecosystem Assessment. (2005). *Ecosystems and human well-being: Synthesis.* Washington, DC: Island Press.

The Natural Step. (2006). *What is sustainability?* Retrieved March 25, 2007, from www.naturalstep.org/com/What_is_sustainability

Roelofs, J. (1996). *Greening cities: Building just and sustainable communities.* New York: Bootstrap Press.

Roseland, M. (1994). Ecological planning for sustainable communities. In D. Aberley (Ed.), *Futures by design: The practice of ecological planning* (pp. 70–80). Gabriola Island, British Columbia, Canada: New Society Publishers.

Sargent, F. O., Lusk, P., Rivera, J. A., & Varela, M. (1991). *Rural environmental planning for sustainable communities.* Washington, DC: Island Press.

Sustainable Community Roundtable Report. (2006). *About the roundtable.* Retrieved March 25, 2007, from www.sustainsouthsound.org/about

Transition United States. (n.d.). *Why transition.* Retrieved March 10, 2010, from http://www.transitionus.org/why-transition

Touart, A. (1998). New partnership to gather economic data on recycling industry. *BioCycle, 39*(10), 6.

Van der Ryn, S., & Calthorpe, P. (1986). *Sustainable communities: A new design synthesis for cities, suburbs, and towns.* San Francisco: Sierra Club Books.

World Business Council on Sustainable Development. (2006). *Development*. Retrieved March 25, 2007, from www.wbcsd.org/templates/TemplateWBCSD5/layout .asp?type=p&MenuId=Njc& doOpen=1&ClickMenu=LeftMenu

ADDITIONAL READINGS AND RESOURCES

Readings

Agyeman, J. (2005). *Sustainable communities and the challenge of environmental justice*. New York: NYU Press.

Agyeman, J., Bullard, R. D., & Evans, B. (2003). *Just sustainabilities: Development in an unequal world*. London: MIT Press.

Beaton, R., & Maser, C. (1999). *Reuniting economy and ecology in sustainable development*. Boca Raton, FL: Lewis Publishers.

Daly, H. E., & Cobb, J. B., Jr. (1989). *For the common good: Redirecting the economy toward community, the environment, and a sustainable future*. Boston: Beacon Press.

Daly, H. E., & Townsend, K. N. (1993). *Valuing the earth: Economics, ecology, ethics*. Cambridge, MA: MIT Press.

Elkington, J. (1998). *Cannibals with forks: The triple bottom line of 21st century business*. Gabriola Island, British Columbia, Canada: New Society Publishers.

Hall, D. R., Kirkpatrick, I., & Mitchell, M. (Eds.). (2005). *Rural tourism and sustainable business*. Bristol, UK: Channel View Publications.

Hawken, P., Lovins, A., & Lovins, L. H. (1999). *Natural capitalism: Creating the next industrial revolution*. Boston: Little, Brown.

James, S., Power, J., & Forrest, C. (2000). *APA policy guide on planning for sustainability*. Retrieved March 25, 2007, from www.planning.org/govt/sustdvpg.htm

Kinsley, M. J. (1997). *Economic renewal guide: A collaborative process for sustainable community development*. Snowmass, CO: Rocky Mountain Institute.

Maser, C. (1996). *Resolving environmental conflict: Towards sustainable community development*. Boca Raton, FL: St. Lucie Press.

Maser, C. (1999). *Vision and leadership in sustainable development*. New York: Lewis Publishers.

Mowforth, M., & Munt, I. (2003). *Tourism and sustainability: Development and new tourism in the third world*. New York: Routledge.

Portney, K. (2005). Civic engagement and sustainable cities in the United States. *Public Administration Review, 65*, 579–591.

Richards, G., & Hall, D. R. (2000). *Tourism and sustainable community development*. New York: Routledge.

Shiva, V. (2008). *Soil not oil: Environmental justice in an age of climate crisis*. Chicago: South End Press.

Wackernagel, M., & Rees, W. (1996). *Our ecological footprint: Reducing human impact on the earth*. Gabriola Island, British Columbia, Canada: New Society Publishers.

Websites

APA Policy Guide on Planning for Sustainability—www.planning.org/policyguides/sustainability .htm. This page provides explanations of unsustainability as well as a guide to achieve community sustainability.

Center for Neighborhood Technology—www.cnt.org. This organization links economic and community development with ecological improvement in an effort to build prosperous and sustainable communities.

Center for Rural Affairs—www.cfra.org. This organization focuses on working to build sustainable rural communities through social and economic justice with environmental stewardship.

Ecoforestry Institute—ecoforestry.ca/default.htm. This site is dedicated to teaching and certifying holistic, ecologically sound forestry practices that protect and restore the sustainability of forests while harvesting forest products.

Institute for Local Self-Reliance (ILSR)—www.ilsr.org. ILSR is a nonprofit research and educational organization that provides technical assistance and information on environmentally sound economic development strategies.

The International Council for Local Environmental Initiatives (ICLEI)—www.iclei.org. ICLEI is an international association of local governments and national and regional local government organizations that have made a commitment to sustainable development. More than 475 cities, towns, counties, and their associations worldwide compose ICLEI's membership. ICLEI works with local governments and provides technical consulting, training, and information services to build capacity, share knowledge, and support local government in the implementation of sustainable development at the local level.

The Natural Step International Gateway Page—http://www.naturalstep.org/en. Provides resources, case studies, and other information for those interested in using The Natural Step process.

Redefining Progress—www.rprogress.org/index.shtml. Redefining Progress works with a broad array of partners to shift the economy and public policy toward sustainability.

Resource Renewal Institute (RRI)—www.rri.org/index.php. RRI is a nonprofit organization founded in 1985 to support innovative environmental management in the United States and worldwide. RRI's main role is to promote the implementation of green plans—long-term, comprehensive strategies designed to achieve sustainability.

Rocky Mountain Institute—www.rmi.org. The mission of this organization is to foster efficient and sustainable use of resources as a path to global security. You can find information on resource-efficient buildings, sustainable economic development, and more general topics, such as water and transportation.

Sustainable America (SA)—www.sustainableamerica.org. SA is a national membership organization that rejects destructive consumption and development patterns and promotes public policies and private actions that support sustainable development.

Sustainable Communities Network—http://www.sustainable.org/. This site provides success stories and resources on community sustainable development.

Sustainable Jobs Fund (SJF)—www.sjfund.com. SJF is a community development venture capital fund and a certified community development financial institution (CDFI) that makes investments in growth enterprises, which create quality jobs in economically distressed regions in the eastern United States.

Sustainable Measures—http://www.sustainablemeasures.com/Indicators/index.html. This website is an excellent resource for communities wishing to develop their own indicators of sustainability. It provides examples, data sources, and other useful resources.

Videos

Affluenza (1997), produced and directed by John de Graaf and Vivia Boe. "A scathingly funny historical documentation of America's consumer society which has won acclaim as 'a film that could change your life.'" Available from Bullfrog Films, P.O. Box 149, Oley, PA 19547; phone: (800) 543-FROG.

Ecological Design: Re-inventing the Future (1995), produced by Brian Danitz and Chris Zelov. A video collection about "what imaginative people in this country are doing, including one of the most effective urban planners in the world." Available from Genius Loci Gallery, 1259 Northampton Street, #340, Easton, PA 18042.

4   The Community Development Process

The community development process can be difficult, time-consuming, and costly. Community residents often are more concerned with daily tasks than thinking about, and coming up with, a vision of their community's future. Residents want their children to go to good schools, they want decent jobs, and they want a safe, clean environment in which to live. Without a vision, however, communities have a limited ability to make decisions about these issues. It is analogous to driving across the country without a map.

Who should determine a community's future other than community residents? A consultant hired by the local government to develop a plan, a state or federal agency making decisions about highway bypasses or wetlands preservation, or a private developer constructing a shopping mall or a residential subdivision could all have a large impact on a community's future. Residents of a community need to participate in and actively envision the future of their community; otherwise, other groups and individuals will determine their future for them.

The community development process can be as important as its products. The process we present in this chapter follows the model in Figure 4.1. The model shows a process that begins with community organizing and moves on to visioning, planning, and finally implementation and evaluation.

There continues to be debate over the importance of process versus outcomes in community development. Some people argue that the goal of community development is to increase public participation and that it does not matter if their efforts are successful or not. Others contend that the ultimate goal is to improve the quality of life in the community, with public participation being simply a means to an end. Our position is closer to the latter view. We focus in this chapter on the process of community development, with the ultimate goal of enhancing community assets. It is difficult to maintain interest and commitment to community development processes if participants cannot point to successes. In the long run, both process and outcomes are essential pieces of community development.

FIGURE 4.1   A Community Development Process

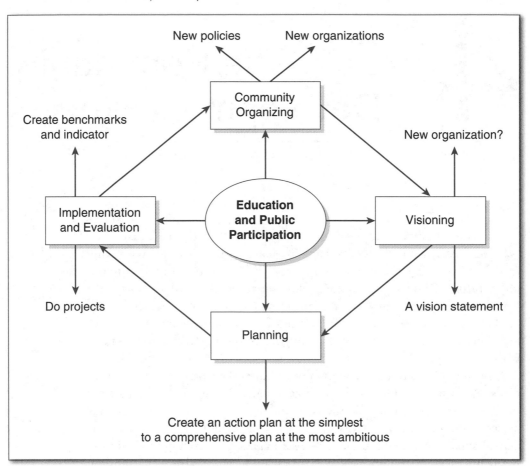

In this chapter, we focus on three areas: community organizing, community visioning and planning, and evaluation and monitoring. In the first section of this chapter, we discuss public participation. We are especially interested in identifying its various forms and techniques for encouraging it.

Public Participation

More than 100 years ago, Alexis de Tocqueville (1904) remarked on the vibrant civil society in the United States, with its remarkable number and mix of voluntary organizations and associations—the types of organizations that are likely to rely on public action. Although the number and mix have shifted since he made his observations, voluntary organizations and associations are still an important part of the fabric of civil society. Although many lament that public participation has declined in the United States, there has been an enormous increase in the number of community-based organizations (CBOs) involved in development over the past two decades.

In most cases, community development practitioners grapple with the issue of participation. How is a community motivated to affect change? How does a community maintain momentum? Who in the community should get involved? To begin the discussion, we address some conceptual issues surrounding public participation.

There are at least four types of public participation: **public action, public involvement, electoral participation,** and **obligatory participation** (Langton, 1978). By examining these differences, we can better understand the community development process and its relationship to and use by CBOs and local governments. From this comparison, public action fits closest to the community development process model. In this type of public participation, the activities are initiated and controlled by citizens, with the intent of influencing government officials and others. Public involvement and obligatory participation, on the other hand, are initiated and controlled by government officials. This type of public participation is growing, however, and can have a meaningful impact on the quality of life and may ultimately lead to a community-initiated effort.

In the community development process model (Figure 4.1), the role of public participation may start with public action and shift to public involvement, depending on the organizational context and "ownership" of the process. Generally, public action is the category of public participation on which CBOs focus.

Sherry Arnstein's (1969) "ladder of public participation" is a useful framework for understanding the role of CBOs in public participation. This ladder has eight "rungs" divided into three sections that illustrate degrees of participation and public power. Arnstein argued that power and control over decisions are necessary ingredients to "real" public participation. The lower two rungs are nonparticipatory participation and are called manipulation and therapy. Examples include public or neighborhood advisory committees or boards that have no authority or power in controlling projects or programs but simply represent a way to vent frustration. The next three rungs illustrate "degrees of tokenism": informing, consultation, and placation. Methods include simple communication tools, such as posters, and more sophisticated tools, such as surveys, meetings, public hearings, and placement of citizens on powerful boards. The final three rungs represent "degrees of citizen power": partnership, delegated power, and citizen control. Here, planning and decision making can have three degrees of power in relation to a citizens group, board, or corporation: shared power between the citizen group(s) and the public authority, authorized power to prepare and implement a plan or program, or empowerment to essentially act as a decentralized local government with full control over particular programs (Arnstein, 1969, pp. 223–224).

Ideally, CBOs attempt to place themselves on the top rungs of the ladder, whereas many local governments conduct their participation efforts at the lower rungs of the ladder. Especially when CBOs are newly established, the original catalyst is often public action, and the desire to maintain public input on a regular basis is strong. In the day-to-day work of CBOs, however, public participation is difficult to maintain for several reasons. First, it increases the complexity of decision making. Developing programs, services, and policies that take into consideration a wide range of interests can be challenging. Second, it is time-consuming and thus can be seen as inefficient. Third, reaction time is slowed, a disadvantage when the organization needs to act quickly to take advantage of a funding deadline. Finally, the demands for funding and reporting require a professional staff (see Chapter 5). Over time, staff may develop expertise and experience, giving them a sense that they know what is best for the community. Thus, CBOs can encounter two pitfalls in relation to public participation: (1) with professionalization, they can lose sight of their community base and at worst become unrepresentative of the community, and (2) due to the funding requirements, their agenda—goals and programs—can become co-opted by external forces.

So far, we have discussed conceptual models and types of public participation that CBOs would fall under, given their purpose. We have yet to ask why people participate. The natural tendency is to think that people get involved because of the importance of the issue—it directly affects them, and they have an interest in finding solutions to the problem. Many community organizers assume that they can increase the level of participation by educating people on the issue and encouraging them to get involved with the effort to address the issue.

Although this approach may work for some people and in some cases, we must recognize that there are many other reasons why people may become involved in a local organization. Many people may become involved because of social relationships. Participation is a way to meet new people and develop new friendships. People may become engaged because a friend or a neighbor is involved in the project. Thus, these social relationships can be a valuable mechanism for encouraging others to participate.

People also may participate because of the kind of activities offered through the organization. Although many residents do not have much time for community activities, others may be looking for new activities. Getting involved in fund raising or planning may provide opportunities for which some people are searching. In many instances, residents have experiences and skills that are underused, and they are seeking opportunities to make better use of these skills.

Although time is cited frequently as the primary reason for lack of participation, it is rarely the real issue. A variety of other constraints may limit participation. Among the most important barriers are lack of child care, transportation, accessibility for the disabled, and interpreters, as well as a lack of advance information. Local organizations need to consider providing services to overcome these barriers if they want to have a diverse set of residents participate in meetings and activities.

Communication is another reason that residents may not participate. This issue may be especially important in communities where there are no local newspapers, radio stations, or television stations. Even in communities where there are adequate communication systems, it may be difficult to reach people in the community. Technology is facilitating the communication in many neighborhoods. Setting up a neighborhood listserv provides up-to-date information on activities in the area. This strategy may be limited in many concentrated poverty neighborhoods and rural areas. Nothing beats face-to-face communication. It may have a more powerful influence on getting people motivated to participate in community events.

Residents also need to see real, direct benefits to participation and that their actions are having an impact. Thus, it is important for community organizers to identify small projects where they can demonstrate success with the community. The community can build off these successes and tackle bigger issues.

Understanding why people do and do not participate in a community development process can help us to identify additional techniques of public participation. There are many techniques, each with varying functions. Depending on what a CBO is trying to accomplish, it will need to choose the appropriate technique for the purpose it is trying to achieve. In Table 4.1, we identify a variety of public participation techniques and their objectives. The table is not exhaustive, but it provides a range of techniques that can be and are used by CBOs and other organizations to achieve different purposes. The choice of the appropriate technique depends on several issues, such as the context for the process, the number of people participating, the available resources, and the participants' level of interest.

Because the choice of issue can affect the level of participation and the likelihood that participants will stay with the organization, the techniques need to focus on accomplishing something. They cannot be seen as meaningless exercises. The technique should be one that helps unite people rather than divide them. Most community organizers begin with small, simple techniques that have a clear outcome. The techniques need to be explained clearly to participants so that they understand clearly the process they will use to make decisions.

Community Organizing

To many, organizing can sound like a daunting task. How does one individual or a small group organize people to change something? As Kahn (1991), a leading authority on community organizing, reminded us, "Organizing doesn't need to be big to be successful" (p. 19). Organizing begins with one person wanting to change one thing. It is a way for people to work together to solve a common problem.

Organizing takes various forms. Union organizing focuses on workers with the same employer or in the same industry. Constituency organizing involves group characteristics, such as gender, race, language, or sexual orientation. Issue organizing addresses a particular concern, such as school,

TABLE 4.1   Public Participation Techniques and Their Functions

Technique	Identify Attitudes and Opinions	Identify Impacted Groups	Solicit Impacted Groups	Facilitate Participation	Clarify Planning Process	Answer Citizen Questions	Disseminate Information	Generate New Ideas	Facilitate Advocacy	Promote Interaction Among Groups	Resolve Conflict	Plan Program	Change Attitudes Toward Government	Develop Support/Minimize Opposition
Arbitration and mediation planning	X							X		X	X			
Citizens advisory board	X			X	X	X	X	X			X	X	X	X
Citizen representatives on policy-making bodies	X			X	X			X					X	X
Community surveys	X		X											
Community training				X	X				X				X	
Drop-in centers		X		X	X	X	X					X	X	X
Focus group	X		X	X		X				X				
Meetings, community sponsored and neighborhood	X		X	X	X	X	X	X					X	X
Meetings, open informational			X		X	X	X						X	
Neighborhood planning council	X			X					X	X			X	X
Ombudsman		X				X	X	X					X	X
Policy delphi	X							X						
Public hearing		X	X	X		X	X						X	
Short conference	X			X	X	X	X	X		X	X	X		X
Task forces			X					X				X	X	X
Workshops	X		X	X	X			X		X	X	X	X	X

SOURCE: Adapted from "Matching Method to Purpose: The Challenges of Planning Citizen-Participation Activities," by J. Rosener, in *Citizen Participation in America: Essays on the State of the Art*, edited by S. Langton, 1978 (pp. 109–122). Lexington, MA: Lexington Books. Reprinted with permission.

taxes, or housing. Neighborhood or community organizing focuses on place and addresses people who live in the same place (Kahn, 1991, p. 70). Community organizing, therefore, is distinct from other forms of organizing because it focuses on mobilizing people in a specific area. Recently, however, there have been successful efforts at blending these various forms of organizing, such as union and community organizing. These efforts attempt to organize workers where they live rather than in the workplace. This strategy has the advantage of obtaining support from local organizations and institutions that would not normally be involved in union organizing efforts. Unions also become more involved in community issues, such as schools, in an effort to garner support from residents.

There are three approaches to problem solving in communities: service, advocacy, and mobilizing. The first two approaches do not involve community residents in problem solving. In fact, residents may never be consulted. Service focuses on the individual, trying to address an individual's problems, such as unemployment, poverty, lack of health insurance, or mobility limitations. Service programs address problems one at a time, not comprehensively, and do not examine or challenge the root causes of those problems. Advocacy is a process where one person or a group of individuals speaks for another person or group of individuals. Advocates can effect change in organizations and institutions on behalf of others. Mobilizing involves community residents taking direct action to protest or support local projects, policies, or programs. Mobilizing is important because it gets people involved in direct action on a problem (Kahn, 1991, pp. 50–51).

CBOs use two different strategies to mobilize residents: social action campaigns and the development model. Social action campaigns are efforts by CBOs that aim to change decisions, societal structures, and cultural beliefs. Efforts at change can be small and immediate, such as getting a pothole filled, or large and long-term, such as promoting civil rights or fair trade practices. Tactics used in social action campaigns include, but are not limited to, appeals, petitions, picketing, boycotts, strikes, and sit-ins (see Case Study 4.1). Some tactics are nonviolent yet illegal and represent a form of civil disobedience (Rubin & Rubin, 1992).

The development model is more prevalent at the community level. Community development corporations (CDCs) represent a type of community organization that uses the development model to achieve community development goals (see Chapter 5 for a discussion of CDCs and other types of CBOs). These organizations focus on providing economic and social services in disenfranchised neighborhoods and communities (Rubin & Rubin, 1992).

Rubin and Rubin (1992) identified several different community organizing models that are used across the United States. Probably the most popular model has been the Alinsky model. The Alinsky model involves a professional organizer, who works with existing organizations to identify issues of common interest in the neighborhood. The Boston model takes a different approach by contacting welfare clients individually at their residences and relies heavily on appeals to the self-interest of each person. In recent years, the Association of

Community Organization for Reform Now (ACORN) has mixed these two models. The ACORN model is based on developing multi-issue organizations that are much more political than the other two models. Another model that has received a great deal of attention in the literature is the Industrial Areas Foundation (IAF) model, which emphasizes the importance of intensive training of organizers. Although this model is a direct descendent of the Alinsky model, it emphasizes the importance of maintaining close ties with existing community organizations as the neighborhood is organized. Each of the models has advantages and disadvantages. The choice of which model to use is based largely on the context, the resources, and the circumstances. We discuss these different models in more detail in the chapter on political capital.

In the next section, we describe a specific process—visioning—that many communities have used to help them define the future. Visioning is not the only process that practitioners use, but it represents one approach in the community development field that helps to focus groups of individuals on the assets of a community. Visioning is making community planning models more open and accessible to the entire community and establishing a more open and democratic process in envisioning a future at the outset of a process.

Community Visioning

Community visioning has become an accepted planning technique. Many communities used this technique to promote broad public participation on the direction a community should move in the future (Shipley & Newkirk, 1998). A visioning process establishes a desired end state for a community, a vision of the future toward which to strive. Shipley and Newkirk (1998) saw vision as "a metaphor that describes social, cultural, and perhaps emotional attributes" (p. 410). They further considered visioning as a way to return to the roots of planning when individuals such as Le Corbusier, Daniel Burnham, John Nolen, and Frank Lloyd Wright had visions of place. The visioning technique, however, strives to establish a vision of place through broad public participation rather than one individual's view. In theory, a community vision occurs through a group process that tries to arrive at a consensus about the future of place. A neighborhood, a whole city, or an organization can use a visioning process.

BOX 4.1 VISIONING DEFINED

Visioning is a process by which a community envisions the future it wants, and plans how to achieve it. Through public involvement, communities identify their purpose, core values, and vision of the future, which are then transformed into a manageable and feasible set of community goals and an action plan.

SOURCE: Green, Haines, and Halebsky (2000, p. 1.2).

A growing number of communities in the United States have been engaged in a formal process to develop an overall image of what their community wants to be and how it wants to look at some point in the future—what we refer to here as community visioning. In this section, we briefly describe the visioning process, how the process differs from other planning efforts, and how visioning is used by communities.

The basic advantage of visioning is that it allows for an expansive, innovative, and proactive future orientation. Visioning focuses on the strengths that must be developed to reach a desired end state. It expands the notion of public participation beyond that of other models and suggests that the community can design and create its own future.

The Roots of Visioning: Context and History

Beginning with the Housing Act of 1954, a debate began about the purpose of public participation and how it was to be included in decision-making processes of local, state, and federal governments (Glass, 1979; Howe, 1992; Meyerson & Banfield, 1955; Rabinovitz, 1969). The acceptance of public participation in government decision-making processes occurred during the turbulence of the 1960s and, in many instances, was mandated as part of the policy-making process.

Especially in professions where public participation was a routine event, such as in urban planning, the ideas of grassroots participation, community organizing, and planning from the bottom up were much discussed. The dominant planning model transformed over time, as ideas about public participation and how it should work were appended to the base model. In the next section, we describe this model and two other planning models that have influenced the process of neighborhood, town, and urban development. Community visioning represents the latest transformation of a general process that ideally strives to involve residents in creating and deciding on their mutual future.

Comprehensive-Rational Planning

Comprehensive-rational planning has been the most common form of planning used in cities, villages, and towns to address their future. The comprehensive-rational model is focused on the production of a plan that guides development and growth. The plan aims at comprehensiveness and implies focusing on the elements/functions of a place (Rittel & Webber, 1973; Wildavsky, 1973). Critics have leveled several criticisms of the model. Among the most important criticisms are that (1) it is impossible to analyze everything at once, (2) "wicked" problems cannot be addressed (Rittel & Webber, 1973), (3) it cannot react swiftly, (4) it is based on assumptions of growth and thus cannot deal effectively with decline or stagnation (Beauregard, 1978),

(5) it is based on past trends and forecasting that prove to be inaccurate, and (6) it is ineffective because the plans rarely reach the implementation stage (Hudson, 1979). Radical critics argue that it supports the accumulation and legitimation functions of the state (Beauregard, 1978; Fainstein & Fainstein, 1982) and is elitist and centralizing (Grabow & Heskin, 1973). Although comprehensive-rational planning has several weaknesses, it still forces residents to consider the interconnections between various elements of a community.

Advocacy Planning

Paul Davidoff (1973) promoted a new model of planning, "Planning Aid," in the 1960s, which was based on the idea of Legal Aid. The process of **advocacy planning** involved advocate planners, representing community groups, and presenting alternative plans to a city council, which decided on the plan or plan elements that were politically feasible, appropriate, and doable. The product of the process would be multiple plans offering different, alternative visions of a community. Advocacy planning promoted a level of public participation unheard of under the comprehensive-rational planning model.

There are several strengths to this model: It focuses on one issue or geographic area, plans are not comprehensive (which makes it less daunting for residents), and the model attempts to bring equality into the planning process by giving poor and disadvantaged groups a voice. The advocacy approach has several weaknesses, however, including the risk of conflicting plans. There also is a risk of being co-opted by a local bureaucracy or a more powerful interest group, or both. How likely is it for a planner in a public planning office to act as an advocate? If planners are outside the system—for example, if they work in a CDC or another CBO—they can be ignored or frozen out of the process and risk having their plans co-opted by political or bureaucratic forces. Nevertheless, community developers closely follow in the footsteps of advocacy planners, precisely because they bring to the conversation alternative ways of looking at projects and proposals.

Strategic Planning

Another model, **strategic planning,** originated in the military and moved into the corporate world, where it was limited to budgeting and financial control. By the 1980s, strategic planning was applied to local governments and nonprofit organizations. Bryson (1995) offered the following general definition of strategic planning: Strategic planning is a "disciplined effort to produce fundamental decisions and actions that shape what an organization is, what it does, and why it does it. . . . [This effort] requires broad yet effective information gathering, development and exploration of strategic alternatives, and an emphasis on future implications of present decisions" (pp. 4–5).

There are many corporate-style strategic planning approaches, but the most well-known and used model in the public sector and within CBOs is the Harvard policy model. This model has been around since the Harvard Business School developed it in the 1920s. SWOT analysis, a systematic assessment of strengths and weaknesses, opportunities, and threats, comes from this model (Bryson & Roering, 1987).

Strategic planning has several strengths. The process aims to build agreement within an organization or a community. It forces the community to ask and answer the questions: "What are our goals and aims?" and "What do we want to accomplish?" These questions encourage communities to think and act strategically—maximizing effectiveness, identifying their comparative advantage, focusing on critical issues, and turning liabilities into assets.

Strategic planning also has several weaknesses. The process is not always well suited to the public sector or CBOs that have multiple objectives and interests. The process may have difficulty satisfying competing and often conflicting demands. In addition, it is internal to the organization, so involving the public may be difficult. The process relies heavily on analyses of the status quo and makes demands for information and data that many communities find overwhelming. It also embraces competitive rather than cooperative behavior.

Charrettes

This physical, design-based, collaborative approach or method allows a community to focus deeply, rather than broadly, on a particular site for arriving at consensus to design and execute a project. Local governments, developers, and CBOs use charrettes to promote creativity in site design despite sometimes overly restrictive zoning regulations and to provide a method of input and discussion about controversial project ideas (La Fiandra, 2006; Lennertz & Lutzenhiser, 2006). A charrette is designed as an intensive and focused process, lasting from 2 to 7 days, and involves a project design team and stakeholders. The essence of a charrette is an iterative design and review process. The multidisciplinary team works in short bursts of time on a project plan, punctuated by stakeholder review sessions. Stakeholders initially operate in a proactive mode helping to frame the project and define broad guidelines. Thereafter, stakeholders react to draft project plans that the charrette team quickly puts together (La Fiandra, 2006; Lennertz & Lutzenhiser, 2006).

Appreciative Inquiry

Appreciative inquiry has a great deal in common with asset-based community development. In the context of community development, appreciative inquiry refers to a process of identifying the strengths and successes that exist in the community. The process was adopted widely by organizations in the 1980s and was adopted in community practice in the 1990s. The appreciative cycle usually consists of the 4Ds: (1) the *discovery* phase, which focuses on identifying accomplishments in the community and analyzing what factors contributed to the success; (2) the *dream* phase requires residents to envision how they could build on these successes to improve the quality of life in their community; (3) the *design* stage involves residents in developing strategies to accomplish goals that were identified in the dream stage; and (4) the final phase is *destiny,* which involves continuous learning and adjusting to carry out the goals.

Visioning

Visioning is an asset-based approach to community development. Community planning and development efforts usually begin with a scan of where the community is headed, which may involve an assessment of demographic, economic, social, and fiscal trends in the area. The next logical step is to develop a common view of where the community should be headed, which usually involves a visioning process. A community may convene a special meeting, or series of meetings, to develop a community vision. The primary product of such an event is a guide for subsequent planning or, in the case of a CBO, program development. Usually, the vision is followed by the development of specific strategies and an action plan the community wishes to follow.

The visioning process focuses on assets rather than the needs of the community. The visioning process begins with identifying an overall community vision and then develops visions in strategic areas (e.g., housing, land use, education, workforce development). Action plans (identifying specific projects, timelines, and individuals, departments, or agencies responsible for completing tasks) are created based on these visions (see Table 4.2). The process requires a substantial commitment by local residents and an ongoing role for facilitation. Individuals trained in facilitation processes could provide the role of ongoing facilitation. CBOs, because of their connection to communities and their experience with different forms of public participation, can play an active and helpful role in a visioning process. Visioning differs from some of the other planning techniques because it usually does not begin with a detailed analysis of trends or rely heavily on data to identify needs. Instead, it focuses on community assets through the values of residents and the visions they have for their community.

Over the past decade, many community development practitioners have turned away from strategic planning and comprehensive planning to visioning methods. One of the reasons for this shift is that visioning does not rely as much on data as the other planning methods do. For example, the heavy emphasis that comprehensive and strategic planning place on providing basic data on the trends and structure of a community frequently overwhelms participants at the

TABLE 4.2   A Visioning Process

Step	Component	Component Explanation
1	Getting started	Coordinating committee forms and begins planning for the first workshop.
2	Community visioning workshop	Coordinating committee facilitates process of preparing a general vision statement and identifies key areas.
3	Establishment of task forces	At workshop, assemble task forces by key area and meet to set action plan.
4	Key area visioning workshops	Each key area task force convenes a community workshop to facilitate a process for preparing a key area vision statement and identifying key subareas.
5	Review of plans and/or programs, etc.	Task forces should review all relevant existing plans, zoning, and subdivision regulations.
6	Data gathering and analysis	Each task force should gather and analyze pertinent data and prepare strategies. Larger task force evaluates data and strategies against general and key area visions.
7	Goal and strategy development	Task forces should develop goals and strategies based on data and vision statements.
8	Community feedback workshop	The coordinating committee should plan on a community-wide workshop to present the general and key area visions and broad strategies.
9	Community feedback workshop Development of action plans	Each task force should prepare action plans based on agreed strategies and goals.
10	Implementation	Undertake action plans.
11	Monitor, evaluate, and revise	The coordinating committee plans a meeting that reviews the activities and accomplishments to date and what activities will be implemented the following year.

beginning of the process and sometimes diverts attention away from the important issues the community is facing. Visioning may involve data collection and analysis, but these tasks usually come after there is some agreement on the direction the community should take and the issues the community is facing (see Case Study 4.1).

For some excellent examples of case studies using the visioning processes, see the database maintained by the Illinois Institute for Rural Affairs (http://www .iira.org/outreach/mapping/communities.asp). This website provides details on the processes used in a wide variety of communities and the outcomes that have been achieved in these cases. Many of these case studies are small towns that have been experiencing decline over the past few decades. These case studies demonstrate how visioning can be implemented in these different contexts.

CASE STUDY 4.1 VISIONING IN WAUSAU, WISCONSIN

The City of Wausau Wisconsin initiated a visioning process to develop strategic goals for the next 20 years. City officials initiated the process, but it eventually gained widespread support among various grassroots organizations in the region. The project developed a consensus around several key issues regarding growth and development in the municipality. The plan that emerged focused on improving bus service to several parts of the city, relocating heavy industry to an industrial park, and several projects related to the physical design of the community.

SOURCE: Green et al. (2000).

Timing and Momentum

One of the issues that communities may face is the question of whether they are ready to begin a visioning process. Should they focus on developing new leaders in the community before engaging in this process? Should they instead develop new and existing organizations that may be needed to implement the community's action plans? Timing and preparedness certainly should be considered before moving ahead with a community visioning process. At the same time, organizational and leadership development are frequent results of visioning efforts. By successfully completing projects that have been identified in the process, communities can develop the capacity to address bigger and more complex issues. Participants may discover along the way that what they really need are more leaders in their community and that they need to invest in a leadership training program. Without initiating the process, this realization may not have occurred.

Keeping the process on track and moving forward can be challenging. It is also one of the chief criticisms of this kind of process. Most visioning guidebooks provide pointers on how to maintain initiative (see Green et al., 2000).

Workshops

To guide the visioning process, three questions can be asked to drive the visioning workshop forward and shape the way in which participants think about their community:

- What do people want to preserve in the community?
- What do people want to create in the community?
- What do people want to change in the community?

One way to help the community develop their vision is to ask them to complete the sentence "In the year 20XX in our community, we would like to see _____." It is useful to look beyond the immediate future and develop the vision for at least a 15-year period. To go beyond 25 years, however, may be difficult for the group to work with in such a session. Case Study 4.2 is a vision statement from one community.

CASE STUDY 4.2 OVERALL VISION STATEMENT: THE TOWN OF STAR PRAIRIE

In the year 2030, the Town of Star Prairie is rural, family friendly, and growing.

The Town of Star Prairie is a rural, green community proud of its heritage and identity. The town has retained its rural character as defined by its rustic nature and its sylvan spaces that are both quiet and peaceful. The town's green spaces are many and varied, ranging from plenty of scenic beauty and quality lakes and rivers to bike and walking trails and parks and playgrounds. Residents have access to public hunting grounds at the old health center site and enjoy fishing on Cedar Lake, considered one of the top fishing lakes in the state of Wisconsin. Part of the town's rural charm is the number of quaint businesses, the museum at the old town hall, and places that people can meet in comfort and openness. The town has maintained its identity in part through its rural character, but it also has an independent government with good communication with other neighboring communities.

The Town of Star Prairie is a family-friendly community. Town residents are proud that parents can bring up their children in a safe and rural quality of life.

The Town of Star Prairie is a growing community. Despite a growing population, the town has retained the quality of its groundwater, in part by its investment in a sewage treatment system for Cedar Lake. Its growth has allowed access to bus and light rail service along the highway to the Twin Cities and the construction and maintenance of good roads.

Natural Resources

In the year 2030, the Town of Star Prairie has preserved and enhanced the quality of its lakes (especially Cedar Lake and Squaw Lakes), groundwater, wetlands, rivers and streams (especially the Apple River and Cedar Creek), and forests and hills through various ordinances and other mechanisms. The town has made efforts to re-create and maintain prairies. The residents recognize that the town's natural resources are important to their quality of life and must be preserved and enhanced. In addition, the town has worked with the county and other jurisdictions to maintain and create quality off- and on-road trails (for hiking, biking, horseback riding), parks (such as Apple River County Park), boat landings, and hunting areas.

Land Use

In the year 2030, the Town of Star Prairie has successfully managed the growth pressure from the Twin Cities by allowing for a mix of housing, open space and recreation, agriculture (especially crop and pasture land), and commercial uses, while still maintaining its rural character. The town regulates this variable land use mix to prevent nuisances, such as noise and odors, and to prevent land and air pollution.

(Continued)

(Continued)

Housing

In the year 2030, the Town of Star Prairie has affordable housing for seniors and others. When subdivisions are built, natural features are preserved and parks are required within them.

Agriculture

In the year 2030, the Town of Star Prairie has an active agricultural industry that especially focuses on plant and tree nurseries, small dairies, and other types of animal production and vegetable production.

Utilities and Community Facilities

In the year 2030, the Town of Star Prairie cooperates with its municipal neighbors. With the City of New Richmond, the recycling center is jointly operated. The town operates a community and senior center. To keep and better our water quality and to maintain water quantity, our more developed lakes, such as Cedar Lake, have rural water systems and sewage treatment facilities. Access to our lakes is easy for all residents from boat landings. In addition, the town has worked with others to maintain its dam and power plant.

Cultural Resources

In the year 2030, the Town of Star Prairie's historical society has a museum at the old town hall and maintains and preserves historical records. The town's historic homes and other structures are maintained and preserved.

Transportation

In the year 2030, the Town of Star Prairie has preserved its rustic roads, such as Old Mill and Brave Drive, and has maintained its road infrastructure. The town has planned and developed additional roads as appropriate for current and future land uses. The town cooperates with the county and others to develop a light rail system to the Twin Cities and a bus system to area communities. The town and the city of New Richmond have developed an agreement to share airport fees. The Cedar Lake Speed Way is closed down at its current location, and the area is redeveloped as part of the park system.

Economic Development

In the year 2030, the Town of Star Prairie has a number of healthy businesses, including small taverns and restaurants, and agriculture-related businesses. Business growth in the town has focused on rural-based businesses. Retail businesses are quaint. The town has achieved this type of business growth through an environmental review process that limits impacts on natural resources and a design review process that helps to maintain the rural character of the community.

NOTE: The second author, Anna Haines, worked with the Town of Star Prairie and the community planning department, which was the basis for this case study.

In Table 4.3, we provide a list of the types of participants that should be involved in a visioning process. Some communities have sought to gain support for their vision by getting it formally adopted by a local government. Formal adoption has several benefits, such as broad dissemination of the vision, increased legitimacy in the community, and possible influence in getting local government officials involved in the implementation stage.

Goals and Strategy Development

Participants in a visioning or planning process usually want to jump immediately into identifying specific projects that could be undertaken by the group. Planning processes in general, and visioning processes specifically, require that broad goals and strategies be identified first before moving too quickly to developing specific projects. These goals and strategies can be introduced to the group or developed within the group itself. Without developing a set of goals and strategies, communities may identify specific projects that are not related to the vision established earlier in the process.

In most visioning processes, the specific goals should be tied directly to the vision statement that has been developed earlier in the process. The goals

TABLE 4.3   Types of Participants

Economic Sectors	Organizations	Government	Personal Factors	Political Views
Agriculture, forestry, and fishing	Art and culture	Elected officials	Race/ethnicity	Conservative/ liberal/ independent
Wholesale	Education	Planning department	Age	Pro-growth/ anti-growth
Construction	Civic	Natural resources	Sex	
Manufacturing	Unions	Transportation	Home ownership	
Transportation and utilities	Youth	Housing	Class	
Finance, insurance, and real estate	Neighborhood	Education	Children	
Services	Social service agencies	Economic development	Length of residence	
Tourism	Health care	Workforce development		
Media	Environmental	Regional planning		
Business type— size, ownership	Recreation			

SOURCE: *From Building Our Future: A Guide to Community Visioning* (Report No. G3708), by Gary Green, Anna Haines & Stephen Halebsky. University of Wisconsin Extension, Cooperative Extension, Madison, WI, 2000. Reprinted with permission.

usually reflect the top priorities that have been identified by participants. These goals and objectives help establish the connections between the vision statement and the specific activities that the community will undertake to achieve that vision.

Action Plan Development

An action plan is a description of the activities needed to be done to move the community toward its vision. For each project that is identified, there should be a detailed plan of what needs to be done, who can do it, when it will be done, what information is needed, and what resources are necessary to implement the strategy. Action plans should be prepared based on agreed-on strategies and goals. In Box 4.2, we provide a description of the types of information needed to prepare an action plan.

BOX 4.2 ACTION PLANNING: BASIS FOR WORKSHEET

Below is a list of the categories and questions that should be asked for each identified project. The purpose of using a worksheet for action planning is to help the CBO or other group to thoroughly analyze and assess how it can start and complete a project. An important facet of this analysis is a political assessment. A formal acknowledgment and assessment of the local political situation can help move projects forward. This assessment will help the CBO or group to decide whether or not it is feasible to move forward on any particular project.

1. *Assess Fit of Vision and Project:* What is your vision theme? What is your project? Why are you doing this project (purpose or desired outcome)? Who will potentially benefit from this project? Who will potentially be harmed by this project?

2. *Analyze the Situation:* Where does this project fit into current community priorities? Are there any groups working on related projects? Have there been past attempts on this or similar projects? Who does it affect positively (individuals and groups)? Who does it affect negatively (individuals and groups)?

3. *Assess Helping and Hindering Forces:* Who are the decision makers (formal and informal, individuals and organizations, internal and external)? Who can help or hinder this project? Who makes the contact? What strategies will we use to influence the decision makers? Who is likely to support the project in the community and who should contact them? What do the people contacted think of the vision and project, what would they like to see as an outcome, and how would they carry out the project? How will you enlist their support? Who is likely to oppose the project and who should contact them? What do the people contacted think of the vision and project and what are their specific objections? What would they like to see as an outcome and how would they carry out the project?

4. *Decide Who Is Going to Do It and How:* Were there any new individuals identified who would be valuable resources for your task force? Are some task force members ready to move on to other projects or do they feel they have made their contribution? Who will coordinate the task force? How often will the task force meet? What subgroups, if any, are needed? How will you keep each other informed? How will you keep the community informed? How will you keep people outside the community informed?

5. *Create a Community Resource Inventory:* What skills, knowledge, linkages (networks), representation, or resources are needed for the CBO or group at this stage of the project? The inventory should cover the following categories of needs: skills and expertise, physical (facilities, equipment), information, finances, and other.

Monitor, Evaluate, and Revise

Communities engaged in development are seldom interested in monitoring their progress and evaluating their efforts. They are primarily concerned with getting things done. There are several reasons, however, why it is useful for a community to measure its progress and evaluate its efforts:

- To keep people involved in the community development process by showing them tangible results of their efforts
- To show foundations, local governments, and other financial supporters that their resources are well spent
- To improve the community's efforts by establishing a reliable system of monitoring progress
- To gain support of the community at large for development efforts by having an effective evaluation system in place

Monitoring is an assessment of the planning process. The purpose of monitoring is to provide indications of whether corrections need to take place in the action plan. For each element of the action plan, communities should ask questions such as the following: Are the deadlines being met? Is the budget appropriate? Is the staffing appropriate? Is the amount of work realistic? Are priorities receiving the appropriate amount of attention? How are we working as a group? Are we learning something important to share? What else do we need?

Evaluation focuses on the specific accomplishments of the process. A distinction should be made between measuring **outputs** and **outcomes**. Outputs are usually things that can be counted that result from the action plan. They are an intermediary measure. Examples of outputs include the number of jobs created, number of houses built, or number of programs developed. Outcomes are usually much more long term and are more difficult to link to the specific elements of the action plan. They are more closely linked to the ultimate objectives identified in the visioning process. Examples of outcomes are decreased levels of poverty or increased levels of personal income, more people accepted into leadership roles, or improved social networks among residents. It is often difficult, however, to make a causal link between outcomes and an action plan. Participants in the visioning process should ask how a community is better off as a result and then try to measure success in terms of goals stated in the action plan.

It is preferable to assess the change in the outputs and outcomes over time. It is important to collect information on the value of the measure at the starting point, often referred to as the baseline. When evaluating change, a community should identify the unit of analysis. The unit of analysis is the basic unit whose properties you choose to measure and analyze. For most communities, the unit of analysis is the neighborhood, the city, or even the county. The decision of what unit of analysis to use may be determined by who is involved in the effort or by data availability. The length of time used to assess change also may vary. The length of time should be based on a reasonable expectation of how long it should take the actions to have an effect. So, if your goal is to create new jobs, you might be able to see the effects of your actions in a few years. Improvement in environmental quality, however, may take a longer period. Thus, the period to be studied may vary by the specific outcomes and impacts that the community wishes to examine.

A written action plan, containing benchmarks or performance indicators, describing the points of success along the way when possible, is essential in monitoring results. Benchmarks are especially useful for long-term projects. For instance, a community may have a long-term vision that involves providing high-quality health care. Reaching this vision may involve a set of goals and strategies that span several years. Knowing the number of people without access to health care or the number of physicians in the community at the start of the project helps local leaders track their progress.

The benchmarks should be reasonable in terms of what can be accomplished in a specified period of time, but, at the same time, benchmarks should keep efforts focused on the ultimate goal(s) in the strategic visioning document. In this regard, photographs of the community when the visioning process started can be useful in making "before" and "after" presentations to show that benchmarks, such as improvements in buildings or streets, have been met. In designing benchmarks or performance indicators, however, community leaders must recognize that community development is not limited to job or income creation; rather, it should include sustainability, historic preservation, health care, education, recreation, and other essential characteristics of a healthy and vibrant community.

Linking benchmarks to each goal provides residents with information about progress in each section of the plan. When one part of the overall effort is not performing well, adjustments can be made to bring it in line without substantially changing the entire approach. Regular reviews of the action plan and comparisons with benchmarks can be very useful. Showing progress on small projects can build confidence and encourage more involvement by residents and businesses.

There are a number of methods of measuring sustainability. One of the most popular methods, because of its ease of use, participatory approach, and accessibility, is sustainability indicators. Many organizations and websites promote the use of indicators to measure and evaluate community sustainability initiatives. The purpose of these techniques is to help communities gather, sort, and analyze data with the purpose of making more informed choices.

Another technique is called ecological footprint analysis. This technique, developed by Wackernagel and Rees (1996), is an accounting tool for estimating resource consumption and waste assimilation requirements of a community, region, or nation. The authors examined Vancouver, British Columbia, Canada and found that the city needs "an area 19 times larger than its 4,000 square kilometers to support food production, forestry products, and energy consumption in the region" (Holtzman, 1999, p. 42). Individuals can measure their own ecological footprint using one of a number of websites. The general idea is to understand the amount of resources a community or individual is using on an annual basis. Indicators enable communities to measure progress toward sustainability.

There are many different frameworks within which to develop sustainable indicators: domain based, goal based, sectoral, issue based, causal, and combination (Maclaren, 1996). A domain-based framework organizes indicators into the three Es: environment, economy, and equity. It allows for and accentuates the links among the three dimensions. Thus, using this kind of framework, one would develop indicators under each of the three dimensions. In contrast, a goal-based framework develops goals first. Then, for each goal, it develops indicators. The sectoral framework is divided by the sectors that an institution, such as a local government, is responsible for maintaining. Typical sectors include housing, welfare, recreation, transportation, and economic development. The strength of this framework is that local government agencies and departments can better monitor their programs. Issue-based frameworks are organized to contend with the issues of the day, such as urban sprawl, crime and safety, or job creation. The weakness of this framework is that the issues are bound to change over time, so the indicators can become irrelevant. The causal framework introduces the notion of cause and effect. Indicators may be difficult to establish, for example, given the complexity of ecological models and the policies that might affect them. Finally, a combination framework can combine two or more of the frameworks. The purpose is to overcome some of the weaknesses of one framework, while taking advantage of the strengths of each (Maclaren, 1996, pp. 190–194).

Choosing a framework and identifying indicators can be a long and intensive process. Many communities use a visioning process to help them establish a community vision, goals, and finally indicators. One way to select indicators is by brainstorming with all interested parties to identify an ideal set. Ways to narrow down a list of possible indicators include looking at data sources, investigating sources of help, and deciding what information is most useful. It is wise to monitor well a few key indicators that provide useful information, rather than monitor poorly a wide variety of indicators. Data may be available for certain indicators but not for others. An indicator that can be supported by available data may be more practical than one that requires extensive data gathering. Another way to narrow down a list of possible indicators is to use evaluation criteria. Box 4.3 provides a list of criteria for narrowing down an indicators list.

BOX 4.3 EVALUATION CRITERIA FOR POTENTIAL INDICATORS

- They reflect stakeholders' concerns.
- They are measurable.
- They are understandable.
- They are comparable and meaningful.
- Data are available to construct them.
- They are targetable and interpretable.
- They have a suitable geographic/temporal scale.
- They are timely and anticipatory.
- They are results oriented.
- They have long-range reliability.
- They are flexible.

Community-Based Research

Frequently, communities decide they need to do some research as part of their planning process. In this section of the chapter, we provide an overview of survey research and participatory action research.

Survey Research

In many cases, communities begin the community development process by conducting a survey. **Survey research** requires community members' time as well as their financial commitment. Before embarking on a survey project, community members need to ask themselves several questions: Do we want to conduct a survey or use another technique to achieve public participation? What is the best way to obtain the needed information? What do we want to know? How will this information be used? Can residents commit sufficient time and money to conduct a survey?

Most communities conduct surveys to collect information on the attitudes, opinions, values, and behavior of local residents on a specific topic. If the goal is to obtain public participation on a policy issue, other techniques may be more appropriate or cost-efficient. For example, it may be quicker and easier to hold public meetings or conduct focus groups. Focus groups may be more appropriate in a situation where you want to understand why people feel they way they do about particular issues. Public meetings provide an opportunity for residents to voice their opinion about issues and listen to the perspectives of their neighbors. A survey instrument may not provide the type of information obtained from these two other techniques.

A community survey may not be appropriate at the beginning of the planning process. If a survey is conducted too early in the process, residents may not have identified all of the issues they want to consider. At the same time, if a survey is conducted too late in the process, residents may feel that their participation is meaningless because the plan has already been worked out. Communities also need to consider whether they have sufficient resources for conducting a survey. Similarly, community leaders must be willing to use the information once it is collected.

There is no single best technique for conducting surveys. The appropriate technique depends on the resources available, the type of information desired, and the sampling strategies. In the following list, we briefly discuss the advantages and disadvantages of three commonly used survey techniques—face-to-face interviews, mail surveys, and telephone surveys:

1. Face-to-face interviews generally provide the best response rate of the three techniques considered, usually more than 70%, and permit the interviewer to use visual aids or fairly complex questions. This technique is often used with long questionnaires as well. Interviewers can follow up on responses to get a better understanding of why a given response is provided. Face-to-face interviews, however, are the most expensive of the three techniques, and there may be more problems with interviewer bias.

2. Mail surveys are probably the most frequently used technique for conducting community surveys, mainly because they are usually the cheapest method of the three considered here. With mail surveys, maps and other visuals aids can usually be included, though the instructions need to be concise and understandable. The response rate for mail surveys varies depending on the number of follow-up letters sent. Many communities will send out only one wave of questionnaires, which generally produces a response rate of 30% to 50% on average. A follow-up postcard can yield another 10%, and a replacement questionnaire will generate another 10% to 20%. There are several disadvantages to using mail surveys: The length of the survey can be more limited than that of other methods, and it is very difficult to ask complex questions in mail surveys.

3. Telephone surveys are used increasingly by communities because they can be done quickly and generally have a higher response rate than mail surveys do. The cost may vary, however, depending on whether or not individuals are sampled in each household. The response rate among telephone surveys is almost as good as face-to-face interviews, and the interviewer has the opportunity to probe for additional comments. One of the chief disadvantages is that interviewers cannot use visual materials or ask complex questions.

Increasingly, communities are using multiple techniques to conduct a survey. So, communities may begin with a mail survey and then contact nonrespondents through either a phone call or face-to-face visit. This approach is obviously much more doable in small neighborhoods and where most residents have listed phone numbers.

Survey research is a valued technique for reaching community residents to obtain their ideas and suggestions. The quality of the data is largely dependent on how much effort goes into the design of the questionnaire and the response rate for the survey. Questions need to be designed to minimize the bias. The credibility of the entire project can be undermined by leading or biased questions. Similarly, every effort should be made to obtain the highest response rate possible. Communication about the purposes of the survey and how the data will be used is crucial.

Participatory Action Research

One method of community-based research is called **participatory action research** (PAR). This method grew out of community development work in developing countries, in particular Latin America and Africa. PAR is an advocacy tool for a grassroots, bottom-up approach to community development that purposefully incorporates participation from disenfranchised or marginalized groups in society—the poor, minorities, women, and children.

PAR is defined by the three words that make it—participation, action, and research. "A hallmark of a genuine participatory action research process is that it may change shape and focus overtime as participants focus and refocus their understandings about what is 'really' happening and what is really important to them" (Wadsworth, 1998, p. 7). Participation involves researchers, funders, and communities—both the people who are researched and the people whom the research is for. In every PAR process, participation must be deeply defined and understood.

Action refers to the researcher's involvement in real projects with participants. It is the opposite of armchair research, which may only use secondary data and not require the researcher to ever leave his or her office. It also does not refer to a researcher in the field gathering primary data through interviews or observations for a great length of time, although both techniques may be used in a PAR process. Action means involvement and working with people in their communities to create change. Research within a PAR process can involve any of the formal techniques used in conventional research projects, but in PAR, for example, residents as participants would derive the questions.

One of the chief advantages of PAR is that communities own the research. They develop the goals, help collect the data, are involved in analyzing the data, and interpret the results. This level of participation by residents helps ensure that the research process is strongly connected to the visioning process, and that the results will be used by participants.

——————————————————————————— **Summary and Conclusions**

In this chapter, we focused on the role of public participation in the community development process and presented visioning as a specific process used by a growing number of communities to guide their futures. The process of visioning lends itself well to using a variety of public participation techniques, as well as including aspects of community organizing. Visioning exercises have become part of general planning processes at the local government level but also are used by voluntary groups and CBOs to guide them in their work in communities and neighborhoods. We would be first to acknowledge that there are a wide variety of processes and tools that are used by community development practitioners. There is no single right method that will work in all communities at all times. As practitioners, we find ourselves adapting the process to different situations and contexts. The model we presented here simply represents a basic process that represents some of the common elements used by practitioners.

As we mentioned at the beginning of the chapter, there continues to be some debate over the importance of process and outcomes in community development. Some practitioners believe that the process is the key and that the eventual outcomes of the process do not matter. Others believe that visible outcomes are all that matter and that the process is relatively unimportant. Probably the most reasonable position to take regarding this debate is that most community development efforts require both a meaningful process that involves residents and tangible products that participants can point to as the result of their effort.

Finally, we argued that community-based research is normally an important element of the community development process. Although participation of residents in the process is often taken for granted in the planning process, the research stage is often handed over to the "professionals." Increasingly, residents are taking back this activity and guiding the research process themselves.

KEY CONCEPTS

ACORN model

Advocacy planning

Alinsky model

Appreciative inquiry

Boston model

Community organizing

Comprehensive-rational planning

Electoral participation

Evaluation

Industrial Areas Foundation (IAF) model

Monitoring

Obligatory participation

Outcomes

Outputs

Participatory action research   Survey research

Public action   Strategic planning

Public involvement   Visioning

QUESTIONS

1. Why is public participation important in a community development effort?

2. What are the four forms of public participation? What are some differences between these forms?

3. How do the forms of public participation relate to the ladder of public participation?

4. What are the different organizing models and how do they differ?

5. What is visioning?

6. How does public participation and visioning relate to the future growth and development of communities?

7. What is community organizing?

8. Define evaluation and monitoring.

9. What are the differences between outcomes and outputs? Give some examples of each.

EXERCISES

1. Contact a CBO to evaluate its community development process. Ask the following kinds of questions: What kinds of public participation techniques did the CBO use? Did the CBO develop a plan? What kind of process was used to create that plan? What kinds of outcomes have occurred? Are any impacts claimed due to the process? Has the CBO developed any indicators to monitor progress?

2. Discuss the advantages and limitations of the CBO's public participation techniques and their planning process and action plan. Discuss the limitations of claiming outcomes and outputs. Discuss how they can make their process broader and more participatory in the future.

3. Identify a federal, state, or local agency that recently conducted a public participation process in your community. An example might be a transportation plan for a city. Evaluate their effort to involve the public in the decision-making process. What were the strengths of the process? What were the weaknesses of the process? How could the process be improved in the future?

4. Help conduct a survey for a neighborhood association. Work with the association in developing the goals of the survey and the appropriate method for collecting the data.

REFERENCES

Arnstein, S. R. (1969). A ladder of citizen participation. *Journal of the American Institute of Planners, 35,* 216–224.

Beauregard, R. A. (1978). Planning in an advanced capitalist state. In R. Burchell & G. Sternlieb (Eds.), *Planning theory in the 1980s: A search for future directions* (pp. 235–254). New Brunswick, NJ: Center for Urban Policy Research, Rutgers University.

Bryson, J. M. (1995). *Strategic planning for public and nonprofit organizations: A guide to strengthening and sustaining organizational achievement.* San Francisco: Jossey-Bass.

Bryson, J. M., & Roering, W. D. (1987). Applying private-sector strategic planning in the public sector. *Journal of the American Planning Association, 53,* 9–22.

Davidoff, P. (1973). Advocacy and pluralism in planning. In A. Faludi (Ed.), *A reader in planning theory* (pp. 277–296). Oxford, UK: Pergamon Press.

de Tocqueville, A. (1904). *Democracy in America.* New York: D. Appleton and Company.

Fainstein, N., & Fainstein, S. (1982). New debates in urban planning: The impact of Marxist theory within the United States. In C. Paris (Ed.), *Critical readings in planning theory* (pp. 147–173). Oxford, UK: Pergamon Press.

Glass, J. J. (1979). Citizen participation in planning: The relationship between objectives and techniques. *Journal of the American Planning Association, 45,* 180–189.

Grabow, S., & Heskin A. (1973). Foundations for a radical concept of planning. *Journal of the American Institute of Planners, 39,* 106–114.

Green, G., Haines, A., & Halebsky, S. (2000). *Building our future: A guide to community visioning* (Report No. G3708). Madison: University of Wisconsin Extension Publications.

Howe, E. (1992). Professional roles and the public interest in planning. *Journal of Planning Literature, 6,* 230–248.

Hudson, B. (1979). Comparison of current planning theories: Counterparts and contradictions. *Journal of the American Planning Association, 45,* 387–398.

Kahn, S. (1991). *Organizing: A guide for grassroots leaders.* Silver Springs, MD: National Association of Social Workers.

La Fiandra, D. (2006). Charrettes in site design and land use regulation. *The Maryland Bar Journal, 39,* 30–35.

Langton, S. (1978). What is citizen participation? In S. Langton (Ed.), *Citizen participation in America: Essays on the state of the art* (pp. 13–24). Lexington, MA: Lexington Books.

Lennertz, B., & Lutzenhiser, A. (2006). A charrette is the best way to share. *Planning, 72,* 44–47.

Meyerson, M., & Banfield, E. (1955). *Politics, planning and the public interest: The case of public housing in Chicago.* Glencoe, IL: The Free Press.

Rabinovitz, F. (1969). *City politics and planning.* New York: Atherton Press.

Rittel, H., & Webber, M. (1973). Dilemmas in a general theory of planning. *Policy Sciences, 4,* 155–169.

Rubin, H. J., & Rubin, I. S. (1992). *Community organizing and development* (2nd ed.). Boston: Allyn & Bacon.

Shipley, R., & Newkirk, R. (1998). Visioning: Did anybody see where it came from? *Journal of Planning Literature, 12,* 407–416.

Wadsworth, Y. (1998). What is participatory action research? *Action Research International,* Paper 2. Retrieved March 2, 2007, from www.scu.edu.au/schools/gcm/ar/ari/arihome.html

Wildavsky, A. (1973). If planning is everything, maybe it's nothing. *Policy Sciences, 4,* 127–153.

ADDITIONAL READINGS AND RESOURCES

Readings

Aspen Institute. (1996). *Measuring community capacity building: A workbook-in-progress for rural communities.* Washington, DC: Author.

Chambers, R. (2005). *Participatory workshops: A sourcebook of 21 sets of ideas and activities.* London: Earthscan.

Christenson, J. A., & Robinson, J., Jr. (Eds.). (1989). *Community development in perspective.* Ames: Iowa State University Press.

Daniels, T. L., & Keller, J. W. (with Lapping, M. B.). (1988). *The small town planning handbook.* Washington, DC: Planners Press.

Emery, M., & Purser, R. E. (1996). *The search conference: A powerful method for planning organizational change and community action.* San Francisco: Jossey-Bass.

Fung, A. (2004). *Empowered participation: Reinventing urban democracy.* Princeton, NJ: Princeton University Press.

Fung, A., & Wright, E. O. (2003). *Deepening democracy: Institutional innovations in empowered participatory governance.* London: Verso.

Holtzman, D. (1999). Economy in numbers: Ecological footprints. *Dollars and Sense, 224,* 42.

Klein, W. R., Benson, V. L., Anderson, J., & Herr, P. B. (1993). Visions of things to come. *Planning, 59*(5), 10–19.

Kretzmann, J. P., & McKnight, J. L. (1993). *Building communities from the inside out: A path toward finding and mobilizing a community's assets.* Evanston, IL: Center for Urban Affairs and Policy Research, Northwestern University.

Maclaren, V. W. (1996). Urban sustainability reporting. *Journal of the American Planning Association, 62,* 184–202.

North Central Regional Center for Rural Development. (2000). *Take charge: Participatory action planning for communities and organizations.* Ames, IA: Author.

Rosener, J. (1978). Matching method to purpose: The challenges of planning citizen-participation activities. In S. Langton (Ed.), *Citizen participation in America: Essays on the state of the art* (pp. 109–122). Lexington, MA: Lexington Books.

Stoecker, R. (2005). *Research methods for community change: A project-based approach.* Thousand Oaks, CA: Sage.

Strand, K., Marullo, S., Cutforth, N., Stoecker, R., & Donohue, P. (2003). *Community-based research and higher education: Principles and practices.* San Francisco: Jossey-Bass.

Wackernagel, M., & Rees, W. (1996). *Our ecological footprint: Reducing human impact on the earth.* Gabriola Island, British Columbia, Canada: New Society Publishers.

Walzer, N. (Ed.). (1996). *Community strategic visioning programs.* Westport, CT: Praeger.

Whitney, D., & Trosten-Bloom, A. (2003). *The power of appreciative inquiry.* San Francisco: Berrett-Koehler.

Websites

Appreciative Inquiry Commons—http://appreciativeinquiry.case.edu/. A good general source of information on using appreciative inquiry.

The Aspen Institute Policy Programs—www.aspeninstitute.org. The Aspen Institute has a website that describes various issues about measuring community capacity. The institute also has a workbook titled *Measuring Community Capacity Building: A Workbook in Progress,* which is very useful.

Axelrod Group—www.axelrodgroup.com. This site provides information regarding the Conference model (an approach that includes the use of Future Search) and follow-up conferences designed to help in the development of an action plan.

Future Search—www.futuresearch.net. This website provides information on Future Search, an organizational development technique of collaborative inquiry that focuses on the future of an organization, a network of people, or a community.

International Association for Public Participation (IAP2)—www.iap2.org. This organization helps people around the world, including communities, to improve their decisions by involving those people who are affected by those decisions. It provides many public participation tools.

Taos Institutue—http://www.taosinstitute.net/. The Taos Institute is an excellent resource for materials and training in the area of appreciative inquiry.

Sites for Data and Tools

American Factfinder—factfinder.census.gov. This is the richest source of data for communities. The U.S. Census Bureau provides detailed household data that can be examined at several different levels of geography. In addition to the decennial census, this site provides access to the American Community Survey, Economic Censuses, and population estimates for communities.

Community Economic Toolbox—www.economictoolbox.geog.psu.edu. For a good source of economic data, the Community Economic Toolbox provides some important indicators of economic change. In addition to economic snapshots, this website supplies communities with basic economic tools, such as location quotients and shift share analyses.

Headwater Economics—http://www.headwaterseconomics.org/eps/. This source provides some unique data analyses for a variety of geographic areas.

Social Explorer—http://www.socialexplorer.com/pub/maps/home.aspx. Provides demographic information in an easily understood format: data maps. They have created hundreds of interactive data maps of the United States.

Sonoran Institute—http://eps.sonoran.org/. Customized socioeconomic profiles at the national, regional, state, county, and community levels.

Videos

Collaborative Planning (1990), produced by the American Planning Association, directed by Edith Nettle. This video "shows how citizens can work together in their communities to plan for the future." Available from Community Services—Washington, 915 15th St. NW, Suite 601, Washington, DC 20005.

5

The Role of Community-Based Organizations

Community development corporations (CDCs) have become the principal organizations for carrying out local development activities in many urban and rural neighborhoods. Many other types of community-based organizations (CBOs) are involved in development activities as well. In this chapter, we review the basic structure and mission of CDCs, **local development corporations (LDCs), neighborhood associations,** and other CBOs. We are especially interested in examining how these organizations operate, how they balance community organizing and development activities, and their effectiveness in generating valuable outcomes and impacts in their neighborhoods and localities. There is no end to the examples of CBOs that we could consider here. Many of these organizations have a more narrow focus and are discussed in the following chapters on community assets.

BOX 5.1 CDC FACTS (2005)

- There are more than 4,600 CDCs in the United States.
- The median age of CDCs is 18 years.
- Two thirds of the CDCs serve one neighborhood or a multineighborhood area smaller than a city.
- Average annual housing production more than 86,000 units.
- CDC activity creates more than 75,000 jobs per year.
- More than 20% of CDCs have more than one business.
- More than 20% of CDCs offer individual development accounts (IDAs).

SOURCE: Community-Wealth.org (http://www.community-wealth.org/strategies/panel/cdcs/index.html).

We focus on CBOs because they play an especially important role in the community development process. Rubin and Rubin (1992, pp. 96–97) suggested that local organizations make community action more effective for several different reasons. First, organizations create power. Government officials are more likely to respond to demands when CBOs represent a large number of people. At the same time, individuals are more likely to participate in a project because they are no longer acting alone. Second, organizations provide continuity. The membership may change, but the organization can continue to fulfill its mission. Continuity also is important for attracting resources, especially from foundations, and for developing ties with government officials. Social movements can be effective but need to institutionalize their efforts in some way. Organizations fulfill that function. Third, organizations help develop expertise, either through collective or accumulated experiences or through obtaining resources to hire experts when needed. In this sense, CBOs can provide a stronger link between local knowledge and technical expertise. Finally, organizations improve the ability of residents to respond to problems more quickly. Without organizations, residents would have to organize and mobilize around new issues each time they develop.

CBOs also stimulate democratic empowerment by providing an incubator for public participation. Residents learn how to participate through their involvement in these organizations. This experience often shapes individual involvement in other organizations and institutions. Participation is a learned skill that is more easily developed in formal and informal organizations. It is through the experience of working through conflicts and different interests in organizations that individuals develop valuable leadership skills that can be used in other settings. Most large, complex organizations (such as schools and the workplace) do not provide rich opportunities to learn democratic principles.

A key advantage of CBOs is that they are embedded in local social networks. As we discuss in the chapter on social capital (Chapter 7), these networks become an important source of information. Social networks also provide resources that enable the organization to function more effectively. For instance, social networks provide the organization with local knowledge that is so critical for implementing programs and delivering services.

The organizations we discuss in this chapter all struggle with some of the major issues affecting community development efforts: how to encourage public participation, avoid becoming too bureaucratic, obtain external resources without losing control over the process, address multiple objectives (e.g., economic, social, environmental) at once, and build the capacity of local residents. Most CBOs begin as nonprofit organizations, but many evolved into for-profit entities as they became established and able to maintain their financial base.

The power of working through existing CBOs is a basic principle in most community organizing efforts. It is important to see the connections between CBOs and asset building strategies. The best example is the Dudley Street Neighborhood Initiative (DSNI). The DSNI was able to obtain support from the City of Boston and negotiate effectively with local foundations through the development of a strong organization. The organization was able to effectively recruit new members, as well as develop strong leadership programs.

Its greatest success was maintaining local control over the community development process, while involving large powerful institutions and organizations (Medoff & Sklar, 1994).

Community Development Corporations

There are more than 2,000 CDCs in the United States today. The National Congress for Community Economic Development (NCCED, 1995) defines a CDC as a private nonprofit entity, serving a low-income community, governed by a community-based board, and serving as an ongoing producer in housing, commercial-industrial development, or business development. The primary goals of CDCs are to serve low-income communities and to empower residents. These dual-purpose goals were the source of much debate in the 1990s.

CDCs are intended to be community-controlled organizations. For most people, this means that the board of directors is drawn from community residents, especially low-income families. There are some reasons to question whether having a representative board really constitutes community control (see the discussion in Chapter 4 regarding the ladder of public participation). For example, the board may not exercise much power and may defer to professional and technical staff to make decisions. Due to the increasingly technical nature of development projects, many board members may feel they do not have the expertise to make independent judgments.

Although CDCs are involved in a wide variety of projects, affordable housing activities have been the most successful and visible. Surveys of CDCs show that more than 90% report that they are engaged in housing, and almost one-half report that they have produced more than 100 units (NCCED, 1995). Between 1960 and 1990, CDCs and other nonprofit developers produced about 736,000 units of federally assisted housing. Housing appears to be the preferred activity for several reasons. For many poor neighborhoods, residents are in dire need of affordable housing. Adequate housing, and the stable resident population it encourages, is a foundation for stimulating business and commercial development in a neighborhood. There are relatively more funding sources for housing in poor neighborhoods than for other types of activities, partially due to the perceived lower risk of housing activities. Most CDCs are able to tap into resources from federal and local governments for financing housing projects. Since 1974, **Community Development Block Grants (CDBGs)** and, more recently (since 1990), the HOME programs have provided steady sources of federal funding for CDCs. The **HOME program,** for example, mandates that at least 15% of each participating jurisdiction's funds be earmarked for nonprofit housing producers. Recently, CDCs have moved increasingly beyond housing into areas such as business development and have been criticized for not proving to be as successful, at least initially (Lemann, 1994).

CDCs claim to provide several advantages in leading the community development effort in localities. First, many CDCs view themselves as involved in comprehensive development—a variety of activities from physical and economic development to the provision of social services and the promotion of cultural activities and the arts. Second, CDCs have the technical expertise to address community problems. Third, CDCs are more entrepreneurial, more efficient, and less bureaucratic than the local, state, and federal government agencies involved in community development. And fourth, CDCs are more equipped to shape the development process according to the community's vision and needs.

Three Generations of CDCs

The origin of CDCs can be traced to Robert Kennedy's tour of Bedford-Stuyvesant and the Special Impact Amendment to the Economic Opportunity Act. The Bedford-Stuyvesant Restoration Corporation is considered the first CDC in the country (see Case Study 5.1). Most of the early CDCs emerged from neighborhood-based political activities and attempted to empower residents. Over time, they began to rely more heavily on paid staff and became a major source of technical assistance in low-income neighborhoods. In this section, we briefly discuss the historical development of CDCs in the United States.

CASE STUDY 5.1 BEDFORD-STUYVESANT RESTORATION CORPORATION (BSRC)

In 1966, New York Senator Robert F. Kennedy visited the Bedford-Stuyvesant neighborhood in Brooklyn. From the 1940s to 1960, the population shifted from 75% White to 85% African American and Latino. The neighborhood suffered from a loss of jobs, disinvestment of local resources, and inadequate public services. With the assistance of local leaders, Senator Kennedy helped establish the Bedford-Stuyvesant Renewal and Rehabilitation Corporation, which eventually became the Bedford-Stuyvesant Restoration Corporation. This organization became the nation's first CDC.

At the core of the CDC's strategies was the improvement of the physical conditions of the neighborhood, which it hoped would improve the likelihood of attracting new businesses and other revitalization efforts. The neighborhood turned its attention to improving basic services, such as garbage collection and infrastructure maintenance, as the first step in improving the physical environment.

One of the first projects was a program to help residents weatherize and renovate the exteriors of their homes. This project had the dual purpose of improving the physical conditions of the community (more than 4,200 housing units were rehabilitated) and generating job opportunities (more than 2,000 temporary and permanent jobs) that gave local residents job experience and training.

> Probably the most visible project of the BSRC was the redevelopment project at Restoration Plaza. The multipurpose complex was an abandoned bottling factory mill. Since 1975, the complex has been the home of a variety of businesses, including commercial banks, utility companies, a grocery store, a theater, and several community-based service organizations. The project became the center of the revitalization efforts in the neighborhood.
>
> For more than 30 years, BSRC has addressed a variety of needs in the Bedford-Stuyvesant neighborhood. It has attracted more than $370 million in investments and provided residents with important jobs skills and experiences.
>
> SOURCE: From "Community Development Corporation Oral History Project," www.prattcenter.

1960s: Activist Organizations

The first CDCs were engaged in housing projects, but their primary focus tended to be on business and workforce development. Community activists founded the first CDCs (fewer than 100) during the 1960s. The first major source of federal funding for CDCs was the **Special Impact Program (SIP)**. This program established block grants to CBOs that would design and implement their own development strategies. The program faced serious opposition from within the Johnson administration, and it has moved from several different agencies (O'Connor, 1999). Eventually, the program was considered a success and was seen as a key element of the place-based development strategies of the War on Poverty. During a 20-year period from 1968 to 1986, the federal government allocated more than $75 million in this program to CDCs.

1970s: Specialization

During the 1970s, the number of CDCs increased to several hundred. Their focus shifted, primarily to housing projects. Groups involved in redlining issues and problems related to urban renewal organized many of the CDCs created during this period (Vidal, 1992). At about the same time, foundations began investing much more in CDCs. The Ford Foundation's **Grey Areas Program** was one the largest and most visible efforts during this period. The Grey Areas Program sought to coordinate service programs among local bureaucracies in an effort to integrate low-income residents into urban society.

1980s and 1990s: Professionalization

In the 1980s, the number of CDCs expanded to more than 2,000. CDCs became increasingly specialized, concentrating on housing activities. CDC staff generally was more professional and played much less of an activist role than they had in the past. One of the most important changes in the community development field during the 1980s was the rise of national financial intermediaries, which served to support CDCs in the area of housing. Three of the most important intermediaries are the **Local Initiatives Support Corporation (LISC)**, the **Enterprise Foundation,** and the **Neighborhood Reinvestment Corporation (NRC)**. These intermediaries provide CDCs with the financial resources, technical assistance, and information that make them much more effective in the field of housing. Some analysts have pointed to a growing tension between CDCs and these intermediaries because of the influence that the control of resources generates (Rubin, 2000). Yet CDCs have benefited from the rise of intermediaries.

The oldest of the institutions providing technical assistance to and support for CDCs is the NRC, which was established in 1978 by Congress in the Neighborhood Reinvestment Corporation Act. NRC provides direct financial assistance, technical assistance in developing local lender pools or acquiring low-cost financing, and assistance in initiating revolving loan funds.

In 1979, the Ford Foundation established the LISC, which has worked with more than 1,000 CDCs to build 53,000 affordable homes and nine million square feet of commercial and industrial space. The LISC provides financial and technical assistance. In 1991, LISC established a demonstration program in three localities (Palm Beach County, Florida; Little Rock, Arkansas; and New Orleans, Louisiana) to test the effectiveness of a consensus-organizing approach to community development (Gittell & Vidal, 1998). This approach was first used in the 1980s in Monongahela Valley, Pennsylvania. Consensus organizing establishes social capital by building relationships inside the community and establishing new relationships with the larger community.

Another intermediary serving CDCs in the United States is the Enterprise Foundation, which was established in 1981 to develop affordable housing in low-income neighborhoods. The Enterprise Foundation has helped develop more than 36,000 homes. It also established a financial subsidiary, which has raised more than $655 million to support low-income housing.

Taken together, these intermediaries have become an important piece of the institutional support for community development in this country. They have been especially effective in providing the financial and technical assistance that CDCs need. At the same time, there is a built-in tension between these support organizations and CDCs. Many CDCs feel these intermediary institutions push them to be more concerned with building houses than community capacity. These intermediaries, however, allow CDCs to learn from one another and provide some of the basic training and skills needed to be effective.

Debates Over CDCs

The shift in the CDCs' mission from activist/organizers to professional/ technical assistance providers has been the source of recent criticism. Stoecker

(1997) raised several questions about the ability of CDCs to adequately deal with the limits that capitalism imposes on these nonprofit organizations. He stated that CDCs have evolved into institutions that support rather than challenge the free market. CDCs are so dependent on external sources of financing that they are pressured to ensure that their projects are profitable rather than addressing the social needs of residents (Marquez, 1993). Probably one of the most frequent criticisms of CDCs is that the institutionalization of these organizations reduces their willingness to fight for basic structural change in the way the federal government deals with poor communities (Piven & Cloward, 1977).

CDCs, however, continue to have their defenders. Goetz and Sidney (1995) argue that CDCs continue to play a significant role in organizing communities. In their study of CDCs in Minneapolis and St. Paul, Goetz and Sidney found that many of the CDCs were politically active, in terms of both gaining support for their projects and addressing broad issues affecting their neighborhoods. Many CDCs channel their political activities through broader coalitions or trade associations involved in nonprofit housing development. Other supporters of CDCs disagree with the distinction between development and empowerment (Rubin, 1994). CDCs may help initiate activist groups in some cases, which essentially buffer them from the politics of the issue (Rubin, 1993).

Stoecker (1997) proposed a new model for CDCs. He argued that community organizing and development functions probably should not, and cannot, occur within the same institutions. CDCs may threaten their investors if the CDCs take a confrontational approach in their organizing efforts. Stoecker argued that separating these functions into different organizations could facilitate local development for several reasons. Community organizing may be more effective when it is loosened from the ties of financial interests. When these functions are no longer tied to one another, community organizing may reflect more accurately the needs of the community than the needs of financial interests. Separating the functions also may allow the development function to operate more efficiently because it would allow organizations to increase their capital capacity by becoming larger and serving several locations. The degree to which this separation has already occurred through other CBOs, such as neighborhood associations that both support and oppose the local CDC depending on the issue, is not well understood.

Another line of criticism focuses on the tendency for CDCs to specialize in housing projects. Vidal (1997) contended that housing is less of a priority for poor neighborhoods today than in the past. Instead, there are pressures to increase the role of CDCs in other areas, such as workforce development and social service delivery. Lemann (1994), however, asserted that CDCs have proven to be relatively successful in the housing arena, but that they are very limited in their ability to successfully promote business or commercial development, training, or even social service delivery. Lemann argued that communities have a very limited ability to affect economic development because of larger economic and political forces affecting the fate of localities.

Although CDCs concentrate on housing, they also provide many services that are not offered by for-profit developers. In particular, they often supplement their real estate activities with tenant or homeowner counseling, property management, and crime prevention (Berger & Kasper, 1993).

The most likely scenario is that CDCs will continue to be involved in housing but will be forced to move into new areas as well. CBOs are well positioned to contribute to local development through such areas as workforce development, social service delivery, and so on. In particular, much more emphasis in the field today is on community or capacity building. CDCs find themselves in a unique position that enables them to build social relationships among various institutions and organizations in the community, which can serve as assets for future development (Gittell & Vidal, 1998).

Local Development Corporations

LDCs can be either profit or nonprofit organizations, although most choose nonprofit status. LDCs are involved in a wide variety of economic development activities, including leasing and improving real property; acquiring property; making equity investments in small businesses; selling notes to finance projects; borrowing and relending money to assist businesses; receiving grants from federal, state, and local agencies; developing industrial parks; establishing and operating small business resource centers (small business incubators); and undertaking historic preservation activities.

No official count of LDCs in the United States exists. Levy (1990) estimated that in the late 1980s, about 15,000 organizations were involved in promoting local economic development. This figure is probably much larger today. In the 1980s and 1990s, economic restructuring, especially in the Northeast and Midwest, provided an incentive for many localities to establish LDCs as a means of institutionalizing their economic development efforts.

LDCs offer several advantages over local governments in conducting economic development activities. First, LDCs can provide a one-stop shop for businesses. Many local governments spread these activities across several agencies and departments, making it difficult for businesses and developers to obtain the information and assistance they need. Second, LDCs provide stronger and more long-lasting relationships between local officials and the business sector. This arrangement, it is argued, makes it more likely that the economic development policies will reflect the community's interests than if either the government or a private development group was responsible for these activities.

Critics, however, see public-private partnerships, such as LDCs, as a way to remove economic development decisions from the public realm, which primarily benefits realtors, land owners, and developers (Logan & Molotch, 1987). Many communities create LDCs to do things to promote development that some local governments may be prohibited from doing, such as lease property to private businesses. LDCs are simply a legal device to accomplish many of these goals for communities.

Most LDCs are relatively small, with a median budget of about $150,000 (Green, Haines, Dunn, & Sullivan, 2002). The average LDC receives more than 60% of its funding from public sources and more than one-third from private sources, with the rest coming from grants and loans. The average LDC has one full-time equivalent paid professional and a half-time paid support staff member.

The boards of directors of LDCs are much less representative of the community than are boards for CDCs. The average board for an LDC is approximately one-third government officials and two-thirds individuals from the private sector, primarily the major businesses in the community. Most board members are White and male. These organizations clearly have a pro-business orientation and typically are not involved with housing, social services, or many of the other activities in which CDCs engage. There is growing pressure for LDCs to be more directly involved in job training and indirectly involved in affordable housing and child care. Especially in periods of tight labor markets, LDCs face more pressure to help existing businesses with the workforce needs than to attract more businesses to the community.

Recently, there has been a push to promote regional, rather than local, economic development. The key argument is that most economies today are more regional in nature. By promoting regional development organizations, it may be possible to avoid some of the hyper-competition between localities for business locations. Many of these regional entities attempt to establish networks of local development organizations and identify areas of collaboration. They also tend to focus on economic development activities that generate less competition, such as business startups and retention.

There are numerous national organizations that support the activities of local development organizations. The International Economic Development Council (IEDC) provides training, technical assistance, and other services to local development professionals. IEDC also provides an accreditation program for economic development professionals. The National Association of Development Organizations (NADO) conducts research, training, and technical assistance for regional development organizations. The Economic Development Administration (EDA) has numerous programs in support of local economic development organizations.

Neighborhood Associations

Logan and Rabrenovic (1990) defined a neighborhood association as "a civic organization oriented toward maintaining or improving the quality of life in a geographically delimited residential area" (p. 68). As with CDCs and LDCs, neighborhood associations saw a period of rapid growth in the 1970s and 1980s. In their study of neighborhood organizations in Albany, New York, Logan and Rabrenovic reported that more than 70% of neighborhood organizations had been established since 1975. Most neighborhood associations were formed as a result of a specific event or issue, with the most common being commercial or industrial development. Disputes over development typically involve rezoning of land from residential to nonresidential uses and often motivate residents to form neighborhood organizations. Some cities have actively promoted neighborhood associations as a way of obtaining public participation on local issues.

Although neighborhood organizations are established because of a specific issue, most take on additional issues. Logan and Rabrenovic (1990) found that several issues dominated the interests of neighborhood organizations in the late 1980s. These issues could be grouped into four broad categories: safety (e.g., police, fire), collective consumption (e.g., parks, playgrounds, streets, garbage collections), lifestyle (e.g., housing, cleanliness of the area, architectural standards), and development (e.g., residential land use changes, impacts of industrial/commercial development).

Who supports and who opposes neighborhood associations? According to Logan and Rabrenovic (1990), local governments were considered a cooperating organization about 50% of the time and a confrontational organization about 43% of the time. Businesses and land developers are much more likely to be seen as opponents rather than cooperators with neighborhood associations.

Why do residents become involved in neighborhood associations? Research shows that length of residence and interests in protecting the value of homes are strong predictors of membership in neighborhood associations. Having children younger than 5 years of age also strongly affects membership in these organizations; presumably, interest in safety and education are the motivating factors in this case.

Oropesa (1989) examined the factors related to the success of neighborhood associations. She asked neighborhood association leaders to indicate how successful their organization had been in addressing the key problems in their neighborhood. Her study considered several possible influences, including the population characteristics of the community (e.g., poverty level, percent of families with children, stability), the resources available to the neighborhood association (e.g., number of members, budget, staff, professionalization of leaders), and the political structure of the association (i.e., how decisions are made). Oropesa found that several internal and external factors influence the effectiveness of associations. Poor neighborhoods were less effective than other types of neighborhoods, primarily because they were less likely to have professional leaders. Neighborhood associations that faced opposition from the city bureaucracy were less successful than those that did not face opposition. Finally, Oropesa looked at the level of democratic decision making in the neighborhood associations and found that organizations that promoted public participation were more successful than those that did not.

Overall, neighborhood organizations tend to be less formal and more specialized than the other two types of CBOs examined in this chapter. They also tend to emphasize community organizing more than development. Most cities have programs that encourage the development of neighborhood organizations because they tend to help establish stronger ties between the local government and residents.

There usually is a tension, however, between neighborhood organizations and local governments. Local governments encourage neighborhood organizations to be active but are usually unwilling to grant much authority or resources to them. One of the central problems is that neighborhood associations are often considered an obstacle to development. Neighborhood organizations can under certain circumstances yield considerable political power in local elections. So, elected officials walk a fine line of trying to obtain their support, while not making them too powerful.

Cities vary widely in their support for neighborhood associations. In some cities, there is financial support and training available to neighborhood associations. Many cities grant neighborhood associations with a certain degree of veto power with regard to development decisions. If a development project is proposed, the neighborhood has a great deal of influence on approval, if it is necessary. This situation, however, always raises the possibility of "not-in-my-backyard" sentiment. Thus, city officials need to balance neighborhood positions with fiscal and economic realities of cities.

CASE STUDY 5.2 SUPPORT FOR NEIGHBORHOOD ASSOCIATIONS IN PORTLAND, MAINE

The City of Portland, Maine, provides a wide variety of services for its neighborhood associations. The city supports a website for neighborhood associations that includes a listserv for e-mail, event calendars, and basic information on each association. The website also provides news and announcements for each of the neighborhood associations. The city manager meets monthly with neighborhood advisory representatives to discuss local issues and concerns. For more information, see: http://www.livinginport land.org/.

Community Youth Organizations

Much of the focus in the field of urban development has been on the problems of youth. The problems and issues of urban youth are well documented. Youth face extremely high unemployment rates and grim job prospects. About half of the minority young men in large cities do not complete high school. Crime and delinquency continue to be major problems, although the rates in most cities declined over the past decade or so, largely because of the aging of the population.

Many factors contribute to the problems of youth. Some analysts have argued that the lack of social institutions in inner cities and the demands on urban families limit the opportunities for youth in these settings (Eccles & Gootman, 2002). Schools are asked frequently to respond to these issues, but they lack the resources needed to adequately address these problems. Youth development has taken a new turn in recent years by focusing on the role of CBOs (McLaughlin, 2000). Most interactions of youth are centered on their neighborhood. Without a strong infrastructure to support youth, social problems will continue to rise among youth. Increasingly, youth programs are seen as an integral feature of successful CDCs in inner cities.

In a comprehensive study of 120 community programs for youth development in 34 cities, McLaughlin (2000) found that youth participating in these programs improved their academic success, life skills, and self-efficacy. Successful programs tend to provide personal attention to youth, feature youth leadership, and build on the diverse set of talents, skills, and interests of youth.

McLaughlin (2000) made several recommendations for improving organizations for youth development. He pointed out that the vast majority of youth programs address the needs of boys, with few programs focusing on girls. Youth programs also frequently have a difficult time accessing resources. Local governments need to recognize that youth programs play an important role in many communities and in some cases are as important as schools.

Wheeler and Thomas (2010) identify several lessons that have been learned from youth community development programs. They suggested that to fully engage in community development efforts, youth must appreciate their own identity and culture. Similarly, youth are too often viewed as problems rather than resources or assets that can contribute to the community. Successful communities have used strategies to engage youth in a meaningful way in the issues that matter to them the most. This means that adults may have to yield some of their control over the process and create real opportunities for youth participation.

One area that has received increasing attention in recent years is the positive role of community service for youth. Students who volunteer for service in community organizations are much more likely to graduate from college (about 20% more likely). Organizations involving youth are much more likely to facilitate volunteerism among youth than other types of organizations.

An important source of funding for out-of-school and community-school programs for youth is the Community Development Block Grant (CDBG) program (Flynn & Perry, 2001). The City of Boston uses CDBG funds to support sports leagues and academic remediation programs for youth. Iowa City, Iowa, used CDBG funds to purchase a vacant lot on which students from the school district built a house as part of the vocational program in the school district. The house was eventually sold and the profits from the sale were returned to the vocational program. The CDGB funds must be used primarily to support low- and moderate-income families and must have a written "citizen participation plan" for the community. These funds can be used for a wide variety of activities, including facilities, services, and programs.

CASE STUDY 5.3 GREATER HOMEWOOD COMMUNITY CORPORATION

Established in 1969, the Greater Homewood Community Corporation (GHCC) has been engaged in a wide variety of youth programs in Baltimore. The majority of youth in this area live in concentrated poverty neighborhoods. These programs include job placement, college preparatory services, leadership training and civic engagement, arts camps, and tennis camps. In addition, the Experience Corps trains 400 older adults to serve in 20 elementary schools and over 7,000 students in Baltimore. The organization combines these activities with their efforts to promote community economic development, adult literacy, and civic engagement throughout the city.

SOURCE: Greater Homewood Community Corporation (http://www.greaterhomewood.org/programs/Neighborhood_Programs).

Faith-Based Organizations

Interest in the role of faith-based organizations (FBOs) in community development has grown rapidly since 2000. In 2001, President George Bush created the White House Office of Faith-Based and Community Initiatives and Centers for Faith-Based and Community Initiatives in 10 federal agencies. The goal of this initiative was to enhance the capacity of faith-based and other CBOs to better meet the social needs of America's communities.

Vidal (2001) identified three types of FBOs involved in community development: (1) congregations, (2) national networks of religious organizations (e.g., Lutheran Social Services and Catholic Charities), and (3) freestanding religious organizations that are neither congregations nor national networks. In a review of the field of faith-based activities, Vidal (2001) found that less than 15% of CDCs are faith based. Also, FBOs are not actively involved in community development, and their activities are limited in scope. Either they donate small amount of cash to service delivery groups or they organize small groups of volunteers to provide a service for a limited amount of time. Vidal concluded that most FBO staff lack the skills and experiences necessary to make significant contributions to community development.

Vidal (2001) recommended that FBOs collaborate with existing CDCs and other nonprofit organizations to deliver services and promote development more effectively. However, FBOs have significant potential, given the resources and population size they represent.

CASE STUDY 5.4 RESCUE ATLANTA:
A FAITH-BASED COMMUNITY DEVELOPMENT ORGANIZATION

Rescue Atlanta is located in the inner city of Atlanta. Like most churches, it holds services on Sunday morning for its membership. But the church does so much more. The organization provides a wide variety of services, including food, shelter, transportation assistance, and medical care, to the homeless and unemployed residents in the area. During the winter season, Rescue Atlanta can house as many as 80 homeless people. The organization also provides outreach to many children in these neighborhoods.

SOURCE: http://www.rescueatlanta.com/Home.html

Community Foundations

A more specialized form of CBO is a **community foundation**. Most community foundations provide philanthropic services to community residents. Their primary function is to pool donations into a larger fund to make grants for charitable purposes. Most community foundations are nonprofit organizations that serve residents in a specific region. Community foundations support a wide variety of local initiatives, such as social service programs and economic development projects.

Community foundations can be distinguished from other philanthropic organizations in three ways (Carman, 2001). First, most large foundations are created through a single donor, such as a family or corporation. Community foundations have multiple donors. Second, community foundations service specific geographic areas. Third, they are public charities and must continuously receive financial support from multiple donors in order to maintain their tax status.

The first community foundation was established in 1914 in Cleveland. Community foundations manage more than $30 billion in charitable funds and serve more than 700 communities across the United States. Most are run by a voluntary board of local citizens but have professional staff that oversee the day-to-day activities of the foundation. There has been a rapid increase in the number of community foundations across the United States. More than half of the community foundations are less than 10 years old.

Successful community foundations must balance the interests of donors with those of the local community. While many of the donors may be community residents, it is not necessarily the case that donor preferences will match community needs. Many community foundations work with existing CBOs, such as community development corporations, to better meet the needs of local areas.

──────────── International Nongovernment Organizations

Nongovernmental organizations (NGOs) play a key role in development assistance from working with multilateral agencies such as the World Bank and bilateral agencies such as USAID. Riva Krut (1997) provided the following definition of an NGO:

> [An NGO is] a category of organizational entities [that was] created at the founding of the United Nations. The category was invented in order to describe a specific relationship between civil organizations and the intergovernmental process, and since then the term has been loosely applied to any organization that is not public. (p. 11)

Edwards and Hulme (1996) made a distinction between NGOs that "are intermediary organizations engaged in funding or offering other forms of support to communities and other organizations" and grassroots organizations (GROs) that "are membership organizations of various kinds" (p. 15). Fisher (1998) offered a similar definition. She defined two types of NGOs in the Third World: GROs and grassroots supporting organizations (GRSOs). GROs are located in communities and have a local membership; GRSOs are located at the national or regional level, are staffed by professionals, and channel international funds to GROs (Fisher, 1998, p. 4). Fisher recognized that there are many different definitions of NGOs. By focusing only on NGOs in the Third World, she defined NGOs as "organizations involved in development, broadly defined." She preferred, however, to recognize GROs as the NGO of preference because they have "locally based memberships" and "work to develop their own communities" (p. 6). GROs come closest to the CBOs we find in the United States.

We should make a distinction between NGOs of the Northern and Southern Hemispheres. Many northern NGOs emerged after World War II to assist in providing aid to European communities devastated by the war. In contrast, some southern NGOs survived colonialism; others were formed only recently and for many different reasons (Nelson, 1995, p. 38). Northern NGOs are located in developed or First World countries, whereas southern NGOs are located in developing or Third World countries. One criticism of northern NGOs is that they rely on the easy availability of funding for humanitarian assistance, rather than keep a focus on the longer term capacity building and institutional development that are necessary to assist people out of poverty (Edwards & Hulme, 1996, p. 6).

NGOs, like most CBOs in the United States, are embedded in a large network of organizations and institutions involved in aid and development. In the next section, we briefly describe some of these networks.

Government policy toward NGOs is wide ranging and depends largely on political factors within a country. Such factors include degree of democratization, stability of the government, strength of political culture and tradition, and ability to implement policy (Fisher, 1998, p. 39). Fisher identified five general government responses or approaches to NGOs that represent a spectrum from most to least repressive. At the most repressive, governments fear NGOs and their activities. These governments can make it difficult for NGOs to work because they may arbitrarily close down NGOs, arrest and imprison their leaders, keep NGOs under surveillance, subject them to harassment, or simply make laws so onerous that NGOs find it difficult to remain open. Another approach has been to ignore NGOs. This approach, according to Fisher, has been the most common one due to many governments' inability to implement policies that affect NGOs and their work. A favored approach by many governments is co-optation. Governments favor some NGOs and not others, give grants to NGOs in an attempt to control them, or create their own NGOs. A fourth approach is to take advantage of NGOs for financial reasons (i.e., to increase the amount of aid and foreign exchange into a country); enhance government legitimacy, military, and security purposes (i.e., to shield the government from ethnic rivalries or guerilla movements); and help in implementing major reforms. The final approach involves cooperation and learning that can be either ad hoc or systemwide, but this is far less common than the other approaches. Governments may use this approach because of budgetary pressures, using NGOs to implement policy by lowering costs or to reach more people, or both (Fisher, 1998, pp. 40–46; Riker, 1995, pp. 28–34).

NGOs function with governments to promote development in several ways. Riker (1995) recognized five approaches: autonomous development that is independent of the central government; partnership in development to minimize duplication of efforts; competition in development; advocacy for government accountability such that NGOs serve as watchdogs and policy advocates; and bypassing the state, which could put NGOs and their programs at risk from a hostile government (pp. 2–22). No single model will work for all NGOs in all regions. There are some general patterns of NGO-government relations in different regions of the world. In Latin America, NGOs have been relatively autonomous. States have seen NGOs as a way to avoid social unrest and respond to the high levels of poverty. In Africa, governments have tried to co-opt large NGOs but tend to leave the smaller NGOs alone. Asian countries have had a more schizophrenic relationship with NGOs. The relationships tend to vary country by country and even agency by agency.

A big question that NGOs face is, who are they accountable to? If they work for and with the poor in developing countries, or at least specific constituencies in specific developing countries, are they accountable to them or are they accountable to the agency that has provided funding for their operations and projects? NGOs are accountable to a variety of institutions—downward to their partners, beneficiaries, staff, and supporters and upward to their trustees, donors, and host governments (Edwards & Hulme, 1996, p. 8). Part of the problem NGOs have is establishing how their performance and thus their effectiveness and impact can be measured. It is difficult to measure societal or organizational changes that may have occurred as a result of an NGO's efforts because of the many other influences—economic, political, social, and technological—that occur on a national and international scale.

CASE STUDY 5.5 NYUMBANI—*WATOTO WA MUNGU* (HOME—CHILDREN OF GOD)

In 1992, Father Angelo D'Agostino, a Jesuit, opened Nyumbani Children's Home to respond to the increasing number of HIV-infected children in Kenya, who are often abandoned or orphaned. Nyumbani provides a home to about 100 children, from birth to their early 20s. They are given "the best nutritional, medical, in particular, anti-retroviral therapy, psychological, academic, spiritual care available and live at Nyumbani until they become self-reliant" (Nyumbani, 2006). To reach more children, Nyumbani started a community-based outreach program to provide services to children and their families infected with HIV/AIDS. This program, called *Lea Toto* ("to raise the child"), began providing services in 1998 and received funding from USAID starting in 1999. They provide the following services: basic medical and nursing care, counseling and psychological support, spiritual guidance, relief for social needs, HIV transmission prevention education, promotion of community empowerment/ownership, voluntary counseling and testing, clinical care for home-bound clients, anti-retroviral treatment (since 2005), training of caregivers, nutritional support, business development training, and income generation activities. They also provide microcredit services to caregivers (Nyumbani, 2006).

The most recent initiative by this organization is Nyumbani Village, whose concept is to create a self-sustaining community for orphans and elders who have been left behind by the "lost generation" of the AIDS pandemic. Approximately 1,000 acres were donated by the Kitui District County Council for the village. Nyumbani expects that about 1,600 people will live in this village once it is completed. The plan is for a grandmother or caretaker to care for 7 to 10 children in each of the 100 dwelling units in the village. Use of locally available resources is the primary operating principle for the operation and construction of Nyumbani Village. This sustainability concept reaches into all that Nyumbani does, from using local labor to creating construction materials on or near site to producing their own food and educating and training through schools and polytechnics.

SOURCE: Nyumbani (2006).

Summary and Conclusions

CBOs play an integral role in the community development process. Successful communities generally have successful organizations representing their interests. Unfortunately, most CBOs pay little attention to organizational processes because they tend to focus on the community's issues. Yet developing an organization that is fair and effective is undoubtedly an important determinant of the viability of a community development process.

CBOs do not fit neatly into traditional categories of organizations. They frequently provide services, but they also are activist organizations promoting social change. They are nonprofit organizations, but they increasingly own and manage property. They rely heavily on government support but at times directly challenge government policies. These contradictions often produce unique challenges for CBOs.

Probably the biggest challenge that CBOs face is the tension between public participation and leadership. The tension here is that if CBOs are successful at getting the community involved, they may lack the leadership to carry through with their objectives. Conversely, strong leadership may be a deterrent for many people to participate in the organization.

Finally, CBOs typically struggle with the meaning of community control. Does it simply mean that the board of directors (and staff) is representative of the community? Does it mean that the board of directors has the authority to set broad policies and make decisions for the organization? Does it mean that residents have an opportunity to make key decisions for the organization? As shown in this chapter, there appear to be several answers to these questions.

KEY CONCEPTS

Community Development Block Grant (CDBG)

Community development corporation (CDC)

Community foundation

Enterprise Foundation

Grey Areas Program

HOME program

Local development corporation (LDC)

Local Initiatives Support Corporation (LISC)

Neighborhood association

Neighborhood Reinvestment Corporation (NRC)

Nongovernmental organization (NGO)

Special Impact Program (SIP)

QUESTIONS

1. Describe the major changes that have occurred in the structure and mission of CDCs in the United States in the past 30 years.

2. What are the major criticisms of CDCs? Do you believe these criticisms are valid? Why or why not?

3. Describe the role that intermediaries play in supporting the activities of CDCs.

4. What are local development organizations and how do they differ from CDCs?

5. In what types of activities do neighborhood organizations get involved? What factors influence their success?

6. What are some different approaches that NGOs can take in working with governments to promote development?

EXERCISES

1. Identify a CDC in your city or region and evaluate the level of community control in the organization.

    a. Review the records of the organization to assess how well the community has been represented on the board. What have been the trends in community participation on the board? Have low- and moderate-income residents been well represented on the board?

    b. Interview the board members and the staff of the CDC to obtain their assessments of community control. Is there agreement or systematic differences between the board and the staff regarding the issue of community control? If there are differences, have there been specific issues where the lack of control was most apparent?

    c. Interview community residents to assess their views of how well the CDC is responding to community needs and issues.

2. Identify a neighborhood organization in your community and interview some members regarding the primary activities of the organization. How has the organization sought to involve residents in their organization? Why was the organization established?

3. Identify a LDC in your area and interview the staff regarding the economic development activities of the organization. What are the sources of funding for the organization? How does it spend its resources?

4. Choose a developing country to study and identify a specific issue within that country (e.g., HIV/AIDS, nutrition, agricultural development, women's rights). Use the Internet to identify the NGOs working on this issue. What is their relationship to the national government? How do the NGOs collaborate with one another? What types of specific programs have they developed? Can you assess the impact of their activities?

REFERENCES

Berger, R. A., & Kasper, G. (1993). An overview of the literature on community development corporations. *Nonprofit Management and Leadership, 4,* 241–255.

Carman, J. G. (2001). Community foundations: A growing resource for community development. *Nonprofit Management and Leadership, 12,* 7–24.

Eccles, J., & Gootman, J. A. (2002). *Community programs to promote youth development.* Washington, DC: National Academy Press.

Edwards, M., & Hulme, D. (1996). NGO performance and accountability. In M. Edwards & D. Hulme (Eds.), *Beyond the magic bullet: NGO performance and accountability in the post-cold war world* (pp. 1–20). West Hartford, CT: Kumarian Press.

Fisher, J. (1998). *Nongovernments: NGOs and the political development of the Third World*. West Hartford, CT: Kumarian Press.

Flynn, M., & Perry, M. (2001). *Using the Community Development Block Grant to support out-of-school time and community school initiatives*. Washington, DC: The Finance Project. http://www.financeproject.org/Publications/Brief8.pdf

Gittell, R., & Vidal, A. (1998). *Community organizing: Building social capital as a development strategy*. Thousand Oaks, CA: Sage.

Goetz, E., & Sidney, M. (1995). Community development corporations as neighborhood advocates: A study of the political activism of nonprofit developers. *Applied Behavioral Science Review, 3,* 1–20.

Green, G. P., Haines, A., Dunn, A., & Sullivan, D. M. (2002). The role of local development organizations in rural America. *Rural Sociology, 67,* 394–415.

Krut, R. (1997). *Globalization and civil society: NGO influence in international decision-making* (Discussion Paper No. 83). Geneva, Switzerland: United Nations Research Institute for Social Development.

Lemann, N. (1994, January 9). The myth of community development. *New York Times Magazine,* pp. 27–31.

Levy, J. M. (1990). *Economic development programs for cities, counties, and towns*. New York: Praeger.

Logan, J. R., & Molotch, H. L. (1987). *Urban fortunes: The political economy of place*. Berkeley: University of California Press.

Logan, J. R., & Rabrenovic, G. (1990). Neighborhood associations: Their issues, their allies, and their opponents. *Urban Affairs Quarterly, 26,* 68–94.

Marquez, B. (1993). Mexican-American community development corporations and the limits of directed capitalism. *Economic Development Quarterly, 7,* 287–295.

McLaughlin, M. W. (2000). *Community counts: How youth organizations matter for youth development*. Washington, DC: Public Education Network.

Medoff, P., & Sklar, H. (1994). *Streets of hope: The fall and rise of an urban neighborhood*. Boston: South End Press.

National Congress for Community Economic Development. (1995). *Tying it all together: The comprehensive achievements of community-based development organizations*. Washington, DC: Author.

Nelson, P. (1995). *The World Bank and non-governmental organizations: The limits of apolitical development*. New York: St. Martin's Press.

Nyumbani. (2006). *Watoto wa mungu*. Retrieved March 25, 2007, from www.nyumbani.org/index.htm

O'Connor, A. (1999). Swimming against the tide: A brief history of federal policy in poor communities. In R. F. Ferguson & W. T. Dickens (Eds.), *Urban problems and community development* (pp. 77–137). Washington, DC: Brookings Institution.

Oropesa, R. S. (1989). The social and political foundations of effective neighborhood improvement associations. *Social Science Quarterly, 70,* 723–743.

Piven, F., & Cloward, R. P. (1977). *Poor people's movements: Why they succeed, how they fail*. New York: Vintage.

Pratt Center for Community Development. (1997). *Community development corporation oral history project*. Retrieved March 6, 2007, from www.prattcenter.net/cdcoralhistory.php

Riker, J. V. (1995). Contending perspectives for interpreting government-NGO relations in South and Southeast Asia: Constraints, challenges and the search for common ground in rural development. In N. Heyzer, J. V. Riker, & A. B. Quizon (Eds.), *Government-NGO relations in Asia: Prospects and challenges for people-centred development* (pp. 15–56). New York: St. Martin's Press.

Rubin, H. J. (1993). Understanding the ethos of community-based development: Ethnographic description for public administrators. *Public Administration Review, 53,* 428–437.

Rubin, H. J. (1994). There aren't going to be any bakeries here if there is no money to afford jelly-rolls: The organic theory of community-based development. *Social Problems, 41,* 401–424.

Rubin, H. J. (2000). *Renewing hope within neighborhoods of despair: The community-based development model.* Albany: State University of New York Press.

Rubin, H. J., & Rubin, I. S. (1992). *Community organizing and development* (2nd ed.). Boston: Allyn & Bacon.

Stoecker, R. (1997). The CDC model of urban redevelopment: A critique and an alternative. *Journal of Urban Affairs, 19,* 1–22.

Vidal, A. (1992). *Rebuilding communities: A national study of urban community development corporations.* New York: New School for Social Research, Community Development Research Center, Graduate School of Management and Urban Policy.

Vidal, A. (1997). Can community development re-invent itself? The challenges of strengthening neighborhoods in the 21st century. *Journal of the American Planning Association, 63,* 429–438.

Vidal, A. (2001). *Faith-based organizations in community development.* Washington, DC: U.S. Department of Housing and Urban Development, Office of Policy Development and Research.

Wheeler, W., & Thomas, A. M. (2010). Engaging youth in community development. In J. W. Robinson & G. P. Green (Eds.), *Introduction to community development: Theory, practice and service-learning* (pp. 209–228). Thousand Oaks, CA: Sage.

ADDITIONAL READINGS AND RESOURCES

Readings

Adger, C. T. (2001). School–community-based organization partnerships for language minority students' school success. *Journal of Education for Students Placed at Risk, 6,* 7–25.

Blakely, E. J., & Aparicio, A. (1990). Balancing social and economic objectives: The case of California's community development corporations. *Journal of the Community Development Society, 21,* 115–128.

Cowan, S. M., Rohe, W., & Baku, E. (1999). Factors influencing the performance of community development corporations. *Journal of Urban Affairs, 21,* 325–339.

DeFilippis, J. (2003). *Unmaking Goliath: Community control in the face of global capital.* New York: Routledge.

Eccles, J., & Gootman, J. A. (Eds.). (2002). *Community programs to promote youth development.* Washington, DC: National Academy Press.

Gast, E. (2005). *Community foundation handbook.* Washington, DC: Council on Foundation.

Gittell, R., & Wilder, M. (1999). Community development corporations: Critical factors that influence success. *Journal of Urban Affairs, 21,* 341–361.

Goetz, E. (1993). *Shelter burden: Local politics and progressive housing policy.* Philadelphia: Temple University Press.

Goetz, E., & Sidney, M. (1994). Revenge of the property owners: Community development and the politics of property. *Journal of Urban Affairs, 16,* 319–334.

Goetz, E., & Sidney, M. (1997). Local policy subsystems and issue definition: An analysis of community development policy change. *Urban Affairs Review, 32,* 490–512.

Lenz, T. J. (1988). Neighborhood development: Issues and models. *Social Policy, 18,* 24–30.

Lowe, J. S. (2004). Community foundations: What do they offer community development? *Journal of Urban Affairs, 26,* 221–240.

O'Brien, D. J. (1975). *Neighborhood organization and interest-group politics.* Princeton, NJ: Princeton University Press.

Powell, W. W., & Steinberg, R. (2006). *The nonprofit sector: A research handbook.* New Haven, CT: Yale University Press.

Rohe, W. M. (1998). Do community development corporations live up to their billing? A review and critique of the research findings. In C. T. Koebel (Ed.), *Shelter and society: Theory, research and policy for nonprofit housing* (pp. 177–199). Albany: State University of New York Press.

Salamon, L. M. (1999). *America's nonprofit sector.* New York: Foundation Center.

Stoecker, R. (1994). *Defending community: The struggle for alternative redevelopment in Cedar-Riverside.* Philadelphia: Temple University Press.

Stoecker, R. (1995). Community, movement, organization: The problem of identity convergence in collective action. *Sociological Quarterly, 36,* 111–130.

Vidal, A. (1996). CDCs as agents of neighborhood change: The state of the art. In W. D. Keating, N. Krumholz, & P. Star (Eds.), *Revitalizing urban neighborhoods* (pp. 149–163). Lawrence: University of Kansas Press.

Villarruel, F. A., Perkins, D. F., Borden, L. M., & Keith, J. G. (2003). *Community youth development: Programs, policies, and practices.* Thousand Oaks, CA: Sage.

Walker, C., & Weinheimer, M. (1998). *Community development in the 1990s.* Washington, DC: Urban Institute.

Wright, E. (1999). *An annotated bibliography for faith-based community economic development.* Washington, DC: National Congress for Community Economic Development.

Websites

Accion International—www.accion.org. This NGO provides small loans and training to poor people who start their own businesses, so they can work their own way out of poverty. It has loaned $2.2 billion to more than 1.6 million poor business owners and has had 98% of its loans paid back.

ActionAid—www.actionaid.org. This organization aims to work with poor and marginalized people to eradicate poverty by overcoming the injustice and inequity that cause it. It has helped about one million people in Africa get better access to health services.

Bridgespan Group—http://www.bridgespan.org. This website provides strategies for building organizations and promoting social change.

CARE International—www.care.org. This private international relief and development agency focuses on improving the lives of people in more than 60 countries by working at the family and community levels on food, health care, shelter, education, and sustainable livelihoods.

Center for Faith Based and Neighborhood Partnerships—http://portal.hud.gov/portal/page/portal/ HUD/program_offices/faith_based. This website is a good portal for basic information on resources and technical assistance that is provided through the Department of Housing and Urban Development.

Faith Based and Community Initiatives—http://www.faithbasedcommunityinitiatives.org/index.htm. This website provides basic information and resources on faith based and community initiatives.

Independent Sector—http://www.independentsector.org. A good general website on improving the effectiveness of nonprofit organizations.

National Congress for Community Economic Development (NCCED)—www.ncced.org. NCCED is the trade association of and advocate for the community-based development industry. The organization represents more than 3,600 CDCs. NCCED serves the community development industry through public policy research and education, special projects, newsletters, publications, training, conferences, and specialized technical assistance.

Neighborhoods Online—http://www.neighborhoodsonline.net/. This website is an online resource center for people working to build strong communities through the United States. It provides information and ideas covering all aspects of neighborhood revitalization.

Pratt Center for Community Development—www.prattcenter.net. This website includes 15 profiles of CDCs written for the CED Oral History Project.

Rural Local Initiatives Support Corporation—www.ruralisc.org/index.html. This organization helps build the capacity of resident-led rural CDCs, increase their production and impact, demonstrate the value of investing in and through rural CDCs, and make the resource and policy environment more supportive of rural CDCs and their work. This organization provides training and technical and financial assistance to 70 CDCs and provides information to more than 1,300 rural CDCs.

Society for Nonprofit Organizations—http://www.snpo.org. Provides resources for building nonprofit organizations.

Videos

Building Hope (1994), produced by Charles Hobson, directed by David Van Taylor (57 minutes). An excellent overview of the history of community development, with special emphasis on the Bed-Stuy Restoration Corporation. Available from Pratt Institute, Center for Community and Environmental Development, 379 Dekalb Avenue, Brooklyn, NY 11205.

Holding Ground: The Rebirth of Dudley Street (1996), produced and directed by Mark Lipman and Leah Mahan (58 minutes). A nice summary of one of the most heralded community development efforts in the United States over the past two decades. Available from New Day Films, 22nd Hollywood Avenue, Ho-Ho-Kus, NJ 07423.

Vietnam's Tram Chim: Pearl of the Mekong (1999), produced by Worthwhile Films. Tram Chim is in the Plain of Reeds, a wetland area devastated during the Vietnam War. Here we see a major conservation project that has succeeded because of the commitment of many people. Available from Worthwhile Films, 605 McMillan Road, Poynette, WI 53955; phone: (608) 635–7170; Internet: www.DANEnet.Wicip.org.

Water for Tonoumassé (1989), produced and directed by Gary Beitel. This film shows the efforts of a group of villagers to get clean water by drilling a well nearby. It chronicles the success of this project, in which women played a key role. Available from Filmakers Library Inc., 124 East 40th Street, New York, NY 10016; e-mail: info@filmakers.com; Internet: www.filmakers.com.

6

Human Capital

Human capital is an essential community asset. In many communities, however, human capital is underutilized. Human capital includes general education background, labor market experience, artistic development and appreciation, health, and other skills and experiences. In this chapter, we focus on the labor market skills of individuals, especially the role of workforce development networks in building these skills. Human capital, however, has benefits beyond simply getting a high-paying job. It is related to other aspects of quality of life as well.

Traditionally, human capital development emphasizes individual approaches. Individuals bear the cost and burden of obtaining education and training. Although many government programs provide job training, they tend to focus on specific populations (e.g., youth, unemployed) and often are not well connected with local labor market conditions. CBOs offer a useful strategy for building these assets in a way that simultaneously improves the mobility of workers while meeting the demands of local employers. The asset-based approach builds on the experiences and interests of individuals and communities and matches them with the needs and opportunities in the region.

Why do communities engage in workforce development? Many communities have limited information on the changing needs of the workforce. Having an adequate, skilled, and trained workforce is a prerequisite for economic development today. Yet communities face several obstacles in developing their workforce. If the community provides training for jobs that are not available locally, workers may move to where the jobs are, leaving the community with the costs and none of the benefits of the training. If the community attracts new employers requiring skills that are not available locally, the employer may have to hire workers outside the community, minimizing the benefits of the new firm. Training institutions have a difficult time gauging the future needs of employers. Much of the training that employers demand is specific and too costly for training institutions to provide. Similarly, the availability and cost of child care and housing in the community may not be adequate to support the workforce. Community organizations can play an important role in making the local labor market more transparent and facilitating the match between the supply of and demand for labor.

BOX 6.1 WORKFORCE DEVELOPMENT FACTS

- Of the 25 occupations expected to be the fastest growing in the next decade, 8 require substantial experience and education and 9 are in health care.
- The average earnings of Whites significantly exceed those of Blacks and Hispanics, but Blacks are increasing their earnings more rapidly than Whites are, though Hispanics are lagging even further.

SOURCE: Judy and D'Amico (1997).

A more fundamental workforce issue facing communities is a collective action problem: There is a general need for skilled workers, but individual firms may be unwilling to train workers because they fear they will lose their investment. Workers are mobile, and they may take their skills to other employers that will provide them with better wages and benefits. Employers often respond to this problem by providing firm-specific training or no training at all. Historically, employers may have been willing to invest in workers because they were likely to benefit from the increases in productivity. This system worked fairly well when individuals worked for one or two employers in their career. Today, workers are much more mobile, and employers tend to hire their skilled workers rather than provide existing workers with training. This system has a difficult time meeting the growing needs for a skilled workforce and overcoming the obstacles that low-income residents face in preparing for the new economy.

CBOs can address many of the obstacles workers, employers, and training institutions face in workforce development efforts. By establishing workforce networks, they can improve the flow of information between employers, workers, and institutions. They can reduce some of the costs, and risks, of training workers by spreading the costs out across several organizations. Finally, CBOs can coordinate some of the other needs of the workforce, including child care, housing, and transportation.

In this chapter, we review the key concepts and issues surrounding workforce development, the major actors and institutions involved, and the primary strategies and tactics for building a local workforce. In addition, we briefly discuss the potential for creating green-collar jobs. Workforce development efforts have changed dramatically in recent years due to welfare reform, the aging of the workforce, and the restructuring of major industries. CBOs are uniquely situated to improve the functioning of local labor markets by providing networks between employers, workers, and trainers.

Workforce Development Issues

Communities face several interrelated challenges regarding **workforce development** issues. Most of these issues are concerned with the supply of and demand for labor, the matching process between job searchers and job opportunities, and the institutions (e.g., vocational training, child care) involved in supporting employers and workers. The following issues are a few that might be addressed:

1. What are the sources of persistent unemployment and underemployment in the community? Are under- and unemployment due to increased skill requirements of employers or the lack of training among workers, or both?

2. Do workers have sufficient information about the location and skill requirements of jobs? Do employers use the appropriate methods for searching for qualified workers in the community?

3. Is job training offered by employers? If yes, what type? If not, why not and what obstacles do employees face in obtaining additional training? What types of programs are available from training institutions in the region and how well do they match the needs of employers and workers in the area?

4. What is the job turnover rate among employers? What are the causes and consequences of this turnover for employers, workers, and the community? What types of programs might reduce the turnover?

5. How many jobs will be created in the area in the next few years and what are the skills, education, and experience requirements for these jobs? How well does the available demand for labor match the available supply of labor in the region?

6. What are the current levels of wages and benefits available to workers in the region? Do the jobs being created by local employers provide a living wage?

7. How many workers are commuting out of the community and what are the skills and experience of these workers? Would these out-commuters be willing to work locally if jobs were available that provided similar wages and benefits?

8. To what extent do the availability and cost of day care in the community present obstacles to residents entering the labor force? Are employers facing any problems in adding additional shifts because of the costs or availability of day care?

9. Do retirees who have significant job experience and skills have opportunities to find meaningful work in the area? Are there jobs for the disabled?

Key Concepts and Debates

Workforce development is a frequently misunderstood term; many people think of it as only job training. Harrison and Weiss (1998) defined workforce development, however, as the "constellation of activities from orientation to the work world, recruiting, placement, and mentoring to follow-up counseling and crisis intervention" (p. 5). Training is only one component of workforce development.

A growing number of CBOs are responsible for workforce development. Probably one of the most publicized models of workforce development is the Center for Employment Training, which is based in San Jose, California, and now operates throughout the western and southwestern United States (Melendez, 1996). This model has three basic functions: enhancing job-specific skills, assisting with job search strategies, and facilitating access to jobs by establishing relationships with employers and providing information on job opportunities. Other models may be organized differently, but they provide essentially the same services (see Case Studies 6.1 and 6.2).

CASE STUDY 6.1 MILWAUKEE JOBS INITIATIVE, INC.

Milwaukee suffers from some of the same problems that affect most major cities—a growing demand for high-skilled workers and a declining demand for unskilled positions. The Milwaukee Jobs Initiative (MJI) was established in 1995 to provide a match between inner-city workers with the broader regional economy, and thus jobs that provide good wages and benefits. The initiative has brought together major businesses, unions, and community organizations to design and implement the project. MJI works on both the demand and supply side of the regional labor market. The initiative is working primarily with three industry sectors: manufacturing, printing, and construction. In these sectors, MJI establishes intermediary organizations that help to improve employment and training in the sector. Because many of the firms in the sector will have similar training and employment needs, MJI can provide an incentive for employers to participate. The organizations identify job openings and workforce development needs and help with systems to train and retain workers for these sectors. MJI also works with community organizations to recruit low-income individuals for good jobs in the region and provides support for them. Since 1997, MJI has successfully placed 368 individuals in jobs that pay an average of $11.12 per hour with access to health benefits. MJI plans on focusing on establishing clear pathways to high-wage employment for central city residents and coordinating the demand for skilled workers throughout the region.

SOURCE: Center on Wisconsin Strategy (1999).

CASE STUDY 6.2 RURAL OPPORTUNITIES INCORPORATED

Rural Opportunities Incorporated (ROI) was established in 1969 to serve as an umbrella organization to provide services to migrant and seasonal farmworkers throughout New York. Today, it has expanded to other states in the region and provides a variety of services, including education, training, child development, health and safety, housing, and real estate development. Its most important program is provided through the National Farmworker Jobs Program (NFJP). Under the NFJP, ROI provides (1) urgent assistance, such as food, shelter, and medical care; (2) skills assessment, placement assistance, and counseling; (3) adult education, such as English as a second language; and (4) traditional occupational training.

ROI fits the hub-spoke model for providing services. It works closely with local businesses, training institutions, public agencies, and other CBOs. Most of ROI's clients are Hispanic. It serves several hundred farmworkers each year. People served by ROI tend to have poor command of English, little education, and practically no job experience outside of agriculture. The holistic approach of ROI seems to work best to provide the variety of workforce services that are needed by this population.

SOURCE: Green (2007).

Human capital theorists argue that variations in earnings are consequences of differences in workers' abilities and skills (Beaulieu & Mulkey, 1995). Individuals can enhance their future earnings by investing in their labor skills (through education and job training). A basic assumption behind **human capital theory** is that individuals will be motivated to increase earnings, which means they will be willing to invest in education and training necessary to improve their position in the labor market. Human capital theory assumes that workers are mobile and will move to other locations with more job opportunities. This individualistic view of education and training tends to ignore the importance of community attachment and ties to family and friends. The theory also assumes that employers do not have any responsibility toward their workers for increasing their skills or education. Some employers, however, may see it as being in their interest to provide job training as a way to increase the productivity of their workforce.

Low-income and minority workers often face obstacles in finding jobs that adequately reward their skills and abilities. In many communities, the available jobs do not match the skills and experience of the local workforce. **Spatial mismatch theorists** suggest that inner-city minorities experience high unemployment rates because the jobs available within their labor market demand advanced skills and education, attributes most inner-city residents lack. Entry-level jobs appropriate for inner-city residents are much more likely to be located in the suburbs. This spatial mismatch leads to lower wages or longer commutes for the poor. The poor suffer not only because of physical isolation from the jobs (lacking transportation to work) but also because of social isolation (lacking contacts to obtain information about these jobs). Kain (1968) argued that the root cause behind the spatial mismatch is residential segregation due to racial discrimination in the housing market. The negative effects of housing segregation are magnified by the decentralization of jobs in most cities.

The occupational and industrial structures in the local area shape the demand for labor as well. It is important to distinguish between occupations and industries to understand these forces. An industrial classification identifies what a worker helps to produce. An occupation is the kind of work the employee does. An occupation is defined as a group of job-related activities that comprise a single economic role directed toward making a living (Hodson & Sullivan, 1990). The U.S. Census Bureau has defined more than 500 occupational categories for analyzing these roles. An industry is the branch of economic activity devoted to the production of a good or a service. The Census Bureau uses more than 200 industrial categories.

A local labor market is defined as the social relations between sellers (workers) and buyers (employers) of labor. Within a community, several labor markets may be operating between buyers and sellers, some involving local markets and others constituting regional or national markets. For example, professionals, such as computer programmers or attorneys, usually compete in a national labor market, while machinists or receptionists may be competing in a local or regional labor market. A local labor market area is difficult to define, especially in rural areas where workers may commute long distances and employers may recruit from surrounding communities. Most workforce development activities focus on the local labor market because the activities will most likely affect unskilled and semiskilled workers.

The labor force participation rate is calculated as the percentage of the population (most government agencies consider only people 16 years or older) in the labor force. Persons not in the labor force consist mainly of students, homemakers, retired workers, inmates of institutions, and others unable or unwilling to seek employment in the reference week (Myers, 1992). The unemployment rate is the percentage of the labor force that is searching for work but is currently unemployed.

Labor markets are portrayed frequently as consisting of individual workers searching for work and employers searching for workers, with no mechanism linking the two together. In many cases, however, workers and employers make use of employment networks or intermediaries. Employment networks are "lines of communication that link many potential occupants of jobs in multiple firms with employers who make decisions to fill those jobs" (Tilly & Tilly, 1998, p. 25).

Theories about how labor markets operate tend to fall into one of three broad categories (supply oriented, demand oriented, or institutionally oriented theories), based on which factors are stressed in explaining the functioning of labor markets. Supply-side theorists emphasize the importance of the number of workers with specific skills at various wage levels as the primary determinants of the functioning of labor markets. These theorists argue that productivity is a function of the skills, knowledge, and experience acquired by workers. Unemployment, underemployment, and poverty are generally explained as results of a lack of investment by individuals in the types of skills that are demanded in the labor market.

A standard set of issues needs to be examined when analyzing the supply of labor in a community, including sociodemographic characteristics of the population (e.g., race, age, gender, income, educational background), work experience, training experience and projected needs, job search strategies, commuting behavior, and wages and benefits received. In addition to this basic information, it is useful to assess the availability of other sources of labor. Are there retired workers interested in reentering the labor market? Are there part-time workers interested in full-time work? Are there workers who are commuting out of the area who might be interested in working locally? Are there workers interested in upgrading their skills to obtain local jobs? Unfortunately, most communities rarely collect this basic level of information about their workforce.

Demand-side theorists emphasize how changes in the structure of occupations, industries, skills, and the location of work shape local opportunities. According to this theory, development depends largely on the creation of new jobs demanding higher skill levels. Demand-side theorists assume that workers have perfect information about the available job opportunities and will seek to obtain the necessary training and education for these jobs.

Most of the information needed to assess the demand for labor can be obtained from employers. Several methods (e.g., phone or mail surveys) could be used to collect this information, but face-to-face interviews are preferable if the resources are available. Among the basic questions that need to be asked are the anticipated number of workers to be hired in the next few years; the training, education, and experience required for these positions; the wages and benefits offered to entry-level workers in these positions; and the methods used to search for workers to fill these positions. In addition, it is useful to collect some information about the basic characteristics of the firms, such as number of employees, the industry, the organizational structure, and so forth.

Although it is useful to collect information on the current demand for workers, it also is helpful to obtain data on anticipated demand to plan for future training needs. Also, it may be useful to collect data on training activities of employers to assess the type of training they are providing and how they provide it to workers. This information should provide an understanding of opportunities for mobility within the area and how training institutions can best supplement training efforts that take place in the workplace.

Institutional theorists of the labor market recognize the importance of supply and demand factors but emphasize the organization of work as a mediating factor. These theories point to the importance of firm size, industrial sector, and other organizational factors in influencing returns on education, skills, and work experience. For example, workers who are employed in large firms and in industries that are highly unionized may obtain higher returns on their human capital than workers in small firms or industries with low levels of unionization.

In addition, **institutional theories** may focus on the organizational support for workers and employers in the region. One strategy for obtaining this information is to collect data from training institutions to evaluate the number of people trained in various occupations, and the level of training provided to these individuals, so that we can assess how well the supply matches the current demand among employers. At a minimum, it is necessary for community leaders to have information on the number of graduates from various training programs and the types of programs that are available.

It also may be useful to examine how other institutions in the community are affecting the workforce. How well do the availability and cost of housing match the current and anticipated demand for workers in the area? For example, are employers adding a large number of low-wage positions even when few affordable houses are available for workers? How many spots are available for children in child care centers in the community and how well does the availability match the local need?

These theories represent different approaches to building local markets. Supply-side theorists suggest that the way to build the workforce is through development of worker skills and productivity. According to supply-side theorists, the availability of a skilled workforce will attract employers to the community, or workers will be more attractive to employers elsewhere and they will move to where the job opportunities are. Demand-side theorists suggest it is better to attract, retain, and develop employers that need a skilled workforce. Communities may provide funding for a targeted industry, help existing employers modernize, and provide capital for new businesses that will hire a skilled workforce. Of course, the supply of and demand for labor are complementary. It is difficult for trained workers to find work if the employers are not demanding those skills. Conversely, a community may be able to provide incentives for a new business to locate there, but the business will need workers who have the required skills and training.

Institutional theorists focus more on how the organizational structure of work may influence the supply of and demand for labor in the community. Here, institutionalists make a distinction between internal and external labor markets. In an **internal labor market,** an employer hires entry-level workers and trains and recruits workers within the firm. Upward mobility for most workers occurs within the firm. A firm relying on external labor markets tends to hire workers who already have the skills and training needed for these positions. Workers wishing to improve their job skills and move to higher paying jobs may have to obtain the training on their own and take a job with another employer. The trend over the past 30 or so years has been for employers to rely increasingly on external rather than internal labor markets. As we discuss later, communities may respond to this problem by identifying the common training needs across groups of employers to ensure an adequate supply of skilled workers for employers or by re-creating internal labor markets across a set of employers in the community (**career ladders**).

———————————————— CBOs and Workforce Development

What role can CBOs play in workforce development? Many of the problems that communities face in building their workforce are difficult to address through the actions of individual businesses or workers. Solutions to these problems may require efforts by groups of employers and workers, along with public organizations. For example, employers may be reluctant to invest in the training of their workforce because they fear they will lose their investment if workers take jobs elsewhere. This dilemma is essentially a collective action problem. It is in the interest of all businesses to have a skilled workforce, but individual firms may be unwilling to take the risk of this investment.

One approach to solving this problem is to build career ladders that link employers together in a labor market to create opportunities for mobility across the labor market rather than within firms (Dresser & Rogers, 1997). In Dane County, Wisconsin, CBOs have established career ladders for unskilled and semiskilled workers in the health care industry. The system is based on the idea that unskilled workers will stay with employers involved in the career ladder program because the program provides them with opportunities for upward mobility. Employers in the system benefit as well. Employers that rely heavily on low-skilled workers are likely to lower their turnover rate, which can be very costly to these firms. They also are more likely to invest in job training because their workers will be more likely to stay with their employer to get access to better paying jobs. Similarly, employers relying on higher skilled workers will benefit from a steady stream of trained workers. CBOs are essential in coordinating these relationships.

There are several other examples of employers working collectively to solve problems in their labor market. Many communities lack adequate child care facilities. It is probably too expensive for most employers alone to provide this benefit to workers, but it may be possible for a group of employers to share the cost of providing child care for their workers' children. Similarly, employers can share the cost of providing transportation by pooling their resources of vans or buses. CBOs can help identify the need, locate resources, and bring employers together to address the need. Currently, there are two community-based strategies for coordinating these activities. Some communities mobilize employers within an industry, such as banking or health care. This strategy assumes that there are common training needs or issues within the industry that can be addressed best through some collective action. Other communities rely primarily on a place-based strategy that brings together employers that are in close proximity to one another. This approach may work best when the community is addressing problems such as child care, which are much more influenced by proximity to employers.

Welfare reform has placed much of the responsibility for assisting the poor on local communities. Many communities are engaged in efforts to prepare former welfare recipients for the workforce, train them, and match them with available jobs. CBOs have strong links with local employers. They may have a better understanding of the needs of local workers than do state and federal agencies. CBOs are able to provide training programs that better reflect the needs of local employers. In addition, they are able to maintain contact and monitor the progress of individuals. CBOs also may be a better source of job information for workers than more formal mechanisms, such as a state job service. Research suggests, however, that minorities, especially Hispanics, suffer when relying on informal networks to search for jobs (Green, Tigges, & Diaz, 1999). Relying on family or friends to search for jobs often leads to lower paying jobs for several reasons. Probably the most important reason is that family and friends have similar employment information as the job seekers do. The best job information system would combine the positive aspects of a formal mechanism for accessing job information with the local knowledge and access of informal networks. CBOs can accomplish this by improving the access to job information for employers and workers, while still serving as a formal source of job information in the local labor market.

Communities are engaged in a variety of activities related to workforce development. For example, numerous communities have initiated school-to-work programs. These programs improve the transition from schools by offering apprenticeships, job shadowing programs, and other initiatives that provide students with information about local job opportunities. Public-private partnerships are critical to organizing and implementing these programs. The vision of the local workforce may require the community to establish new programs or provide greater coordination of what is already happening in the community. Or the workers' vision may lead to identifying the need for new programs. An inventory of current activities may provide useful information on what programs are already in place and how the action plan could build on these activities.

Residents in most communities have a wide range of untapped skills and experiences, that could contribute to community development. CBOs are critical institutional mechanisms for identifying these assets, matching them to local needs, and overcoming the obstacles to building human capital. For example, a community that has recently lost a major manufacturing firm in the machine tool industry may have many workers with skills that would be appropriate and useful for another industry, such as plastics molding. Local knowledge of these assets and experiences is crucial to linking human capital with employment possibilities.

Context for Workforce Development

The United States relies heavily on a market approach for matching workers to jobs. Workers obtain education and training based on their interests and their expected outcomes of these investments. Employers move to a region with only a limited amount of information on the labor supply or the skills of the workforce. Workers enter the labor market with imperfect information on available jobs in the region and often with little idea of the job requirements. In reality, many workers rely heavily on social contacts to find jobs and to obtain information about the nature of those jobs. These social ties also are important for employers, who thereby obtain some information about workers as well.

The primary purpose of most federal training programs is to assist disadvantaged workers, especially unemployed and dislocated workers. One of the first general training programs was the Comprehensive Employment and Training Act (CETA) of 1973. The 1982 Job Training Partnership Act (JTPA) later replaced this program. One of the advantages of JTPA programs was that they were relatively decentralized, giving Private Industry Councils (PICs) greater flexibility in developing programs to meet local needs. PICs were organizations that represented local businesses, unions, and institutions involved in training. These organizations were responsible for designing the public programs that provided resources for training. The PICs had much more business participation than many of the previous training programs. The Workforce Investment Act established Workforce Investment Boards that now replace PICs.

Recently, there has been an interest in programs that provide a much more coordinated approach to linking training with job opportunities at a very early stage. The School-to-Work Opportunities Act of 1994 and the Carl D. Perkins Vocational and Applied Technology Education Act of 1990 provide the basis for school-to-work programs as key labor force strategies. School-to-work programs are designed to increase educational and career opportunities for young people by establishing learning partnerships between employers and schools (Fitzgerald, 1997).

Two recent policy changes at the national level enhanced the role of community-based development organizations in workforce development. First, in 1996, Congress passed the Personal Responsibility and Work Opportunity Reconciliation Act. This legislation ended the program known as Aid to Families with Dependent Children (AFDC) and replaced it with a program called Temporary Assistance to Needy Families (TANF). Under TANF, welfare assistance is no longer an entitlement program. Welfare benefits are time limited and are closely tied to work requirements that are intended to move welfare recipients off welfare and into the labor force.

Second, the Workforce Investment Act of 1998 is one of the most comprehensive workforce education and training programs ever passed by the U.S. Congress. This act, along with the Personal Responsibility and Work

Opportunity Reconciliation Act, has provided new opportunities for community-based development organizations in addressing the needs of workers. The Workforce Investment Act has made great strides in providing a more coherent system for employment and training in the United States. It has attempted to improve the system, however, through a formal bureaucratic structure and has done very little to encourage the Workforce Development Boards to reach out to CBOs. A major element of the act is that each board must contract with local organizations to provide many of the services and training programs. Pitcoff (1998) argued that the Workforce Investment Act presents some challenges to CBOs. One challenge is that nonprofit organizations will have difficulty competing against for-profit trainers because of their emphasis on strict performance standards. CBOs are likely to take on tougher cases and to deal with a broader set of worker issues.

This brief review of programs suggests that there is a growing recognition that training programs need to be linked closely with employers and workers. The Workforce Investment Act of 1998 places more emphasis on this feature than any previous training program. This emphasis on accountability and local ties places CBOs at the forefront of job training.

Training programs in the United States have been criticized for being isolated from mainstream workers and employers (Osterman, 1988). Most training programs in the United States were established at the federal level with fairly standard implementation policies. There has been growing criticism of the multitude of federal training programs, which do not appear to be coordinated or focused on specific community needs (Grubb & McDonnell, 1996). High schools still provide some job-specific education, but increasingly vocational schools, community colleges, and postsecondary institutions are responsible for providing vocational education. Although there is a potential for duplication in effort among all these programs, CBOs play a special role in coordinating these programs (Grubb & McDonnell, 1996). CBOs can provide an informal channel of information between employers, training institutions, and workers that will improve the matching process in the local labor market. In the next section, we outline different models for organizing these training efforts around CBOs.

Key Actors and Institutions

Bennett Harrison and Marcus Weiss (1998) identified three prevalent models for workforce development networks: (1) hub-spoke employment training networks with a focal CBO as the hub, (2) peer-to-peer employment training with webs of CBOs, and (3) intermediary employment training networks with intermediaries (e.g., community college, public-private authority, development finance institution) at the hub. These models are ideal types (there is a lot of variation in how these networks are actually structured in the real world). We outline these models in Figures 6.1, 6.2, and 6.3.

In the hub-spoke employment training network, the CBO is at the center of the network and provides information and ties to providers and resources. In the peer-to-peer model, a group of CBOs provide this function. One of the chief obstacles in this model is providing collaboration and coordination across the various organizations. And, in the intermediary employment training model, the CBO is linked with local governments and employers through an intermediary, such as a regional development organization.

Examples of the hub-spoke networks include the San Jose–based Center for Employment Training (CET) and Project QUEST in San Antonio. Both of these programs have been replicated around the country. Examples of the peer-to-peer networks are the Chicago Jobs Council, the Pittsburgh

FIGURE 6.1   Hub-Spoke Employment Training Networks With Focal CBO as the Hub

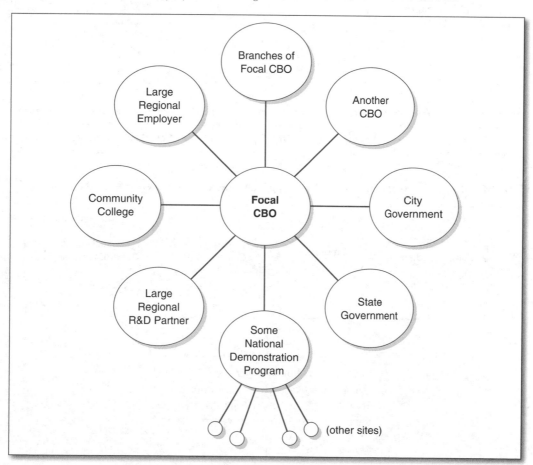

FIGURE 6.2   Peer-to-Peer Employment Training Networks

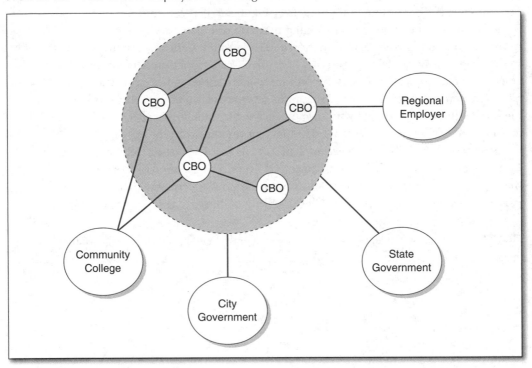

FIGURE 6.3   Intermediary Employment Training Networks With Intermediaries as the Hub

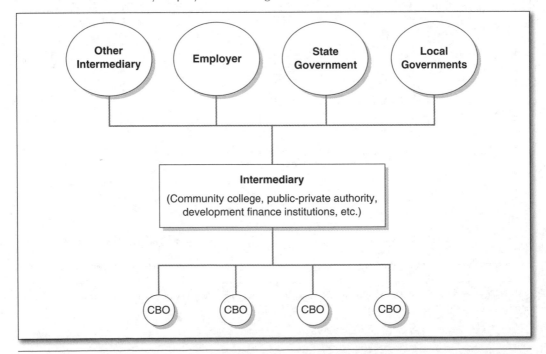

Partnership for Neighborhood Development, and the Business Outreach Centers of New York City. An example of the regional intermediary model is Lawson State, a Black community college in Birmingham, Alabama, that is providing technical assistance to small- and medium-sized businesses in the region.

Probably the most common form of workforce development network is the hub-spoke network. The San Jose CET model has been widely adopted across the United States. It requires less coordination than the other types and more easily links employers with training. Although these workforce development networks have grown in popularity, the evidence is unclear at this point whether they can be successful over time.

Aside from their central role as sources of information and contacts, CBOs can broaden the available training and services to workers. The structure of the workforce development network may influence the breadth and depth of training offered to workers. Training institutions can be captured by local employers and can fail to address the broader workforce development needs for the community. Networks that have CBOs at the center tend to offer broader training to workers than do those with technical colleges or other training institutions at the center (Green, 2007). Similarly, the structure of the network may influence employer participation. If the network is highly centralized or if large firms dominate the decision making, then small firms may be reluctant to participate and invest in the workforce development effort.

Data on Local Labor Markets

A community may decide that it wants to collect information on the local labor force to develop a plan or a vision of its workforce. There exists a wealth of data on employers and workers. Most of the data are now easily accessible through the Internet or through universities or state agencies (see the list of websites at the end of this chapter for several widely used sources). In addition, the community may decide that it is necessary to collect some of their own information on the labor market. Collecting data may be expensive and time-consuming, but it may be the only way to understand what is happening in a CBO's local labor market area. Also, the data will be more current.

A CBO might consider gathering and analyzing data for four broad issues:

1. What is the local labor market?

2. What is the current demand for labor in the region and how is it likely to change in the future?

3. What is the current supply of labor in the region and how is it likely to change in the future?

4. How are local institutions (e.g., training and educational institutions, temporary agencies, local job centers) affecting the match between the supply of and demand for labor in the region?

Most communities do not constitute a local labor market area. A local labor market area is difficult to define, especially in rural areas where workers may commute long distances and employers may recruit from surrounding areas. The size of labor markets may vary by region. Probably the most useful data to help define the local labor market are the Place of Work Data for Municipalities and Counties. These data permit CBOs to evaluate where and how many workers commute to work. By looking at commuting data, CBOs can see where local employers draw workers from and where local residents work. CBOs can also obtain some of this information by asking local employers to identify the zip code of local workers' residences. Based on this information, CBOs may decide to include an adjacent county or region as part of their local labor market area.

In many cases, it is probably sufficient to consider the county as the local labor market area. In some rural areas, this approach might not work—for example, in a rural community that is proximate to a metropolitan area. In these counties, a large proportion of workers typically commute into the urban areas, so it makes sense to include this broader region as part of the local labor market. Another exception would be a rural area that is extremely sparse in its settlement pattern, with few employment opportunities in the local area.

It is important for a community to identify what the local labor market is if it is to understand the factors influencing the supply of and demand for labor in the area. By focusing on commuting rates, CBOs also can see how mobile the workforce is in an area. It is important to recognize that local labor markets do not exist for some professions—these professions are in national or regional labor markets. A good example might be a professional position, such as a physician. Most other workers, however, are influenced by the conditions affecting the local labor market area.

Several data sources exist for analyzing the composition of the industrial base, wages, and occupational structure of local labor market areas. Some of the most widely used sources are the County Business Patterns (CBP), the Bureau of Economic Analysis (BEA), and the Department of Labor. The CBP is published by the U.S. Department of Commerce and includes employment in business categories (Standard Industrial Codes, which are broken out into two, three, and four digits). The data include employment covered by FICA but not government employment or self-employment. The BEA provides data on county population, personal income, and per capita income.

Developing Goals and Strategies

On the basis of data analyzed through this process, communities can identify the most appropriate strategy for building a local labor force. Communities can develop a workforce "vision" along the lines of the process identified in Chapter 4. In the following section, we describe five basic goals and specific strategies that communities can adopt. Communities may identify additional goals and strategies as well.

Preparing the Future Workforce

To have a productive workforce and employers that are competitive in the global marketplace, it is essential that workers have the basic skills necessary in the workplace today. This goal may require businesses to become much more involved with schools and to forge productive partnerships with school systems. Some younger workers may need basic skills, such as how to interview for jobs and how to plan their careers. The specific tactics to be considered include the following strategies:

- *Increase exposure to issues concerning careers and work in or before high school.* Many communities are accomplishing this goal by asking local employers to visit with students and discuss the types of work available and the training and education required for these jobs.
- *Develop an understanding of all career and postsecondary educational options.* There is increasing concern that students are not being exposed to the variety of postsecondary educational opportunities that are available to them. Several states are beginning to develop programs that better communicate the opportunities to students at an early stage of their educational career.
- *Strengthen career and technical education.* One of the issues here is the need to have a strong educational base to build on for an entire career, with special emphasis on math and reading skills.

Sustaining the Workforce

To attract and retain qualified workers, communities need to address the obstacles that many workers face in obtaining additional training or searching for jobs. Most of the obstacles are related to child care, housing, or transportation, although there are others that may be important. The following strategies can help communities overcome these obstacles:

- *Develop partnerships for child care availability.* In most cases, employers cannot afford to provide on-site child care for their employers, but there may be opportunities for a group of employers to cooperate and provide more child care opportunities in the community.
- *Create family-friendly work environments.* CBOs can help employers identify ways to make their work environment more family friendly, such as providing flexible hours or allowing parents to use sick days when their children are sick.

- *Increase efforts and assistance to employers to retain employees.* Workforce development efforts are emphasizing programs designed to help employers reduce their turnover. One example of a program that could be offered by communities is an educational program on how to conduct exit interviews, which help employers better understand why workers leave their firms.
- *Develop partnerships for increased training efforts in the workplace.* As we discussed earlier, sectoral and place-based strategies for collaborative efforts to provide training help overcome some of the disincentives for individual employers to provide training.
- *Assess and provide resources for transportation availability.* Some communities have been able to develop van pools or a busing system to attract workers from other areas or to help local workers commute to jobs outside the local community.
- *Provide affordable housing closer to businesses.* An employer-assisted housing program (discussed in Chapter 7) is one way to accomplish this.
- *Offer postemployment assistance to reduce turnover.* This strategy could involve courses on budgeting and money management, home-work balance, and so on.

Upgrading the Workforce

A key to improving the productivity of employers and increasing the earnings of workers is improving the education and training in the community. Several strategies may be necessary to upgrade the workforce. In many cases, it may be in the interest of all employers in the community to upgrade the workforce but not in the interest of any single employer to invest in the training because they may lose their investment. Community strategies need to address this basic problem. The following strategies are a few examples:

- *Improve the success rate for completing education and training.* This goal may be accomplished by linking students with employers before students complete their training. These links may improve students' motivation for completing the work.
- *Upgrade the workforce through funding and resource shifts.* State governments may be reluctant to provide resources for individual employers, but they may respond to groups of employers that have common training needs and have a major affect on a region's economy.

Expanding the Workforce

A major obstacle in many communities is the lack of workers, especially workers with the skills demanded by local employers. Communities may consider a variety of tactics to expand the workforce to meet these needs:

• *Develop partnerships that address barriers to expanding the labor pool.* For example, groups of employers (and local governments) may work together to provide a transportation system that helps workers commute from areas in the region that may not be facing such a high demand for workers.

• *Expand efforts to attract qualified workers needed to meet employer demands.* CBOs can help employers with the screening and matching process to ensure that workers are qualified to meet the demands of available jobs.

• *Increase efforts to connect education with the world of work.* Apprenticeships and school-to-work programs provide excellent ways of increasing this connection.

Promoting Entrepreneurship

Programs promoting entrepreneurship, especially among women and minorities, have proliferated over the past few decades. Citizens with the vision and ability to start and run a business represent human capital resources that are very important to community welfare. The small business option may be pursued increasingly by women for noneconomic reasons, such as flexibility or accessibility, especially in areas where child care and employment options are more limited (Tigges & Green, 1994). Minorities frequently turn to the small business option because of the obstacles they face in the local labor market. Communities can encourage and support entrepreneurship with a variety of mechanisms:

• *Establish loan funds for start-up and working capital.* In Chapter 8, we discuss several types of loan programs that can benefit small businesses at the start-up stage. In particular, many communities have initiated revolving loan funds as a strategy for this type of development.

• *Provide training programs that build the managerial skills of entrepreneurs.* In particular, communities are becoming involved in helping small businesses with managing their links to suppliers and consumers.

• *Provide technical assistance, such as information and educational programs, to entrepreneurs.* Small business incubators provide an excellent way of providing some of this assistance.

Green-Collar Jobs

One area of workforce development that has received a great deal of attention in recent years is the prospect of developing green-collar jobs (Jones, 2008). Growing concern with climate change and other environmental problems, coupled with the need to create more and better job opportunities, has generated interest in new jobs that improve environmental quality while providing pathways out of poverty for low-skilled, low-income earners.

There is no consensus in the literature on how to define green-collar jobs. A broad interpretation of green jobs includes all existing and new jobs that contribute to environmental quality. This definition suggests that green-collar jobs directly contribute to improving environmental quality but would not include low-wage jobs that provide little job mobility. Most discussions of green-collar jobs do not refer to positions that require a college degree, but they typically involve training beyond high school. Many of the positions are similar to skilled, blue-collar jobs, such as electricians, welders, carpenters, and so on. The difference is they apply these skills to green industries. Examples of green industries might include smart grid construction; expansion of freight and passenger rail; wind, solar, and biofuel production; and energy efficiency industries.

Many of the green job strategies outlined are demand driven. These types of strategies are seen as crucial to the successful development of the green economy because they provide a stable, secure funding environment for companies to take root and grow in. There are probably many more strategies than are discussed here, but these are the core considerations for most communities.

1. *Energy efficiency and green buildings.* Approximately 40% of our energy use is associated with buildings. Energy efficiency is seen as a powerful strategy to grow green-collar jobs because of the potential demand for energy audits and retrofits that exists in neighborhoods, schools, and businesses across the entire United States. Communities can drive green-collar job creation tied to efficiency and green building by crafting policies to improve their own facilities. The jobs related to energy efficiency are often concentrated in traditional building trades and construction industries.

2. *Renewable energy.* Renewable energy is growing rapidly as an alternative to fossil fuel usage. It is seen as a significant generator of green-collar jobs both in terms of manufacturing and in terms of design, installation, and servicing of the systems themselves. Communities can promote renewable energy development through conventional means such as offering tax incentives, credits, and other mechanisms to encourage renewable energy manufacturing in their own backyards. They can also develop creative financing mechanisms that provide incentives to homeowners and businesses to deploy renewable energy on site.

3. *Smart grid.* The current electrical grid is widely seen as a barrier to achieving significant improvements in both energy efficiency and renewable energy growth. The system prevents the full deployment of wind, for example, because the transmission lines simply do not exist to connect our

nation's largely rural high plains wind resource to our urban population centers. The grid is also highly localized and disjointed, which prevents the effective movement of power throughout the country when demand exceeds supply in a given region. A newer, more modern smart grid can take advantage of recent improvements in information technologies to better manage electrical loads. Jobs in this sector will involve the development, construction, and maintenance of this new grid.

4. *Environmental management.* This strategy is often not equated with green-collar jobs but is so broad that it has tremendous potential to grow them. Included in this category would be many technologies that directly benefit the natural environment, including water, solid and hazardous waste, and air quality technologies, among others. We are reluctant to include the recycling industry, although many states and localities have been very successful in promoting recycling programs.

Many of these strategies are particularly appealing because they are demand driven, which means that local elected officials can create the demand for green industry by simply shifting their regulatory and purchasing policies to achieve their green job and environmental goals. Communities that can weave together a policy framework with broad-based support will likely be at a significant advantage in terms of creating a business environment that encourages green industry development. Local efforts at promoting green-collar jobs can be especially effective if they invest in groups of firms that can be linked through a chain of waste and products. So, for example, it may appropriate for CBOs to link wood products firms with other firms that could use their waste products. This approach creates "virtuous cycles of innovation and growth" in the community.

Summary and Conclusions

Matching the demand for and supply of labor in a region can be a difficult challenge. In some communities, there may be unemployed or underemployed workers who cannot find entry-level jobs. In other cases, employers may not find enough workers with the skills and training needed for positions. There are serious limits with market solutions and government training programs in addressing these problems. CBOs can play an integral role in solving the training and matching problems in low-income neighborhoods, and we believe CBOs are critical to implementing an asset-based approach to community development. CBOs have knowledge of the skills and experiences of the local workforce and the needs of local employers. They also have a better understanding of the problems that constrain the functioning of the local labor market, such as the lack of child care or transportation. CBOs also can provide a good channel for information.

Federal and state policies are increasingly recognizing the important role of CBOs in workforce development. Increasingly, policies such as TANF emphasize the comprehensive nature of workforce development. It is no longer sufficient just to train workers—and then expect they will have access to jobs. Instead, these programs need to be comprehensive and address the housing, transportation, and child care needs of workers. The Workforce Investment Act offers new opportunities for CBOs to become key actors in the workforce development effort.

Finally, federal policy has moved toward greater involvement of local actors and institutions in developing training programs. Policy makers recognize that local residents need to be involved in designing these programs and that one standard model will not work in a wide variety of settings.

KEY CONCEPTS

Career ladders	Internal labor market
Demand-side theorists	Labor force participation rate
Employment networks	Local labor market
Green-collar jobs	Occupation
Human capital theory	Spatial mismatch theorists
Industry	Supply-side theorists
Institutional theories	Workforce development

QUESTIONS

1. What is the difference between job training and workforce development?

2. Compare and contrast traditional models of workforce development with community-based approaches.

3. Compare and contrast three prevalent models of workforce development networks: hub-spoke employment training networks, peer-to-peer employment training, and intermediary employment training.

4. What are the four main types of information communities need to assess their labor market situation?

5. What are the broad goals and strategies frequently used by CBOs to build their local labor force?

EXERCISES

1. Analyze some aspects of your local labor market.

   a. Define the area of your local labor market. How far do most workers commute and how far do employers recruit in the region? You can use census data to examine the commuting patterns.

   b. Identify the major employers in your community. Try to find out the types of jobs they have available, the starting wages and benefits for these jobs, and the types of skills and experience needed for these jobs.

   c. Identify local institutions involved in training and collect information on the types of programs available, the number of graduates in each program, and any plans for new programs in the area.

   d. What gaps do you see in the supply of and demand for labor in the region? How well do the job openings match the skills and experiences of workers?

2. Using census data and other local sources of information, try to determine what a living wage would be in your community. What percentage of the population in the community is not earning a living wage?

3. Try to identify the green-collar jobs in your community. What are the training and educational requirements for these jobs? What training programs are available in your region for these jobs?

REFERENCES

Beaulieu, L. J., & Mulkey, D. (Eds.). (1995). *Investing in people: The human capital needs of rural America.* Boulder, CO: Westview Press.

Center on Wisconsin Strategy. (1999). *Milwaukee jobs initiative.* Madison, WI: Author.

Dresser, L., & Rogers, J. (1997). *Rebuilding job access and career advancement systems in the new economy.* Madison: Center on Wisconsin Strategy, University of Wisconsin–Madison.

Fitzgerald, J. (1997). Linking school-to-work programs to community economic development in urban schools. *Urban Education, 32,* 489–511.

Green, G. P. (2007). *Workforce development networks in rural areas: Building the high road.* Cheltenham, UK: Edward Elgar.

Green, G. P., Tigges, L. M., & Diaz, D. (1999). Racial and ethnic differences in job search strategies in Atlanta, Boston and Los Angeles. *Social Science Quarterly, 80,* 263–278.

Grubb, W. N., & McDonnell, L. M. (1996). Combating program fragmentation: Local systems of vocational education and job training. *Journal of Policy Analysis and Management, 15,* 252–270.

Harrison, B., & Weiss, M. (1998). *Workforce development networks: Community-based organizations and regional alliances.* Thousand Oaks, CA: Sage.

Hodson, R., & Sullivan, T. A. (1990). *The social organization of work.* Belmont, CA: Wadsworth.

Jones, V. (2008). *The green collar economy.* New York: HarperCollins.

Judy, R. W., & D'Amico, C. (1997). *Workforce 2020: Work and workers in the 21st century.* Indianapolis, IN: Hudson Institute.

Kain, J. (1968). Housing segregation, Negro employment, and metropolitan decentralization. *The Quarterly Journal of Economics, 82,* 175–197.

Melendez, E. (1996). *Working on jobs: The Center for Employment Training.* Boston: Mauricio Gaston Institute.

Myers, D. (1992). *Analysis with local census data: Portraits of change.* Boston: Academic Press.

Osterman, P. (1988). *Employment futures: Reorganization, dislocation, and public policy.* New York: Oxford University Press.

Pitcoff, W. (1998). Developing workers: Community-based job training brings families out of poverty. *Shelterforce Online, 102.* Retrieved March 10, 2006, from www.nhi.org/online/issues/102/jobs.html

Tigges, L. M., & Green, G. P. (1994). Small business success among men- and women-owned firms in rural areas. *Rural Sociology, 59,* 289–310.

Tilly, C., & Tilly, C. (1998). *Work under capitalism.* Boulder, CO: Westview Press.

ADDITIONAL READINGS AND RESOURCES

Readings

Andersson, F., Holzer, H. J., & Lane, J. I. (2005). *Moving up or moving on: Who advances in the low-wage labor market.* New York: Russell Sage Foundation.

Applebaum, E., Bernhardt, A., & Murnane, R. (2003). *Low-wage America.* New York: Russell Sage Foundation.

Bartik, T. J. (2001). *Jobs for the poor: can labor demand policies help?* New York: Russell Sage Foundation.

Bernhardt, A., Morris, M., Handcock, M. S., & Scott, M. A. (2001). *Divergent paths: Economic mobility in the new American labor market.* New York: Russell Sage Foundation.

Berry, D. E. (1998). The jobs and workforce initiative: Northeast Ohio employers' plan for workforce development. *Economic Development Quarterly, 12,* 41–53.

Fitzgerald, J. (1998). Is networking always the answer? Networking among community colleges to increase their capacity in business outreach. *Economic Development Quarterly, 12,* 30–40.

Gibbs, R. M., Swaim, P. L., & Teixeira, R. (Eds.). (1998). *Rural education and training in the new economy: The myth of the rural skills gap.* Ames: Iowa State University Press.

Goldstein, D. (2007). *Saving energy, growing jobs.* Berkeley: Bay Tree Press.

Holzer, H. J. (1996). *What employers want: Job prospects for less-educated workers.* New York: Russell Sage Foundation.

Kazis, R., & Miller, M. C. (2001). *Low-wage workers in the new economy.* Washington, DC: The Urban Institute Press.

Luce, S. (2004). *Fighting for a living wage.* Ithaca, NY: Cornell University Press.

Melendez, E. (Ed.). (2004). *Communities and workforce development.* Kalamazoo, MI: W. E. Upjohn Institute for Employment Research.

Melendez, E., & Harrison, B. (1998). Matching the disadvantaged to job opportunities: Structural explanations for the past successes of the Center for Employment Training. *Economic Development Quarterly, 12,* 3–11.

Molina, F. (1998). *Making connections: A study of employment linkage programs.* Washington, DC: Center for Community Change.

Streeck, W. (1989). Skills and the limits of neo-liberalism: The enterprise of the future as a place of learning. *Work, Employment and Society, 3,* 89–104.

Wilson, W. J. (1996). *When work disappears.* New York: Knopf.

Websites

ALMIS—www.doleta.gov/almis/index.htm. The U.S. Department of Labor, Employment and Training Administration sponsors America's Labor Market Information System (ALMIS). This website offers information about ALMIS projects, upcoming events, and state-maintained bulletin boards, products and services, labor market information contacts, and news releases of interest to the LMI community. In addition to web links to various states' websites, there are also links to national statistics sources.

Community Economic Toolbox—http://www.economictoolbox.geog.psu.edu/. This useful website provides you with the ability to develop an economic snapshot of communities, calculate location quotients and shift-share analyses, and develop living wage estimates for your region.

Downtown and Business District Market Analysis—http://www.uwex.edu/ces/cced/dma/. This website provides a tool for using geographic information systems and market data to identify business opportunities in small towns.

Employee Benefits Survey—http://www.bls.gov/ncs/ebs/. This survey provides comprehensive data on the incidence and detailed provisions of selected employee benefit plans in small, medium, and large private establishments, and state and local governments.

Employment Cost Trends—http://www.bls.gov/ncs/ect/. The employment cost trends program produces two ongoing surveys: the Employment Cost Index (ECI) and Employers' Costs for Employee Compensation (cost levels). The ECI measures the change over time in the cost of labor, including the cost of wages and salaries and employee benefits. Cost levels data provide average costs per hour worked for wages and salaries and specific benefits.

Employment Projections—http://www.bls.gov/emp/. The Office of Employment Projections develops and publishes estimates on the economy and labor market 10 to 15 years into the future. Included are projections of the labor force, potential gross domestic product, industrial output, and employment by industry and occupation.

Green Collar Association—http://www.greencollar.org. This website is a primary source of information on the green economy and green-collar jobs.

Living Wage Calculator—http://www.livingwage.geog.psu.edu/. This is a useful site to help you identify the components for calculating a living wage.

National Center for Education Statistics (NCES)—http://nces.ed.gov/. This website offers access to data sets, reports, guides, and research studies. Several NCES reports are available in their entirety: *The Condition of Education, The Digest of Education Statistics, Projections of Education Statistics,* and *Youth Indicators.*

National Longitudinal Surveys (NLS)—http://www.bls.gov/nls/. The Bureau of Labor Statistics sponsors the collection and production of data from the NLS. Each survey gathers information on the labor market experiences of five groups of American men and women at multiple points in time. Each of the NLS groups consists of 5,000 or more members.

Occupational Compensation Survey—http://www.bls.gov/ocs/. These annual or biennial surveys provide information on average weekly or hourly earnings for selected occupations in the nation and certain metropolitan areas, as well as related benefits data for white- and blue-collar workers.

Social Explorer—http://www.socialexplorer.com/pub/home/home.aspx. This is a very useful website that allows you to present demographic data in data maps. The site is interactive and allows you to customize maps as well.

U.S. Bureau of Economic Analysis (BEA)—http://www.bea.gov/. BEA is a major producer and compiler of economic, business cycle, and labor market data. BEA has built a large online source for this data compiled from more than 50 federal agencies, called STA-TUSA. This is a fee-based site.

U.S. Bureau of Labor Statistics (BLS)—www.bls.gov. The BLS site is a major source for national labor market information, and it has data sets for state and metropolitan areas. This is a large and complex website containing hundreds of data sets, including local area unemployment statistics, industry employment estimates, and projections.

U.S. Census Bureau—www.census.gov. The Bureau of the Census website contains data from all of the bureau's data collection efforts: the Decennial Census, the Current Population Survey, the economic censuses, and the monthly economic surveys. It is a large and complex site of data, including population estimates and projections and data related to migration, journey to work, income and poverty, educational attainment, and much more.

Videos

The Greening of Southie (2008), directed by Ian Cheney and produced by Curt Ellis. Available from Bullfrog Films, PO Box 149, Oley, PA 19547; phone: (800) 543–3764.

Green Jobs: Hope or Hype (2008), NOW on PBS. Available from PBS at: http://www.pbs.org/now/shows/522/index.html.

7

Social Capital

Community development practitioners have long recognized the importance of social relationships in organizing and mobilizing community
residents, as well as contributing to the success of projects. People frequently
become involved in community-based organizations (CBOs) because their
friends or neighbors are involved or they want to meet new people. Who
becomes involved often will shape the direction and the outcomes of the
development effort. Similarly, community residents often depend on neighbors and families for assistance. CBOs can help build on these relationships
and social ties in their efforts to promote development.

Social scientists consider these social relationships and ties as a form of capital (referred to as social capital) that facilitates collective action in communities.
Social capital can be considered an asset that contributes to the development
of other forms of community capital—human, financial, physical, political,
cultural, and environmental. Social capital also may directly affect individual
well-being through its effects on health and happiness, education, and children's
welfare (Putnam, 2000). In this chapter, we examine the role of social relationships and networks in the community development process. We are especially
interested in how we can build the types of social relationships and networks that
will serve as assets in the community development process in the future.

BOX 7.1 SOCIAL CAPITAL FACTS

- The number of Americans attending public meetings dropped from 22% in 1973 to 13% in 1993.
- Union membership declined from 33% in 1953 to 16% in 1992.
- Membership in the League of Women Voters has declined 42% since 1969.
- Membership in the Parent-Teacher Association (PTA) has declined from 12 million in 1964 to 7 million today.
- Membership in the Jaycees is down 44% since 1979.
- Membership in the Masons is down 39% since 1957.

SOURCE: Putnam (2000).

In Chapter 1, we distinguished between the concepts of community of place and community of interest. Community of place refers to social relationships in a particular locality, whereas community of interest refers to social relationships based on a common set of interests. Communities of interest are promoted through professional associations and national organizations associated with specific issues (e.g., environmental protection, abortion rights). Although social capital can refer to both types of communities, we focus in this chapter on the nature of social capital in communities of place. Like other community assets, the match between the demand for and supply of social resources may be weak. In particular, individuals may be forming more social ties and networks around their community of interest than their community of place. Clearly, there are many examples of neighborhoods and communities that rally around local issues, such as the siting of a hazardous waste site or the location of a "big box" store, such as Wal-Mart or Home Depot. Mobilization, however, does not necessarily institutionalize these localized relationships in most communities. Our discussion of social capital focuses on long-term social relationships that build expectations and reciprocity.

CASE STUDY 7.1 SOCIAL CAPITAL IN A SEGREGATED COMMUNITY

The town of York, Alabama, experienced economic decline for decades. In the mid-1980s, the community began to develop an arts movement, which included a new arts center, support for local artists, and events focusing on promoting the local art scene. The new energy in the community was accomplished by bridging the arts interests of both the Black and White communities in York. The art movement in York had some success in breaking down racial barriers in the community by bringing together people around a common interest in the arts. The experience led to a new, more inclusive vision of the community.

SOURCE: Blejwas (2010).

Social Capital Definition and Issues

Social relationships and networks serve as a form of capital because they require investments in time and energy, with the anticipation that individuals can tap into these resources when necessary. The more individuals invest in these resources, the more they are likely to receive benefits in the future. These resources are referred to as social capital. Social relationships are considered capital because they can be productive and improve the well-being of residents.

Social capital has been defined in a variety of ways (cf. Coleman, 1988; Putnam, 1993b; Temkin & Rohe, 1998). There is a common emphasis, however, on the aspects of social structure (trust, norms, and social networks) that facilitate collective action. The most frequently used indicators of social capital are voter turnout, newspaper readership, participation in voluntary organizations, and attendance at meetings in local organizations. Others have looked, however, at the specific structures of social networks and ties of individuals and communities as indicators of the level of social capital (Green, Tigges, & Diaz, 1999). For community development practitioners, both types of social capital can be important.

As indicated in Box 7.1, there is growing evidence that Americans are becoming less involved in local associations and organizations. This trend has resulted in the loss of social capital in neighborhoods and communities. Putnam (2000) argued that there are several plausible reasons for the decline in social capital:

- *Increased time pressures*—people don't have as much time for meetings and participation in local activities. One of the major factors here is that adults are working more hours at their jobs, which may take away time that could be devoted to community organizations.
- *Residential mobility*—because people move more frequently than they used to (today people move, on average, every 7 years), they are probably less involved and attached to their community. Most research shows that the number of years living in a neighborhood is positively correlated with community attachment and involvement.
- *Increased labor force participation of women*—women are disproportionately involved in community organizations. Because women are much more likely to be employed than they have been in the past, they probably have less time for participation in these organizations and activities.
- *The growth of the welfare state*—in the past, communities relied heavily on voluntary organizations to provide social support. Many of these activities have been replaced by the welfare state in the past 50 years, therefore usurping a primary mechanism for civic involvement.
- *Erosion of the civic culture in the 1960s*—many social analysts have argued that the culture of the 1960s emphasized individualism rather than social responsibility.
- *The growth of suburbs*—recent critics of suburbs have argued that suburban development fosters alienation and individualistic behavior and therefore undermines civic culture. A couple of attributes of suburban life are particularly important, such as heavy reliance on automobiles (commuting) and land use patterns that reduce social interaction.
- *Generational effects*—there is substantial evidence that a decline in organizational participation has taken place over the past few generations that cannot be explained by the aging process.
- *Television*—many people blame television for the lack of community involvement because television viewing takes people's time away from community activities. It also is a passive activity that may lead to social alienation.

After careful consideration of the possible explanations, Putnam (2000) eliminated all except television and generational effects. First, television requires large amounts of time. The average household watches television for several hours per day—time that may have been devoted to civic organizations and associations in the past. Second, television may affect the outlook of viewers, increasing their pessimism about human nature and inducing passivity. Individuals who are more pessimistic about their ability to change things will probably be less involved in local organizations and associations. Finally, there is some evidence that television may have especially negative effects on children. Television viewing may increase aggressiveness and reduce school achievement, which may be related to participation in local organizations. If Putnam is correct, the way to increase social capital is to lure people away from TV and back into social arenas. Today, individuals (especially teenagers) spend much more time with computers and the Internet. The important question is whether this technology will facilitate or constrain the development of social capital. Social blogs and Internet forums can promote greater interaction among individuals with common interests. This technology could build social capital in communities of place but is most likely to encourage the development of communities of interest.

Putnam's (2000) research also shows that the generation that came of age after World War II was much more engaged in local organizations than were the generations that followed. His interpretation of these results is that the experience of World War II contributed to the high level of participation among this generation.

Although there has been an erosion of membership in most organizations in the United States in the past 40 to 50 years, there also has been growth in the number of advocacy groups (e.g., Sierra Club, National Organization for Women, and AARP). These organizations, however, limit the role of member participation; the primary element of membership is the financial support necessary for the organization to pursue its goals. There also has been growth in nonprofit organizations and local support groups, which are really not associational organizations. They may address community issues, but they do not directly involve their membership in shaping the activities of the organization. Thus, although there has been a proliferation of advocacy groups and national organizations that are issue oriented, these organizations do not enhance the social capital of communities or enhance the community's capacity to act collectively.

So, what are the implications of this research on social capital for community development practitioners? There is clearly a need to build new opportunities for social interaction that will generate trust and reciprocity among residents. Traditional strategies of building voluntary organizations and promoting leadership and citizenship through them probably will be less effective than they have been in the past. New technology that promotes social networks and interaction can play a role, but it must still be supplemented with face-to-face opportunities for interaction. These technologies must also be place based to effectively promote community development programs. Finally, this research points to some of the negative aspects of social capital that result from the racial, class, and gender segregation of social networks. Successful community development strategies need to identify strategies for overcoming this segregation. Many times it is important to identify common interests rather than focus on specific goals or strategies.

Several questions related to social capital should be considered in the community development field: Are social relationships and networks a form of capital or resources that can serve as assets in developing a community? Can social relationships and networks affect community development efforts? Do these social ties facilitate or impede development? What are some of the effects of strong and weak social ties on community development efforts? Can communities build social networks and ties to enhance their chances of development? What are some of the negative aspects of social capital in community development?

Key Concepts and Debates

The concept of social capital has been applied to a variety of issues: families and youth behavior problems, schooling and education, work and organizational issues, democracy and governance issues, and general collective action problems. In general, the literature has pointed to the importance of social capital in addressing common problems that are not easily resolved by individual actions. In this sense, social capital is central to building other forms of capital (human, financial, physical, environmental, cultural, and political) because of the limits of individual actions in solving these collective problems.

One important distinction is between *bonding* and *bridging* social capital. Bonding capital refers to bringing people together who already know each other with the goal of strengthening the relationships that already exist. Granovetter (1974) also made a distinction between strong and weak ties. Strong ties involve large investments of time and energy, whereas weak ties are basically acquaintances. Strong ties may be helpful for gaining access to emotional support and help in the case of emergencies. Weak ties may be especially aid in finding jobs or housing. Bridging capital brings together people or groups who did not previously know each other with the goal of establishing new social ties to provide new information, access additional social networks, and fill the "structural holes" in the system of networks in the community (Burt, 1992). Woolcock (1998) also referred to linking capital, or the ties between people in communities and their local organizations.

There are both advantages and disadvantages to promoting bonding capital. Increasing the level of interaction between those who already know each other may improve information flows, raise the level of reciprocity, and generate

greater trust among individuals. At the same time, increasing the density of relationships (the frequency of interaction among people who already know each
other) may make it less likely that a network will reach out to individuals not
in the network. In this sense, strong social ties may fragment the community
and make it more difficult to achieve collective action.

The development of bridging capital addresses these concerns by encouraging the formation of new social ties and relationships. These issues are especially important when considering community leadership. There are several
advantages to having a broad set of leaders rather than the same set of individuals serving as leaders in a variety of organizations. New leaders may
bring new information and ideas, as well as additional contacts and resources
that may not be available in existing networks.

How does social capital benefit individuals? Social relationships can provide both emotional and instrumental support. Emotional support includes
advice, support, and friendship. Instrumental support includes material aid
and services, information, and new social contacts. More specifically, instrumental support includes activities such as taking care of children, providing
transportation to someone, or lending money to someone. The types of inter-
personal contacts that provide the bulk of emotional and instrumental support
are with kin (family), friends, and neighbors. Institutions, such as churches,
however, may play a strong role in providing emotional and instrumental support in some neighborhoods. Many times churches are able to combine this
type of support with assistance in housing and job training as well.

Several factors may influence the extent to which individuals rely on informal sources of support. For example, individuals with few economic resources
may need to rely more heavily on social ties to compensate for their lack of
resources in the marketplace. The poor, therefore, may have to rely on informal
arrangements for child care and other services, rather than purchasing these services. The poor, however, tend to rely heavily on family and friends, who may
have few resources themselves to support them. Thus, the poor are faced with
a greater need for instrumental support, but fewer sources are available in their
network to help them.

Racial and ethnic differences frequently exist in the size and density of
social networks and the frequency of social interaction (Taylor, 1986).
Whites have the largest networks, followed by Hispanics, and then African
Americans. Most accounts of these racial and ethnic differences emphasize
the importance of culture and values in explaining the differences, although
some point to differences in family structure and social class as key factors
(Hofferth, 1984). Networks of African Americans have a lower proportion of
kin than do those of Whites, whereas sex diversity is highest in the networks
of Whites, even when kin/nonkin composition is controlled (Marsden, 1987).

Research also suggests that although women generally have smaller social
networks, they place greater emphasis on close relationships than do men
(House, Umberson, & Landis, 1988). Women generally are more likely than
men to seek or accept informal support, even when controlling for need.

Finally, Wilson (1987) argued that the structure of ghetto neighborhoods is the ultimate case of the different forms of social capital between African Americans and Whites. Neighborhoods with high concentrations of poverty isolate their residents from social contacts with mainstream society. Thus, African Americans in the inner city seldom have ties with friends or relatives in more stable areas of the city or in the suburbs. The high concentration of poverty affects not only the nature of the social relationships but also people's attitudes toward work and information about job opportunities outside the neighborhood.

This discussion suggests that community development efforts may face serious obstacles in developing social capital in poor and minority communities. The poor may be more dependent on social relationships to meet their needs, but family and friends may have fewer resources to support them. Some groups, such as Hispanics, maintain very strong social ties and seldom have ties to individuals outside their local neighborhood or family. In many urban neighborhoods, the loss of social institutions has made it more difficult to develop social capital. Ironically, this may suggest the need to broaden residents' social ties to individuals outside their neighborhood or family.

A related concept is **multiplexity**. Verbrugge (1979) defined multiplexity as the overlap of roles, exchanges, or affiliations in social relationships. Having a close friend who also is a coworker or neighbor is an example of a multiplex relationship. Coleman (1988) viewed multiplexity in social relationships as enriching social capital because it allows social organization to be appropriated from one situation to another. For example, if people are bound together by emotional ties, they can exchange information about job openings or job expectations. This multiplexity may enhance the normative and informational functions of social capital. Individuals who are strongly tied to job searchers through multiple relationships, however, are likely to have similar experiences and characteristics as the job searchers and therefore will probably not gain much new information (Granovetter, 1974).

Putnam (1993a) found that social capital is highly correlated with economic development. Regions in Italy with high levels of social capital have more economic development (higher quality jobs and income) than those with low levels of social capital. Putnam has been criticized for his argument about the relationship between social capital and economic development. The link between strong and vibrant civic organizations, economic growth, and development is tenuous. Although aspects of social capital, such as voting and participation in civic organizations, may help establish democratic institutions, making a link between these activities and economic development at the regional and local level is problematic. There are so many other factors affecting a region's economy that it would be difficult to identify the relative influence of social capital.

Critics also have argued that social capital cannot be built or destroyed quickly. They contend that though people may be less tied to their local neighborhood, they have become more involved in professional organizations and other organizations that represent their interests. This view suggests that the concept of community has become more liberated and based on people with similar interests. A liberated community may contribute to an increased number of bridging ties for individuals.

Is this version of community the same as the ties that bring together people in a neighborhood? Although individuals may still be active in regional and national organizations, and developing social ties with people outside their local neighborhood or community, it is not the same. Interacting with others by Internet or phone may not produce the same set of shared norms, expectations, and reciprocity that develops through face-to-face interaction with neighbors and other community residents. More important for community development, involvement in these communities of interest does not provide participants with as much experience at resolving conflicts and differences of opinion among community members. Communities of interest focus on the fairly narrow interests that bind them. Communities of place are faced with a broad set of issues and sets of interests that are much more likely to be different. Although communities of interest may establish social networks that prove to be useful, they do not provide some of the other benefits that are gained through the development of a community of place.

Another issue that community development practitioners need to consider is the negative side of social capital (Portes & Landolt, 1996). In some cases, the strong bonds and social ties that exist among individuals may prove to be an obstacle to development. A couple of examples may help demonstrate this point. Many minority groups that rely heavily on family and friends to find jobs through their networks may lack different sources of job information. The ties to the larger, mainstream economy may be lacking, which produces obstacles to job seekers' mobility.

Another example of the limits of strong social capital is the role that social networks play in helping small entrepreneurs in many cities (Waldinger, 1995). Ethnic entrepreneurs may benefit by serving an ethnic economy because it helps them establish a client base and market. Dependence on the ethnic economy alone, however, may be limiting and restrict the ability of entrepreneurs to enter new markets outside their niches.

These examples suggest that the major weakness of social capital may be in cases where there are primarily strong ties and an absence of weak ties. One could imagine cases, however, where neighborhood residents lack the strong ties necessary to provide emotional and instrumental assistance. Gangs also contain social capital, but they do not necessarily generate benefits for their community. So how can practitioners counteract the dark side of social capital? It is much more difficult to cross racial, ethnic, and class lines in community organizing and development. The Industrial Areas Foundation (IAF) has had some success in organizing across racial and ethnic lines around school reform in Texas. This model has not been as successful in other regions, however. A key element to the success of the IAF in addressing the negative aspects of social capital is the IAF process that emphasizes common interests as the basis for any organizing effort. In contexts where there is less potential for common ground, however, it may be more difficult to overcome this aspect of social capital.

A more fundamental critique, however, is that social capital cannot adequately challenge larger structural forces, especially those of capitalism, that tend to work against poor communities (Stoecker, 2004). This critique charges that social capital theories are largely apolitical and emphasize cooperation over conflict. This position, however, assumes that social capital is necessarily apolitical, which we do not believe is the case. Collective action, which is so critical to social movements and political action, is often built on social networks and trust, which are generated through social capital. That is not to say that social capital can replace political organizations and activities. The evidence suggests, however, that social capital can facilitate political participation. In this regard, social capital is a necessary, but not sufficient, condition for political organization in poor communities (Saegert, Thompson, & Warren, 2001).

In the following section, we discuss the unique role that CBOs can play in developing social capital, especially bonding capital. We tend to agree with Putnam's (2000) assessment that social capital can more easily be destroyed than created. We discuss some specific strategies CBOs use to facilitate social capital development and address some of the negative aspects of these strategies.

CBOs and Social Capital

Community residents need a place to permit social interaction. Social gatherings are a frequently used method for creating that space. This is why community buildings, recreational centers, and other public buildings (e.g., schools) are so critical to the development of communities. Community organizations can promote social gatherings as a way to develop informal and formal networks. New urbanists have argued that the physical design of communities has a major influence on social relationships (Katz, 1994; Kunstler, 1993). They have been critical of the sprawling pattern of metropolitan settlement that has developed over the past 40 years. New urbanist communities are designed with the intention of promoting social interaction in a variety of ways. Mixing of residential and commercial uses tends to decrease traveling time to work, which increases opportunities for community participation. The new urbanist design also tends to promote social interaction through the building of porches and patios in front of houses, where families will most likely interact with their neighbors.

Also, CBOs can use public debate to encourage participation. Visioning sessions (discussed in Chapter 4), for example, offer a venue for residents to identify shared purpose and common concerns. These opportunities to develop a vision of the community are most important in planning for development of the community. Some communities are experimenting with using new technology, especially the Internet, to create more dialogue among community residents. These opportunities also enable residents to learn how to deal with conflict and differing values and cultures.

Third, CBOs can promote social capital by ensuring that they have a diverse leadership, rather than relying on the same individuals all the time. This practice can help promote community norms for public life—everyone is expected to participate, and everyone has access to leadership roles.

Putnam (2000) also suggested that there is a role for CBOs in the arts and cultural programs as a means for promoting social capital. In particular, he emphasized the need to promote cultural activities, such as group dancing, community theater, and song festivals. These types of community recreation were once popular throughout the United States and played an especially important role in bringing together diverse sets of citizens.

Social Capital and Local Economic Development

How does social capital affect local economic development? To examine this relationship, we need to consider both micro and macro forces. Micro factors are those specific social ties and networks among residents. It is useful to distinguish between intracommunity ties (integration) and extracommunity networks (autonomy). Both types of social capital may improve the prospects for local economic development. Intracommunity ties are beneficial because they allow individuals to draw on the social resources in their community and increase the likelihood that the community will be able to address adequately collective concerns in their community. Extracommunity networks are an equally important source of social capital (Flora, Green, Gale, Schmidt, & Flora, 1992). These social ties provide access to external resources that may facilitate the development process. For example, many communities may need to access external sources of information or financial capital that are not available locally. Extracommunity networks also provide new ideas that can stimulate development activities locally.

In addition to these intra- and intercommunity networks, two macro aspects of social capital can affect local development. First, the level of social ties that connect citizens and public officials, referred to as synergy, can affect local development. There may be several ways to create synergy, such as through public hearings and listening sessions, public-private development partnerships, and citizen-appointed boards. Social capital theorists argue that in communities with more interaction between citizens and public officials, there is a greater likelihood of public trust in local government officials and accountability of public officials.

Another macro element of social capital refers to the organizational integrity of the local government. Organizational integrity refers to the institutional coherence, competence, and capacity of the local government. Organizational integrity is a form of social capital because it affects how citizens interact with their local government and the amount of trust they have in it. If the local government is arbitrary and has a limited capacity to deal with local issues, citizens are less likely to support government programs.

Thus, social capital is highest when the organizational integrity of the local government is high and there is a high level of synergy between citizens and public officials. This situation is referred to as a development state. Other possible combinations of organizational capacity and synergy are less desirable.

Assessing Social Capital

As we indicated earlier, various indicators have been used to measure social capital. Among the most common indicators are voter turnout, newspaper readership, participation in voluntary organizations, and attendance at meetings of local organizations. These definitions are based largely on the approach toward social capital taken by Putnam (1993b, 2000). These indicators of social capital are narrow and in many cases are not very useful for community-based development organizations. A more useful method might be the definition of social capital used by Temkin and Rohe (1998). They distinguished between two aspects of social capital: sociocultural milieu and institutional infrastructure.

Sociocultural milieu is defined as having four elements: (1) the feeling that the community is spatially distinct, (2) the level of social interaction among residents, (3) the degree to which residents work and socialize in the community, and (4) the degree to which residents use neighborhood facilities. Most of these data are not available from existing sources and must be obtained through surveys of residents or records from local organizations.

Institutional infrastructure also includes four elements: (1) the presence and quality of neighborhood organizations, (2) voting by residents, (3) volunteer efforts, and (4) visibility of the neighborhood to city officials. Again, these data may be obtained through surveys and organizational records.

Summary and Conclusions

Although debates about the definition and importance of social capital in national development continue, there is much more consensus about the importance of these resources in community development. One of the obstacles to community development has been the dependence on social ties and networks outside one's community. The loss of local organizations and institutions in communities has facilitated this change. The establishment of local organizations that encourage local exchanges and interaction is crucial to the development of social capital in communities. At the same time, greater reliance on social ties and networks outside the locality may not actually undermine social capital. Because residents now have access to more information and resources, these bridging ties may be more useful for the development of the community. The challenge is to create a common vision that will harness these resources.

The other obstacle that communities face with regard to social capital is how to overcome the negative effects of social capital. Many communities have a core set of residents who are connected strongly to one another and have a disproportionate influence over local policies and activities. In particular, local developers and realtors may work together to promote their narrow interests against the general welfare of the community. They clearly have developed a strong basis for social capital, but it may undermine attempts to promote community development. These negative effects of social capital need to be addressed by encouraging more widespread involvement in community activities and policies.

Finally, social capital is a critical resource that can shape, and be shaped by, other community assets. Access to capital is dependent on social ties and contacts in many neighborhoods. Job information is strongly influenced by who one knows. Social interaction in neighborhoods can be shaped by the physical characteristics of the community. Access to power can also be determined by social resources that individuals have. Finally, cultural capital is strongly related to social ties.

KEY CONCEPTS

Bonding capital	Organizational integrity
Bridging capital	Social capital
Institutional infrastructure	Sociocultural milieu
Integration	Strong ties
Linking capital	Synergy
Multiplexity	Weak ties

QUESTIONS

1. What is the definition of social capital? What are some key indicators of social capital? What are some of the trends in terms of the level of social capital in the United States?

2. What are the major criticisms of the concept of social capital?

3. What can CBOs do to promote social capital?

4. How does social capital affect local development? What are the micro and macro forces that affect the relationship between social capital and local development?

EXERCISES

1. Identify a local volunteer organization in your community that has been active for several years. Go back through the records of the organization and examine the membership trends, meeting-participation trends, and the social backgrounds of the leadership of the organization over the years.

2. Among the major volunteer organizations in your community, identify the leaders, such as the board of directors, of each organization. How much overlap is there in the leadership between these organizations? Try to identify common organizational ties among these individuals to assess the diversity of the leadership in your community.

3. Work as a group of students and ask individuals to identify the social characteristics (gender, race, and ethnicity) of five people (not related) whom they can count on for support and help. Next ask students to identify the social characteristics of individuals who helped them get their last job. Compare and contrast the size, structure, and composition of the networks of individuals in each group. What does this exercise reveal about the social networks of the group?

REFERENCES

Blejwas, E. (2010). Asset-based community development in Alabama's Black Belt: Seven strategies for building a diverse community movement. In G. Green & A. Goetting (Eds.), *Mobilizing communities: Asset building as a community development strategy* (pp. 48–67). Philadelphia: Temple University Press.

Burt, R. (1992). *Structural holes: The social structure of competition.* Cambridge, MA: Harvard University Press.

Coleman, J. S. (1988). Social capital in the creation of human capital. *American Journal of Sociology, 94*(Suppl.), 95–120.

Flora, J. L., Green, G. P., Gale, E. A., Schmidt, F. E., & Flora, C. B. (1992). Self-development: A viable rural development option? *Policy Studies Journal, 20,* 276–288.

Granovetter, M. (1974). *Getting a job: A study of contacts and careers.* Cambridge, MA: Harvard University Press.

Green, G. P., Tigges, L. M., & Diaz, D. (1999). Racial and ethnic differences in job search strategies in Atlanta, Boston and Los Angeles. *Social Science Quarterly, 80,* 263–278.

Hofferth, S. (1984). Kin networks, race, and family structure. *Journal of Marriage and the Family, 46,* 791–806.

House, J. S., Umberson, D., & Landis, K. (1988). Structures and processes of social support. *Annual Review of Sociology, 14,* 293–318.

Katz, P. (1994). *The new urbanism: Toward an architecture of community.* New York: McGraw-Hill.

Kunstler, J. H. (1993). *The geography of nowhere: The rise and decline of America's man-made landscape.* New York: Simon & Schuster.

Marsden, P. V. (1987). Core discussion networks of Americans. *American Sociological Review, 52,* 122–131.

Portes, A., & Landolt, P. (1996). The downside of social capital. *The American Prospect, 26,* 18–23, 94.

Putnam, R. D. (1993a). The prosperous community: Social capital and public life. *The American Prospect, 13,* 35–42.

Putnam, R. D. (1993b). *Making democracy work: Civic traditions in modern Italy.* Princeton, NJ: Princeton University Press.

Putnam, R. D. (2000). *Bowling alone: The collapse and revival of American community.* New York: Simon & Schuster.

Saegert, S., Thompson, J. P., & Warren, M. R. (Eds.). (2001). *Social capital and poor communities.* New York: Russell Sage Foundation.

Stoecker, R. (2004). The mystery of the missing social capital and the ghost of social structure: Why community development can't win. In R. Silberman (Ed.), *Community-based organization in contemporary urban society: The intersection of social capital and local context* (pp. 53–66). Detroit, MI: Wayne State University Press.

Taylor, R. J. (1986). Receipt of support from family among Black Americans: Demographic and familial differences. *Journal of Marriage and the Family, 48,* 67–77.

Temkin, K., & Rohe, W. (1998). Social capital and neighborhood stability: An empirical investigation. *Housing Policy Debate, 9,* 61–88.

Verbrugge, L. M. (1979). Multiplexity in adult friendships. *Social Forces, 57,* 1286–1309.

Waldinger, R. (1995). The "other side" of embeddedness: A case-study of the interplay of economy and ethnicity. *Ethnic and Racial Studies, 18,* 555–580.

Wilson, W. J. (1987). *The truly disadvantaged.* Chicago: University of Chicago Press.

Woolcock, M. (1998). Social capital and economic development: Toward a theoretical synthesis and policy framework. *Theory and Society, 27,* 151–208.

ADDITIONAL READINGS AND RESOURCES

Readings

Cohen, J., & Rogers, J. (1992). Secondary associations and democratic governance. *Politics and Society, 20,* 393–472.

DeFilippis, J. (2001). The myth of social capital in community development. *Housing Policy Debate, 12,* 781–806.

Edwards, B., Foley, M., & Diani, M. (Eds.). (2001). *Beyond Tocqueville: Civil society and the social capital debate in comparative perspective.* Lebanon, NH: University Press of New England.

Fernandez, R., & Harris, D. (1992). Social isolation and the underclass. In A. Harrell & G. Peterson (Eds.), *Drugs, crime, and social isolation: Barriers to urban opportunity* (pp. 257–293). Washington, DC: The Urban Institute Press.

Field, J. (2004). *Social capital.* New York: Routledge.

Fukuyama, F. (1995). *Trust: The social virtues and the creation of prosperity.* New York: Free Press.

Gittell, R., & Vidal, A. (1998). *Community organizing: Building social capital as a development strategy.* Thousand Oaks, CA: Sage.

Halpern, D. (2004). *Social capital.* London: Polity.

House, J. S. (1981). *Work, stress, and social support.* Reading, MA: Addison-Wesley.

Lin, N. (2001). *Social capital: A theory of social structure and action.* New York: Cambridge University Press.

McPherson, M., Smith-Lovin, L., & Brashears, M. E. (2006). Social isolation in America: Changes in core discussion networks over two decades. *American Sociological Review, 71,* 353–375.

Portes, A. (1998). Social capital: Its origins and applications in modern sociology. *Annual Review of Sociology, 24,* 1–24.

Putnam, R. D. (1995). Bowling alone: America's declining social capital. *Journal of Democracy, 6,* 65–78.

Putnam, R. D. (1996). The strange disappearance of civic America. *The American Prospect, 24,* 34–48.

Putnam, R. D. (2007). "E Pluribus Unum." *Scandinavia Political Studies, 30,* 137–174.

Verba, S., Schoolman, K., & Brady, H. (1995). *Voice and equality: Civic voluntarism in American politics.* Cambridge, MA: Harvard University Press.

Wilson, W. J. (1996). *When work disappears: The world of the new urban poor.* New York: Knopf.

Websites

Robert D. Putnam—www.BowlingAlone.com. This website provides important resources for analyzing social capital and includes the data used by the author in his book *Bowling Alone.*

Saguaro Seminar (Harvard University)—http://www.hks.harvard.edu/saguaro/. This is an ongoing seminar that is designed to improve the measurement of social capital and civic participation. In includes lots of data and information on social capital measurement.

Worldbank—http://web.worldbank.org/WBSITE/EXTERNAL/TOPICS/EXTSOCIAL DEVELOPMENT/EXTTSOCIALCAPITAL/0,,menuPK:401021~pagePK:149018~piPK:149093~ theSitePK:401015,00.html. This site is an excellent resource for social capital research. It includes references, data, published and unpublished papers, questionnaires, web guides, and more.

Videos

Social Capital and Sustainability: The Community and Managing Change in Agriculture, produced and directed by Dan Mundt, Publication EDC-88. This video links social capital with sustainability in agriculture. Available from Iowa State University Extension Publication Distribution, 119 Kooser Drive, Ames, IA 50011.

8

Physical Capital

Sense of a place is shaped by the local physical capital: its roads, buildings (houses, businesses, warehouses), and other physical features (railroad tracks, bridges, vacant land). In the context of community development, physical capital refers to buildings (houses, retail stores, factories) and infrastructure (roads, water, sewers). When physical capital (e.g., a house) is constructed, an individual or a household is making an investment and expects a return on that investment, whether it is going to be sold later for profit or heirs will inherit it. This investment, however, provides a return to other community residents as well. One unique aspect of physical capital is its immobility. Although on occasion houses are moved, water and sewer lines replaced, and factories razed, these are costly endeavors. To a great degree, physical capital endures over a long time and is rooted in place. Thus, the quality of local physical capital is important within a community development context and in relation to other forms of community capital. The slow recovery of New Orleans from Hurricane Katrina's destructive force, which damaged 204,737 housing units in Louisiana alone (U.S. Department of Housing and Urban Development, 2006, p. 1), reminds us of the importance of physical capital to a community.

BOX 8.1 HOUSING FACTS

- Housing is the single largest form of fixed capital investment in the United States (Green & Malpezzi, 2000).
- As of 2006, the rate of homeownership in central cities was 54.6% (U.S. Census Department, 2006).
- As of 2006, a total of 75.6 million people and families owned their homes (U.S. Census Department, 2006).
- In 2003, 5.18 million U.S. households with extremely low incomes had worst-case needs, defined as unassisted renters with very low incomes (below 50% of area median income) who pay more than half of their income for housing or live in severely substandard housing (U.S. Department of Housing and Urban Development, 2003).

(Continued)

(Continued)

- More than one third (36%) of households with worst-case housing needs are families with children (U.S. Department of Housing and Urban Development, 2003).
- Of the 5.18 million households with worst-case needs, 2.76 million are White, non-Hispanic households; 1.04 million are Black, non-Hispanic households; and 1.04 million are Hispanic households (U.S. Department of Housing and Urban Development, 2003).
- Between 1991 and 1995, the nation lost 337,000 unsubsidized units that were affordable for renters with extremely low incomes (Joint Center for Housing Studies of Harvard University, 1999).
- Almost 3.9 million unsubsidized renters with extremely low incomes spent more than 50% of their incomes on rent in 1995. But in 1994, for the total population, personal consumption expenditures on housing accounted for 14.9% of household budgets (Joint Center for Housing Studies of Harvard University, 1999).

Communities face a wide variety of issues with respect to their physical capital. Transportation is a critical challenge for many communities. Potential transportation issues include building new roads, creating or improving public transportation, or developing bike paths. Many projects are simply too big for neighborhoods or even cities to tackle. Even with big projects, neighborhoods should participate in transportation decisions. The Intermodal Surface Transportation Efficiency Act (ISTEA) has several provisions that mandate local participation in transportation decisions. Transportation issues are intimately tied to land use, infrastructure, economic development, and environmental decisions made by communities.

Another critical issue is the public infrastructure. Four key elements of the infrastructure are (1) water resources, (2) sewer systems, (3) stormwater facilities, and (4) solid waste collection and disposal. Beyond these basic elements, communities are challenged by the opportunities associated with broadband Internet service. Approximately one-third of the U.S. population is still without access to broadband services. Many of these services are provided by municipal governments. In some cases, the services (e.g., solid waste collection/disposal and Internet services) are contracted out to private firms. Privatization makes it much more difficult for residents to influence decisions regarding these services.

In this chapter, we focus our discussion on housing. Why housing? Affordable housing has been one of the chief concerns among community-based organizations (CBOs) in the United State for decades, and it is a core issue for most communities. We examine several questions related to affordable housing: Why is affordable housing important within a community development context? How do communities create affordable housing? What role do CBOs play in the provision of affordable housing? We also review the key concepts and issues surrounding affordable housing, the major actors and institutions, and the primary strategies and tactics for making housing more affordable, accessible, and available in a community. CBOs, because of their unique relationship with communities, can help establish networks that are part of a broader affordable housing strategy while addressing local housing concerns and providing information on affordable housing to a broad array of actors and institutions. There is a consensus that the way housing markets operate makes it difficult to provide affordable housing and that the federal government is relying increasingly on CBOs to meet these needs.

Housing Issues

Housing is an important feature of any community and in many ways defines it. Housing is where people live; it is the private spaces for our families and friends to share common concerns. Housing quality and its physical appearance matter. It can provide a community with a positive image, suggesting that the community cares about place, and it can obviously affect the value of homes. Housing is a major component in the bundle of goods that define social and economic well-being for American families. It is an indicator of the social status of families and individuals. It is the largest investment most people make and comprises the majority of most families' net worth. It is also the largest part of most households' budgets, generally around 20%, but often a third or more for families of limited means (Clay, 1992, p. 93). Finally, housing is intimately linked to the other amenities associated with the neighborhood in which it is located. It is connected to neighbors and friends, the natural environment, and consumption (shopping and services).

Efforts to produce and renovate affordable housing are place-based strategies in community development. Although the construction of affordable housing benefits those individuals who may reside in those units, housing is tied to a particular community, a neighborhood. A house cannot be easily moved, although it can be rehabilitated. If vacant land is available, new housing can be constructed.

The Problem

In most communities, there are a range of housing types from apartments and manufactured homes to townhomes and duplexes to single-family homes that can span from the very small and modest to the very large and luxurious. A variety of housing options are available for the diverse range of incomes, tastes, and values that exist in most communities. Many people, however, experience a number of problems related to housing:

• The cost burden of housing is excessive, approaching 40% to 50% (often as high as 70%) of an individual's or family's income.

• Housing may be overcrowded or physically inadequate, lacking indoor plumbing and heating, for example.

• First-time buyers may have difficulty in making the transition to home ownership.

- Homelessness is a widespread and increasing problem (see Box 8.2).

- Special needs groups (e.g., people with AIDS) and migrant farmworkers have difficulty obtaining housing.

- Few housing options may be available as people make the transition from one life phase to another.

- Rural areas often have an older housing stock, in conjunction with the nonadoption and nonenforcement of codes, a lack of plumbing, a lack of lending institutions, lower family incomes combined with uncertain futures, and few qualified builders and craftspeople.

- Subtle and pervasive forms of housing discrimination have kept communities segregated along racial lines. Racial segregation has affected the neighborhoods where people live and their choice of available housing in terms of types, tenure, and cost.

- Sprawl adds to the cost of providing services and often the price of a home.

BOX 8.2 HOMELESSNESS

In the United States, the risk of homelessness is relatively high among poor households, with about 1 in 10 poor adults and children experiencing homelessness every year. Communities generally use a two-pronged strategy to deal with homelessness: helping people leave homelessness and preventing people from becoming homeless.

The causes of homelessness are unclear, but studies have found factors that can lead to homelessness. These factors include but are not limited to adults with mental health, substance abuse, and other problems.

The effects of homelessness on children and adults are grim. Children suffer worse health issues, more developmental delays, and more anxiety, depression, and behavior problems than children who are housed. Homeless children also have poorer school attendance and performance and suffer additional negative conditions. Homeless adults suffer from poor health and myriad other issues.

SOURCE: Burt, Pearson, and Montgomery (2005).

Housing problems can be divided into four general issues:

1. **Housing affordability** refers to the median housing costs within a community in relation to household income. Housing is considered affordable when households do not pay rents that exceed 30% of household income.[1]

2. **Housing adequacy** refers to the physical condition of the housing stock and its age.

3. **Housing availability** is the housing stock and its distribution by type (e.g., single family, multifamily).

4. **Housing accessibility** refers to institutional barriers or other issues, such as racial segregation, financing, and local regulations, which can make access to particular types of housing difficult (Bogdon, Silver, & Turner, 1994).

In the following section, we focus on the concepts behind these issues. We need to understand how the housing market operates to understand how to address housing issues.

-- **Key Concepts and Debates**

To understand housing in any community, one needs to understand the local housing markets. A housing market occurs within a region and is shaped by an interaction of demand, supply, and institutional forces. These forces include the number and characteristics of households and their purchasing power, the composition and condition of the existing housing stock, the type of tenure, the degree of household formation, the ability to pay for housing of decent quality, the extent of poverty, and the degree of government subsidies and the regulatory environment (Huttman, 1988, pp. 6–7). Other factors shaping the housing market include the abundance of or restraints on economic resources, the general money market situation, land availability, construction technology, costs of building and maintaining housing units, and the cost of land (Huttman, 1988, pp. 8–9).

In Table 8.1, we outline each phase of housing production in the left-hand column. In the middle column are the influences on each phase. It should be noted that virtually all the influences listed are institutional (i.e., formal and informal rules, laws, and regulations). Although regulations and laws are critical in keeping the housing market functioning in a fair and efficient manner, it should be noted that regulations can create perverse incentives. For example, home ownership rates can decline under stringent regulatory environments, and more regulations can increase house prices (Green & Malpezzi, 2000). The right-hand column outlines the players involved in each phase of the process.

The institutions (informal and formal laws and regulations) that affect the housing market are key factors in understanding how housing markets work in particular communities. Regulations, such as zoning, subdivision regulations, and building codes, are important factors in housing construction. Most local jurisdictions have regulations in place that are necessary to ensure the welfare and safety of the public. Do these regulations allow for alternative development models, such as cluster housing or mixed-use development? Regulations can also lead to patterns of segregation or exclusion (zoning of large lots, zoning insufficient land for multifamily dwellings) by race or income. Another primary obstacle for many individuals and families in owning a home is access to capital or the issues of housing finance (Chapter 9 focuses on financial capital).

TABLE 8.1   Major Influences and Participants in the Housing Market

Market Phase	Influences	Participants
Preparation: land acquisition, planning and zoning amendments	Real estate law Recording regulations and fees Landowners Banking laws Zoning Subdivision regulations Private deed restrictions Public master plans	Developers Lawyers Real estate brokers Title companies Architects and engineers Surveyors Planners and consultants Zoning and planning officials
Production: site preparation, construction, and financing	Banking laws Building and mechanical codes Subdivision regulations Utility regulations Union rules Rules of trade and professional associations Insurance laws Laws controlling transportation of materials	Developers Lending institutions Federal Housing Administration (FHA), Veterans Administration (VA), or private mortgage insurance companies Contractors Subcontractors Craftsmen and their unions Material manufacturers and distributors Building code officials Insurance companies Architects and engineers
Distribution: sale (and subsequent resale or refinancing)	Recording regulations and fees Real estate brokers Real estate law Transfer taxes Banking laws Rules of professional associations	Developers Lawyers Lending institutions Title companies FHA, VA, or private mortgage companies
Service: maintenance and management, repairs, and improvements and additions	Property taxes Income taxes Housing and health codes Insurance laws Utility regulations Banking laws	Owners Maintenance firms and employees Property management Insurance companies Utility companies Tax assessors

Market Phase	Influences	Participants
	Union rules	Repair people, craftspeople, and their unions
	Rules of trade and professional associations	Lending institutions
	Zoning	Architects and engineers
	Building and mechanical codes	Contractors
	Laws controlling transportation of materials	Subcontractors
		Material manufacturers and distributors
		Local zoning officials
		Local building officials

SOURCE: From *Shelter and Subsidies: Who Benefits From Federal Housing Policies,* by H. Aaron, Washington, DC: Brookings Institution Press (1972). Reprinted with permission of the Brookings Institution Press.

Economists argue that markets, when operating correctly (i.e., uninhibited by regulation), will produce the right mix of housing types and prices (availability and affordability). If markets were producing the right mix of housing, however, we would not see issues of affordability, availability, adequacy, and accessibility continue to plague local housing markets. Markets cannot rectify this situation for several reasons. First, private housing developers often are unwilling to rehabilitate or construct new housing in low-income neighborhoods or communities. Second, developers cannot make a reasonable profit when construction costs are high because of labor and materials and when the available buyers are unwilling or cannot afford to buy in a particular neighborhood at a particular price. Third, private housing developers can create higher profit margins by producing middle- and high-income housing units in new subdivisions (previously farms or green space) than by rehabilitating or constructing affordable housing. Fourth, regulations can produce perverse incentives, or at least not the right incentives for creating affordable housing. Some economists argue that eliminating regulations would allow developers and therefore the housing market to operate more efficiently and effectively.

An important process that occurs within local housing markets is filtering. Filtering is a key concept for understanding changes in the housing market. It is the process by which high-income households buy and move into new homes, leaving behind a house that is bought by someone of slightly lesser means, who in turn leaves behind a house that is bought by someone of lesser means. This process filters houses downward from richer to poorer families.

Myers (1990) noted that there are three interacting components in the definition of filtering: change in occupancy (turnover), declining price, and declining income (p. 276). Baer and Williamson (1988) identified several criticisms of the filtering model: (a) absorption rates of new units to filter down are inadequate;

(b) the correlation between decreasing quality/cost of units and age is not inevitable; (c) discrimination makes minorities, particularly African Americans, more dependent than others on the filtering process; (d) owners and renters may exhibit different behaviors in the filtering process; and (e) overproduction of new units at the top may mean that new units compete with older units at the same value and represent an income loss to owners (p. 131).

The concept of filtering is useful and explains some of the dynamics in the housing market. The criticisms noted earlier, however, are important, especially for racially segregated neighborhoods. CBOs, especially if they are in neighborhoods that are experiencing a filtering process, may be able to slow it through their efforts. Another dimension to the housing market is the effect of immigration. Box 8.3 discusses some recent research on immigration and housing.

BOX 8.3 IMMIGRATION AND HOUSING

Immigrants are admitted into the United States every year; those who enter and stay illegally number about 1.5 million, give or take some unknown number (Borjas, 2002, p. 1). Immigrants are increasingly a factor in understanding home ownership rates and housing demand. Borjas's analysis of census data found a "home ownership gap" between immigrant and native households that expanded from a 12-percentage-point gap in 1980 to a 20-point gap by 2000 (p. 3). He also found that "more recent immigrant waves have lower home ownership rates than earlier groups" (p. 3). It appears that an important factor in home ownership is location, such that ethnic enclaves operate to increase demand for owner-occupied housing. Immigration plays an important role in the demand for rental and owner-occupied housing. Understanding the role of immigration in housing is critical for the success of neighborhoods and communities and for the success of immigrants in other aspects of community.

Another key concept is **dual housing market.** Some analysts argue that the supply of subsidized housing has created a dual housing market: that is, the creation of two markets operating side by side, one that operates for private market units and the other for public housing units. In reality, both private and public sector housing are supported by subsidies (Huttman, 1988, p. 4). Forms of **public housing** are direct governmental allocations, whereas private housing receives governmental support from guarantees on housing mortgages and insurance and, most important, through favorable tax deductions for homeowners.

The Debate Over Affordable Housing

In discussions of housing policy, analysts turn to whether affordable housing is a supply or demand problem and whether a supply-side or demand-side solution is needed. The federal government originally saw the problem as a supply problem and called for public housing as a solution. From the 1960s to the present, the federal government has shifted its position to the demand side. The shift from a **supply-side model** to a **demand-side model** means that the nature of the problem and the range of possible solutions are viewed differently. Under a demand-side model, it is assumed that there is an adequate supply of housing, but low-income households do not have adequate incomes to afford available units. The solution is to help households by supplying them with vouchers, for example, so that they can meet the costs of housing.

The key question is whether supply- or demand-side housing assistance is more efficient and cost-effective and whether it achieves the goals of housing policies. One argument is critical of demand-side housing assistance, such as federal Section 8 certificates or vouchers. The criticism is that Section 8 programs may benefit property owners more than renters. Rents are at their highest level in more than 20 years, we have lost 1.4 million low-rent housing units (that have not been replaced), and many renters reside in structurally inadequate units (Nenno, 1996, p. 137). There is counterevidence to suggest, however, that rents in real terms are no higher than they were 30 years ago (Green & Malpezzi, 2000). One of the problems is that in the 1960s and 1970s, many cities, through redevelopment efforts, began to eliminate **single-room occupancy** housing (SRO) through demolition and conversion of those buildings to other uses. SROs were an important source of low-cost housing in many downtown areas of major cities. A number of cities now have programs to create or preserve SROs. There is a Section 8 SRO program that provides rent subsidies to tenants in newly rehabilitated SROs (Goetz, 1993).

In contrast, critics of supply-side housing assistance find evidence that housing conditions are improving and that some areas have high vacancy rates. This leads to the conclusion that the problem is rent burden. Thus, the need is for certificates or vouchers, not providing housing per se.

Another important debate in the community development and housing literature is the level and scope of government and community involvement in housing markets. The federal government, as we explained in the previous discussion, has both direct and indirect effects on housing. Indirect effects come from the use of taxation (tax credits and deductions) and regulations that actually dwarf the effects of public production. Since Nixon's New Federalism and Reagan's more accelerated efforts at devolution, the federal government has used **block grants** (in which the federal government provides general guidelines for the use of funds, allowing local governments some discretion over how funds are used) rather than **categorical assistance** (in which the federal government allocates funds for specific programs, allowing little or no discretion over how funds are used) to help fund what were federal government functions for 50 years, including welfare assistance, housing, and urban development. Public housing has been one important source of affordable housing.

The United States now produces fewer than 30,000 new public houses or federally subsidized units each year compared to an average of more than

150,000 units per year in the late 1970s. Subsidized units formerly not only served to fill the critical gaps of low-income housing supply but also represented a major resource for minority households (Clay, 1992, p. 99).

The federal government has moved away from producing public housing to making funds available to lower levels of government and to organizations. One argument for this policy change is that lower levels of government are more aware of their citizens' needs and can be more responsive and innovative in delivering services. Although devolving responsibility to lower levels of government may make sense theoretically, in practice state and local governments do not have the resources to assume the same levels of activity that the federal government undertook in the past. State and local governments vary in the types of housing policies they use and in their levels of financial and technical support. Even so, the trend is to retreat from direct housing provision, in the hopes that the private sector and CBOs will respond, given the right incentives.

In the next section, we review a chronological history of housing policy in the United States to bring a contextual dimension to the previous discussion and prepare for the following section on the efforts of CBOs.

The Federal Government's Role in Housing

The federal government first became involved directly in the housing market at the turn of the century. It played two critical roles. One role was to help ensure that home ownership was widespread by creating subsidies for middle- and upper-income households.[2] The second role was to directly provide housing to low-income households.

During the Depression, almost all home mortgages were in default, and 1,000 foreclosures a day occurred (Goetz, 1993, p. 20). The federal government acted on a variety of fronts to help the country through the crisis. Organizations were created from 1932 to 1934 to refinance troubled mortgages (Home Owner's Loan Corporation), to address a lack of mortgage insurance (Federal Housing Administration), and to provide funds for home lending (Federal National Mortgage Association) (O'Connor, 1999, p. 91). The creation of these organizations subsidized middle- and upper-income households. In later years, subsidizing homeowners continued. The tax code provides a major subsidy to middle- and upper-income home owners. Home owner deductions dwarf all other housing expenditures, and the overall pattern of benefits from government housing aids is inequitable (Dolbeare, 1986, pp. 264–268). In general, the income tax system benefits owners over renters and benefits higher income home owners over lower income home owners.

The U.S. Congress affirmed the goal of a decent home and suitable living environment for every American family in the Housing Act of 1949 and reaffirmed it in subsequent housing acts in 1968 and 1990. Over time, a myriad of programs addressed affordable housing and urban development under the U.S. Department of Housing and Urban Development, by one estimate about

200 programs (Van Vliet, 1997). As we already suggested, the trend in these programs is away from providing public housing and toward funding CBOs.

The purpose of urban renewal (1949–1974) was slum clearance and reuse of land, part of which would be designated for public housing. Despite thousands of projects and more than 400,000 dwelling units on committed land, critics of urban renewal claimed that it eliminated more affordable housing than it ever produced, was used as an economic development tool to revitalize downtown land, and benefited urban real estate interests (Nenno, 1997, p. 30). Urban renewal was criticized for destroying working-class neighborhoods, and displacing poor people and people of color from their neighborhoods without providing adequate assistance to relocate (Goetz, 1993, p. 23; Marcuse, 1986, p. 254; O'Connor, 1999, p. 97). The Model Cities Program (1966–1974) carried out demonstrations, including constructing housing projects in selected blighted areas to revitalize them in their entirety. It was believed that a comprehensive approach was needed to eradicate blight. The program failed due to the high number of eligible communities and a lack of funding.

The **Community Development Block Grants (CDBGs)** program was established under President Nixon when several programs were consolidated into a single program (urban renewal, Model Cities, neighborhood facilities, open space, water and sewer, and public works assistance). These grants were allocated to cities and urban counties by a formula based on need. Smaller places and rural areas had to compete within their state under a state CDBG program. Over time, CDBG funds have been increasingly used for gap financing in private or nonprofit affordable housing developments.

> It is clear that cities could not pursue housing activities at anywhere near current levels without CDBG support. Three-quarters of officials in cities reported that CDBG was their primary housing resource. CDBG remains critical to city housing rehabilitation efforts. (Nenno, 1996, p. 40)

Although urban renewal, Model Cities, and CDBG are important programs for provision of affordable housing, the Department of Housing and Urban Development (HUD) has had many specific programs directly related to housing provision. Housing assistance through HUD ranges from public housing (a supply-side program) to **Section 8** and **HOME** (demand-side programs). Public housing assistance was directed at very-low-income families by the late 1960s. In 1974, Congress created the Section 8 private leasing programs. These programs provided a cash-based housing allowance for qualifying families, based on a percentage of median income. The Section 8 program supported both new construction and existing, rehabilitated housing. By 1983, the new construction portion of the program was canceled and was replaced with the Housing Development Action Grant (HODAG). HODAG lasted for 6 years until 1989, when it too was canceled. Section 8 has played and continues to play an important role by giving a housing allowance to eligible and certified low-income tenants who can search for rental units that meet certain physical standards. Landlords receive the difference between 30% of the tenant's adjusted income and the fair market rent (Green & Malpezzi, 2000, p. 88). In theory, a low-income family, for example, has a much wider choice of housing; the rental housing market is opened up to a much greater degree than is possible without the allowance.

The Low Income Housing Tax Credit (LIHTC) is an important element in affordable housing provision. Through its use, an average of 1,300 projects and 56,000 units are placed in service annually (Abt Associates, 1996, p. 3.1). The LIHTC was created by the Tax Reform Act of 1986 and renewed in Congress in 1992.

> The LIHTC provides a federal income tax credit . . . for ten years to private investors who provide equity capital for new construction or the cost of substantially rehabilitated affordable housing units. The credit applies to the proportion of units occupied by eligible low-income households. (Rosen & Dienstfrey, 1999, p. 450)

LIHTC has become the primary subsidy tool for low-income housing production. The program provides the equivalent of more than $3 billion in annual budget authority to state housing agencies. This program is another important funding source for CBOs, and these organizations are responsible for about 25% of LIHTC production overall. CBOs produce about 30% of LIHTC units in metropolitan areas and about 29% in suburbs; however, they produce only about 8% in nonmetropolitan areas (Abt Associates, 1996, p. 4.6).

In 1990 the National Affordable Housing Act was passed. Under this act, the HOME program was established.

> It is a formula allocation program (based on comparative local housing needs rather than an application grant program) intended to support a wide variety of state and local affordable housing programs. . . . HOME funds can be used for acquisition, construction, reconstruction, and moderate or substantial rehabilitation, and also for tenant-based rental assistance. (Nenno, 1996, p. 133)

The HOME Program, or HOME Investment Partnerships, under HUD, operates as a grant program for states and local governments for the purpose of increasing home ownership and affordable housing opportunities for families with low or extremely low incomes. Under the HOME program, the American Dream Downpayment Initiative, through local jurisdictions, helps low- and very-low-income families with down payments, closing costs, and rehabilitation assistance. Other uses of HOME program funds include tenant-based housing assistance and new construction of housing.

An important piece of the National Affordable Housing Act was housing vouchers that go directly to the tenant rather than the landlord, as in Section 8.

This program allows tenants to shop for rental housing that costs more than their voucher, in which case they need to pay the difference or choose to shop for units that are less than their voucher, in which case they can keep the savings. Another important part of this program is that 15% of its funds are set aside for CBOs that develop housing.

The 1990 act also included the Homeownership and Opportunity for People Everywhere (HOPE) program. Under Secretary Kemp of HUD, the goal of the HOPE program was to empower low-income persons by assisting them in owning a home. HOPE concentrated on selling public housing to residents, assisting ownership for families in FHA-distressed multifamily properties, and promoting home ownership of publicly held, single-family properties through nonprofit organizations, among other elements (Nenno, 1996, pp. 86–87).

In the early 1990s, the federal government launched one of the most ambitious programs related to public housing. HOPE VI (Homeownership and Opportunity for People Everywhere) represented a major shift in how public housing was implemented. Prior to the program, public housing was concentrated in poor neighborhoods. Many of the housing projects were deteriorating, and the residents were socially isolated from the larger community. HOPE VI provided new funds for physical revitalization of public housing properties, along with supportive services:

> Since 1992, HUD has awarded 446 HOPE VI grants in 166 cities. To date, 63,100 severely distressed units have been demolished and another 20,300 units are slated for redevelopment. As of the end of 2002, 15 of 165 funded HOPE VI programs were fully complete. The billions of federal dollars allocated for HOPE VI have leveraged billions more in other public, private and philanthropic investments. (Popkin et al., 2004, p. 2)

A major element of the program, however, is the deconcentration of the poor. To accomplish this, the program helps the poor relocate to better neighborhoods and encourages mixed-income developments to replace distressed public housing projects. Research on the effects of this program is mixed (Popkin et al., 2004). There is substantial evidence, however, that children who live in more mixed-income developments tend to do better in school. Critics of HOPE VI charge that it "has paved the way for rapid demolition without building new units." Another criticism is the program "offers municipalities an easy way to tear down low-income units without adequately replacing them" (Venkatesh & Celimli, 2004, p. 3).

The Bush administration tried to eliminate HOPE VI in every budget, but because of bipartisan support from its beginning in 1992, the program has been maintained, although at lower funding levels (Venkatesh & Celimli, 2004, p. 3). It is likely that the Obama administration will continue support for HOPE VI. Case Study 8.1 discusses Chicago's Plan for Transformation, which used HOPE VI funds.

CASE STUDY 8.1 CHICAGO, PUBLIC HOUSING, AND HOPE VI

Chicago's Housing Authority (CHA) in the 1970s managed almost 40,000 public housing units. Cabrini Green and Robert Taylor Homes are two notorious examples of the failure of Chicago's public housing program. Like many other cities, high-rise buildings were constructed to house low-income families. HUD deemed most public housing units in Chicago nonviable after decades of deterioration and slated many buildings for demolition. In 1999, the CHA developed the Plan for Transformation (PFT), which at its heart aimed to turn around Chicago's philosophy about public housing. Rather than segregating people by income and race, the CHA aims to develop mixed-income communities that include moderately priced homes and market-rate homes as well as units priced for public housing residents. CHA's primary work under the PFT is to build or rehabilitate 25,000 housing units by 2009. The CHA has razed complexes such as Robert Taylor Homes and on the same site constructed "new mixed-income communities with contemporary town homes and low-rise buildings" (Chicago Housing Authority, 2003, p. 1). In the process of razing and creating homes, many families have had to find temporary housing. Once the new units are complete, relocated residents can apply to return to the new developments. All residents must comply with a range of rules, two of which are passing a drug test and obtaining employment (Chicago Housing Authority, 2003, p. 2). City agencies offer support services to residents to help them meet these goals.

As of August 2006, more than "2,000 economically diverse families" (Metropolitan Planning Council, 2006) occupied these developments. These mixed-income developments are expected to house 15,000 families by 2009. However, it appears that many families will not return to their old neighborhoods. Although 75% of families want to return, Venkatesh and Celimli (2004) predict that "fewer than 20 percent will be able to return because units for poor families do not meet demand and the eligibility rules for poor families are prohibitive" (p. 2).

Chicago has transformed its public housing policy, but there are winners and losers. Only time will tell whether the CHA's mixed-income developments will function.

SOURCES: Chicago Housing Authority (2003); Metropolitan Planning Council (2006); Venkatesh and Celimli (2004).

The Obama administration initially proposed replacing the HOPE VI program with a new set of policies, referred to as Choice Neighborhoods. Congress, however, decided to keep both programs. Choice Neighborhoods will provide grants to help revitalize and manage improvements of public and HUD-assisted housing developments. The program has been funded at $65 million for FY2010. It is anticipated that the Choice Neighborhoods program will be linked to a variety of other nonhousing funds as well. Successful applicants to the Choice Neighborhood program may have a competitive advantage for these other programs.

The history discussed in this chapter focused on programs that aimed to create housing units through either supply- or demand-side policies. Another important piece of legislation—the **Fair Housing Act**—has influenced housing in this country. The Fair Housing Act was enacted in 1968 because of widespread racial segregation that has been and continues to be a problem in this country. The central feature of this act was to legally prohibit housing discrimination on the basis of race, religion, nationality, sex, disability status, or family status.

> The Act was, in theory, the pinnacle of civil rights reform in this country, because it offered equal access to a home, a mortgage, and neighborhoods that accompanied equal access to the voting booth, education, jobs, hotels, and other major arenas of life. (Goering & Squires, 1999, p. 1)

Some states and localities have extended the federal legislation to include age, ancestry, sexual orientation, lawful source of income, or marital status. More recently, states and localities have passed legislation prohibiting discrimination on the basis of arrest record, political beliefs, personal appearance, military record, or student status. There are some exceptions to this legislation, including senior citizen housing, groups homes, and units owned by religious organizations.

In assessing what the act has accomplished, even with amendments in 1988 that gave stronger enforcement powers to the secretary of HUD and the attorney general, national and local housing audits have found widespread discrimination (Kushner, 1995). It is estimated that from 2 to 10 million cases of housing discrimination occur each year in the United States (Feagin, 1999, p. 82).

Community-based organizations have become involved in fair housing issues. Many cities have established "Fair Housing" associations that assist residents in claims of discrimination. They may provide legal assistance and educational programs. In addition, CBOs conduct "audits" to provide evidence of discrimination. An audit typically uses testers to see if landlords, realtors, or lenders behave differently based on race or some other social category. So, for example, White and Black couples may inquire about a rental apartment. If the landlord treats the testers differently, it can be used as evidence of discrimination. This strategy has been used effectively in many cities as a means of enforcing the Fair Housing Act.

The Role of CBOs in Housing Provision

So far, we have shown that there have been two primary approaches to address the problems of affordable housing: federal government programs and markets. A third approach that has gained momentum and popularity is the use of CBOs to address housing issues. Many actors and institutions are involved in the private housing market, as illustrated in Table 8.1. Note that no CBOs are mentioned. Nevertheless, CBOs involved in housing need to understand how the private sector housing market works if they are to participate in the development or rehabilitation of affordable housing. Like the private housing market, CBOs act as the developer in the first three stages of housing development and often take on various roles in the fourth phase, service, particularly maintenance and property management.

Models of Community-Based Housing Provision

Private sector housing developers are reluctant to construct affordable housing, especially in neighborhoods that have high rates of unemployment, poverty, minorities, crime, and other social problems. CBOs have stepped in as developers to provide affordable housing in many neighborhoods where the private sector has assumed either that the process of filtering is taking care of the low-cost portion of the market or is simply ignoring that part of the market. CBOs are well situated to respond to housing needs in a community or neighborhood. They are physically located within the community or neighborhood and can listen and respond to neighborhood needs. They are connected to local voluntary organizations as well as governmental bodies, financial institutions, and philanthropic organizations. Without financial support from government and other sources, however, CBOs could not act as suppliers of affordable housing. Part of the strength of CBOs is the active membership of people in the community who are involved in deciding on the CBOs' roles and activities.

There are many organizational models for community-based housing provision. They are not mutually exclusive within a community; all can exist and produce affordable housing within a community. Community development corporations (CDCs) are the most common organizational model outlined. Other CBOs are important in providing both affordable and alternative forms of housing, such as community land trusts (CLTs) and cooperative housing (cohousing).

CDCs are vital players in community development, especially in the housing sector. CDCs are involved in many kinds of activities, with housing development and rehabilitation dominating their work. Even though CDCs contribute only a small portion of the total number of housing units constructed per year, they meet the needs that the private sector does not (Squires, 1994, p. 61). By the early 1990s, CDCs had produced about 320,000 units of affordable housing (Sullivan, 1993, p. 1). (See Case Studies 8.2 and 8.3.)

CASE STUDY 8.2 CDCs: A RURAL EXAMPLE—SOUTH EAST ALABAMA SELF-HELP ASSOCIATION

Formed in 1967 to help small farmers in a 12-county area of southeast Alabama, the South East Alabama Self-Help Association (SEASHA) realized that housing development funds were more readily available than funds for cooperative farming and that a major problem in the area was the lack of decent, affordable housing. The organization's first initiative was part of a HUD-financed national experiment to design and build a prototype home for low-income people. HUD discontinued the program, but SEASHA learned enough to continue on its own. Within 12 years, SEASHA had constructed 269 single-family garden-style homes for low- and moderate-income families. Another successful experiment was a 100-unit rental complex for elderly and disabled residents. SEASHA linked a range of auxiliary services to the apartment complex. It created a subsidiary, SEASHA Homes, that has constructed more than 300 new single-family homes, rehabilitated 75 existing homes, and constructed 192 multifamily apartments for elderly and disabled citizens. The organization makes use of subsidies offered through HUD and Farmers Home Administration programs to make the homes affordable for low-income families.

SOURCE: From "Community Development Corporation Oral History Project," www.pratt.edu/picced/advocacy/bsrc.htm, February 1997. Pratt Institute Center for Community and Environmental Development, Brooklyn, New York. Copyright 1997 by the Pratt Institute Center for Community and Environmental Development. Reprinted with permission.

CASE STUDY 8.3 CDCs: AN INNER-CITY EXAMPLE—NEW COMMUNITY CORPORATION

In 1969, about a year after its creation, New Community Corporation (NCC) began to plan its first housing project, New Community Homes. NCC, located in Newark's Black inner city, successfully reached out to neighboring White suburban communities and created the New Community Foundation, raising funds for its project. As part of the planning for the project, 60 families living in public housing were asked to participate in a process to develop the housing project. Their design was unlike any the state had seen and went against specific state rules for costs of low-rise housing. However, the state agreed to build the 120-unit New Community Homes project as planned, and the project was opened in 1975. With this success, NCC completed five major building projects over a 5-year period, creating an additional 829 units of affordable housing. In 1989, NCC built a transitional housing facility for previously homeless families. By 1992, NCC employed 1,200 people and owned and managed more than 2,500 housing units.

SOURCE: From "Community Development Corporation Oral History Project," www.pratt.edu/picced/advocacy/bsrc.htm, February 1997. Pratt Institute Center for Community and Environmental Development, Brooklyn, New York. Copyright 1997 by the Pratt Institute Center for Community and Environmental Development. Reprinted with permission.

Housing establishes a foundation for other community activities, such as economic development and social services. It is a visible product, so CDCs can establish a viable track record. Financial tools are more readily available for housing than for other community activities as well (Rosen & Dienstfrey, 1999, p. 439; Stoutland, 1999, p. 202). To get a housing project off the ground, many CDCs rely on five to seven sources of funds (Rosen & Dienstfrey, 1999, p. 445).

There are two types of CLTs: conservation trusts, which focus on land conservation and do not promote development, and CLTs that focus on housing and community development (White & Matthei, 1987). CLTs separate ownership of the house from the property it is on, thereby retaining ownership of the land in trust and according the benefits of home ownership to families. Keeping the land in trust removes it from the speculative market. Residents do not own the land; the title to the land is held in trust for the community by the CLT. Residents lease the land from the CLT, which acts as the legal instrument to allow the CLT to control the resale price of the home. CLTs figure the maximum resale price of the land each year by considering the initial investment, the increase in local wages, plus any improvements made. The buyer can expect a fair return on his or her investment, and the resale price restriction guarantees that the home remains affordable for future buyers (Goetz, 1993).

Shared housing is an important way for low-income households and families to afford housing in many communities. "Shared housing combines common facilities for joint use and shared responsibility for governing this use" (Hemmens, Hoch, & Carp, 1996, p. 1). Many types of shared housing are found in communities. Many forms are informal arrangements and can sometimes be illegal: That is, they do not conform to zoning regulations or building codes. Shared housing occurs when neighborhood or community demographics and economic needs do not mesh with the available housing stock and its price. Shared housing ranges from co-ops to accessory apartments to group homes and condominiums. Several variations are possible, as evidenced by the list of shared housing in Box 8.4, but these various forms need varying kinds of institutional/legal and financial support. Many types of shared housing are supported and created by CBOs, who can act as developer, advocate, or financier.

BOX 8.4 KINDS OF SHARED HOUSING

- Shared
  - Collective
  - Co-op
  - Condo
- Private
  - Boarding
  - Rooming
  - Single-room occupancy
  - Accessory
  - Echo (temporary housing built as an accessory unit onto a single-family home)
- Institutional
  - Congregate
  - Transitional
  - Women's shelter
  - Group homes

SOURCE: Hemmens et al. (1996).

Collaborative housing (cohousing) is a form of shared housing. A group of people buy, design, and construct a group of housing units and share community buildings and open space. This movement started in Denmark and only moved to the United States during the 1990s. The first cohousing community was built in 1991 in Davis, California. Cohousing communities have several characteristics: participatory process, intentional neighborhood design, extensive common facilities, and complete resident management (Levinson, 1991). Like other alternative organizational forms, cohousing faces financial hurdles, specifically construction financing, and sometimes zoning problems, depending on state and local laws as well as attitudes of planning boards and local councils (Levinson, 1991). Many cohousing communities are concerned with affordability issues. These communities have used government subsidies to make some units in affordable for low- and middle-income households. Other ways to make cohousing communities affordable for low- and middle-income households are to build in rural areas or on urban in-fill land, build on a large scale to achieve economies of scale, develop densely, use sweat equity, and use prefabricated parts.

Employer-assisted housing reminds people of the idea of company towns, but today employer-assisted housing "means the offering of one or more housing benefits to non-management workers" (Schwartz, Hoffman, & Ferlauto, 1992, p. 4). Although relocation packages for management have been standard fare in corporations for a long time, helping nonmanagement employees with buying a house or renting is a fairly new idea. Part of the reason for this new benefit is the realization that many communities offer housing only at prices unaffordable to workers. Companies find it difficult to retain loyal and qualified employees, so they have turned to benefit packages to address the affordable housing problem that these employees face. In these programs, employers help pay interest charged to home buyers or the down payment required on the new home. In general, there are two categories of employer-assisted housing: demand-side programs that enable employees to buy housing available on the market and supply-side housing programs that produce housing units for employees. Many large employers use these programs to stabilize neighborhoods that surround them and revitalize the housing stock.

The problem with these programs, particularly demand-side programs, is that many people like their benefits portable: In other words, people like the option of getting another job in another city or town and taking their pension with them. Nevertheless, these programs provide an option to employers in difficult labor market situations with tight housing markets. Several states now have employer-assisted programs that help subsidize employers for these programs. Research has shown, however, that the programs tend to pay for themselves by reducing the employee turnover rate because workers are required to pay back the subsidy if they leave their employer within a set period, such as 3 to 5 years.

Mutual housing associations are more widely used in Western Europe but are becoming more prevalent in the United States. These organizations are structured as nonprofits, with tenants controlling their rental housing. Like CLTs, mutual housing associations aim to take affordable housing units out of the market to prevent speculation and keep those units affordable to low-income residents over a long period of time (Hovde & Krinsky, 1997; White & Matthei, 1987).

Limited-equity cooperatives aim to control price through cooperation with other homeowners. They are based on the idea of a housing cooperative, which is a nonprofit association of members who jointly own the building in which they live. Members purchase "shares" that convey the right to occupy a particular unit. Limited-equity co-ops are attempts to control escalating housing costs by controlling equity appreciation (Goetz, 1993, p. 89).

Housing trust funds use the idea of dedicating specific revenue sources to a particular function. Since the 1980s, with the housing crisis fueled by federal devolution, states, cities, and counties have turned to dedicating funds for housing purposes. Real estate transfer taxes and linkage fees (fees paid by commercial and industrial development to offset the impact of additional employees on the local housing supply) are examples of such revenue sources (Brooks, 1997, p. 230). Housing trust funds exist across the United States, with well over 100 in operation. They have several common characteristics: a dedicated source of revenue that acts to remove the need for funding from an annual budgetary process, local programs, a large amount of variation in program requirements, an assumption that other financial institutions are involved in affordable housing projects and that the housing trust fund is not the sole financier, a dedication to housing, and an allocation of housing to low- and very-low-income households (Goetz, 1993, pp. 101–104).

The Impact of CBOs

The preceding discussion identified a variety of CBOs involved in housing issues, especially related to supply. The remaining question is how effective are CBOs in the delivery of housing? Interestingly, CBOs' delivery of housing about equals the federal government's production or output during the same period. This means that CDCs have developed a production capacity about equal to HUD's (Goetz, 1993, p. 118). Another source of affordable housing is manufactured homes, which are produced by the private sector. Private housing starts represent the largest output of units, representing almost 2% of the housing stock in any given year. All other housing output is far less than 1% of the total housing stock.

If CBOs are producing far less than 1% of the current housing stock, does this mean they are ineffective or inefficient? These data can lead one to believe that CBOs have little impact on communities, but one would be ignoring the context within which CBOs operate. Most CDCs and CBOs operate in communities with difficult conditions: poverty, unemployment, building abandonment, disinvestment, crime, and pollution. Also, one would be ignoring the comprehensive approach that many CBOs bring to community development. That CBOs are having an impact in neighborhoods and communities with these conditions should be seen as an accomplishment. For the lives that CBOs touch, for the people who live in the homes that CBOs are building, in neighborhoods where a variety of projects are taking place along with housing, such as job training, open space improvements like community gardens, recreational programs, social services, health care services, and day care provision, CBOs make an impact and a difference.

Subprime Mortgages and the Housing Crisis

The housing crisis that emerged in the United States during 2007 has been traced to the large number of subprime mortgages that were made over the preceding decade. **Subprime loans** are usually defined as loans that are considered high risk, based on the lack of capital, high debt-to-asset ratio, or blemished credit history. Many of these loans have adjustable rates that increase after a few years. During much of the decade prior to the collapse of the housing market, credit markets were less regulated and there was a surplus of capital in most regions. The result was that many questionable home mortgages were made and sold on secondary markets. The subprime crisis began in late 2006 with a growing number of foreclosures. In 2008, more than 2.9 million home foreclosures were reported in the United States. California and Florida led the country with the largest number of foreclosures. As the number of foreclosures increased, several large financial institutions collapsed under the weight of the collapsing markets for home mortgages.

The collapse of the subprime capital market led to a spike in the number of housing foreclosures. Although the foreclosures were widespread, the largest concentrations were in California, Florida, Arizona, and Michigan. In many inner-city neighborhoods, the majority of homes were abandoned, leading to further decline in housing values. Several Midwestern cities, such as Detroit and Cleveland, experienced extremely high rates of foreclosure as well.

The Neighborhood Stabilization Program (NSP) was established to stabilize communities that have experienced high rates of foreclosures and abandonment. The program was passed by Congress in 2008 as part of the Housing and Recovery Act. NSP is administered as a component of the CDBG program. States and localities that receive the funds must use at least 25% of the funds to purchase and redevelop abandoned homes or foreclosed properties. The income of new owners must not exceed 50% of the area median income.

It is unclear what the long-term consequences of the subprime mortgage crisis will be for communities. One possibility is that credit for housing will be extremely tight for decades. This will likely make it difficult for families to purchase homes. Home ownership has been a central issue for the field of community development. It is likely many organizations will shift their focus to rentals in the future as a means of providing housing. Finally, the effects of the subprime mortgage crisis will be with communities for at least the next decade. As the value of homes declines in some neighborhoods, other neighborhoods will bear some of the cost of the crisis as their property taxes increase to cover the loss.

Green Building

Green building refers to construction practices that are environmentally responsible and resource-efficient throughout a building's life cycle from siting to design, construction, operation, maintenance, renovation, and deconstruction (U.S. Environmental Protection Agency, 2010). The primary goal of green building is to minimize the impact of the built environment on human health and the natural environment. Green building attempts to achieve these goals by efficiently using energy and other resources and reducing waste, pollution, and environmental degradation.

The U.S. Green Building Council (USGBC) has established a set of standards for green building, called **Leadership in Energy and Environmental Design (LEED)**. These standards include six standards covering all aspects of the development and construction process. There are points awarded for various practices, with the total of 100 points possible. Presumably, consumers will be willing to spend more on housing and other buildings with a higher LEED score.

Summary and Conclusions

Housing has become the "meat and potatoes" of community development work. It is an area where CBOs can have an impact and show success and where the federal government was willing to lend a hand in promoting these activities. Some critics have charged that CBOs have focused too much on housing issues and should diversify their activities and pay more attention to community organizing issues. Other critics claim that housing is one of the few things that CBOs can do effectively and that they should stay focused on these issues and stay out of the economic development realm. Bockmeyer (2003) posited that reliance on CBOs actually "undermines collective action by encouraging inter-group competition, and discourages smaller organizations that focus on housing advocacy" (p. 76). Bratt and Rohe (2004) reinforced Bockmeyer's housing devolution theory. They found that overall, the number of CDCs continues to grow, but this growth has masked the mergers, downsizing, and shutting down of CDCs.

CBOs will most likely continue to be the lead actors in housing markets in most low-income neighborhoods. They now have the experience, funding, and skills to carry out these activities in these difficult settings. There probably is a need for CBOs to focus on the production of rental units rather than almost exclusively on home ownership. This shift could be facilitated by considering some of the alternative housing models that have been discussed here.

Of course, one of the major limitations of housing projects developed by CBOs is that CBOs do not address the racial segregation of neighborhoods, which limits the opportunities of low-income residents. These issues can best be addressed through regional strategies and policies.

KEY CONCEPTS

Block grants

Categorical assistance

Community Development
    Block Grants (CDBGs)

Demand-side model

Dual housing market

Fair Housing Act

Filtering

Green building

HOME

HOPE VI

Housing accessibility

Housing adequacy

Housing affordability

Housing availability

Leadership in Energy and
    Environmental Design (LEED)

Physical capital

Public housing

Section 8

Single-room occupancy

Subprime loans

Supply-side model

QUESTIONS

1. Why is housing and its quality important in and to communities?

2. What is a housing market?

3. What are the forces that affect a housing market?

4. What is the difference between supply- and demand-side policies?

5. What is filtering and why is it important?

6. Why are CDCs important actors in the affordable housing market?

7. Discuss another type of CBO and its role in community housing.

EXERCISES

1. Examine organizations in your community that are interested in housing issues. What aspects of housing does each organization focus on? Do organizations compete or are they involved in a network—that is, do they work cooperatively or competitively? Why?

2. Sample term paper question: Choose a community in your state. Examine the housing market, particularly for affordable housing, and the organizations involved in delivering affordable housing. Use the following questions to guide you:

    a. What is the current demand for housing in the community and region and how is it likely to change in the future?

    b. What is the current supply of housing and how is it likely to change in the future?

    c. How are the private and public sectors meeting the supply and demand for housing? Is there an unmet demand?

3. Identify any LEED-certified buildings in your community. Talk with the developers of this building about the differences in this building and other projects in which they have been involved. How does this building compare with regard to cost and energy consumption?

NOTES

1. If we agree that housing or shelter is a necessity, some would say a right, then the question is, how can low-income households in particular afford shelter? And what percentage of income devoted to housing is excessive? When you look at the income distribution in the United States, you find that the lower the income, the higher the percentage of income devoted to housing. A common rule of thumb is that spending more than 30% of household income on housing implies that it is not affordable. HUD uses this rule of thumb in its official calculations. This is a normative policy decision. For an argument about what is affordable, see Green and Malpezzi (2000).

2. Green and Malpezzi (2000) noted that not all homeowners benefit from the mortgage interest deduction. A married couple's itemized deductions need to be more than the standard deduction of $7,500.

REFERENCES

Aaron, H. J. (1972). *Shelter and subsidies: Who benefits from federal housing policies?* Washington, DC: Brookings Institution.

Abt Associates, Inc. (1996). *Development and analysis of the national low-income housing tax credit database.* Washington, DC: U.S. Department of Housing and Urban Development.

Baer, W. C., & Williamson, C. B. (1988). The filtering of households and housing units. *Journal of Planning Literature, 3,* 127–152.

Bogdon, A., Silver, J., & Turner, M. A. (1994). *National analysis of housing affordability, adequacy, and availability: A framework for local housing strategies.* Washington, DC: U.S. Department of Housing and Urban Development.

Borjas, G. J. (2002). *Homeownership in the immigrant population* (Working Paper No. 02–01). Washington, DC: Research Institute for Housing America.

Bratt, R. G., & Rohe, W. M. (2004). Organizational changes among CDCs: Assessing the impacts and navigating the challenges. *Journal of Urban Affairs, 26,* 197–220.

Bockmeyer, J. L. (2003). Devolution and the transformation of community housing activism. *The Social Science Journal, 140,* 175–188.

Brooks, M. E. (1997). Housing trust funds: A new approach to funding affordable housing. In W. Van Vliet (Ed.), *Affordable housing and urban redevelopment in the United States* (pp. 229–245). Thousand Oaks, CA: Sage.

Burt, M. R., Pearson, C. L., & Montgomery, A. E. (2005). *Strategies for preventing homelessness.* Washington, DC: U.S. Department of Housing and Urban Development, Office of Policy Development and Research.

Chicago Housing Authority. (2003). *The CHA's plan for transformation.* Chicago: Author.

Clay, P. L. (1992). The (un)housed city: Racial patterns of segregation, housing quality and affordability. In G. C. Galster & E. W. Hill (Eds.), *The metropolis in black and white: Place, power and polarization* (pp. 93–107). New Brunswick, NJ: Rutgers University, Center for Urban Policy Research.

Dolbeare, C. (1986). How the income tax system subsidizes housing for the affluent. In R. G. Bratt, C. Hartman, & A. Meyerson (Eds.), *Critical perspectives on housing* (pp. 264–271). Philadelphia: Temple University Press.

Feagin, J. R. (1999). Excluding Blacks and others from housing: The foundation of White racism. *Cityscape, 4,* 79–91.

Goering, J., & Squires, G. (1999). Guest editors' introduction: Commemorating the 30th anniversary of the Fair Housing Act. *Cityscape, 4,* 1–17.

Goetz, E. G. (1993). *Shelter burden: Local politics and progressive housing policy.* Philadelphia: Temple University Press.

Green, R. K., & Malpezzi, S. (2000). *A primer on U.S. housing markets and housing policy.* Bloomington, IN: American Real Estate and Urban Economics Association.

Hemmens, G. C., Hoch, C. J., & Carp, J. (1996). Introduction. In G. C. Hemmens, C. J. Hoch, & J. Carp (Eds.), *Under one roof: Issues and innovations in shared housing* (pp. 1–16). Albany: State University of New York Press.

Hovde, S., & Krinsky, J. (1997, March/April). Watchful stewards: Mutual housing associations and community land trusts preserve affordable housing. *Shelterforce.* Retrieved March 19, 2007, from www.nhi.org/online/issues/92/mha.html

Huttman, E. (1988). Introduction. In E. Huttman & W. Van Vliet (Eds.), *Handbook of housing and the built environment in the United States* (pp. 1–20). Westport, CT: Greenwood.

Joint Center for Housing Studies of Harvard University. (1999). *The state of the nation's housing, 1999.* Cambridge, MA: Author.

Kushner, J. A. (1995). *Fair housing: Discrimination in real estate, community development, and revitalization* (2nd ed.). Colorado Springs, CO: Shepard's/McGraw-Hill.

Levinson, N. (1991). Share and share alike. *Planning, 57,* 24–26.

Marcuse, P. (1986). Housing policy and the myth of the benevolent state. In R. G. Bratt, C. Hartman, & A. Meyerson (Eds.), *Critical perspectives on housing* (pp. 248–263). Philadelphia: Temple University Press.

Metropolitan Planning Council. (2006). *CHA plan for transformation update.* Retrieved March 30, 2007, from www.metroplanning.org

Myers, D. (1990). Filtering in time: Rethinking the longitudinal behavior of neighborhood housing markets. In D. Myers (Ed.), *Housing demography: Linking demographic structure and housing markets* (pp. 274–296). Madison: University of Wisconsin Press.

Nenno, M. K. (1996). *Ending the stalemate: Moving housing and urban development into the main-stream of America's future*. Lanham, MD: University Press of America.

Nenno, M. K. (1997). Changes and challenges in affordable housing and urban development. In W. Van Vliet (Ed.), *Affordable housing and urban redevelopment in the United States* (pp. 1–21). Thousand Oaks, CA: Sage.

O'Connor, A. (1999). Swimming against the tide: A brief history of federal policy in poor commu-nities. In R. F. Ferguson & W. T. Dickens (Eds.), *Urban problems and community development* (pp. 77–137). Washington, DC: Brookings Institution Press.

Popkin, S. J., Katz, B., Cunningham, M. K., Brown, K. D., Gustafson, J., & Turner, M. A. (2004). *A decade of Hope VI: Research findings and policy challenges*. Washington, DC: The Urban Institute.

Pratt Institute Center for Community and Environmental Development. (1997). *Community devel-opment corporation oral history project*. Brooklyn, NY: Author.

Rosen, K. T., & Dienstfrey, T. (1999). The economics of housing services in low-income neighbor-hoods. In R. F. Ferguson & W. T. Dickens (Eds.), *Urban problems and community development* (pp. 437–472). Washington, DC: Brookings Institution Press.

Schwartz, D. C., Hoffman, D. N., & Ferlauto, R. C. (1992). *Employer-assisted housing: A benefit for the 1990s*. Washington, DC: Bureau of National Affairs.

Squires, G. D. (1994). *Capital and communities in black and white: The intersections of race, class, and uneven development*. Albany: State University of New York Press.

Stoutland, S. E. (1999). Community development corporations: Mission, strategy, and accomplish-ments. In R. F. Ferguson & W. T. Dickens (Eds.), *Urban problems and community development* (pp. 193–240). Washington, DC: Brookings Institution Press.

Sullivan, M. L. (1993). *More than housing: How community development corporations go about changing lives and neighborhoods*. New York: New School for Social Research, Community Development Research Center, Graduate School of Management and Urban Policy.

U.S. Census Department. (2006). *Housing vacancies and homeownership, third quarter, 2006*. Washington, DC: Author.

U.S. Environmental Protection Agency. (2010). *Green building*. http://www.epa.gov/greenbuilding/pubs/about.htm

U.S. Department of Housing and Urban Development. (2003). *Affordable housing needs: A report to Congress on the significant need for housing: Annual compilation of a worst case housing needs survey*. Washington, DC: Author.

U.S. Department of Housing and Urban Development. (2006). *Funding for recovery in the hurri-canes' wake: Part 1: Research works, 3, 9*. Washington, DC: Author.

Van Vliet, W. (1997). Learning from experience: The ingredients and transferability of success. In W. Van Vliet (Ed.), *Affordable housing and urban redevelopment in the United States* (pp. 246–276). Thousand Oaks, CA: Sage.

Venkatesh, S., & Celimli, I. (2004, November/December). Tearing down the community. *Shelterforce Online, 138*. Retrieved March 21, 2007, from http://www.nhi.org/online/issues/138/chicago.html

White, K., & Matthei, C. (1987). Community land trusts. In S. T. Bruyn & J. Meehan (Eds.), *Beyond the market and the state: New directions in community development* (pp. 41–64). Philadelphia: Temple University Press.

ADDITIONAL READINGS AND RESOURCES

Readings

Baker, A. (1992). This land is not for sale. *Social Policy, 22,* 25–35.

Belden, J., & Weiner, R. (1995). *A home in the country: The housing challenges facing rural America.* Washington, DC: Fannie Mae Office of Housing Research.

Bratt, R., Hartman, C., & Meyerson, A. (Eds.). (1986). *Critical perspectives on housing.* Philadelphia: Temple University Press.

Calem, P. S., Gillen, K., & Wachter, S. (2004). The neighborhood distribution of subprime mortgage lending. *Journal of Real Estate Finance and Economics, 29,* 393–414.

Dolbeare, C. (1990). *Out of reach: Why everyday people can't find affordable housing.* Washington, DC: Low Income Housing Information Service.

Ferguson, R. F., & Dickens, W. T. (1999). Introduction. In R. F. Ferguson & W. T. Dickens (Eds.), *Urban problems and community development* (pp. 1–31). Washington, DC: Brookings Institution.

Ferguson, R. F., & Stoutland, S. E. (1999). Reconceiving the community development field. In R. F. Ferguson & W. T. Dickens (Eds.), *Urban problems and community development* (pp. 33–75). Washington, DC: Brookings Institution.

Foote, C. L., Gerardi, K., Goette, L., & Willen, P. S. (2008). *Subprime facts: What (we think) we know about the subprime crisis and what we don't* (Public Policy Discussion Papers No. 08–2). Boston: Federal Reserve Bank of Boston.

Gramlich, E. (1991). *Comprehensive housing affordability strategies: A citizen's action guide.* Washington, DC: Center for Community Change.

Pennington-Cross, A., & Ho, G. (2008). Predatory lending laws and the cost of credit. *Real Estate Economics, 36,* 175–211.

U.S. Department of Housing and Urban Development. (2008). *Unequal burden: Income and racial disparities in subprime lending in America.* Washington, DC: U.S. Department of Housing and Urban Development Office of Policy Development and Research. Retrieved February 4, 2010, from http://www.huduser.org/portal/publications/fairhsg/unequal.html

Vidal, A. (1992). *Rebuilding communities: A national study of urban community development corporations.* New York: New School for Social Research, Community Development Research Center, Graduate School of Management and Urban Policy.

Zukin, S. (2010). *Naked city: The death and life of authentic urban places.* New York: Oxford University Press.

Websites

American Housing Survey—http://www.huduser.org/portal/datasets/ahs.html. A good source of data on housing conditions in several cities and regions.

American Planning Association—www.planning.org/. This site offers a variety of information about the association. It has a large publications list that is very useful for all kinds of planning-related issues. Another useful site is that of the association's Planning Advisory Service (PAS), whose reports can be accessed at www.planning.org/pas/passtuff3.htm.

Co-Housing Network—www.cohousing.org. This coalition promotes cohousing and helps people start cohousing communities.

Enterprise Foundation—www.enterprisefoundation.org. The Enterprise Foundation was started in 1982 by James Rouse, a real estate developer known for, among other projects, the development of Inner Harbor in Baltimore. The organization's purpose is to bring lasting improvements to distressed communities. It is a national, nonprofit housing and community development organization.

Fannie Mae Foundation—www.fanniemaefoundation.org. The mission of this foundation is to transform communities through innovative partnerships and initiatives that revitalize neighborhoods and create affordable home ownership and housing opportunities across America.

Farmworkers and Colonia Communities—www.hud.gov/groups/colonias.cfm. This section of the HUD home page contains listings and links to a wide variety of resources for individuals and organizations interested in farmworker housing.

Green Globe Certification—http://www.greenglobecertification.com/. Alternative certification process for green building.

Home Mortgage Disclosure Act (HMDA) Data—http://www.ffiec.gov/hmda. The Home Mortgage Disclosure Act (HMDA), enacted by Congress in 1975 and implemented by the Federal Reserve Board's Regulation C, requires lending institutions to report public loan data. In this section of the website, you can find out more about the regulation and its interpretation.

Housing Assistance Council—www.ruralhome.org. The Housing Assistance Council is a national nonprofit corporation created in 1971 to increase the availability of decent housing for rural, low-income people.

iGreenBuild—http://www.igreenbuild.com/. Provides articles, videos, and commentary about green building delivered to you from experts in LEED certification, sustainable design, renewable energy, green building materials, and hundreds of other environmentally friendly design and construction-related categories.

Internet Resources for the Built Environment—www.cyburbia.org. This site has a directory with more than 7,500 links. There is a planning resource directory, which has a list of housing-related sites. Also, an architectural resource directory focuses on buildings, construction, historic preservation, and green architecture.

Local Initiatives Support Corporation—www.lisc.org. This national intermediary was started with a $10 million grant from the Ford Foundation and six *Fortune* 500 companies for the renovation of 100 neighborhoods. The purpose of LISC is to assist CDCs that are committed to comprehensive residential and commercial development. LISC helps CDCs redevelop neighborhoods and communities in urban and rural settings.

The National Housing Conference (NHC)—www.nhc.org. This organization is a diverse coalition of housing leaders from the public and private sectors. Since 1931, the NHC has worked to forge consensus and develop innovative approaches to meet our nation's housing needs.

National Housing Institute (NHI)—www.nhi.org. This nonprofit organization focuses on affordable housing in a community context. NHI publishes *Shelterforce,* which is available by subscription either online or in hard copy. NHI searches for innovative strategies, unique partnerships, and effective ways to organize low-income communities.

National Low Income Housing Coalition—www.nlihc.org. This organization was established in 1974 and is dedicated to ending America's affordable housing crisis. The NLIHC is committed to educating, organizing, and advocating to ensure decent, affordable housing within healthy neighborhoods for everyone. The website provides information on housing affordability across most areas of the United States.

Neighborhood Reinvestment Corporation—www.nw.org/network/home.asp. The Neighborhood Reinvestment Corporation, a national nonprofit, was created in 1978 by the Neighborhood Reinvestment Act (Public Law 95–557) to revitalize communities. It is a national intermediary and supports local CBOs.

The Neighborhood Reinvestment Training Institute—www.nw.org/. This organization provides train-
    ing to CDCs and other CBOs that are committed to community development—in particular,
    affordable housing, neighborhood economic development, and the quality of community life.
NeighborWorks America—http://www.nw.org/network/home.asp. This national nonprofit organi-
    zation works on issues related to affordable housing. It has developed partnerships with more
    than 230 community-based organizations to provide training, education, and resources on
    affordable housing issues.
Racial Residential Segregation—http://enceladus.isr.umich.edu/race/racestart.asp. A good source of
    data and research on racial residential segregation at the University of Michigan.
U.S. Environmental Protection Agency—http://www.epa.gov/greenbuilding/pubs/about.htm. A good
    resource on green building.
U.S. Department of Housing and Urban Development—www.hud.gov. This site lists all of the avail-
    able programs from HUD. It also has information on mortgages, best practices, and so forth.
    Another site of interest is HUD User (www.huduser.org), which is the primary source for fed-
    eral government reports and information on housing policy and programs, building technology,
    economic development, urban planning, and more.
U.S. Green Business Council—http://www.usgbc.org/

Videos

Homes and Hands: Community Land Trusts in Action (1998), produced by Women's Educational
    Media, directed by Helen S. Cohen and Debra Chasnoff. This video features the stories of CLTs
    in Durham, North Carolina; Albuquerque, New Mexico; and Burlington, Vermont. Available
    from the Institute for Community Economics, 57 School Street, Springfield, MA 01105–1331;
    phone: (413) 746–8660.
Regulations and Affordable Housing (1990), produced by the American Planning Association. This
    training video focuses on innovative regulations and local trust funds. Available from the
    American Planning Association, 122 S. Michigan Ave., Ste. 1600, Chicago, IL 60603; phone:
    (312) 786–6344.

9

Financial Capital

Poor and minority communities generally lack access to financial capital. Why are they disadvantaged in credit markets? Is it a problem of collateral or the credit history of the residents in the community? Or is it a result of the discriminatory practices of lending institutions in the area? What can community-based organizations (CBOs) do to address these problems?

BOX 9.1 FINANCIAL CAPITAL FACTS

- The homeownership rate in 2001 was 74.3% for non-Hispanic Whites, 48.4% for non-Hispanic Blacks, and 47.3% for Hispanics.
- In 2000, Black applicants for mortgages were twice as likely as White applicants to be rejected for a loan.
- In 2000, Hispanic applicants for mortgages were more than 40% more likely than White applicants to be rejected for a loan.

SOURCE: Ross and Yinger (2002).

In this chapter, we examine why credit markets do not respond the needs of poor and minority communities. Many poor and minority communities are creating alternative credit institutions (e.g., community development credit unions, community development banks, revolving loan funds, and microenterprise loan funds) to address their credit needs. We evaluate whether these community development credit institutions are able to overcome the obstacles that businesses and individuals face in these communities. We also assess how these local institutions can be strengthened.

One of the basic assumptions of the asset-based development approach outlined in this book is that there are existing resources in most communities that are underused. This is especially the case when we look at the availability of financial capital. In even some of the poorest communities, family savings are deposited in institutions that invest the capital outside the area.

The savings are never used to help promote development in the community. These assets need to be mobilized to serve local needs. One of the problems is that the returns on these investments are often higher when invested outside rather than inside the community. The alternative community credit institutions examined here seek to reinvest these resources in the community to promote development. They are still driven by profits, but with the constraint that the capital be invested at the source. In other words, they attempt to create a balance between economic and social objectives of investing.

Like the other community assets discussed in this book, there is a strong relationship between financial capital and other forms of capital. Much of the focus on physical capital has been on developing financial mechanisms to provide affordable housing. Human capital strategies focusing on self-employment often emphasize the importance of debt and equity capital to help new businesses start and grow. Strategies for building environmental capital also rely heavily on developing pools of capital to purchase land. Finally, social capital is often intimately tied to access to financial capital in many communities. In many ways, financial capital is the lifeblood of communities.

Financial Capital Issues

Communities face a variety of issues related to credit. Most of these issues are concerned with the demand for and supply of financial capital and the institutions involved in the credit market. Among the most important issues are the following:

1. Do consumers and firms have an adequate supply of credit in the community? Is the cost of credit an obstacle for consumers and firms? If there is a problem, is long-term or short-term credit the problem?

2. What types of credit are being demanded by consumers and firms? What have been the experiences of consumers and firms in trying to obtain credit in the community?

3. What is the structure of credit institutions in the community? How much competition is there among lenders? What is the history of branch openings and closings in the community?

4. How well are local credit institutions meeting the needs of local residents? What portion of the assets of credit institutions are invested locally?

5. How well do credit institutions that serve a community market their services and products? How aware are residents of the available credit services and products?

6. Are minorities, women, or small businesses discriminated against in the local credit market?

————————————————————————— **Key Concepts and Debates**

Economic theory suggests that markets are the most efficient means of allocating credit. There are several reasons that capital markets may not operate efficiently and may deny credit to low-income and minority individuals, to small businesses, and to residents in poor neighborhoods who are deserving of credit. The following reasons are among the most important:

1. *Incomplete information.* Lenders have imperfect or incomplete information about loan applicants. They have a difficult time evaluating the risk involved in making loans. If lenders rely on the willingness to pay interest charges as an indicator of risk, they may make loans that are too risky. If they use collateral as their primary indicator, they may not be taking enough risk. Instead, lenders often use indicators such as the neighborhood one lives in or a business's location as a means of assessing the risk of a loan. This strategy typically works against minorities and low-income individuals as well as people who live in poor neighborhoods.

2. *Transaction costs.* One reason borrowers may be disadvantaged in credit markets is because of the transaction costs involved. Transaction costs are the costs associated with reviewing and structuring an investment or loan. The administrative costs of making large loans are about the same as making small ones. Banks also make more profit off large residential and commercial loans than they do off smaller ones. The result is that banks may prefer to make loans to wealthier applicants than to small businesses or poor applicants.

3. *Regulation.* Banking regulations may affect the ability of lending institutions to take risks. Regulators may encourage lenders to rely more heavily on collateral as a determinant in the loan process, which may work against low-income and minority loan applicants. Conversely, regulators may attempt to create more competition in local capital markets, which might improve access to credit in poor and minority neighborhoods.

4. *Bias/discrimination.* Studies continue to show that some lenders discriminate against minorities and minority communities. There are two different types of studies that demonstrate this finding. Some studies were based on audits of bank loan applications of White and Black applicants with similar credit histories. The studies found that Whites are more likely than Blacks to receive loans. Second, statistical studies using data from the Federal Reserve have shown that Whites are more likely than Blacks to receive loans. Critics of these statistical studies, however, point out that they do not consider the credit history or success rates of applicants.

5. *Competition.* Finally, credit markets may not work properly in some communities because of the lack of competition. Communities with only a few lenders may not face enough competitive pressure to efficiently allocate credit. This issue may be especially important for rural communities that are relatively isolated and may only have one or two banks.

When we discuss community credit needs for poor and minority communities, it is important to distinguish between equity and debt capital. **Equity capital** is a direct and permanent investment, such as cash or other assets (e.g., land, buildings), in a project. As a result of the investment, the investor can claim a portion of the earnings after the project pays its debts. Equity capital is usually the long-term operating funds for a business. **Debt capital** is the short-term credit. Normally, credit institutions tend to specialize in providing either equity or debt capital, not both. Another type of capital that is somewhat related to equity capital is venture capital. **Venture capital** is usually an investment in a high-risk enterprise in the form of equity. The investment is often associated with a new product or service, and the investor takes a risk to receive a high return on this new market.

There are several approaches to dealing with market imperfections in credit markets, most involving some mix of government regulations and market-driven programs. The first approach, a pure market approach to solving the credit problems of poor and minority neighborhoods, focuses on removing the obstacles to the flow of capital into and out of these communities, such as the lack of competition among financial institutions or regulatory constraints that make it difficult to take risks on the investments in these communities. The assumption is that the market will correct the uneven investment of capital when poor neighborhoods become attractive for capital investment. One of the major factors affecting the flow of capital across neighborhoods is the cost and availability of land. As land becomes more costly in other areas of cities, poor neighborhoods become more attractive for investment. The gentrification process, however, may not benefit the local residents who wish to remain in the neighborhood. Gentrification can lead to higher tax rates because of the increasing demand for services and may ultimately push out residents who live on a fixed income.

The second approach is to use regulations to influence the allocation and pricing of credit. One example is the **Community Reinvestment Act of 1978 (CRA)**. During the 1970s, banks and thrift institutions were charged with redlining in allocating credit. **Redlining** is arbitrary geographic discrimination in the granting of credit. Redlining was seen as contributing to the economic decline of many minority neighborhoods. In response to such charges, Congress passed the CRA to encourage financial institutions to meet the credit needs of local communities. Banks are evaluated on their lending practices. For example, regulators will examine whether the banks are providing services and making loans to residents in all neighborhoods of their market. Regulators also look at the extent to which banks contribute to community development. The CRA rating may influence the willingness of the regulators to permit the bank to merge with other banks or establish new branches.

Another example of a regulatory approach is to provide private institutions with incentives for investing in minority and low-income communities. Some states have developed linked deposit programs that provide banks with deposits from state government if the banks are meeting certain criteria for lending in desirable areas. Another example is to provide loan guarantees to businesses and individuals in communities that have been identified as being underserved with respect to credit.

A third approach to improving the access to credit in minority and poor communities is to assist in the development of community credit institutions that focus on development in a geographic area. Examples of these types of institutions are community development credit unions (CDCUs), revolving loan funds (RLFs), community development loan funds, and microenterprise loan funds. These institutions allocate credit differently from private lenders for several reasons. First, because they are more actively tied to CBOs, they have more complete information on the risk of loan applicants, which may increase the level of lending in these areas. Second, although these institutions are interested in profit making, they also have social objectives. Most of these institutions only make loans to applicants in a geographic area or to individuals who may have less access to credit, such as low-income women, in the case of some microenterprise loans, or small businesses, in the case of revolving loan funds. Although market and regulatory approaches to addressing the credit needs of poor and minority communities may have some impact on the flow of capital, community-based credit institutions offer the most promise because they consider community at the heart of the investment decision.

Community Credit Institutions

There are several examples of community development loan funds. In this section, we focus on the most popular ones: CDCUs, community development loan funds, microenterprise loan funds, and RLFs. We discuss the distinguishing characteristics of these institutions, provide some examples, and evaluate their performance in poor and minority communities.

CDCUs are credit unions that have a geographic or associational bond in areas where most members have low incomes. There are approximately 400 CDCUs in the United States, ranging in size from $25,000 to $30 million in assets. Many CDCUs are organized by neighborhood residents to address credit needs that are not being met by commercial lending institutions. The organizational structure of a CDCU is essentially the same as any other credit union—a nonprofit cooperative governed by its member-elected board of directors. A cooperative form of organization is owned and controlled by the people who use the services (see Case Study 9.1).

CASE STUDY 9.1 CDCUs: LOWER EAST SIDE PEOPLE'S FEDERAL CREDIT UNION

This credit union was established in response to a branch bank closing in the Lower East Side of New York City. The neighborhood used the CRA to challenge the Manufacturers Hanover Trust Company's decision to close the branch and received the vacated building for 3 years, rent free, plus a $100,000 deposit in the credit union.

One of the persistent criticisms of credit unions has been that they operate like commercial banks and have less interest in social objectives than they did in the past. CDCUs are more immune to this criticism than are other types of credit unions because CDCUs limit their investments to the community or neighborhood they serve. Probably the main limitation of these organizations is that there are so few of them.

Community development loan funds are privately owned, nonprofit organizations that make loans to assist low- and moderate-income people, women, and minorities in obtaining housing and jobs. These institutions serve as financial intermediaries that accept loans from socially motivated investors and reinvest in CBOs and projects. These funds often support nontraditional investments, such as land trusts, cooperative housing developments, and others. As a result, many of the loans carry a higher risk than is acceptable to most commercial banks (see Case Study 9.2).

CASE STUDY 9.2 COMMUNITY DEVELOPMENT BANKS: THE NEW HAMPSHIRE COMMUNITY LOAN FUND (NHCLF) AND THE BOSTON COMMUNITY LOAN FUND (BCLF)

The NHCLF has been operating since 1983. NHCLF takes investments from socially oriented investors and church groups and makes loans to CBOs, such as tenant groups, community land trusts, housing cooperatives, and community development corporations. The average loan ranges from $40,000 to $100,000. The BCLF was established in 1985 by a coalition of religious institutions and community leaders. BCLF focuses on developing and preserving housing for low-income people in Boston. It also provides technical assistance to groups, so they can become qualified developers and borrowers.

Community development loan funds are proliferating across the country (Parzen & Kieschnick, 1992). Some of these loan funds are limited to cities or neighborhoods, such as the Boston Community Loan Fund; and some make loans available at the state level, such as the New Hampshire Community Loan Fund. Probably the most well-known community development loan fund in the United States is the South Shore Bank in Chicago (Taub, 1988). This bank has served as a model for many of the loan funds developed in the past couple of decades.

The Clinton administration had plans to fund several hundred community development loan funds, but it never received much political support for the project. Although there are some very successful cases of community development loan funds, they are scattered around the nation and only a few communities have them.

Microenterprise loan funds are not-for-profit corporations that make very small, short-term loans for debt capital to microenterprises. The primary purpose of microenterprise loan funds is to provide opportunities to the poor and underemployed by developing business skills and establishing small businesses that require small amounts of capital to operate.

CASE STUDY 9.3 ASSET BUILDING IN NATIVE COMMUNITIES

The Four Bands Community Fund is a 501(c)(3) nonprofit corporation serving the residents of the Cheyenne River Reservation in rural western South Dakota. The fund was established in 2000 to provide business loans, training, and consulting to residents of the reservation. Clients are required to obtain training and consulting as a condition for their loan. In addition, they have begun entrepreneurship programs for youth. In the first 8 years of operation, Four Bands provided training programs to 1,531 clients, contributed more than $75,000 in savings match for the Individual Development Account (IDA) program, and approved over 120 loans for a total of $669,000. The program generated almost 200 jobs on the reservation.

SOURCE: DeWees and Sarkozy-Banoczy (2010).

Several U.S. funds were adapted from the Bangladeshi Grameen Bank, which creates small groups to provide loans. The Grameen Bank has made loans to more than 700,000 of the poorest women in Bangladesh. The average loan is $67. The repayment rate is 98%, and the average interest rate is 16%. The bank uses a personal sense of obligation as a tool to encourage loan repayment, relying explicitly on peer pressure. Potential borrowers join small groups, which make credit available to any member of the group, contingent on repayment of loans by every member. The peer group concept appears to work best when the groups range from five to eight members. The Grameen Bank has had a 2% loan loss rate, which is much lower than the loss rate for most commercial banks, which is 3% to 4%. Most of the U.S. programs that have used this model, however, may have loan losses as high as 10% in the early years, but most get down to 2% to 5% within 5 to 10 years.

Some of the U.S. microenterprise loan funds rely on the Grameen principles and some do not. Examples of microenterprise funds in the United States are the Lakota Fund, Women's Venture, and the Good Faith Fund. See Case Study 9.3 for a description. Most of these programs limit the size of a loan to $25,000 and serve a limited population.

Microenterprise loan funds face several obstacles. First, because the businesses participating in these programs are so small, most start out in their homes.

Many municipalities prohibit home work. Adding expenditures for rent and other associated costs may be too much of an obstacle for microenterprises.

Second, licensing requirements may be prohibitive for many microenterprises. In some urban areas, the costs of licenses would be equivalent to the maximum size of loans permitted under the loan fund.

Third, because many of the microenterprise loan funds focus on helping individuals make the transition from welfare to work, there are often bureaucratic obstacles that borrowers face. In some cases, individuals may run the risk of losing their public aid if their business begins to show a profit. There needs to be a transition period where profits from the business are not counted against any support that borrowers may be receiving from public aid.

Finally, most microenterprise loan funds are simply not large enough to become self-sustaining. Because of the administrative costs and the turnover in credit, a loan fund must be fairly large to support itself. Assuming that the loan fund charges an average interest rate of 16% and sets aside reserves for a 7% loss rate, the break-even point would be an $8 million loan fund, which is much larger than most microenterprise loan funds. Using a microenterprise loan fund in an area where the population is large usually means that the fund will face some serious obstacles. In most cases, the loan funds are actually subsidized by foundations or government sources.

Most of the early microenterprise loan funds were started in developing countries. These experiences produced several important lessons about what makes these loan funds work properly. The evidence suggests that they should be demand driven, which means that providing loan funds to a business for which there is no market is not going to work. Also, most of these businesses will never graduate to commercial banks, so the loan programs need to be flexible enough to meet the needs of these businesses as they change and grow.

RLFs are designed to provide financing of housing and business development, frequently using loan terms that are not available through conventional lenders. As the loans are repaid, the money returns to the fund to be loaned out again. Many RLFs are funded by government programs. Community Development Block Grants (CDBGs) are a major source of funding for RLFs throughout the United States. Generally, RLFs do not make as many small and high-risk loans as other types of programs, such as microenterprise loan funds. A recent study by the Corporation for Enterprise Development (CFED) found that, among the RLFs they studied, a median of 276 jobs per fund had been created (Levere, Clones, & Marcoux, 1997).

CASE STUDY 9.4 REVOLVING LOAN FUNDS

Thief River Falls, Minnesota

In the late 1980s, when Land O'Lakes announced that it was closing its turkey processing plant, which affected not only workers at the plant but also 32 area turkey growers who faced the loss of their market, the community began seeking other options. The city established an RLF to help start Northern Pride, Inc., a grower-owned cooperative that purchased the processing facility outright and ran it as a for-profit corporation. Much of the grant came from the Economic Development Administration as well as other sources.

Glacier Garden Rainforest Adventures

The Juneau Economic Development Council made a $300,000 loan to construct a greenhouse and provide site preparation for landscaping and construction of cart pathways. The facility gives tourists and local residents an opportunity to observe the rainforest environment with a tour guide/naturalist who is familiar with the flora and fauna of the area. Private financing matched the RLF dollars 2 to 1. The new businesses created 4 full-time and 23 part-time jobs.

There are numerous examples across the country of successful RLFs. Two interesting examples are the fund established by Thief River Falls, Minnesota, which has focused on new industry to replace jobs that have been lost, and the Glacier Garden Rainforest Adventures in Juneau, Alaska (see Case Study 9.4). Among the various community development credit institutions examined here, RLFs have probably proven to be the most successful and widely adapted throughout the United States. Part of their success is due to the funding base for these loan funds and the ease at which they can be replicated.

———————— Context for Community Credit Institutions

One of the major reasons for the growing interest in local credit markets has been the **deregulation** of the banking industry during the past 20 years. The merits of banking deregulation have been widely debated. Proponents contend that deregulation has improved efficiency and competition in banking markets and has placed banks on a level playing field with nonfinancial institutions that have entered banking markets. As a result, banks are able to provide a wider variety of services and charge less for services and credit.

Critics of deregulation claim that banking deregulation has increased the concentration of financial resources, ultimately leading to higher costs for banking services and credit. In addition, banking deregulation is alleged to have an especially deleterious effect on poor and minority communities because lending institutions can more easily shift credit to growing areas. As local banks have merged with larger banks, there has been a net flow of capital out of poor communities because the banks now can get a higher return on their capital by investing outside these communities.

Banking deregulation has focused on three issues: interest charges, geographic restrictions, and the types of services offered by financial institutions. Prior to 1980, Regulation Q placed a ceiling on the interest rates commercial banks could pay on deposits. Regulation Q was removed because of increased competition for capital from funds from newly developed alternative investment instruments (e.g., money market funds). With the elimination of Regulation Q, commercial banks are allowed to compete for deposits. This provides savers the opportunity to earn more but increases borrowers' interest rates. One of the unintended consequences of this act, however, was that lending institutions began competing more through prices, and some took more risk in their investments to cover the additional costs.

The second element of banking deregulation has concerned geographic limitations on the activities of lending institutions. Prior to the mid-1980s, banks were not permitted to cross state lines. The spark for merger mania was the Supreme Court's decision in 1985 that interstate banking was constitutional. Today, we have effectively created interstate banking across the country.

Finally, prior to the 1980s, nonfinancial institutions were immune from banking regulations because they were not considered banks by the regulators. Commercial banks are defined as institutions that take deposits and make loans; if a firm only meets one of these criteria, it is not considered to be a commercial bank. In the 1980s, firms such as Sears and Merrill Lynch began entering the financial arena by making loans. Financial institutions asked regulators for permission to become more involved in activities not related to finance, such as real estate, insurance, and securities. Thus, the wall that had divided nonfinancial and financial institutions since the Depression was eliminated. This wall had reduced the risk in the financial sector, which had been a major factor in the Depression of the 1930s.

Ironically, the deregulation of the 1980s, which was perceived to be so threatening to low-income and minority neighborhoods, actually turned out to be an important resource for CBOs to pressure banks to lend more in their area. The federal agencies that must approve the bank mergers require that the lending institutions demonstrate that they are meeting the credit needs of the communities they serve. CBOs have used this provision to challenge the practices of lending institutions, and as a result the lending institutions have made available relatively large amounts of credit for community development purposes.

Another piece of legislation that influenced the field of community development banking in the 1990s was the Community Development Banking and Financial Institutions Act of 1994 (the CDFI Act). The purpose of the act was to create a fund for community development financial institutions (CDFIs). The fund assists CDFIs through equity investments, capital grants, loans, and technical assistance. The support can be used for a wide variety of community development activities, including housing for low-income people, businesses owned by low-income people, financial services, commercial facilities promoting job creation or retention, and technical assistance.

The CDFI fund was originally set up as an independent agency but was eventually placed in the U.S. Treasury Department. In its first three rounds, the CDFI awarded more than $119 million to 122 awardees; $58 million to 172 banks, thrifts, and CDFIs for lending in low-income communities under the Bank Enterprise Award program; and $3 million to 70 organizations in the Technical Assistance Component funding.

To be eligible for a CDFI fund award, an organization must meet six criteria:

1. Its primary mission must be community development.

2. It must serve an investment area or targeted population.

3. It must provide development services and equity investments or loans.

4. It must maintain accountability to residents of its investment area or targeted population.

5. It cannot be a public agency or institution.

6. It must be primarily a financing entity.

The issue of banking regulation became a particularly important issue in the financial crisis of 2007–2008. Several major financial institutions had to receive bailouts from the federal government in order to stay in business. The primary problem was that many of these institutions were pulled down by the subprime mortgage crisis (discussed in a previous chapter). Many financial institutions participated in secondary markets without full understanding of the loans that were being sold in these markets. Many of these loans would lead to foreclosures and the banks held the notes. In addition, banks had been permitted to engage in activities not directly related to finance as a result of deregulation. The previous restrictions on banks had limited bank activity in fairly risky investments. The end result was that the credit markets dried up. Businesses and consumers had a very difficult time obtaining access to credit. Most community development financial institutions were in better shape because they were not directly affected by these activities. But because many of them relied on these larger institutions to gain access to capital, they were also affected by the crisis.

Key Actors and Institutions

Several federal agencies are responsible for regulating lending institutions in the United States: the Comptroller of the Currency, the Board of Governors of the Federal Reserve System, the Federal Deposit Insurance Corporation, and the Office of Thrift Supervision. The reason there are so many agencies involved in the regulation of lending institutions is that they all have some impact on capital markets in the United States. The primary arena in which these agencies affect CBOs is through the CRA. Several states have become much more active in this arena and have developed policies beyond the federal CRA.

Some states are engaged in efforts to improve the social responsibility of commercial banks. A few states have enacted reinvestment laws that establish a quid pro quo policy. For example, in New York, banking powers are linked to CRA activity; with a better rating, banks are allowed to invest a larger portion of their assets in real estate. In Massachusetts, CRA ratings are tied to eligibility to receive deposits of state funds. In Maine, financial institutions acquiring in-state banks are required to demonstrate that the transaction will lead to a net increase in funds to the state and will benefit the communities being affected.

Other states have developed new institutions to provide credit to underdeveloped sectors and regions and to small businesses and minority groups. State programs range from seed capital and venture capital programs to small business and home mortgage loan programs. A central concept behind many of these financial institutions is the pooling of risk. Capital access programs and business industrial development corporations are two examples of innovative institutions designed to fill the credit gap of poor communities.

One mechanism for directing capital to borrowers who have difficulty obtaining loans from commercial banks and venture capitalists is a **Business Industrial Development Corporation (BIDCO)**. BIDCOs use an approach referred to as a risk return initiative. Developed in the early 1970s, BIDCOs are structured to meet the financial needs of small businesses that fall into this credit gap. They use two different means of channeling credit to businesses. First, BIDCOs can make Small Business Administration (SBA) loans and sell the guaranteed portion on the secondary markets. By selling these loans, it is possible to leverage capital up to 10 to 1. Second, BIDCOs can borrow from private sources and make non-SBA loans.

Another example of a state credit institution is a Capital Access Program (CAP). CAPs are based on a different principle than are traditional types of insurance or guarantee programs. CAPs are based on a portfolio or pooling concept. An example of this program is the Loan Loss Reserve Program developed by the Michigan Strategic Fund. Under this program, a special reserve is established for banks participating in the program to cover loan losses. The reserve is established through matched payments made by the borrower and the bank.

In addition to these state and federal agencies, numerous intermediary organizations have emerged to help neighborhoods and communities with their credit problems. One of the premiere organizations in the country is the Woodstock Institute in Chicago. This organization has worked for years with Home Mortgage Disclosure data to design CRA programs and initiatives.

Other national organizations are more specialized. For example, the National Association of Development Organizations (NADO) provides a training program for revolving loan managers. The Association of Community Organizations for Reform Now (ACORN) is a coalition of low- and moderate-income people with members in 26 states. The organization has worked to eliminate redlining practices in many cities. The National Association of Community Development Loan Funds serves as a resource center and an advocate for issues related to community development loan funds.

Many other communities are developing informal support networks for entrepreneurship and economic development. Entrepreneurial clubs provide entrepreneurs with information on funding and other issues that they face as they attempt to grow their businesses. Club meetings provide an environment where entrepreneurs can safely share their ideas and problems and meet other entrepreneurs who are facing some of the same obstacles.

Community Economic Development Finance

In addition to CDFIs, many other financial mechanisms can be used to promote community development. In this section, we briefly describe some of the most commonly used financial tools. Many of the more traditional incentives are direct loans or loan guarantees to developers or businesses. Other common tools include property tax abatements, land subsidies, and investment tax credits.

One of the most popular tools is tax incremental financing (TIF). This tool is used most often to promote development or redevelopment in an area that is not likely to attract investment. Paetsch and Dahlstrom (1990) defined a TIF as "a technique used to disperse the costs of development to those government agencies that will benefit from the increased tax base that a TIF project will generate" (p. 83). In most cases, a TIF area is defined and the taxes on the property are frozen in that area for the life of the project. The revenue generated from the development is channeled to the appropriate taxing authority. Most often, property owners make payments for the amount of taxes abated to a fund that reimburses the developer for approved project costs. The specifics of TIF programs differ significantly across states.

TIFs have frequently been criticized. They can be very complex to use and require some professional expertise to negotiate deals with developers. The TIF process can be time-consuming, and many developers are unwilling to stay with the process. They are often used for development projects in areas that are not truly blighted.

The tax-exempt industrial development bonds (IDBs) is another controversial financial tool used by many communities today. State and local governments often use tax-exempt bonds to finance schools, roads, and other infrastructure needs. During the past 30 years, however, states and localities have used tax-exempt bonds to finance private development projects. Throughout the 1980s, the federal government attempted to restrict the use of the bonds, but localities used them increasingly to compete for business development projects.

There has been a great deal of criticism of these financial tools in recent years. One of the chief concerns is whether the subsidy provided by states and localities is actually necessary for business development. Would businesses have located or expanded in the community without the subsidy? Some research suggests that these incentives play a minor role compared to proximity to markets, the quality of the workforce, and access to business services. A second concern is that these subsidies may ultimately have a limited effect on the poor and unemployed in the community. Finally, the growing competition among states and localities for economic development may raise the levels of subsidies beyond the benefits they ultimately receive from the development.

Predatory Lending

Many communities struggle with issues related to predatory lending. The concept of **predatory lending** lacks a precision definition (Goldstein, 1999; Temkin, 2000). There is probably some overlap between predatory lending and subprime loans. It is probably best to consider predatory lending as a category of subprime lending. Most analysts suggest the definition should include at least the following characteristics: (1) high interest rates, (2) abusive conditions on borrowing (e.g., prepayment penalty, balloon payments, and additional fees and charges), (3) fraudulent behavior (e.g., failure to fully explain the terms of the loan), and (4) the loans are targeted to homeowners on the basis of specific characteristics (e.g., race, ethnicity, age).

There are several difficulties in developing policies to address predatory lending. Many predatory lending practices may fall into a grey area. Lenders may rationalize the high interest rates they charge because of the credit history of applicants. There is not much evidence that the rates many lenders charge can be justified by the creditworthiness of applicants. Many borrowers may not be experienced enough to raise questions about all of the loan terms. In addition, there are very little data on interest rate charges, creditworthiness of applicants, and the specific terms of loans.

The lack of data on predatory lending presents obstacles to addressing the problem. Mortgage foreclosures have tended to be concentrated in some of the poorest neighborhoods with large concentrations of minority households. Many of the lenders do not have to report their practices through the Home Mortgage Disclosure Act because they are not legally defined as banks (collecting deposits *and* making loans). One of the key issues is whether various neighborhoods are being targeted by predatory lenders. Another issue is that predatory lending needs to be viewed in its entirety. Additional information is required about the creditworthiness and credit history of borrowers to completely understand the nature of the loan.

Individual Development Accounts

An increasingly important tool to develop wealth in poor neighborhoods is the **Individual Development Account (IDA)**. General asset-building strategies have been around for more than 60 years, but the IDA programs can be traced to the late 1980s. In the early 1990s, there were several pieces of legislation that laid the ground for the growth of IDAs. For example, the Family Self-Sufficiency Act of 1990 permitted residents in public subsidized housing to accumulate assets while maintaining their eligibility for housing. Similarly, in the welfare reform act of 1996, Congress decided not to count savings from IDAs as part of the asset limits for eligibility for welfare. In 1998, Congress provided $125 million for IDA demonstration projects. Iowa was the first state to pass an IDA program as part of its welfare reform legislation. Many other states have since followed with similar programs.

There are several sources of funding for IDAs, including the federal government, financial institutions, and private foundations. The central idea of this tool is to provide matched savings accounts for low-income individuals. These funds can only be used for the purchase of assets, such as homes, education/training, or to start a new business. Account holders are usually required to attend some financial education classes or programs in order to be eligible. Typically, IDA funds are limited to a few thousand dollars, but the match can be as much as $4 to $5 for every dollar saved from earnings. Evaluation studies suggest that IDA programs have a powerful influence on the ability of low-income residents to save and build assets (Boshara, 2005; Mills, Patterson, Orr, & DeMarco, 2004).

One of the limitations of IDAs is that they may not be consistent with other community development objectives. Many of the programs encourage homeownership, but they do not limit where one purchases the home. So, in many cases, community development corporations using this tool may actually be encouraging residents to move out of their neighborhood as they purchase a home elsewhere. Generally, IDAs are not able to influence the larger housing market that may be affecting the ability of residents to purchase a home. This may be especially important in gentrifying markets where housing values may be increasing faster than savings rates.

Assessing Local Credit Markets

There are two basic components to any assessment of credit markets: the supply of and the demand for credit in the community. In addition, any analysis must begin by identifying the market area for credit institutions. One way of identifying the market is to use CRA statements to identify the service area of local lending institutions. This area should be about the same for most services.

There are many data sources on capital markets, and one of the most widely used is the data provided through the Home Mortgage Disclosure Act (HMDA). Financial institutions are not required to disclose much about their lending practices. HMDA requires that banks and thrifts with more than $10 million in deposits in Metropolitan Statistical Areas (MSAs) report (1) the annual number and volume of residential loans, (2) the volume and amount of mortgage loans by census tract and zip code in MSAs, and (3) the aggregate number and volume of mortgage loans outside the MSA. The HMDA was recently amended by the Financial Institutions Reform, Recovery, and Enforcement Act (FIRREA) to expand disclosure requirements. FIRREA requires lenders to disclose the race, sex, and income of loan applicants and recipients. HMDA data are of little value to rural communities because information on capital flows outside MSAs is not provided by lending institutions.

The CRA also requires lenders to provide information on their activities. Four agencies regulate lending institutions: the Comptroller of the Currency, the Board of Governors of the Federal Reserve, the Federal Deposit Insurance Corporation, and the Office of Thrift Supervision. These regulators require the following items in a CRA statement:

1. A delineation on a map of each community served by the institution. The overriding concern is that the banks are not arbitrarily excluding certain neighborhoods from their area.

2. A list of the specific types of credit that the institution is prepared to offer in each community.

3. A copy of the CRA notice indicating where to get copies of the statement, written comments, and the institution's lending performance.

4. Information on efforts to assess and to help meet the credit needs of the community.

The regulators consider a number of additional pieces of information in their evaluation of lending institutions. Examiners consider the institution's attempts to assess credit needs, the marketing of credit services, the geographic distribution and record of opening and closing offices, discrimination and other illegal credit practices, and participation in community development and redevelopment projects/programs.

The CRA, along with HMDA, was designed to address the problems of redlining neighborhoods based on race or economic class. National organizations concerned with redlining, such as the National Center for Policy Alternatives, the Center for Community Change, and the Woodstock Institute, have recognized that the CRA taps only a small segment of the financial industry, and they have argued that nonregulated institutions should also be monitored. These organizations contend a broader approach to monitoring is needed.

Several other data sources on lending institutions may be useful. Several guides provide basic information on the practices of lending institutions. One of the problems with using secondary data sources to analyze the performance and behavior of lending institutions is that the data are reported by bank and not by branch. This means that if there are only branch banks in a neighborhood or community, examining the lending patterns of those institutions is impossible. HMDA requires banks to report lending by census tract, but it does not require this of all banks, and this information is not available from other types of lenders. Obviously, an alternative is to collect your own information on lending patterns, but this can be very costly and time-consuming for community organizations.

Strategies for Building Local Credit Markets

Communities may adopt several strategies for building their local credit markets. In this section, we identify some of the most common strategies.

Build CDFIs

CBOs can play an important role in helping to build community credit institutions. Most of the institutions that have been discussed in this chapter could be operated by CBOs, but they may need help with technical assistance or funding. Many financial intermediaries exist for this purpose. Some community development corporations have established revolving loan funds to help revitalize their neighborhoods. In some cases, the loan funds have eventually spun off into separate organizations. There are advantages, at least initially, for a CDFI to be affiliated with a CBO that has an established reputation and can help build the financial base and links to borrowers. The Community Development Block Grant Program is another source of funding for revolving loan funds.

In many cases, community development financial institutions are able to receive funding from national foundations that are interested in supporting poor and minority neighborhoods. Most of the community development financial institutions rely on these foundations for continual support.

Another emerging source of support for community development financial institutions, however, is community foundations (see Chapter 5). Community foundations are looking to find new strategies for supporting local efforts to support businesses and families. Community foundations have been especially interested in supporting microenterprise loan funds.

Pressure Local Credit Institutions to Serve Community

Experience with the CRA suggests that communities can achieve important results by challenging the lending practices of local credit institutions. CRA challenges require a rigorous analysis of the lending practices of these institutions and evidence that the community is being underserved. CBOs also have found that it frequently takes a well-organized effort to make lenders respond to local credit needs. Some financial institutions, however, are looking for ways to demonstrate that they are serving their local communities, and CBOs should take advantage of these resources. Lenders contend that the CRA regulations are ambiguous, and community organizations can educate them on areas where they can invest in the community with relatively low risk.

Over the years, community organizations have used the CRA to encourage local lenders to invest in a wide variety of community development projects. Many times, the banks making the investments either have received poor CRA ratings or are seeking to merge with another bank. Providing evidence of support for community development efforts is important information in receiving approval from federal regulators.

Use Informal Credit Markets

Some communities have been successful at promoting informal credit markets to address local needs. One of the most likely sources is angel funds. Increasingly communities and regions are helping to organize groups of investors willing to provide capital for a business start-up. **Angel investors** usually provide the capital in exchange for ownership equity in the firm. In many cases, angel investors are retired entrepreneurs or executives who have some knowledge of the industry or business activity in which they are investing. Often, angel investors can provide a bridge between loans from family and friends to formal venture capital funds. CBOs can play an integral role in matching borrowers with available capital. These organizations can help identify available sources of financial capital and make them go to work in the local community.

Identify External Sources of Credit

Most borrowers find credit in their local communities. Those who have a specialized need, however, may find intermediaries outside the community that can serve them. One example would be a worker-owned firm. There are several credit sources for these types of institutions. For example, the Ohio Employee Ownership Center helps train workers to become owners and helps them find sources of funding to purchase the firm for which they work. The National Cooperative Bank provides funding for worker-owned cooperatives. There are several private venture capital firms that specialize in employee ownership, including Churchill Capital's Churchill ESOP Capital Partners, Keilen and Company's KPS Special Situations Fund, and American Capital Strategies. CBOs, again, can play a special role in helping match these intermediaries with local firms.

Summary and Conclusions

There continues to be concern among policy makers and community activists that poor and minority communities suffer from a lack of capital. Some people contend that the credit gap is due to discriminatory lending practices of financial institutions. Others argue that the credit gap is due to the risk of investing in these neighborhoods. In response to these problems, a variety of community credit institutions have been created. Our brief review suggests that government programs and market-based solutions have not adequately addressed credit problems in these communities. Over the past few decades, community credit institutions have emerged to fill this need.

Although some of these models are very promising, most of the evaluations of these institutions suggests that they have only had limited impact on the credit markets in poor and minority communities. Although they have been able to funnel more dollars into poor neighborhoods, they have not come close to meeting the demand for credit in these areas. In many cases, the community credit institutions have received a substantial amount of support from foundations and the federal government, but they have not proven to be sustainable. The evidence also suggests that these institutions are supplemented with technical support and other types of assistance to communities.

KEY CONCEPTS

Angel investors

Business Industrial Development
   Corporation (BIDCO)

Community development
   credit union (CDCU)

Community development loan fund

Community Reinvestment
   Act of 1978 (CRA)

Debt capital

Deregulation

Equity capital

Home Mortgage Disclosure Act (HMDA)

Individual Development Account (IDA)

Linked deposit programs

Microenterprise loan fund

Predatory lending

Redlining

Revolving loan fund (RLF)

Tax incremental financing (TIF)

Transaction costs

Venture capital

QUESTIONS

1. What are some of the explanations for why minorities and residents in low-income neighborhoods are disadvantaged in capital markets? What are some strategies that communities can use to address these problems?

2. What are some distinguishing features between a traditional commercial lender and a community development loan fund?

3. What have been the major elements of financial deregulation over the past two decades? What have been the implications of deregulation for poor and minority communities in the United States? How can deregulation be used to the advantage of these communities?

4. What strategies can communities use to build local capital markets? Provide some concrete examples in your area of these activities.

EXERCISES

1. Go to your local bank and obtain a copy of their Community Reinvestment Act Performance Evaluation. Examine the statement and answer the following questions:

   a. How is your bank rated by lending, investment, and service?
   b. What is the relevant market for this institution?
   c. What is the bank's loan-to-deposit ratio?
   d. What are its lending patterns in low-income areas?
   e. What types of community development loans has this institution made?
   f. Does the bank service all parts of its market?
   g. What is the overall assessment of the community development activities of this bank?

2. Analyze the local credit market in your community. What are the various types of institutions supplying credit in the community? How well do these institutions serve the community? How well does the supply of credit match the demand? Are there any credit gaps that you can find in the community?

3. Meet with some local businesses and discuss their experiences with obtaining credit from local banks and other lenders. Do they believe that there are major obstacles to obtaining credit in the local community? Has the lack of credit ever prevented them from expanding into new markets and growing their business? If so, how have they responded to these problems?

REFERENCES

Boshara, R. (2005). *Individual development accounts: Policies to build savings and assets for the poor.* The Brookings Institution, Policy brief: Welfare reform & beyond #32. Retrieved June 15, 2010, from http://www.brookings.edu/~/media/Files/rc/papers/2005/03childrenfamilies_boshara/pb32.pdf

DeWees, S., & Sarkozy-Banoczy, S. (2010). Investing in the double bottom line: Growing financial institutions in native communities. In G.P. Green & A. Goetting (Eds.), *Mobilizing communities: Asset building as a community development strategy* (pp. 14–47). Philadelphia: Temple University Press.

Goldstein, D. (1999). *Understanding predatory lending: Moving towards a common definition and workable solutions.* Joint Center for Housing Studies of Harvard University. Retrieved June 15, 2010, from http://www.jchs.harvard.edu/publications/finance/goldstein_w99–11.pdf

Levere, A., Clones, D., & Marcoux, K. (1997). *Counting on local capital: A research project on revolving loan funds.* Washington, DC: Corporation for Enterprise Development.

Mills, G., Patterson, R., Orr, L., & DeMarco, D. (2004). *Evaluation of the American dream demonstration: Final evaluation report.* The Ford Foundation and Charles Stewart Mott Foundation. Retrieved June 15, 2010, from http://csd.wustl.edu/Publications/Documents/Abt_ADD_Final_Report.pdf

Paetsch, J. R., & Dahlstrom, R. K. (1990). Tax increment financing: What it is and how it works. In R. D. Bingham, E. W. Hill, & S. B. White (Eds.), *Financing economic development: An institutional response* (pp. 82–98). Newbury Park, CA: Sage.

Parzen, J. A., & Kieschnick, M. H. (1992). *Credit where it's due: Development banking for communities.* Philadelphia: Temple University Press.

Ross, S. L., & Yinger, J. (2002). *The color of credit: Mortgage discrimination, research methodology, and fair-lending enforcement.* Boston: MIT Press.

Taub, R. P. (1988). *Community capitalism.* Boston: Harvard Business School Press.

Temkin, K. (2000). Subprime lending: Current trends and policy issues. *The NeighborWorks Journal, 18,* 38–41.

ADDITIONAL READINGS AND RESOURCES

Readings

Bates, T. (1993). *Banking on Black enterprise: The potential of emerging firms for revitalizing urban economies.* Washington, DC: Joint Center for Political and Economic Studies.

Caftel, B. J. (1978). *Community development credit unions: A self-help manual.* Berkeley, CA: National Economic Development and Law Project.

Center for Responsible Lending. (2009). *8 signs of predatory lending.* http://www.responsiblelending .org/mortgage-lending/tools-resources/8-signs-of-predatory-lending.html

Dominguez, J. (1976). *Capital flows in minority areas.* Lexington, MA: Lexington Books.

Dreier, P. (2003). The future of community reinvestment: Challenges and opportunities in a changing environment. *Journal of the American Planning Association, 69,* 341–353.

Engel, K., & McCoy, P. (2004). Predatory lending: What does Wall Street have to do with it? *Housing Policy Debate, 15,* 715–751.

Foote, C. L., Gerardi, K., Goette, L., & Willen, P. S. (2008). *Subprime facts: What (we think) we know about the subprime crisis and what we don't* (Public Policy Discussion Papers No. 08–2). Boston: Federal Reserve Bank of Boston.

Ho, G., & Pennington-Cross, A. (2006). The impact of local predatory lending laws on the flow of subprime credit. *Journal of Urban Economics, 60,* 210–228.

Hogwood, A. W., Jr., & Shabecoff, A. (1992). *Lending for community economic development: A guide for small town and rural lenders.* Washington, DC: Community Information Exchange.

Parzen, J., Shabecoff, A., Vandenberg, L., & Berman, G. (1990). *Capital and communities: A community guide to financial institutions.* Washington, DC: Community Information Exchange.

Retsinas, N. P., & Belsky, E. S. (2008). *America's rental housing: The key to a balanced national policy.* Joint Center for Housing Studies, Harvard University, 2008. Retrieved February 3, 2010, from http://www.jchs.harvard.edu/publications/rental/rh08_americas_rental_housing/index.html

Rosen, D. P. (1988). *Public capital: Revitalizing America's communities.* Washington, DC: The National Center for Policy Alternatives.

Sherraden, M. (1991). *Assets and the poor: A new American welfare policy.* Armonk, NY: M. E. Sharpe Publishers.

Squires, G. D. (Ed.). (1992). *From redlining to reinvestment: Community responses to urban disinvestment.* Philadelphia: Temple University Press.

Squires, G. D. (1994). *Capital and communities in black and white.* Albany: State University of New York Press.

Squires, G. D. (1999). The persistence of housing discrimination: The indelible color line. *The American Prospect, 42,* 67–70.

Squires, G. D. (Ed.). (2003). *Organizing access to capital: Advocacy and the democratization of financial institutions.* Philadelphia: Temple University Press.

Squires, G. D., & O'Connor, S. (2001). *Color and money.* Albany: State University of New York Press.

Sumell, A. J. (2009). The determinants of foreclosed property values: Evidence from inner-city Cleveland. *Journal of Housing Research, 18,* 45–61.

Turner, M. A., & Skidmore, F. (1999). *Mortgage lending discrimination: A review of existing evidence.* Washington, DC: Urban Institute.

White, K. (1987). *The community loan fund manual.* Springfield, MA: Institute for Community Economics.

Websites

Assets for Independence Resource Center—http://idaresources.org/. A good resource for communities considering the IDA model for promoting assets.

Center for Social Development (Washington University)—http://csd.wustl.edu/AssetBuilding/overview/Pages/default.aspx. This website provides some excellent resources on IDAs in different contexts. It also includes several papers on policies related to IDAs.

The Coalition of Community Development Financial Institutions—www.cdfi.org. This website provides information for those interested in CDFIs. The coalition was developed in 1992 as an ad hoc policy development and advocacy initiative and represents more than 350 CDFIs in 50 states. The coalition is a primary source of information about CDFIs for the general public, the media, public officials, and the private sector.

Community Reinvestment Fund (CRF)—www.crfusa.com. The CRF is a nonprofit organization that provides a secondary market for economic development loans. This website also provides information and resources for lenders, such as information on fair lending, lender liability, and housing-related sites.

The Enterprise Development—www.enterweb.org/communty.htm. This website is an excellent resource for information on a wide variety of programs related to community economic development, including financing.

The Federal Financial Institutions Examination Council (FFIEC) website on the Home Mortgage Disclosure Act (HMDA)—http://www.ffiec.gov/hmda/. This rich data source provides detailed data on home mortgage loans by census tract throughout the United States. The data are available at several different levels and for several different years.

Federal Reserve Board/Community Revinvestment Act (CRA) Performance Ratings—http://www.federalreserve.gov/DCCA/CRA/crarate.cfm. The Federal Reserve regularly rates commercial lending institutions regarding their community revinvestment activities. You can obtain the full reports from lending institutions at this website.

National Community Capital Association—http://www.opportunityfinance.net/. The National Community Capital Association is a membership organization of nonprofit groups that invest in poor communities.

National Credit Union Administration—http://www.ncua.gov/index.html. This website provides data and other information on federal and state-chartered credit unions across the country.

National Federation of Community Development Credit Unions—www.natfed.org. This website provides basic information on and resources for CDCUs.

Social Investment Forum—http://www.socialinvest.org/areas/SRIGuide/community.htm. This website is an online guide to social investment. It provides information on how to investigate the investments of lending institutions. The website also provides some good information on community banks, community credit unions, community loan funds, and microenterprise lenders.

Woodstock Institute—www.woodstockinst.org. The Woodstock Institute is a Chicago nonprofit organization that works to promote community reinvestment and economic development in lower income and minority communities. The institute engages in applied research, policy analysis, technical assistance, public education, and program design and evaluation. Its primary activities are CRA and fair lending policies, financial and insurance services, CDFIs, and economic development strategies.

Videos

Faith, Hope, and Capital: Banking on the "Unbankable" (2000), produced by Tenth Street Media, Inc., directed by Lynn Adler and Jim Mayer (Item #BLV10148). This video examines the workings of CDFIs. It provides case studies of several institutions that provide capital and technical assistance to businesses in poor and neglected communities. Available from Films for the Humanities and Science, P.O. Box 2053, Princeton, NJ 08543–2053.

Subprime Solution? (2008). This PBS video looks at how a nonprofit organization, Just Price Solutions, looks at how community-based organizations can address the subprime credit crisis, as well as problems of "creditworthiness" in poor neighborhoods. The video is available at http://www.pbs.org/now/shows/426/.

10 Environmental Capital

What is environmental capital? To review, capital in the context in which we have defined it is a type of community asset that can be employed to produce more assets; individuals or businesses should not equate capital with just wealth generation. Others use the term *assets* as a way to examine, analyze, and create community. Kretzmann and McKnight (1993) now are well known for their asset-based approach to community development. Ferguson and Dickens (1999) also spoke of community development assets as different forms of capital: physical, human, social, financial, and political. They captured Kretzmann and McKnight's definition within these different forms of capital. Ferguson and Dickens, however, ignored an important form of capital: environmental capital. Increasingly, community-based organizations (CBOs) are faced with issues related to their natural environment. In this chapter, we discuss some of the dilemmas, strategies, and tactics involved in the community-based efforts to build a community's environmental capital.

Environmental capital includes several aspects of a community's base of natural resources: air, water, land, flora, and fauna. Why do communities need to be concerned about environmental capital? There are several possible reasons. First, communities need to be concerned about the ecological functions that natural resources play, such as flood control, water catchment, and waste assimilation. Second, natural resources have direct use value, primarily as marketed outputs (e.g., timber, crops, renewable energy) and unpriced benefits (e.g., recreation and landscape). Finally, natural resources may have nonuse values, such as the ability to pass on a natural area for future generations or simply the satisfaction that is derived from knowing that the natural resources are being preserved. Because natural resources may produce a variety of values, it is important to consider the best use of the resources for the long-term viability of a community.

We need to make a few comments at the outset about the relationship between natural resources and economic development. In the past, natural resources have been viewed primarily in terms of their productive value, but increasingly communities are considering the consumer value of their natural resources and viewing their natural resources as amenities. **Amenities** are natural and manmade features of a community that cannot be re-created or transferred to other communities. Examples of an amenity would be a wildlife ecosystem, a recreational area, a historical site, or even the social and cultural traditions of a community. Amenities are usually restricted in an absolute sense, and once the consumer value has been destroyed, it is impossible to restore the amenities' initial value.

What is the relationship between amenities and economic development? Most people immediately think of the first scenario, in which development leads to the destruction of an amenity. An example might be a development project that is proposed for a wetland site. There are, however, other possible relationships between amenities and economic development. In some cases, nondevelopment can lead to the destruction of amenities. For example, the loss of people in some rural areas may lead to the loss of farms and the landscape that so many people appreciate. Another possibility is that preservation or promotion of amenities can lead to nondevelopment. Residents may limit economic activities or take land out of the market to preserve natural resources. Finally, preservation or promotion of amenities can promote higher levels of development, as in the case of a recreation area.

For many, the natural environment is in the background of communities. People accept its existence without thinking about it. In a city, suburb, or village, it is more obvious to observe what is going on in the downtown area or with new housing developments. People generally do not notice when a wetland is filled in or a few trees are felled for a new industrial or residential development. Many communities, however, are beginning to recognize that wisely managed natural resources, a community's environmental capital, play a major role in community satisfaction and economic development.

Few communities have considered the complicated needs of natural systems included within their political boundaries. Numerous laws, strategies, and programs address parts of a community's ecological support system (e.g., sewage treatment districts, shore-land preservation regulation, priority watershed plans, lake management districts, farmland preservation zoning, well-head protection zones). In contrast to these local **regulatory** and **management approaches,** CBOs can offer an alternative approach to protecting a community's environmental capital, especially in places that do not have the broad support necessary for protecting key environmental resources.

Many minority and poor communities face a disproportionate number of environmental problems; this situation is referred to as **environmental racism.** Many of these communities have become sites for hazardous waste or illegal dumps (Bullard, 1994). Residents in these communities often suffer from high rates of cancer and other diseases. These communities are mobilizing around the environmental problems in their communities.

In this chapter, we examine why CBOs are sometimes better able to address a community's environmental capital than either government or market-based strategies. We also examine the kinds of obstacles and issues that CBOs need to address to become more effective and successful in considering environmental capital issues. We focus on community land trusts and other types of local organizations to illustrate how CBOs can address environmental capital issues, particularly the issue of sprawl and open space. In particular, we are interested in how CBOs can promote development that benefits the economy, the community, and the environment.

Forms of Environmental Capital

Depending on where your community is located, the natural environment may play a role in local image and quality of life. Many communities rely on their local environmental capital for beauty, as an economic resource, or for recreational opportunities. Your community probably has some connection with its environmental capital, whether for tourism, industry, or recreation.

Local environmental capital provides important functions to communities. Undeveloped lands, especially wetlands, act as flood control and part of a system of water storage. Trees and plants hold soils in place and act as air purifiers. Natural areas also provide aesthetically pleasing environments and, if large enough, provide plant and animal diversity. Finally, natural areas provide opportunities for economic development and recreation, education, and spiritual enrichment.

Communities have changing relationships with their local natural resources. During the early history of many communities, economic development probably was based on the extraction of natural resources. Change is a part of natural ecosystem dynamics, but air, water, land, or an ecosystem can become degraded through human activities. **Surface water** (lakes, rivers, and streams) may degrade over time: Algae blooms can occur regularly, or water can become murky or overly acidic—clear and lifeless. Closely allied with degradation is the depletion of natural resources. Depleted systems have fewer of the species that made them ecosystems, and the relationships and connections that make them systems can start to disintegrate.

Pollution is often the source that degrades natural resources. Pollution comes from point and nonpoint sources. **Nonpoint source pollution** is the most difficult to address; it cannot be traced to a specific source. Urban streets and agricultural fields are common sources of nonpoint pollution. **Point source pollution**, in contrast, is specific output from a production process and can be traced to its source. Some examples of point source pollution are manufacturing firms, such as paper plants, or utilities, such as coal-fired power plants. Clean water and air are used as part of the production process, but the output of water or air is "dirtier" than it was when it was used as an input. Reduction, degradation, or loss of natural resources also translates to loss of beauty and loss of ecosystem functions, such as air and water purification, sediment filtration, and water flow control. The following sections describe environmental resources that are important to communities.

Aesthetic Qualities/Scenic Resources

The **aesthetic qualities** of natural resources and the built environment are important aspects of a community. Aesthetic qualities of the built environment can be enhanced by selective emphasis on certain natural features, such as preservation of a scenic waterway or the use of prairie plants, native trees, and native shrubs in community plantings. The built environment can enhance the natural beauty of surrounding resources by emphasizing building materials and colors that blend with local scenery. Variety and unique features are important components of aesthetic quality. Examples of unique features might include forests, farmland, wetlands, and prairies; small communities; urban communities; utilities; highways; water-related areas, such as streams, rivers, and lakes; landforms, such as hills, cliffs, plains, valleys, and glacial features; and view potential, such as vistas and panoramic views.

Agricultural Land Resources

Productivity and size are two important aspects of a community's agricultural resource. Potential productivity for traditional agricultural activities can be determined through a review of agricultural land: slope, available water, soil particle size, amount of organic matter, depth of root zone, permeability of soils, depth to groundwater table, and length of growing season. Productivity can be judged by comparison to an indicator crop or use of an agricultural lands rating system. Size of the land also may be important for agricultural purposes. Some crops and farming practices require the use of large equipment or other management practices that can govern optimal size for a farm unit.

Geographic Setting and Soils

The topography, drainage patterns, soil characteristics, mineral deposits, and other geological features of a community can influence and be influenced by a whole variety of activities within the community. Geological and geographical considerations affect community aesthetics, wildlife habitat, economic resources, location of roads, soil erosion, surface water runoff, and many other land use factors. Geology also affects the community water supply.

Understanding the **geographic setting** involves mapping watersheds and subsurface geology and their drainage patterns; mapping geological phenomena, such as outcrops, bluffs, cliffs, glacial features, sand dunes, and caves, for their significance from both aesthetic and wildlife habitat perspectives; and identifying local rock types and deposits.

Human Health/Environmental Hazards

Air quality, water quality, climate, and noise issues are now considered when assessing natural resources. Air quality concerns are part of the landscape no matter where you live in the United States. Urban areas are at greatest risk of noncompliance with air standard regulations. Pesticide use and other agricultural activities in rural areas, construction, nonmetallic mining, and vehicle exhaust, however, all contribute to air pollution.

Careful monitoring of community human health categories is needed to ensure fair distribution of community businesses or services that have an impact on local air, water, or noise quality. Although a site may be ideal for the location of a business, factory, or highway in economic terms, it may not be ideal in ecological terms: A change in local air, water, or noise may have an impact on the health of surrounding human, plant, or animal communities.

Plant Communities

Natural vegetation provides local scenery and contributes to the quality of life in a community. Vegetation is also significant for the role it plays in an area's ecology and the maintenance of an adequate water supply. Ecological interactions include soil quality, wildlife habitat, nutrient cycling, and climate impacts. Presence or absence of vegetation and the type of vegetation affects the ability of the land to absorb water and to conserve soil and nutrients. Identifying current plant communities and evaluating their aesthetic, recreational, ecological, and conservation effects assist communities in discovering where change should be encouraged and where it should be avoided. The character of plant communities can be summarized by reviewing such qualities as size, frequency of occurrence, diversity, fragility, significance, plant community/species types, age of plants, canopy cover and openings, density of plant stands, signs of physical or insect damage, and location in relation to other features.

Wildlife and Wildlife Habitat

Wildlife includes turtles, snakes, salamanders, frogs, toads, fish, birds of prey, songbirds, waterfowl, and insects. All need a natural resources habitat appropriate to their food, resting, mating, and shelter needs. The amount and characteristics of the habitat space vary from animal to animal. Birds and animals travel along corridors of habitat that also include flight paths. For some species, these corridor habitats are also vital to their survival. Undisturbed areas have many benefits for the community as well as the wildlife, such as education, nature study, outdoor enjoyment, and comparative information.

Surface Water Resources/Water Supply

Surface water resources are integral to numerous natural systems. They replenish atmospheric water lost in precipitation and accept surface runoff. Plant and animal ecosystems are dependent on a certain quality, temperature, rate of flow, and volume of water. Lakes, rivers, and streams are a source of drinking water for humans; a source of water supply for agriculture, industry, and tourism; an avenue for transportation and waste disposal (industrial, agricultural, utility, sewer, and urban runoff); and a source of recreation and passive enjoyment.

Evaluation of surface water features considers alteration of lakes, rivers, or streams as a result of human activity; scarcity of quality surface water; water resource hazards, such as flooding; and resource sensitivity, such as areas where increased shore-land development would be incompatible or would degrade the water resource and its accompanying role in the natural system.

Groundwater/Water Supply

Agriculture and many other industries depend heavily on large supplies of high-quality groundwater. For small communities and rural homes, groundwater is the only economical source of high-quality water for domestic use. For example, in rural areas, nitrogen and phosphorus can affect water quality. Quality and availability of groundwater can vary locally, on a site-to-site basis, depending on the specific geologic and hydrologic conditions of the area. Groundwater is sensitive to local contamination, depending on pollutant characteristics and soil permeability. Once present in groundwater, pollutants travel with or through the groundwater, depending on their chemical characteristics.

The supply of groundwater is not infinite. It must be recharged through the hydrologic cycle. Precipitation percolates into the ground or enters the ground from surface water bodies. Poorly constructed wells, improper well spacing, and excessive pumping can lead to pronounced decreases in water storage, interference between wells, interchange of water between aquifers or basins, and interference with surface water levels. Evaluation of groundwater supplies should consider supply and uses, sensitivity and threats, and hazards.

Although people continue to improve their understanding of the components of natural systems and their potential benefits, communities must still proceed with caution in local management decisions. People now know, for example, that wetlands serve important functions. Wetlands help to maintain water quality, reduce the chances of flooding, offer habitat for numerous species, and provide a source of water in dry years. In the past, soils present in wetland areas were valued primarily for their agricultural potential.

Wetlands often were drained for the perceived economic benefit of crop sales. The loss of potential long-term economic and environmental benefits from water quality/quantity protection, aesthetic appeal, and recreation uses was ignored. Thus, decisions about a community's environmental capital can have both short- and long-term effects.

———————————————— **Land Use and Environmental Capital**

Many human-related activities affect local environmental capital. In this section, we examine two distinct problems that can affect a community's environmental capital. One problem, which exists on the fringes of urban America, is called sprawl. The other problem, which exists in central cities and other locations of the United States, is vacant land resulting from deindustrialization and depopulation of central cities. Two important issues involving vacant land are abandoned buildings and brownfields. In the next few sections, we define and discuss these terms and examine how CBOs are addressing these issues.

Sprawl

BOX 10.1 SPRAWL FACTS

- By some estimates, the amount of land covered by urban and suburban development has increased by nearly 300% since 1955, while population has increased by only 75% (Ewing & Kostyack, 2005, p. viii).
- From 1970 to 1990, Detroit's population shrank by 7%, but its urbanized area increased by 28%. Pittsburgh's population shrank 9% in the same period, while its area increased by 30%. Chicago's population increased between 1970 and 1990 by 1%; meanwhile, its urbanized area grew by 24%. Phoenix sprawl provides a similar picture: While its population grew 132% from 1970 to 1990, Phoenix's urbanized area grew by a significant 91% (Sierra Club, 2001).
- Sprawl-like development can use many more resources—five times more pipe and wire, five times as much heating and cooling energy—than urban living. Sprawl also uses 35 times as much land, and it requires 15 times as much pavement, as compact urban living (Sierra Club, 2001).
- Between 1982 and 2003, more than 35 million acres of land were developed (U.S. Department of Agriculture, 2003).
- Three-fifths, or 60%, of the nation's rarest and most imperiled species are found within designated metropolitan areas, with the 35 fastest growing large metropolitan areas home to nearly one-third (29%) of these species (Ewing & Kostyak, 2005, p. viii).

Sprawl is one of the biggest threats to a community's environmental capital. Sprawl can be defined as low-density, often residential development, on the fringe of or beyond the border of suburban development (Office of Technology Assessment, 1995). Existing laws and regulations, such as local land use planning efforts, have inadequately protected the natural environment from sprawl (Daniels & Bowers, 1997).

BOX 10.2 CHARACTERISTICS OF SPRAWL

- Unlimited outward extension
- Low-density residential and commercial settlements
- Leapfrog development
- Fragmentation of powers over land use among many small localities
- Dominance of transportation by private automotive vehicles
- No centralized planning or control of land uses
- Widespread strip commercial development
- Great fiscal disparities among localities
- Segregation of types of land uses in different zones
- Reliance mainly on the trickle-down or filtering process to provide housing to low-income households

SOURCE: PlannersWeb (2000).

Several factors contribute to sprawl. Zoning policies frequently discourage higher density development and mixed-use development projects. Highway building provides an incentive for families to move to the suburbs and commute to their jobs. Housing policies have provided a powerful incentive for the growth of the suburbs and exurbs. Competition for tax revenue among municipalities encourages businesses to move out to the suburbs, where the costs of doing business may be lower. Finally, social and economic conditions in the inner city, such as property values and concentrated poverty, may discourage compact development.

What are the impacts of sprawl? There are several problems associated with sprawl. Many people point to the tendency for sprawl to contribute to a loss of a sense of place because the development looks the same across most communities. Sprawl means a loss of land, especially of prime farmland adjacent to cities. There continues to be concern that sprawl increases costs to local government because services must be provided over a larger area rather than to a more dense settlement. Sprawl increases auto dependence and associated fuel consumption, which contributes to air pollution and other environmental problems. Outward expansion of cities tends to lead to abandonment of the inner city, which tends to create greater racial segregation. Finally, sprawl has been found to contribute to the loss of wildlife habitat and wetlands (PlannersWeb, 1999).

Several strategies deal with sprawl, including creating a sense of place, preserving open space and farmland, concentrating growth and investment, changing transportation strategies and priorities from automobile dependence, and establishing regional cooperation. Case Study 10.1 describes a growing practice of encouraging higher density development. Two additional strategies—smart growth and new urbanism—have generated advocates, websites, and research. In the following section, we discuss these two strategies.

CASE STUDY 10.1 CLUSTER DEVELOPMENT

When the Lowcountry Open Land Trust received a conservation easement on the 314-acre former cotton plantation located on Wadmalaw Island and known as Oakhart, the family agreed to cluster a development of no more than seven houses on a 30-acre area, leaving more than 85% of the farm permanently undeveloped and available for forestry, agriculture, and recreational uses. Existing zoning regulations would have allowed construction of approximately 70 houses. The conservation easement is the 15th received by the Lowcountry Open Land Trust on Wadmalaw Island, bringing the land conserved there to more than 2,500 acres. Lowcountry Open Land Trust has conserved more than 18,800 acres of open space on the coast of South Carolina.

SOURCE: Land Trust Alliance (1999b).

Smart Growth and New Urbanism

There are two strategies presented in the literature as possible solutions to sprawl—smart growth and new urbanism. Generally, both strategies aim at tackling sprawl in metropolitan areas. *Smart growth* is a new term for an old idea—growth management, which is a strategy that communities have used for approximately 40 years. Growth management evolved over time, and one could argue that smart growth is its latest evolution. States and metropolitan areas that have experienced rapid growth rates—Florida, Oregon, and New Jersey, to name a few—use many growth management techniques. Some of the primary tools used in growth management include zoning, development buffers, purchase of development rights programs, urban growth boundaries, minimum density requirements, cluster development, and exclusive agricultural zoning. Over time, as more communities grew more rapidly than usual—and the growth spread outward more quickly than seen previously—growth management was repackaged and expanded into the smart growth movement.

Like definitions of sprawl, there are no agreed-on definitions of smart growth. Common characteristics among the various definitions include a call to end sprawl and a new vision of urban/suburban collaboration and regional growth management (Gillham, 2002, p. 157). Most definitions depend largely on whether an organization favors development or conservation. Embedded in many definitions are the following ideas: (a) acknowledgment of continued construction of single family homes, (b) importance of balancing development with natural resources, (c) importance of managing growth rather than stopping it, (d) recognition that cities are important to quality of life, (e) recognition that new development patterns that favor compact and walkable/bikeable communities are possible and allow for a wider range of transportation choices, and (f) recognition that intergovernmental cooperation is a key factor in addressing growth.

BOX 10.3 SMART GROWTH PRINCIPLES

- Create range of housing opportunities and choices
- Create walkable neighborhoods
- Encourage community and stakeholder collaboration
- Foster distinctive, attractive communities with a strong sense of place
- Make development decisions predictable, fair, and cost effective
- Mix land uses
- Preserve open space, farmland, natural beauty, and critical environmental areas
- Provide a variety of transportation choices
- Strengthen and direct development toward existing communities
- Take advantage of compact building design

SOURCE: Smart Growth Online (2006).

Nevertheless, a consortium of organizations developed 10 smart growth principles (see Box 10.3). A key idea behind these principles is the need to balance development with the protection of natural resources, such as farmland, forests, and wetlands. Table 10.1 outlines a few policies for each principle. The tools can be implemented at the local government level and are appropriate for metropolitan areas in addition to small towns and rural areas.

In addition to smart growth, another strategy for contending with sprawl, new urbanism, has gained currency within the past decade. The new urbanism concept generally focuses on the neighborhood or town scale, on new areas of development, and almost exclusively on physical design. Seaside and Celebration, Florida, are examples of new urbanist developments. These developments aim to produce compact, livable communities. An idea that stems from new urbanism is called **traditional neighborhood development**, or TND.

Generally, TNDs occur on greenfield sites (i.e., undeveloped land, including agricultural fields). Ideally, they could be built on brownfield sites (previously developed, vacant, or polluted sites) within cities. Rather than allowing a 200-acre subdivision with 100 houses evenly spread over that land, with garages and roads dominating the feel of the development, a TND would bring the houses closer together, add a small retail district with the

TABLE 10.1 Smart Growth Implementation Tools

Goals	Tools
Promote mixed land uses	• Adopt codes, such as the traditional neighborhood ordinance, that can parallel existing codes. • Use flexible zoning tools, such as overlay zones or planned unit developments.
Take advantage of compact building design	• Use public meetings to educate community members about the relationship among transportation, density, and compact building options. • Ensure a sense of privacy and safety through design of homes and yards.
Create a range of housing opportunities and choices	• Revise zoning and building codes to permit a wider variety of housing types. • Plan and zone for affordable and manufactured housing developments in rural areas.
Create walkable communities	• Adopt design standards for streets that ensure safety and mobility for pedestrian and nonmotorized modes of transport. • Identify economic opportunities that stimulate pedestrian activity. • Connect walkways, parking lots, greenways, and developments.
Foster distinctive, attractive communities with a strong sense of place	• Preserve scenic vistas through the appropriate location of telecommunication towers and improve control of billboards/signage. • Preserve historic buildings or structures that are valued by the community. • Encourage outdoor art, such as sculptures, murals, and other examples of creative expression.
Preserve open space, farmland, natural beauty, and critical environmental areas	• Expand use of innovative financing tools to facilitate open space acquisition and preservation, such as a purchase of development rights program. • Include a green infrastructure plan in your comprehensive plan. • Create a network of trails and environmental corridors/greenways. • Partner with nongovernmental organizations, such as land trusts, to acquire and protect land.
Strengthen and direct development toward existing communities or development	• Institute regional tax base sharing to limit intergovernmental competition and to support schools and infrastructure throughout the region. • Create incentives for contiguous development or limitations on scattered development.

(Continued)

TABLE 10.1 (Continued)

Goals	Tools
Provide a variety of transportation choices	• Finance and provide incentives for multimodal transportation (biking, walking, driving, snowmobiling, cross-country skiing, etc.) systems that include supportive land use and development.
Make development decisions predictable, fair, and cost effective	• Display zoning regulations and design goals in pictorial fashion to better illustrate development goals. • Conduct impact analyses or cost of community service studies, or both, on proposed developments. • Strive for one-stop shopping for development-related permits.
Encourage community and stakeholder collaboration in development decisions	• Conduct community-visioning exercises to determine how and where the community should grow. • Include the public and stakeholders often and routinely in each step of the planning process.

SOURCE: Haines (2003).

possibility of apartments above stores, de-emphasize cars and roads by creating alleys and placing garages in the rear of lots, and focus attention on people through sidewalks, front porches, and small lot sizes. This development option is important because it potentially provides consumers with additional choices about the kind of suburban development in which they choose to live.

Another concept that has received attention in recent years is green infrastructure. Green infrastructure encompasses a wide range of landscape elements, including natural areas, private conservation lands, and public and private working lands of conservation value. It also incorporates outdoor recreation and trail networks. This movement ultimately is responding to sprawl and its consequences. Green infrastructure plans and planning occur at a landscape scale, attempt to reduce landscape fragmentation, and maintain biodiversity on a regional scale (McDonald, Allen, Benedict, & O'Connor, 2005).

Sprawl and smart growth represent two opposing and contrasting patterns of development along a continuum. Communities have not consciously chosen the path to sprawl, but communities now have the opportunity to consciously choose an alternative path. Altering a community's growth pattern away from sprawl toward one that preserves, maintains, and creates a sense of place and better balances development with natural resources and open space will not be an easy or simple task. However, in making visions and plans, and choosing tools that can achieve those visions and then abiding by them, communities can begin to create healthy and vibrant places to live and work.

Brownfields

BOX 10.4 VACANT LAND AND BROWNFIELDS: THE FACTS

- In a recent U.S. Conference of Mayors survey of 231 cities, 210 cities estimated that they collectively had more than 21,000 brownfield sites ranging in size from a quarter of an acre to 1,300 acres. The General Accounting Office has estimated that there are more than 450,000 brownfield properties across America, in every state of the union.
- Philadelphia, Pennsylvania, has 15,800 parcels of vacant land and 27,000 vacant structures.
- New Orleans, Louisiana, contains 14,000 vacant lots.
- Chicago, Illinois, has 70,000 vacant lots.
- Milwaukee, Wisconsin, has 2,500 acres of vacant land or 4 square miles, or 4%, of total land area.
- St. Louis, Missouri, contains 13,000 tax-delinquent parcels or 1,200 acres, or 3%, of total land area.
- Trenton, New Jersey, has 900 acres or 18% of total land area.
- Detroit, Michigan, contains 46,000 city-owned vacant parcels and 24,000 empty buildings.
- Twenty-eight states now have brownfields redevelopment programs to clean up abandoned and often polluted industrial sites.
- Every dollar of public money spent for a brownfields development effort leveraged an average $2.48 in private sector funds.

SOURCE: Sierra Club (1999, 2006).

Part of the sprawl debate is the issue of brownfields. Due to deindustrialization and depopulation of central cities, thousands of structures and acres of land have been abandoned in the past 30 years. With this abandonment have come a number of problems for residents in these areas, including health issues, visual blight, increased crime and safety issues, lost tax revenue, public expenditures related to demolition of buildings, and contaminated land.

Brownfields are especially a problem because of the cost and legal liability issues associated with cleanup. The U.S. Environmental Protection Agency (EPA, 2006) defined a brownfield as "a property, the expansion, redevelopment, or reuse of which may be complicated by the presence or potential presence of a hazardous substance, pollutant, or containment" (p. 1). The EPA reported that there are more than 450,000 brownfields in the United States (EPA, 2006). To make these brownfield sites more attractive to developers, the federal and state governments have created programs that limit liability and mitigate the risk and costs of cleanup. These programs address key barriers to the cleanup and redevelopment of brownfields.

At the federal level, in such agencies as the General Service Administration, the Treasury Department, the EPA, the U.S. Department of Housing and Urban Development (HUD), and the Economic Development Administration, brownfields programs create incentives for redeveloping these contaminated areas. In addition, most state governments have brownfields or voluntary cleanup programs. The latest brownfields law, passed in 2002, called the Small Business Liability Relief and Brownfields Revitalization Act, expanded the EPA's programs by increasing funding availability for projects, clarifying liability issues, and assisting states and tribes to expand their programs. In 2006, the EPA budgeted $210 million for brownfields programs. Prior to this law, anyone associated with a contaminated site, at any point in time, could be held liable, in perpetuity, for the cleanup costs associated with it. Public funding has resulted in $6.5 billion in private investments for cleanup and redevelopment and an estimated 25,000 new jobs (EPA, 2006, p. 1).

Another dimension of brownfields is environmental justice. This movement is much broader than a focus on brownfields alone. The EPA (1998) defined environmental justice as "the fair treatment and meaningful involvement of all people regardless of race, ethnicity, income, national origin, or educational level with respect to the development, implementation, and enforcement of environmental laws, regulations and policies" (p. 2). This movement exists and remains important because of the correlation between environmental hazards and pollutants and social and demographic characteristics of areas. One report carried out by the Government Accounting Office (GAO) found that "rates of poverty increased as one moved closer to the facility spatially" (Zilney, McGurrin, & Zahran, 2006, p. 52) and were "perfectly linear." Another study prepared by the United Church of Christ Communion in 1987 "found that communities with the highest percentage of minorities had the highest concentration of hazardous facilities" (Zilney et al., 2006, p. 52).

This correlation can be given at least two spins. One spin is that the correlation happened by accident—that industries generally locate where land is inexpensive. In turn, it means that land adjacent to heavy industry is also inexpensive, making it affordable for people who cannot live in other, more costly sections of a metropolitan area. Another far more negative spin on this correlation is that location and regulatory decisions purposefully locate polluting industries near existing low-income neighborhoods, for example, because residents of these areas are the least likely to advocate against these types of decisions. With much less political capital than other wealthier and Whiter neighborhoods, these neighborhoods have little chance to fight against industrial location decisions. Many CBOs act as advocates for residents in neighborhoods where brownfields are an issue and when new facilities are suggested. CDCs throughout the country are addressing brownfield sites in a number of ways (see Case Study 10.2).

CASE STUDY 10.2 BROWNFIELDS PROJECTS IN CHICAGO

In Chicago, Bethel New Life is a CDC that focuses in a holistic manner on the community it serves. They have undertaken many brownfields projects. Bethel New Life is a faith-based, community-directed CDC that uses an asset-based approach to community development. Bethel recently partnered with the American Planning Association, with the help of an EPA grant, to help "community groups in low-income communities develop a new set of 'eyes' to see brownfield sites as opportunities" (American Planning Association, 2006). In this 3-year project, the two partners will create a training program and workbook for CBOs and planning departments.

Bethel has used planning techniques to identify the most reusable properties in their neighborhood, and neighborhood participation has helped the organization identify possible projects. Bethel has linked its work in brownfields to job training and placement and economic development. As of 2006, Bethel has focused on sustainable community development. Its approach is one of advocacy that incorporates tenets of smart growth with participatory action research. In its projects, Bethel focuses on transit-oriented design, energy efficiency, environmental friendliness, and greening and traffic calming. According to Bethel, in its conversion of three brownfield sites, it "created an environmental careers ladder including asbestos removal, lead abatement, hazardous waste handling and horticultural specialists" (Bethel New Life, 2006).

SOURCE: Bethel New Life (2006).

The Roles of Government and the Market

Environmental capital has been addressed primarily through debates about who should have control over natural resources—the government, individuals, or corporations operating in the free market—and what are the best ways to maintain, conserve, and protect those resources—manage, regulate, or buy and sell.

The Government

Mazmanian and Kraft (1999) identified three environmental epochs. The first epoch, from the early 1970s to the early 1980s, was characterized by **command-and-control regulation.** The aim during this period was to clean up the nation's polluted waterways, air, and land, at the same time protecting the nation's natural resources. Critics of this approach charged that it was costly, inefficient, inflexible, reliant on remedial measures rather than preventive actions, complex in its rule-making process, cumbersome, and adversarial and that it used a piecemeal approach (Mazmanian & Kraft, 1999, p. 4). There seems to be a consensus, however, that this approach made large strides toward cleaning up environmental problems in the United States.

In the second epoch, business interests and others were very critical of this stringent regulatory approach and the overreliance on command-and-control regulation. This epoch, which began in the 1980s and extended into the 1990s, shifted to a more market-based approach that was flexible and used incentive-based techniques, was cost-efficient, and shifted responsibilities for compliance and enforcement to the state and local levels.

The third epoch, beginning in the 1990s and continuing today, emphasizes sustainability. The ultimate responsibility for regulating and managing the natural resources lies with the local government; the federal government acts as a guiding force and as oversight. In this epoch, public-private partnerships and local-regional collaborations are the predominant organizational means for implementing community sustainability objectives (Mazmanian & Kraft, 1999, pp. 10–12).

As this third epoch evolves, the federal government continues to approach natural resources in two fundamental ways: management and regulation. The agencies that take a management approach fall under the Departments of the Interior and Agriculture and include the Forest Service, the Bureau of Land Management, and the National Park Service. Under these agencies and a few others, the federal government owns about 630 million acres or about one third of the land area of the United States. These agencies manage environmental resources for timber, grazing, minerals, and recreation. Generally, they manage large tracts of land, most located in the western United States and beyond community boundaries. Thus, communities concerned with their local environmental resources do not turn to these agencies except in specific circumstances. For example, the Urban and Community Forestry program of the Forest Service is involved with educating citizens and creating partnerships to assist communities in planting or managing urban forests.

The regulatory approach is exemplified in the work of the EPA. The EPA was established in 1970 as a regulatory and enforcement agency. Some of the more well-known environmental laws under their jurisdiction are the Clean Air Act, the Clean Water Act, the Endangered Species Act, the National Environmental Policy Act, and the Occupational Safety and Health Act. The agency has shifted to acting as an environmental watchdog, making sure that specific industrial plants are not polluting and that local governments in large metropolitan areas, such as Los Angeles, are implementing plans to clean up their air. When it comes to assisting communities that are interested in preserving their local natural resources, the EPA also acts as an educator, a facilitator, and a technical resource. Thus, the EPA encourages local governments and CBOs to create ways to protect their environmental resources.

The Market

In contrast to the federal or state governments attempting to preserve the environment, the market could be left to operate unregulated (Gordon & Richardson, 1997). Some argue that all environmental resources should be bought and sold like other commodities. The Cato Institute, for example, proposed that all federally owned lands should be auctioned off and that these lands would be better managed both financially and ecologically through the free market (Anderson, Smith, & Simmons, 1999). The free market, however, tends to favor short-term decisions and those that bring a profit to the individual. Because land is a commodity, under a free market system it is understood that it should be developed to its highest and best use (Ewing, 1997).

Under this scenario, the most expensive land markets are in downtown central business districts, and land prices decrease as one moves away from the center of a city. It is relatively easy to value land in terms of its development potential, but valuing land, such as wetlands, prairie, and forests, in terms of its unique environmental or aesthetic attributes is far more difficult. Economists are trying to understand the value of natural resources through a variety of techniques. Environmental groups, however, generally object to the notion that natural resources can have values (prices) established for them.

In this section, we argued that neither the government nor the market is adequate to the task of addressing environmental capital in communities. Generally, the government, particularly both federal and state governments, operates at a level that does not take into account community-level natural resources. They are too small to manage, and sometimes are too small to regulate, even though a particular natural resource may be an important asset to a community. The market also has difficulty with accounting for natural resources for their environmental value rather than their monetary value, so the market cannot be trusted to manage a community's environmental assets.

With the present institutional setting, sprawl will continue, if not actually promoted, and with less financial support from federal and state governments, other organizations need to fill the gap to conserve and preserve natural resources. Land trusts and CDCs are two types of organizations that are concerned with their community's environmental capital. In the next section, we examine how CBOs represent an alternative to government and to the market in managing, conserving, and preserving environmental assets.

Community-Based Organizations

Among the organizations interested in protecting a community's environmental capital and dealing with sprawl are CBOs, such as CDCs and community land trusts. For the most part, environmental organizations in the United States have taken the lead in addressing concerns over the conservation, preservation, and degradation of natural resources. Many national environmental organizations, such as the Sierra Club, the Audubon Society, and the Nature Conservancy, have local chapters that address local concerns or issues. However, local chapters of national organizations may not always have place as their chief concern; the larger organization and its interests may matter more. We are interested in CBOs that are rooted in a place, are supported by residents, and have as their missions a focus on the community as a geographic entity.

Specific issues become important to communities for a variety of reasons. In the next section, we address debates on two problems, sprawl and abandonment of land (e.g., brownfields) and buildings that are taking place simultaneously; however, sprawl is occurring primarily at the intersection between urban and rural places, and abandonment of land and buildings is occurring primarily within cities. Although we can find sprawl occurring on the outskirts of small rural communities in counties that are experiencing rapid growth and we can find brownfields in rural areas, these two phenomena occur mostly in suburbs and inner cities.

CBOs in such places as Detroit, Michigan; Atlanta, Georgia; Ventura, California; Houston, Texas; Racine, Wisconsin; Jefferson Parish, Louisiana; Oakland, California; and St. Louis, Missouri, are coming up with ways to deal with sprawl, vacant land, and brownfields, while preserving the natural environment. One particularly popular organization is the community land trust.

What Is a Community Land Trust?

A land trust is a nonprofit, voluntary organization that works with landowners to protect land, usually open space and green space. Land trusts use a variety of techniques to protect land, such as conservation easements. The first land trust was created in Massachusetts in 1891. According to Alderich and Wyerman (2006), as of 2005 there were more than 1,667 land trusts in the United States. In 1985, there were only 743.

BOX 10.5 EXAMPLES OF KINDS OF LAND PROTECTED BY LAND TRUSTS

- Wetlands
- Wildlife habitats
- Ranches
- Shorelines
- Forests
- Scenic views
- Farms
- Watersheds
- Historic estates
- Recreational areas

SOURCE: Land Trust Alliance (1999a).

Some of the diverse purposes of these organizations are to protect open space and green places threatened by sprawl and development, save individual landowners money, protect local quality of life, create affordable housing, and ensure a safe, reliable, and affordable food supply. Local land trusts have protected more than 4.7 million acres, and national land trusts have protected an additional 13 million acres of forests, wetlands, farmland, and greenways (Fisher & MacDowell, 1999). Increasingly, land trusts are used to purchase and develop brownfields. Because individual developers are not likely to take the risk in investing in these projects, land trusts can overcome some of the obstacles to developing the community.

Land trusts vary in their size, scope, mission, staff (volunteers or experts), boards of directors, and membership. They receive funds from members, land donors, other nonprofits, government agencies, foundations, and corporate partners (Fisher & MacDowell, 1999).

What Do Land Trusts Do?

A land trust "works to conserve land by undertaking or assisting land transactions with landowners in order to permanently protect the natural, scenic, agricultural, historic or cultural attributes of their land" (Fisher & MacDowell, 1999, p. 1). Land trusts accomplish this objective by obtaining some degree of legal control over the land. Community land trusts typically acquire and hold land but sell off any residential or commercial buildings that are on the land. In this way, the cost of land in the housing equation is minimized or eliminated, thus making the housing more affordable.

Land trusts face four challenges in their operations: raising funds, educating landowners about the financial benefits of land preservation, assisting communities in creating land protection strategies, and selecting the "right" projects (Daniels & Bowers, 1997). Several regional and national organizations have been established to help land trusts address these challenges.

The primary tool used by land trusts is a conservation easement. This tool coincides with the general organizational philosophy of a voluntary approach to land management (Daniels & Bowers, 1997). Other tools advocated by land trusts to landowners to preserve their land include an outright donation to the land trust, a bequest or donation of conservation easements, or the sale of land at below-market value.

A conservation easement is a legal agreement by a landowner to protect permanently open space. The first conservation easement was prepared by Frederick Law Olmstead, Sr., in the 1880s to protect parkways in and around Boston (Land Trust Alliance, 1999a). The Tax Reform Act of 1976 explicitly recognized conservation easements as tax-deductible donations. As of 1999, all states have enabling legislation in place for conservation easements. Conservation easements can be legally complex and if not done well can be challenged in court successfully. Land trusts that accept land through a conservation easement should be prepared to enforce it. There are also agricultural conservation easements that are designed to protect farmland. These types of conservation easements are important in that they keep farmland in agricultural use and productivity (American Farmland Trust, 1999). (See Case Studies 10.3, 10.4, and 10.5.)

**CASE STUDY 10.3 BUYING
A CONSERVATION EASEMENT OR SAVING FARMLAND FOREVER**

The Wisconsin Farmland Conservancy, dedicated to keeping farming alive in northwestern Wisconsin, helped to raise $30,000 in 1997 to buy a conservation easement on the 40-acre, community-supported Common Harvest Farm near Osceola, near the growing Minneapolis–St. Paul, Minnesota, corridor. The money ensured that Dan Guenthner and Margaret Pennings, who had been tenant farmers on five farms consumed by sprawl over the past decade, would be able to farm as long as they wished. The conservation easement guarantees that the land will be protected as a farm forever.

SOURCE: Land Trust Alliance (1999a).

CASE STUDY 10.4 BEQUEATHING LAND

Lamenting that neighboring farms with views of the Smoky Mountains are quickly being transformed into cookie-cutter subdivisions, Jim and Gail Harris instead wrote their wills to bequeath their 400-acre farm near Knoxville to the Foothills Land Conservancy. The conservancy accepted a revocable trust on the farm, which land trust officials estimate will be worth several million dollars by the time it passes on to the conservancy. Then the Foothills Land Conservancy will either maintain or lease the farm or permanently protect it with a conservation easement before selling it.

SOURCE: Land Trust Alliance (1999a).

CASE STUDY 10.5 USE OF SALES TAX TO BUY A CONSERVATION EASEMENT

Using funds from a 1% sales tax that Gunnison County, Colorado, voters passed in 1997, as well as donations from area businesses and other sources, the Gunnison Ranchland Conservation Legacy as of November 2006 has protected 15,355 acres. "The waiting list includes 18 families with another 13,000 acres" (Gunnison Ranchland Conservation Legacy, 2007). Ultimately, the fledgling land trust hopes to complete conservation easement agreements, to be held by organizations such as the Colorado Cattlemen's Agricultural Land Trust, on much of the 65,000 acres of prime ranch land in the county. Already, the land trust's Ranchland Protection Program, which purchases development rights from willing landowners, has protected a 12-mile ribbon along Tomichi Creek.

SOURCE: Land Trust Alliance (1999a).

Why Do People Choose to Use Land Trusts?

For some people, saving specific pieces of land is important for what that land and the uses on it contribute to the community. For example, in

New York City, Mayor Rudolph Guiliani planned to auction 115 lots throughout the city where community gardens had been functioning. The Trust for Public Land and the New York Restoration Project purchased the land to preserve the community gardens (Enzer, 1999). Other people donate a conservation easement or bequeath land to a land trust because they have a special connection to their piece of property and want it to remain undeveloped.

Do Land Trusts Work?

If someone donates a conservation easement, will it be enforced? First, if the amount of land is any indication of success, the Land Trust Alliance estimated that 37 million acres of land is being protected through land trusts (Alderich & Wyerman, 2006). This figure is relatively small and covers only some of the most threatened land. Second, many of these organizations and the key tool they use, conservation easements, are relatively new. Recently, easement violations have sent land trusts to court in an effort to protect conservation easements. Enforcement of easements will be the true test of whether land trusts are considered successful in their mission. Thus, for many land trusts, it is too early to tell whether they can be considered successful because the original owner who made the conservation easement continues to enjoy the land.

Given the amount and types of land that are protected through these tools, at this early stage land trusts can be considered successful in their limited, yet important, purpose. Land trusts have only had a marginal impact on development processes because they control such a small amount of land. Yet there is a growing interest in using land trusts to preserve open space (as a result of development pressures) and to deal with abandoned property and structures in inner cities.

The number of land trusts involved in brownfield redevelopment is growing. Land trusts face several obstacles in these projects. The most difficult problem is the fear of legal liability. Federal legal liability is a result of the Comprehensive Environmental Response, Compensation and Liability Act (CERCLA)—usually referred to as the Superfund. Usually, landowners who did not know about the contamination are not legally responsible, but there can be cases where they will be held liable. Second, most land trusts lack funds for remediation costs. Finally, land trusts still face difficulty in finding end users for the land.

One of the most successful efforts by a land trust to acquire and own land that was a brownfield is the Dudley Street Initiative (see Case Study 1.1 in Chapter 1). The organization was able to receive the power of eminent domain from the city of Boston to acquire vacant land and buildings in its neighborhood. The land was eventually used for affordable housing projects. Several intermediary organizations are emerging to deal with the financing needs of redevelopment of brownfields.

Summary and Conclusions

A community's environmental capital is diverse because it comprises the entire range of natural resources within a community, from water to air to land and more. Environmental capital is complex, both in how it operates within a community and in how it works to preserve, conserve, and use that capital appropriately and with care. Because of this diversity and complexity, this chapter focused only on land and touched on only a couple of issues, sprawl and brownfields, that can affect environmental capital in its entirety. Further, it focused only on ways that one kind of CBO can address some of the concerns associated with sprawl and brownfields.

The federal government has refocused its approach to managing and regulating natural resources and is acting as a technical resource and as enforcement oversight rather than as a top-down command-and-control regulator. The market, or private sector approaches, especially as it relates to community environmental capital, is not acting to preserve or conserve specific natural resources, instead tending to use and possibly abuse them. Thus, as in other areas of communities, CBOs are becoming an alternative organizational means of accomplishing community environmental goals.

KEY CONCEPTS

Aesthetic qualities	Groundwater
Amenities	Land trust
Brownfields	Management approaches
Command-and-control regulation	Point and nonpoint source pollution
Conservation easements	Regulatory approaches
Environmental capital	Sprawl
Environmental justice	Surface water
Environmental racism	Traditional
Geographic setting	neighborhood development

QUESTIONS

1. Name three problems that can threaten a community's environmental capital.

2. Why are natural resources or the environment used in conjunction with the term *capital?* Is this a contradiction?

3. Why are CBOs an appropriate organizational level for dealing with a community's environmental capital?

4. What is sprawl? What causes sprawl? What are some strategies to deal with sprawl? Can New Urbanism contribute to social capital?

5. What is a brownfield? What are three "causes" of brownfields?

6. What is environmental justice? What are some of the factors contributing to environmental justice?

EXERCISES

1. Find out if there is a land trust organization in your community. What does it do? What kinds of land has it preserved? How did the land trust do it? What kinds of tools did it use?

2. Are there any brownfields or abandoned buildings in your community? If there are, what is being done to redevelop them? Have any brownfields been redeveloped in your community in the past? How was it done? Which organizations were involved? Did any CBOs get involved?

3. What are the forms of environmental capital in your community? Is any organization taking care of parts of it? What is that organization doing? How successful is it in conserving or preserving environmental capital?

REFERENCES

Alderich, R., & Wyerman, J. (2006). *2005 National land trust census report.* Washington, DC: Land Trust Alliance.

American Farmland Trust. (1999). Good deals: Colorado farm hedges out sprawl. *LandWorks Connection, 11,* 5–6.

American Planning Association. (2006). *Creating community-based brownfields redevelopment strategies.* Washington, DC: Author.

Anderson, T. L., Smith, V. L., & Simmons, E. (1999). *How and why to privatize federal lands* (Report No. 363). Washington, DC: Cato Institute.

Bethel New Life. (2006). *Sustainable development.* Chicago: Author.

Bullard, R. D. (1994). *Dumping in Dixie: Race, class and environmental quality* (2nd ed.). Boulder, CO: Westview.

Daniels, T. L., & Bowers, D. (1997). *Holding our ground: Protecting America's farms and farmland.* Washington, DC: Island Press.

Enzer, M. (1999). Land trust, actress save NYC community gardens. *American Forests, 105,* 11.

Ewing, R. (1997). Is Los Angeles-style sprawl desirable? *Journal of the American Planning Association, 63,* 107–126.

Ewing, R., & Kostyack, J. (2005). *Endangered by sprawl: How runaway development threatens America's wildlife.* Washington, DC: National Wildlife Federation.

Ferguson, R. F., & Dickens, W. T. (Eds.). (1999). *Urban problems and community development.* Washington, DC: Brookings Institution.

Fisher, J., & MacDowell, M. (1999). *Land trusts: A new strategy for private lands conservation in Latin America.* Arlington, VA: The Nature Conservancy.

Gillham, O. (2002). *The limitless city: A primer on the urban sprawl*. Washington, DC: Island Press.

Gordon, P., & Richardson, H. W. (1997). Are compact cities a desirable planning goal? *Journal of the American Planning Association, 63,* 95–106.

Gunnison Ranchland Conservation Legacy. (2007). Home page. Retrieved March 27, 2007, from http://www.gunnisonlegacy.org

Haines, A. (2003). Smart growth: A solution to sprawl? *The Land Use Tracker, 2*(4), 1–4.

Kretzmann, J. P., & McKnight, J. L. (1993). *Building communities from the inside out: A path toward finding and mobilizing a community's assets*. Evanston, IL: Northwestern University, Center for Urban Affairs and Policy Research.

Land Trust Alliance. (1999a). *Land trusts: The front guards of land protection*. Washington, DC: Author.

Land Trust Alliance. (1999b). *Land trusts succeed every day*. Washington, DC: Author.

Mazmanian, D. A., & Kraft, M. E. (1999). The three epochs of the environmental movement. In D. A. Mazmanian & M. E. Kraft (Eds.), *Toward sustainable communities: Transition and transformations in environmental policy* (pp. 3–41). Cambridge, MA: MIT Press.

McDonald, L., Allen, W., Benedict, M., & O'Connor, K. (2005). Green infrastructure plan evaluation frameworks. *Journal of Conservation Planning, 1,* 12–43.

Office of Technology Assessment. (1995). *The technological reshaping of metropolitan America* (OTA-ETI-643). Washington, DC: Government Printing Office.

PlannersWeb. (1999). *Problems associated with sprawl*. Burlington, VT: Author.

PlannersWeb. (2000). *How do you define sprawl?* Burlington, VT: Author.

Sierra Club. (1999). *The costs and consequences of urban sprawl*. San Francisco: Author.

Sierra Club. (2001). *A complex relationship: Population growth and suburban sprawl*. San Francisco: Author.

Sierra Club. (2006). *Toxics: Brownfields*. San Francisco: Author.

Smart Growth Online. (2006). *Principles of smart growth*. Washington, DC: Sustainable Communities Network.

U.S. Department of Agriculture. (2003). *National resources inventory, 2003, annual NRI*. Washington, DC: Natural Resources Conservation Service.

U.S. Environmental Protection Agency. (1998). *Final guidance for incorporating environmental justice concerns in EPA's NEPA compliance analyses*. Washington, DC: U.S. Government Printing Office.

U.S. Environmental Protection Agency. (2006). *About brownfields: Brownfields cleanup and redevelopment*. Washington, DC: Author.

U.S. Environmental Protection Agency, CONCERN, Inc., Community Sustainability Resource Institute, & Jobs and Environment Campaign. (1995). *Sustainability in action: Profiles of community initiatives across the United States*. Washington, DC: Environmental Protection Agency.

Zilney, L. A., McGurrin, D., & Zahran, S. (2006). Environmental justice and the role of criminology: An analytical review of 33 years of environmental justice research. *Criminal Justice Review, 3,* 47–62.

ADDITIONAL READINGS AND RESOURCES

Readings

Agyeman, J., Bullard, R. D., & Evans, B. (2003). *Just sustainabilities: Development in an unequal world*. Cambridge, MA: MIT Press.

Beckerman, W., & Pasek, J. (2001). *Justice, posterity, and the environment*. New York: Oxford University Press.

Buckingham, S., & Turner, M. (2008). *Understanding environmental issues.* London: Sage.

Cole, L. W., & Foster, S. R. (2001). *From the ground up: Environmental racism and the rise of the environmental justice movement.* New York: New York University Press.

Daniels, T. L., Keller, J. W., & Lapping, M. B. (1995). *The small town planning handbook* (2nd ed.). Chicago: American Planning Association.

Pellow, D. N., & Brulle, R. J. (2005). *Power, justice, and the environment: A critical appraisal of the environmental justice movement.* Cambridge, MA: MIT Press.

Rhodes, E. K. (2005). *Environmental justice in America: A new paradigm.* Bloomington: Indiana University Press.

Sargent, F. O., Lusk, P., Rivera, J., & Varela, M. (1991). *Rural environmental planning for sustainable communities.* Washington, DC: Island.

Schlosberg, D. (2009). *Defining environmental justice: Theories, movements, and nature.* New York: Oxford University Press.

Shiva, V. (2008). *Soil not oil: Environmental justice in an age of climate crisis.* Boston: South End Press.

Sierra Club. (2001). *Costs of sprawl.* San Francisco: Author.

Smart Growth Network. (2002). *Getting to smart growth: 100 policies for implementation.* Washington, DC: ICMA.

U.S. Environmental Protection Agency. (1997). *Community-based environmental protection: A resource book for protecting ecosystems and communities* (EPA 230-B-96–003). Washington, DC: Author.

White, K., & Matthei, C. (1987). Community land trusts. In S. T. Bruyn & J. Meehan (Eds.), *Beyond the market and the state: New directions in community development* (pp. 41–64). Philadelphia: Temple University Press.

Websites

American Farmland Trust—www.farmland.org. This organization's mission is to work to stop the loss of productive farmland and to promote farming practices that lead to a healthy environment. Its site includes a current legislative agenda, conferences, tools and resources, and an online store with a publications section.

Community Coalition for Environmental Justice—http://www.ccej.org/. The mission of this organization is to achieve environmental and economic justice in low-income communities and communities of color. It believes that everyone, regardless of race or income, has the right to a clean and healthy community.

Environmental Justice Foundation—http://www.ejfoundation.org/. This foundation provides training and educational material on environmental justice issues, primarily for communities and organizations in the global South.

Environmental Justice Resource Center at Atlanta University—http://www.ejrc.cau.edu/. A comprehensive resource for those interested in environmental justice issues.

International Economic Development Council—www.iedconline.org. This site provides information on brownfields and many other issues pertinent to economic development.

Land Trust Alliance—www.lta.org. The Land Trust Alliance promotes voluntary land conservation and strengthens the land trust movement by providing the leadership, information, skills, and resources land trusts need to conserve land for the benefit of communities and natural systems.

Sierra Club: Environmental Justice and Community Partnerships—http://www.sierraclub.org/ej/. This program of the Sierra Club provides resources for exploring the relationship between social and environmental justice, as well as support for community action.

Smart Growth Network—www.smartgrowth.org. This website provides comprehensive information on smart growth activities and databases.

Sprawl Watch Clearinghouse—www.sprawlwatch.org. The Sprawl Watch Clearinghouse's mission is to make the tools, techniques, and strategies developed to manage growth, accessible to citizens, grassroots organizations, environmentalists, public officials, planners, architects, the media, and business leaders.

The Trust for Public Land—www.tpl.org. This is a national land trust organization working to preserve land, open space, gardens, greenways, and riverways.

Urban Land Institute—www.uli.org. This organization's primary interest is in land use policy and real estate development. It publishes many useful publications, such as *Urban Land and Smart Growth*. The institute conducts many useful workshops and conferences on a variety of land use and real estate issues.

U.S. Environmental Protection Agency (EPA)—http://www.epa.gov/oecaerth/environmentaljustice/. The EPA website information and resources on environmental justice issues.

U.S. Environmental Protection Agency-Green Communities—www.epa.gov/greenkit/. This site provides a step-by-step guide for planning and implementing sustainable actions. It provides a multitude of information on tools, resources (financial, data, and other), and case studies.

Videos

Flow (2008), directed by Irena Salina and produced by Steven Starr. The film examines the worldwide crisis in water. Available from Oscilloscope Laboratories: http://www.oscilloscope.net/.

In Our Own Backyard: The First Love Canal (1982), produced by Lynn Corcoran. Depicts the first brush the United States had with toxic waste at Love Canal. Available from Bullfrog Films, 372 Dautrich Road, Reading, PA 19606; phone: (610) 779–8226; fax: (610) 370–1978.

Laid to Waste (1997), produced and directed by Robert Bahar and George McCollough. Provides an excellent case study of a community fighting against a hazardous waste site. Available from University of California Extension, Center for Media and Independent Learning, 2000 Center Street, CA 94704.

Ours to Decide (1999), produced and directed by Dorrie Brooks. Available from Shebang Media, 710 Woodward Drive, Madison, WI 53704; e-mail: shebang@execpc.com; Internet: www.execpc.com/7Eshebang.

11

Political Capital

What is power? In the context of our discussion about asset building and community development, it means influence over major development projects and other issues affecting the quality of life of residents. Social scientists have debated the definition of power for decades. For some, power is the ability to influence community decision making. Others argue that power is expressed frequently in ways that are more indirect. It may involve nondecisions as well. For example, decisions about where and when development occurs may actually be made by individuals behind the scenes who make their interests and preferences known to public officials but are not directly involved in the decision. Individuals may be influenced subtly by the **anticipated reaction** or by the agenda-setting activities of others. The sociologist Max Weber defined power broadly as the ability to influence others, despite resistance. This definition seems to include both decisions and nondecisions.

Power is at the heart of political capital. Political capital is defined as access to decision making. It is important to make a distinction between instrumental and structural political capital. Instrumental political capital consists of resources that actors can use to influence policies in their own interest. Structural political capital refers to attributes of the political system that shape participation in decision making. In this chapter, we examine both dimensions of political capital.

Power too often is viewed in negative terms. Often, it is considered something that others have that is used for self-interest rather than for public good. For community organizers, however, power cannot be avoided. It is a basic element of a democratic society. Power can be used constructively by ordinary people. To do so, however, requires an understanding of what power is and how it can be used and controlled. In this chapter, we discuss several issues: how community power is measured and conceptualized, what power is used for, and how organizations can use different strategies to build political capital.

BOX 11.1 POLITICAL CAPITAL FACTS

- The percentage of eligible Americans choosing to vote in presidential elections declined from 62.8% in 1960 to 48.9% in 1996.
- The percentage of Americans attending a public meeting about town on school affairs has declined by 35% since the early 1970s.
- The percentage of Americans attending a political rally or speech has declined by 34% since the early 1970s.

SOURCE: Putnam (2000).

Key Concepts and Debates

Much of the social science literature on community power has focused on **elite theory**. Hunter's book, *Community Power Structure* (1953), is considered a seminal study in the field. His study of Atlanta examined how power was concentrated in the hands of a small group of individuals who influenced the major decisions affecting the city. In this case study, it was the large corporations in Atlanta that shaped the broad political and economic decisions. Hunter relied primarily on a reputational approach (see the description of this method later in this chapter) to analyze how local business people were able to exert influence over local government decisions.

Hunter's (1953) findings were extremely controversial at the time because they implied that local governments were not democratic, but were captured by local elites. In response to these claims, Dahl (1961) published *Who Governs?* In this book, Dahl criticized not only the theoretical basis of Hunter's work, but also the research methods he used in Atlanta. Dahl studied local decision making in New Haven, Connecticut. He argued that power was widely dispersed and local elected officials tended to be the primary decision makers (**pluralist theory**). This study sparked a major debate among social scientists over the methodological and conceptual bases of community power.

This debate over community power led to decades of research about power. Much of the earlier research focused on who influenced decisions affecting the community. Later, there was much more interest in nondecisions and the ways in which informal influence could be exerted. For example, decision makers may be influenced by the anticipated reaction of powerful actors in the community. This influence is much more structural as it does not involve individuals directly exerting influence over decisions.

The controversy over community power shifted to an interest in the consequences of power for communities. One of the key theories to directly examine this issue was growth machine theory (Logan & Molotch, 1987). **Growth machine theory** posits that land-based elites in communities profit from the increased intensification of land uses. The imperative in most communities is growth. Key members of the growth machine include land developers, politicians, local media, and utility companies. The chief conflict in communities is between those who are primarily interested in land as exchange value (profit/rent derived through the exchange of land) and those who view land as use value (providing basic needs of shelter and security, as well as meeting other social needs). Growth, according to this theory, tends to benefit the land-based elite, while contributing to environmental and social problems and creating fiscal stress because of the additional services and infrastructure needed to support growth. Although growth machine theory focuses on the political and economic forces that affect decision making, it also includes the supporting pro-growth ideology that exists in most communities. Logan and Molotch (1987) also argue that the local growth machine is so powerful that efforts to manage growth so as to protect the environment and provide benefits to the working-class are largely ineffective.

Growth machine theory differs from elite theory in that the source of power is land ownership, or class, rather than authority in organizations, or status. Growth machine theory also goes beyond answering the question of who has power and asks what power is used for in the community. The assumption is that community power is used to promote growth and that growth most often does not benefit residents. Instead, growth generates increased rent (income) for the growth machine. The ideology of growth, however, legitimates the decisions made by local government officials and other policy makers. The growth machine does not necessarily have to exert active control of government decisions. In many cases, local officials find it in their political interest to promote growth.

A less deterministic approach to community power is Stone's (1989) urban regime theory. A regime is defined as the informal arrangements that support the formal workings of the local government. Rather than assume that government officials always respond to growth interests, Stone developed a more nuanced view of power in his analysis of Atlanta (the site of Hunter's earlier study). Local government officials often turn to large corporations, developers, and real estate professionals because of the resources they can provide. Politicians view these financial resources as critical to achieving their objectives and ultimately to getting reelected. Public officials, however, may turn to other organized interests (e.g., neighborhood associations) if these interests can provide public officials with other resources they may need. The key is that these interests must be well organized. The reason that politicians frequently turn to corporate interests is because they are well organized and hold more resources in most instances.

Stone (1989) identified three types of regimes: corporate, prevailing, and caretaker. Corporate regimes are characterized by a central concern with the interests of large corporations and developers. These regimes most closely resemble the growth machine, as defined by Logan and Molotch (1987). Large corporations and developers hold financial and political resources that help government officials achieve their goals. In particular, government officials benefit if they can show that they have facilitated job growth in their community. In this sense, the corporate regime creates mutual benefits for both corporations and officials. Corporate regimes usually emphasize the exchange value of land. In addition, the type of growth most often associated with the corporate regime does not provide economic benefits for the people most in need, such as the unemployed, underemployed, and low-wage workers.

The prevailing coalition is oriented toward progressive policies that expand social services and housing options to low-income and diverse populations. Cities with prevailing coalitions are normally characterized as having strong neighborhood associations, but they are also more likely to exist in college towns and other places with more progressive environments. These organizations can provide politicians with power and help them achieve their political goals. Prevailing coalitions often push for no-growth or stringent environmental policies that limit the activities of corporations or developers. There is considerable debate in the literature regarding whether these policies can effectively counter the power of the growth machine in the long run. There are, however, numerous case studies of effective neighborhood organizations at least forcing politicians to respond to their interests in the development process. Swanstrom (1988) documents the mobilization of a local neighborhood association in Cleveland to support Mayor Kucinich. This regime was able to pass several progressive policies in the city before corporate interests were able to organize an effort to elect a different mayor.

Caretaker regimes tend to be located between these two regimes, balancing the dual goals of keeping taxes and services to a minimum while passively promoting growth. Government officials in caretaker regimes tend to be most influenced by the small business sector and homeowners. They tend to exist in many suburban and rural areas. Government officials tend to emphasize low taxes over job growth and there tend to be fewer perceived benefits of supporting corporate or developer interests.

Regime theory offers a more contingent theory of power than the other theories we discuss here. The overriding tendency in the United States is toward corporate regimes. Large corporations have the financial resources that governmental officials need to be successful, but some progressive regimes have been established. Several examples of progressive regimes include Berkeley, California; Madison, Wisconsin; Santa Cruz, California; and Burlington, Vermont. These are all fairly small cities and university towns. It is not clear whether they provide a viable model for larger cities and those with higher poverty rates. At a minimum, these cases suggest that community organizing and power do matter.

In the next section, we review the different methods for analyzing a local power structure. Such an analysis may serve several purposes. It can be useful for residents or community organizers who wish to promote change in their community or neighborhood. Also, it may be useful for those who want to bring about change in the local power structure.

Methods

There are three common methods for analyzing community power structure: reputational, positional, and decision making. The reputational approach relies on informants to identify influential people in the community. This method assumes that people in formal authority do not necessarily exert power in the community. Some power actors may be less visible and exert influence indirectly. Informants are usually people who are knowledgeable about local affairs and issues, such as bankers, elected officials, union leaders, ministers, journalists, and business leaders. In this approach, no rule mandates how many people should be interviewed and how the questions should be asked. In most cases, at least a dozen people in a neighborhood are interviewed, and more if the community is large. Informants are asked to list the most influential people in the community, including those who may not be in positions of formal authority. After interviewing people and comparing lists, it is possible to identify those mentioned consistently across lists as holding power. The advantage of this approach to measuring power is that it identifies a wide scope of power actors, especially those in several different areas of the community and those who do not occupy formal positions. It also is relatively easy to identify the formal power structure through this method. The disadvantages are that reputed power actors may not actually exercise power and the method fails to identify specialized power actors for specific issues, such as economic development and education. Also, residents may be less reluctant to identify the informal power structure, such as that of gang members and leaders.

A second method for analyzing the local power structure, the positional approach, identifies persons in important formal positions of power. The positional approach usually begins by identifying the key institutions in the community. In most cases, these institutions include large businesses, educational and health facilities, religious organizations, and civic organizations. The assumption one makes in this approach is that individuals who occupy key positions in these institutions are influential because of their control over organizational and institutional resources in the community. These institutions often employ a large number of workers, purchase a significant amount of goods and services in the region, and are involved in the major economic and political issues facing the community. This approach can be completed relatively quickly because power actors are visible and easily identified. Positional analyses, however, focus primarily on the potential for exercising power rather than on whether an individual actually uses those resources. Also, this method does not adequately consider informal sources of power in the community.

The third approach to examining the local power structure is to analyze events or issues over time. These events could have occurred in the past, or they can be current issues. By identifying individuals or groups that tend to win on most critical decisions affecting the community, it is possible to identify the person or group who exercises power and to identify the power exercised across issues. It is difficult, however, to gain a thorough understanding of the behind-the-scenes aspects of these decisions. This method also ignores actors who are able to keep certain issues from emerging on the local agenda.

This discussion of the different methods of measuring community power does not imply that it is necessary to choose only one method. In fact, it often makes sense to combine methods to generate an accurate assessment of the local power structure. There is usually more overlap between the reputational and positional methods (as much as 0.75 agreement) and much less between the decision-making and reputational or positional methods. One strategy for combining methods would be to use elements of both the reputational and the decision-making methods. In using this strategy, one might begin with a reputational approach but then ask about a specific issue or controversy in the community. This approach might help informants go beyond generalities and the people involved in the decisions and whether these people are involved in multiple issues.

As one might expect, a strong relationship exists between the methods used to measure community power and the type of power structure found. Researchers using a positional method tend to find that community power is concentrated in a few hands. Decision-making methods generate findings that support the pluralist view of power. Reputational methods focus primarily on perceptions of influence, and decision-making methods examine issues and the variety of actors trying to influence local decisions. None of these approaches focus on what power is used for in the community.

One of the issues that all three methods face is that they focus largely on decisions. Power, however, can be expressed through nondecisions as well. One usually thinks of power as the ability to make decisions, although it can be exercised by shaping what does not happen in the community. A couple of examples may help illustrate the importance of nondecisions. One example is the problem of anticipated reaction. Power of the dominant group may be such that potential opponents consider it wise not to raise complaints or challenge decisions because they fear repercussions. Another example is the exclusion of potentially contentious issues from the political agenda by defining them as illegitimate demands. In both of these situations, power is being exercised, but not through actual decisions. Most methods for measuring community power cannot adequately examine these situations.

Community-Based Organizations and Political Capital

This review of the social science literature on community power suggests that the central debate has been whether power is concentrated in the hands of a few or widely distributed through the community. Elite theorists argue that in most communities the business elite has disproportionate power.

Pluralists tend to see power as much more fluid, with no single group able to exert power consistently over major policies. In this section, we discuss the experience of community-based organizations (CBOs) in building power. Most of the social science literature is skeptical that CBOs can effectively counter the influence of business elites or successfully pressure elected officials to address CBOs' concerns. We focus on several successful models that have been used in a wide variety of contexts.

Community organizing has its roots in the social movements of the 1960s. Many of the leaders of the past 30 years have been trained or were involved in the civil rights movement or the antiwar movement (especially Students for a Democratic Society) or both. Two important community organizations emerging from these movements are the Industrial Areas Foundation (IAF) and ACORN. In the following sections, we discuss the differences in tactics and strategies of these two organizations and briefly analyze other significant models of community organizing.

Stoecker (2001) identified three types of community organizing models: **power models, development models,** and **information models.** The premise of power models is that the poor need to be organized to gain power. The focus, then, is on mobilizing the poor to act collectively in their common interest. Stoecker differentiated between power models that emphasize the institutional basis for organizing and individual approaches. The IAF is a good example of the institutional approach, while ACORN is an individual-based approach to organizing. Institutional approaches tend to work from existing organizations, whereas individual-based organizations emphasize building new organizations for the poor.

Development models typically emphasize substantive issues and stress the importance of bringing people together and helping them help themselves. The asset-based development approach discussed employs this model. Most CDCs also tend to operate under this model.

The third community organizing model is the information model, which is most often associated with Paulo Freire and Myles Horton and others like them. This model stresses the importance of education in understanding community problems, ultimately leading to community action. This model falls between the power and development models in its approach toward organizing and issues.

In the next section, we briefly describe the power and information models. We use the IAF and ACORN as examples of the power model and the Highlander Center as an illustration of the information model. The development model was described in more detail in the beginning of the book.

Power Models

A central figure in the history of community organizing is Saul Alinsky (1971). Alinsky established the IAF in 1941. The fundamental purpose of the IAF is to build organizations that use power. The basic principles of Alinsky's approach are outlined in his book *Rules for Radicals*. Alinsky is best known for his confrontational tactics in organizing and engaging the poor in politics. Alinsky began his work in community organizing with the Back of the Yards neighborhood program in Chicago. Ed Chambers has headed the IAF since Alinsky's death in 1972. IAF remains the oldest and largest organizing institution in the United States. In the past 30 years, thousands of citizen leaders have participated in and completed the 10-day organizer training.

The IAF has evolved since the 1970s to include 55 local organizations, operating in 21 states. Three IAF organizations that have received a great deal of attention in recent years include the Citizens Organized for Public Service (COPS) in San Antonio, Texas; the Baltimoreans United in Leadership Development (BUILD) in Maryland; and the Queens Citizens Organization (QCO) in New York. The IAF is currently focusing on several common issues across the local organizations, including living wage campaigns, job training, public education, and affordable housing.

CASE STUDY 11.1 COMMUNITIES ORGANIZED FOR PUBLIC SERVICES (COPS)

Communities Organized for Public Service (COPS) is an organization of 26 parishes in the predominantly Hispanic, low-income west side and south side of San Antonio. Founded in 1974, it is the oldest of the IAF organizations in Texas. Mark Warren's (2001) book, *Dry Bones Rattling: Community Building to Revitalize American Democracy*, provides an excellent overview of the project. Part of the success of COPS has been its ability to organize across racial and ethnic lines on several issues. The following examples are among its successes:

- Established a $10 million Housing Trust Fund to finance affordable housing in inner-city neighborhoods
- Organized the San Antonio Education Partnership to guarantee jobs and scholarships to high school seniors from poor neighborhoods
- Created a community policing strategy with three neighborhood storefront police stations and a neighborhood foot patrol program
- Blocked a proposal to sell the municipally owned electric utility to private interests, which would have significantly increased utility rates

One of the guiding principles of Alinsky's (1971) style of organizing is that self-interest, not altruism, should be the primary incentive for organizing people to take action. Altruism may get people interested in the issues for a while, but self-interest is much more sustainable.

The IAF uses a standard process in their effort to build broad-based citizens' organizations. The process usually begins with one-on-one meetings (called relational meetings) with organizational leaders. The relational meeting is not about pushing an agenda, but instead, organizers learn about the aspirations and values of individuals. The goal is to look for interests, talents, and values that connect people across the community. This stage of organizing can be time-consuming and last more than a year. It is important work, however, in understanding the grounding of a broad-based organization.

Broad-based organizations consist of a variety of affiliates that are dues-paying organizations. These are multi-issue organizations, and the IAF must find common ground across organizations. Critical to the success of these efforts, is the role of paid organizers.

Although there is a great deal of emphasis on identifying common ground, conflict is at the heart of the IAF's strategy. The goal is to make change, and change requires building power and ultimately conflict. Good organizers choose tactics that make people feel uncomfortable and elicit a reaction. It is important to anticipate the reaction and plan accordingly. One of the distinguishing characteristics of Alinsky's (1971) influence on the IAF model is the emphasis on organization rather than ideology. The goal is not a social movement but an organization that deals with specific community issues.

Another power model, ACORN, began in 1970 as part of the National Welfare Rights Organization (NWRO). The leader of the NWRO at the time, George Wiley, attempted to broaden the approach of the organization to economic justice issues by sending an organizer, Wade Rathke, to Little Rock, Arkansas. Their goal was to organize welfare recipients and workers around issues related to education, health care, and housing. They targeted the poor and welfare recipients and encouraged them to establish themselves as a multi-issue organization.

The goal of ACORN is to build a mass community organization to develop sufficient power to achieve individual member interests. Today, ACORN has more than 150,000 family members in more than 450 neighborhood organizations in 60 cities. ACORN uses a relatively standard model for organizing neighborhoods. Rather than mobilizing residents through existing neighborhood organizations (e.g., churches or unions) like the IAF does, ACORN organizes through a door-to-door campaign. It claims to organize the unorganized. The process starts with research and analysis of the problem. ACORN organizers attempt to identify allies for the campaign. Existing neighborhood organizations may be seen as allies, but they usually do not play a formal role in establishing priorities. Another important distinction between ACORN and the IAF is that ACORN uses electoral politics as a key element of their strategy, whereas IAF does not. For example, ACORN regularly supports political candidates who support its interests and programs.

Organizers generally make between 20 and 40 individual contacts per day during the organizing drive. Each contact is spoken with twice and receives two letters and a phone call in a 6-week period. Then the organizer identifies 10 to 15 people in the area who have leadership potential.

Next, an organizing committee is established. The committee identifies the initial issues to be addressed by the organization, collects dues, and involves members in its activities. The organizing committee holds a neighborhood meeting where the history and role of ACORN is explained. The neighborhood residents discuss the issues and select one issue to examine in more detail. After researching the problem, the organization moves toward collective social action. ACORN relies heavily on creative confrontation that polarizes organized low-income residents and "monied" interests.

In recent years, ACORN has focused on several key issues affecting low-income communities: predatory lending, living-wage laws, school quality, affordable housing, community investment, utility costs, and child care. Although most of ACORN's efforts are truly grassroots driven, the group also has a national agenda on some key issues, such as predatory lending.

ACORN suffered a serious setback in 2009 when an undercover videotape exposed ACORN staff encouraging residents to commit fraud. Fundraising for the national organization collapsed, and the future of ACORN is unclear. Many local chapters have changed their name due to the bad publicity. It is likely that local ACORN chapters will continue to survive, but their activities have been significantly curtailed by these set of events.

In addition to the IAF and ACORN, several other organizations use somewhat similar strategies and tactics for organizing. The Gamaliel Foundation was established in 1968 to organize homeowners against the redlining practices of savings and loans on Chicago's west side. The organization has since grown to include more than 60 affiliates in 21 states. The goal of the Gamaliel Foundation is to establish regional organizations in the major metropolitan areas of the United States to address issues related to inequality, concentrated poverty, and segregation. The Gamaliel Foundation has a national leadership and training program for regional leaders.

CASE STUDY 11.2 GAMALIEL FOUNDATION

In recent years, the Gamaliel Foundation has expanded its original mission to focus on three specific issues: (1) to develop a national campaign around the civil rights of immigrants; (2) to provide a broader linking structure for local, progressive organizations; and (3) to focus on urban problems through a regional/metropolitan lens. The Gamaliel Foundation works with faith-based community organizations to build their leadership and capacity.

SOURCE: http://www.gamaliel.org/default.htm

The Pacific Institute for Community Organization (PICO) uses some of the same tactics as the IAF by working through congregations. Headquartered in Oakland, California, PICO is a national network of faith-based organizations focusing on affordable housing, health care, public schools, and redevelopment issues. It claims to have about 1,000 member organizations, representing about one million families in about 150 cities. PICO conducts a national leadership development seminar twice a year that provides an intensive 6-day program.

The Direct Action Research and Training Center's (DART) goal is to establish congregation-based community organizations to confront economic and social injustice. The DART network includes about 20 member organizations in six states, most of which are religious congregations. DART has been most active in living wage campaigns, educational reform, drugs and crime, affordable housing, and community policing. The key element of DART's strategy is to bring together congregations and identify common goals and issues they can address.

Information Models

Most information models are premised on the simple idea that education can be a progressive force for social change. Although there are many intellectual influences on this model, John Dewey's work is considered an important foundation. Education, according to Dewey, is a key element to promoting democracy. The most famous example of the information model for community organizing is the Highlander Center in Monteagle, Tennessee. The Highlander Center was established in 1932 by Myles Horton and Don West to help organize the labor movement in the South. Highlander workshops focused on training people as union leaders in key industries, such as coal, textile, and lumber. The Highlander Center became a central organization of the Committee for Industrial Organization (CIO) in the South.

By the 1950s, the center had turned its attention to the civil rights movement and focused its work on school desegregation and voting rights. The center established Citizenship Schools, which helped African Americans learn to read so they could pass required literacy tests to become eligible voters in the South.

In recent years, the Highlander Center has focused on a wide variety of problems, such as land ownership, environmental degradation, and poverty in Appalachia. There are several common elements to the center's approach to these problems. The Highlander Center recognizes the transformation potential of education and develops programs that build leadership and address key problems in society. The center also relies heavily on participatory research that engages local citizens in understanding the issues their communities face. In its work on land ownership, the center has helped hundreds of community activists and others compile a database of landowners in Appalachia. This approach empowers local citizens and grounds the research in community needs.

CASE STUDY 11.3 HIGHLANDER RESEARCH AND EDUCATION CENTER

The Highlander Center works with grassroots organizations working toward social, economic, and environmental justice throughout Appalachia and the South. It currently has two broad sets of objectives: (1) to develop the capacity of marginalized communities and (2) to build multi-issue cross-constituencies that will help mobilize progressive groups in the region. A key element to the success of the Highlander Center has been the promotion of popular education, which focuses on adult education on a wide variety of social and economic issues. Currently they have programs emphasizing democratic facilitation, education for immigrants and indigenous populations, literacy initiatives, and community-based research by high school students.

SOURCE: http://www.highlandercenter.org/index.html

Summary and Conclusions

Power is a central feature of the community development process. Understanding how to work within a community's power structure or how to organize to gain power is critical to the success of community development projects. In some cases, it is important to understand who is exercising power so as to gain access to resources and influence and thus address community problems. In other instances, it is essential to know how to organize and mobilize residents to gain political power.

Community power is an asset that exists in most communities through its organizations, associations, and institutions. The institutional model sees these organizations as latent sources of power that can bring people together to solve public issues and problems. There are often many obstacles to realizing this potential, however. Organizations are often turf conscious and may be reluctant to coordinate their activities with other community organizations. Race, ethnicity, and class differences may be difficult to overcome. Finally, organizational leaders may be reluctant to mobilize residents because this mobilization might lead to changes in power relations within the organization itself.

Despite numerous examples of successful community organizing, it is still difficult work that typically requires a talented organizer to be successful. Although there may be common values and concerns across organizations and associations in a community, most people focus on organizations' differences rather than their similarities. Community organizing is very time-consuming, and there seems to be less tolerance for this aspect.

For many activists, the ultimate goal is to organize into a broader movement that supports the interests of poor and low-income people. Several organizations we discussed have established national networks that enable communities to learn from one another and provide support. Delgado (1986) argued that there are three primary obstacles to community organizations' impact on national policy. First, community organizations need resources for mobilizing residents as well as maintaining ties with other organizations. Second, to have an impact, community organizations need to have a national presence, such as through electoral politics. Finally, opposition to community organizations, especially by government officials, influences how successful organizations are in building a broader movement.

KEY CONCEPTS

Anticipated reaction

Decision-making method

Development models

Elite theory

Growth machine theory

Information models

Pluralist theory   Regime

Positional method   Regime theory

Power models   Reputational method

QUESTIONS

1. What is community power and what are some of the problems and issues in measuring it?

2. How would you characterize the differences between community leadership and power?

3. Research suggests that the reputational approach to measuring power tends to lead to the conclusion that an elite structure of power exists, whereas decision-making approaches generally conclude that pluralism exists at the local level. Why do you think there is such a strong link between the methods used to analyze community power and the findings regarding the structure of power?

4. What do you think are some of the strengths and weaknesses of institutional and individual approaches to the power model of community organizing? Are there differences in success in terms of the context or issues? Explain.

5. In this book, we distinguish between the concept of community development and community organizing. Do you see any potential for merging these two approaches with any of the models of community organizing discussed in this chapter?

6. Compare and contrast the different organizations involved in promoting community organizing.

EXERCISES

1. Analyze the local power structure in a community using the three methods for measuring power (reputational, positional, and decision making) discussed in this chapter. Compare and contrast your results. Is there any overlap in the findings? How would you characterize the differences?

2. Congregations play a central role in the institutional approach to community organizing. Identify some congregations in your community and interview their leaders about their role in addressing social and economic justice in their community. How much interaction do they have with other congregations and what issues are they currently working on in the community?

3. Identify an issue that has been contentious in your neighborhood or community (it is best to choose one that is not currently the hottest topic). List the organizations involved in the controversy. Interview some of the organizational leaders to gain an understanding of their interests and positions regarding this controversy. Are there any key organizations not involved in the controversy? Interview their leaders to provide an explanation for their lack of involvement.

4. Identify a community organizing effort in your area. Interview the staff and discuss the mission, strategies, and tactics of the organization. What has been done to build the capacity of the organization? What specific issues has this organization taken on in recent years?

REFERENCES

Alinsky, S. D. (1971). *Rules for radicals: A pragmatic primer for realistic radicals.* New York: Vintage Books.

Birner, R., & Wittner, H. (2000). *Converting social capital into political capital: How do local communities gain political influence? A theoretical approach and empirical evidence from Thailand and Columbia.* Retrieved August 17, 2006, from dlc.dlib.indiana.edu/documents/dir0/00/00/02/21/dlc-00000221–00/birnerr 041300.pdf

Dahl, R. (1961). *Who governs?* New Haven, CT: Yale University Press.

Delgado, G. (1986). *Organizing the movement: The roots and growth of ACORN.* Philadelphia: Temple University Press.

Hunter, F. (1953). *Community power structure: A study of decision makers.* Chapel Hill: University of North Carolina Press.

Logan, J. R., & Molotch, H. L. (1987). *Urban fortunes: The political economy of place.* Berkeley: University of California Press.

Putnam, R. D. (2000). *Bowling alone: The collapse and revival of American community.* New York: Simon & Schuster.

Stoecker, R. (2001). *Report to the West Bank CDC: Primer on community organizing.* Retrieved May 26, 2006, from http://comm-org.wisc.edu/cr/crreporta.htm

Stone, C. (1989). *Regime politics.* Lawrence: University of Kansas Press.

Swanstrom, T. (1988). *The crisis of growth politics: Cleveland, Kucinich, and the challenge of urban populism.* Philadelphia: Temple University Press.

Warren, M. R. (2001). *Dry bones rattling: Community building to revitalize American democracy.* Princeton, NJ: Princeton University Press.

ADDITIONAL READINGS AND RESOURCES

Readings

Bobo, K., Kendall, J., & Max, S. (1991). *Organizing for social change.* Santa Anna, CA: Seven Locks Press.

Castells, M. (1983). *The city and the grassroots.* Berkeley: University of California Press.

Chambers, E. T. (2003). *Roots for radicals: Organizing for power, action and justice.* New York: Continuum.

Domhoff, G. W. (1983). *Who rules America now?* Englewood Cliffs, NJ: Prentice-Hall.

Ferman, B. (1996). *Challenging the growth machine.* Lawrence: University of Kansas Press.

Gaventa, J. (1982). *Power and powerlessness: Quiescence and rebellion in an Appalachian valley.* Urbana: University of Illinois Press.

Gecan, M. (2002). *Going public.* Boston: Beacon.

Jacobs, D. (Ed.). (2003). *The Myles Horton reader: Education for social change.* Knoxville: University of Tennessee Press.

Jonas, A. E. G., & Wilson, D. (1999). *The urban growth machine: Critical perspectives two decades later.* Albany: State University of New York Press.

Kahn, S. (1991). *Organizing: A guide for grassroots leaders.* Washington, DC: National Association of Social Workers.

Mills, C. W. (1956). *The power elite.* New York: Oxford University Press.

Mollenkopf, J. (1983). *The contested city.* Princeton: Princeton University Press.

Molotch, H. (1976). The city as a growth machine. *American Journal of Sociology, 82,* 309–330.

Molotch, H. (1999). Growth machine links: Up, down, and across. In A. Jonas & D. Wilson (Eds.), *The urban growth machine: Critical perspectives, two decades later* (pp. 247–265). Albany: State University of New York Press.

Osterman, P. (2002). *Gathering power: The future of progressive politics in America.* Boston: Beacon.

Sen, R. (2003). *Stir it up: Lessons in community organizing and advocacy.* San Francisco: John Wiley.

Shaw, R. (1996). *The activist's handbook: A primer.* Berkeley: University of California Press.

Stone, C. (1980). Systemic power in community decision making: A restatement of stratification theory. *American Political Science Review, 74,* 978–990.

Stone, C., & Sanders, H. (1987). *The politics of urban redevelopment.* Lawrence: University Press of Kansas.

Warner, K., & Molotch, H. (2000). *Building rules: How local controls shape community environments and economies.* Boulder, CO: Westview.

Wilson, D. (2007). *The urban growth machine.* Albany, NY: SUNY Press.

Wood, R. L. (2002). *Faith in action: Religion, race, and democratic organizing in America.* Chicago: University of Chicago Press.

Websites

ACORN—www.acorn.org. This website is a good source for a description of the various ACORN campaigns around the United States.

COMM-ORG (The On-Line Conference on Community Organizing and Development)—http://comm-org.wisc.edu/index.html. This is a wonderful website that provides course syllabi, papers, and an electronic newsgroup for community organizers. It also identifies resources, such as videos, books, and data, that may be useful for organizers.

Community Organizing Toolbox—www.nfg.org/cotb. This is another excellent website for community organizers. It provides interesting case studies, tools, and other material that may be helpful to students and others entering the field of community organizing.

Direct Action and Research Training (DART) Network—www.thedartcenter.org. The DART Network is a congregation-based organization focusing on social justice issues. In addition to providing basic information on the organization, this website provides very detailed instruction on how people can involve their congregation in the network and their activities.

Gamaliel Foundation—www. gamaliel.org/default.htm. This website provides information on the programs and activities of the Gamaliel Foundation and its affiliates.

Highlander Research and Education Center—www.highlandercenter.org/default.asp. The Highlander Center is the premier education center for workers involved in economic and social justice. This website is an excellent source for information on the history of the center as well as its current activities.

Industrial Areas Foundation (IAF)—www.industrialareasfoundation.org. This is the most comprehensive site for a description of IAF activities. It provides a history of the organization and information about their activities and their local affiliates.

Interreligious Foundation for Community Organization—http://www.ifconews.org. The Interreligious
    Foundation for Community Organization is an ecumenical organization working on social justice
    issues, especially in Latin America. The site provides a description of some of their main programs.
PICO National Network—www.piconetwork.org. This site makes available news and discussions of
    the activities of state PICO federations, as well as information on their major focus areas.
Who Rules America?—http://sociology.ucsc.edu/whorulesamerica/. This is a comprehensive website
    development by sociologist William Donhoff on power structure research. It provides discussion
    papers, case studies, and full references on research into the power structure of communities in
    America.

Videos

The Democratic Promise: Saul Alinsky and His Legacy (1999), produced and directed by Bob Hercules
    and Bruce Orenstein, narrated by Alec Baldwin; produced for Independent Television Service
    (ITVS). Available from University of California Extension, Center for Media and Independent
    Learning, 2000 Center Street, 4th Floor, Berkeley, CA 94704; phone: (510) 642–0460.
Taken for a Ride (1996), produced and directed by James Klein and Martha Olson. Available from
    New Day Films, 220 Meyran Avenue, Pittsburgh, PA 15213; phone: (412) 681–7117.

12

Cultural Capital

The arts are an important part of many communities with music festivals, craft fairs, theater, dance, and many other events and activities. A recent survey of public participation in the arts found that approximately 40% of the population participates in some form of arts and cultural activities (National Endowment for the Arts, 2003). The arts and cultural activities with the highest level of participation were visiting museums and attending musical concerts and plays. More broadly, a community's cultural resources, such as historic buildings, archaeological sites, museums, farmers' markets, and ethnic festivals, in many ways define and bring identity to a community. Unfortunately, cultural resources are often viewed as something consumed by the rich and not related to middle-class and working-class residents.

Many communities are subsidizing the support for art museums and concert halls as part of their economic development strategy. The arts are seen increasingly as a necessary tool for the growth machine in many cities (Whitt, 1987; Whitt & Lammers, 1991). To attract major corporations and residents to inner cities, local government officials have promoted performing arts facilities. The assumption is that corporate officials would not consider moving to a city that lacks adequate facilities for the arts. There is no doubt these projects have an economic impact on the community, especially through retail sales and property values. This view of the arts in economic development is limited. There are a wide variety of cultural assets that communities should consider. Our intention in this chapter is to broaden the definition to include all forms of cultural assets that can contribute to community development.

With Richard Florida's (2002) work, the arts, and more broadly the creative economy, have brought new appreciation and recognition to culture and the arts in communities. The arts have taken on new meaning for places and their role in communities, especially from an economic perspective. Community and economic development professionals and urban and regional planners have new inspiration to rethink community and retool their arsenal as they promote, revive, and build community. In this chapter, we review Florida's argument and discuss some of the criticism of his thesis. We believe that the arts do not represent the only cultural assets, but they do provide excellent examples of how these assets can be mobilized.

This chapter takes a community- or place-based examination of cultural capital and focuses on how the arts are used and what they bring to community development. Box 12.1 offers several estimates related to the economic impact of the arts in the United States.

BOX 12.1 ARTS FACTS

- There are 578,587 arts-centric businesses in the United States, employing 2.965 million people.
- Arts-centric businesses represent 4.4% of all businesses and 2.2% of all jobs in the United States.
- The number of arts-centric businesses grew by 5.5% from 2002 to 2005, compared to a growth rate of 3.83% for all U.S. businesses.
- As of 2000, in terms of economic impact, the nonprofit arts industry generated $134 billion in total economic activity by arts organizations and their audiences.
- From consumer spending on the arts, about 4.9 million full-time equivalent jobs and $24.4 billion in federal, state, and local government annual revenues were generated.

SOURCE: Americans for the Arts (2002, 2003).

Cultural Capital Definition and Issues

Our initial discussion defines meanings of cultural capital, and then we move into a more focused discussion on the arts. The meaning of the word **culture** is a challenging one. Anthropologists and sociologists have wrestled with a definition of culture for a long time, and it is safe to say that there is no agreement on the definition within the anthropological community. That said, from a cultural anthropology perspective, culture is a system of meanings that is learned within a particular group or society.

Sociologists debate the meaning of culture as well. One sociologist provides an interesting way to view cultural capital. Bourdieu (1986) argued that there are three fundamental forms of capital: economic, social, and cultural. Economic capital is what most people recognize as a functioning economy (i.e., converting money from or into goods and services). Social capital in Bourdieu's perspective is essentially social obligations and ties. Finally, cultural capital represents forces such as family background and educational qualifications that can be converted into economic capital and help to explain the structure and function of a community.

From a community development perspective, Bourdieu's (1986) explanation of cultural capital is useful to structure how one thinks about this type of capital. Bourdieu refines cultural capital into three states: embodied, objectified, and institutionalized. The embodied state of cultural capital refers to legacy, the values and traditions that people inherit or learn from their family and community. Communities regularly recognize their unique histories through celebrations and local historical societies. As communities have changed, celebrations of new cultures present in a community have become common.

The institutionalized state represents the learned form of culture that occurs through academic qualifications. The public school system is one obvious way in which children are acculturated into U.S. society and into local society as well. Other forms of schooling from day care to technical colleges to parochial schools to universities operate similarly.

Bourdieu's (1986) objectified state is the type of cultural capital that many people probably connect with and understand most readily as culture: cultural goods, such as paintings, books, handicrafts, machines, and other material goods that are produced in a particular time and perhaps a particular place. The objectified state is represented within community development as arts councils and foundations and other mechanisms to produce and celebrate material objects and media.

Another way in which to think about cultural capital is to examine its effect on other forms of capital. The next section raises a number of concepts and issues that intersect with human and physical capitals in particular.

Key Concepts and Debates

One important way in which community-based organizations (CBOs) recognize cultural capital is by evaluating its impact on the local economy. Although CBOs have used the arts as one way to build community, it is probably Richard Florida's (2003) book, *The Rise of the Creative Class*, that pushed the arts to the forefront in economic development discussions recently and has done the most to initiate excitement, discussion, and controversy within communities. Economic development agencies and other CBOs have taken note of Florida's argument. He contended that communities ignore quality of place and the people they retain and attract at their peril by qualifying that "regional economic growth is powered by creative people" (p. 249). Through this argument, he defined a new class of workers, the creative class, who are attracted to and stay in communities that create and maintain high-quality places. Florida divided the creative class into two groups of occupations: the creative core and creative professionals. The creative core includes architects, engineers, scientists, educators, artists, musicians, entertainers, and others "whose economic function is to create new ideas, new technology and/or new creative content" (p. 8). Creative professionals include people in business and finance, law, health care, and related fields. He estimated that the creative class comprises 30% of the U.S. workforce, with the creative core making up about 12%.

Around the world, communities have been trying to measure the creative class and find ways to increase it. Researchers at Michigan State University recently examined the contribution of the creative class to that state (Fernandez, Garg, & LaMore, 2005). The researchers focused on a conservative definition of the creative class, as reflected in Box 12.2. Americans for the Arts (2002,

2003) took a similar conservative definition of **creative industries,** which includes the following industrial classifications: museums and collections; performing arts; visual arts and photography; film, radio, and TV; design and publishing; and arts schools and services. Confining a study of the creative class to those occupations that only have obvious ties to culture and creativity is one response to criticisms leveled at Florida's (2002) thesis about the extent of the creative class.

BOX 12.2 CULTURAL INDUSTRY CATEGORIES

- Applied arts
  - Architectural services
  - Interior design services
  - Industrial design services
  - Graphic design services
  - Other specialized design services
  - Advertising agencies
  - Display advertising
  - Photographic services

- Performing arts: music, theater, dance
  - Performing arts companies
  - Dance companies
  - Musical groups and artists
  - Other performing arts companies
  - Musical instrument manufacturing
  - Promoters of performing arts events

- Visual arts
  - Art dealers
  - Camera and photographic supplies stores
  - Photographic film, paper, plate, and chemical manufacturing
  - Agents and managers for artists
  - Lead pencil and art goods manufacturing
  - Printing and related support activities

- Literary arts
  - Libraries and archives
  - Book publishers

- Media
  - Cable and other program distribution
  - Motion picture and sound recording industries
  - Prerecorded CD, tape, and record repairing

- Heritage
  - Museums
  - Historical sites
- Support
  - Fine arts schools
  - Independent artists, writers, and performers

SOURCE: Fernandez et al. (2005).

Another thesis of Florida's (2002) concerns quality of place. He used four measures to derive a creativity index to prioritize places according to their degree of creativity. Florida's measures include the creative class share of the workforce; innovation, measured as patents per capita; high-tech industry; and diversity, measured by the Gay Index. By pulling data together for large metropolitan regions, Florida found that cities ranking highest on the index were San Francisco, California; Austin, Texas; Boston, Massachusetts; and San Diego, California. At the bottom of the ranking of large regions (47th, 48th, and 49th places) are Las Vegas, Nevada; Norfolk, Virginia; and Memphis, Tennessee. Through this analysis, Florida derived three areas of concentration for economic development programs, which he calls the three *T*s of economic development: technology, talent, and tolerance. Regional growth stems from these essential ingredients and their interrelationships. When a region is missing one of the three *T*s, regional growth will be hindered. It is not clear from Florida's work whether one ingredient is more or less essential at any given time or place.

Perhaps the most controversial aspects to Florida's (2002) argument are his suggestions that communities that are tolerant of diversity and that attract a bohemian group are more likely to be economically successful in the long run. It's not that critics find his creativity index objectionable; it is the lack of actual economic indicators that show, in fact, that the highest ranking creative regions are doing well. Kotkin (2005) believes that communities need to be careful with economic development initiatives and stick to what he calls the basics: jobs, good neighborhoods and schools, and decent infrastructure. He does not think that an art museum will solve, for example, Detroit's problems. Kotkin's argument oversimplified Florida's multipronged approach to encouraging a creative economy. Whether economic development initiatives should focus on the basics or something else, such as creativity or knowledge, many of the arguments about cultural capital recognize that skilled people and quality places are important to overall community health and vitality.

As recognized in Florida's (2002) view, skilled people are necessary for a creative economy. One perspective on workforce development is to focus on youth. The federal organizations as well as smaller, local organizations, such as the Boys and Girls Clubs, have emphasized the arts in their programming. The idea behind these youth arts programs is to take at-risk youth and involve them in activities that bring focus, perseverance, and self-discipline—not to mention creativity—to their lives. Some statistics show that youth engaged in arts programs have higher graduation rates and improved academic performance. Case Study 12.1 highlights the work of an arts apprenticeship program.

CASE STUDY 12.1 YOUTH AND ARTS PROGRAMS

Manchester Craftsmen's Guild, a center for arts and learning, is a partner of the Pittsburgh Public Schools dedicated to the advancement of young people's potential through creativity, communication and mentoring. Youth programs stress that success is based not only on skill and knowledge, but also on attitude and performance. Many of our alumni have gone on to successful careers in the arts, business, communications and other fields. Young people involved in MCG learn to become creative and intellectual risk-takers. For the past ten years, more than 75% of graduates have gone on to four-year colleges and other career academies. Manchester Craftsmen's Guild students have been invited to participate in conferences on leadership, technology and entrepreneurship. Additionally, they have won thousands of dollars in scholarships dedicated to the arts and community involvement.

Most programs are free to Pittsburgh teens and enrollment is simple. After school, transportation via yellow bus is offered from each of Pittsburgh's public high schools at least one day/week. Additionally, students may access free transportation tickets for use on public buses.

Manchester Craftsmen's Guild's nationally recognized after-school arts program for high school students has been designed to educate and inspire any young person who has an interest in the arts and creative self-expression. Each of the many and varied studio courses and workshops offer great opportunities for skill development, critical thinking, experiential learning and preparation for careers and higher education. Individualized mentoring, portfolio development, educational travel, service learning and scholarship opportunities round out the MCG experience.

SOURCE: Manchester Craftsmen Guild. Pittsburgh, PA. www.manchesterguild.org/youth/youth.htm. Copyright 2006 by the Manchester Craftsmen Guild. Reprinted with permission.

Thus, human capital represents another connection with cultural capital. Although skilled people and jobs are critical factors in community development, another factor is the place itself—how physical form influences the quality of relationships, the local economy, and many other aspects of community. As a transition into the next section of this chapter, the case study on Portland, Oregon, offers an example of a community that is integrating many forms of community capital in a successful way and where cultural capital plays an important role. The next section focuses on the intersection between culture and place.

CASE STUDY 12.2 PORTLAND, OREGON

Portland ranked very high on many of the "creativity" indices cited by Florida, and 16th overall, and is rapidly gaining ground. It is now in the top ten cities nationally, and first among its West Coast neighbors, in attracting young adults. As such it provides a compelling case study of the factors—including a burgeoning cultural scene—which interweave in communities that are attracting talent and building creative economies. The following descriptions are based on observations, interviews, and conversations with cultural and community leaders.

First, the cultural attributes that contribute to Portland's distinctiveness and vibrancy:

- *Variety*. Portland has developed a larger and more diverse mix of cultural organization, artists, and cultural projects than any like-size city and many much larger ones. There is an especially large number of mid-sized and smaller organizations— several dozen—encompassing gritty, avant garde theatre, film, video and new media, new music, contemporary dance, performance art, poetry slams, chamber music, etc. Many are barely clawing out an existence and need more support but they add enormous range, interest, and quality to the cultural scene.
- *Diversity*. The large number of established and visible ethnic organizations belies Portland's "white bread" image and helps to presage and celebrate the demographic changes that are rapidly reshaping the city—and its tolerance for differences.
- *Live*. The music scene is robust and diverse. On any night of the week, dozens of clubs offer top quality local and touring talent spanning every musical genre. Two monthly gallery walks overflow into surrounding sidewalks throughout the city. Live music and festivals are featured every weekend during the summer in the city's two large parks as well as neighborhood and regional parks.
- *Contemporary*. Dozens of artists of all disciplines are making and eagerly presenting art. And audiences are eager for the new and novel.
- *Ubiquitous*. Portland's public art program—one of the earliest, largest, and most innovative—has, literally, changed the face of the built environment and provided enormous opportunities for artists. It can be seen throughout the city.
- *Still Growing*. From just a few "mainstays" in the early 1990s to more than 50 and counting, the gallery scene has exploded, offering a diverse range of opportunities for individual artists to exhibit and engage the public with new work. The number of arts organizations and artists has continued to increase dramatically, even during the economic downturn.

Looking more deeply, there are defining characteristics of Portland's cultural scene that make it particularly attractive to creatives and which illustrate approaches that other cities may wish to consider. These emblematic features have to do with boundary crossing, definitions of culture, and the promotion of inter-connections.

- Numerous organizations promote multidiscipline or cross discipline artistic expression— fomenting collaborations and new ways of thinking—and marketing geared to attracting younger audiences. This is occurring across the cultural spectrum from the

(Continued)

(Continued)

Oregon Symphony's multi-discipline *Nerve Ending* concerts, to the Portland Institute for Contemporary Arts' stunning new international *TBA Festival,* to small "guerilla" organizations taking over huge industrial warehouses for genre-breaking exhibitions, installations, and performance art, to a new design festival, *PDX DNA.*

- Informal arts activities thrive: temporary **public art** installations, gallery walks, street festivals (including a growing network of farmers markets which integrate performance and impromptu exhibits), and many arts spaces that sponsor project based collaborations.
- There is a blur between nonprofit and commercial creative industries and this creates many opportunities. Encouraged by longstanding public policy and practices, architectural firms routinely utilize artists on their design teams. Other creative service industries such as design firms, film companies, and advertising agencies regularly tap artists, actors, and musicians for creative input along the spectrum from product development to marketing. It is not a coincidence that many nonprofit arts organizations have also included examples of industrial design in exhibitions.
- Many creative service industry professionals lead double lives as creatives on both sides of the commercial/nonprofit boundary: a world-class software engineer who dances in a contemporary dance troupe; an advertising copywriter who also writes and performs for a contemporary theatre company; or a leading marketing consultant who composes and performs new music. Portland is teeming with such examples.
- The imperative of creativity has yielded a climate in which individual artists are now routinely asked to be on civic planning task forces reaching far beyond culture to economic development, urban design, tourism, and other issues.
- This boundary crossing makes for culturally rich districts and neighborhoods where creative service companies exist side by side with artist studios, galleries, restaurants, nonprofit performance spaces, and night clubs—several have emerged, with and without formal support—over the last decade. Symbiotic relationships abound and contribute to a lively, ever changing street scene.

Creatives eschew boundaries. They want multiple opportunities and entry points across the spectrum of the creative sector—lots of ways to be involved and interact with other creatives in seeking expressive outlets and interesting experiences. Portland offers ample opportunity.

Interviews, research, and observation also suggest several critical "infrastructural" attributes—in addition to its beautiful setting and moderate climate—that contribute to Portland's attractiveness to creatives.

- Land use and urban growth policies, zoning codes, and an early commitment to public art have yielded a compact, human scale, pedestrian-oriented urban form, and promoted decent to good design.

- Portland preserved its attractive and livable inner city neighborhoods and much of its older housing and building stock. In part because of this, Portland is still the cheapest major urban area to live and work in on the West Coast. Several light industrial and warehouse districts have become havens for artists and creative industries needing inexpensive, flexible space. As Jane Jacobs famously said, "New ideas require old buildings."

- Sustainable growth and green economic development policies have yielded the highest recycling rate in the country, green space set-asides (Portland has more square miles of park land, per capita, than any other major city in America), and many other attributes which rank high among the values and livability priorities of creatives.

- Portland is still relatively easy to navigate, despite dramatic population growth. The region has invested in a multi-model transportation system that encompasses mass transit, safe walking routes, bicycle paths, and—still—relatively short automobile drive times. There is a concentration of creative activity in its dense, urbanized areas, making it very accessible.

- It's easy to find out about what's going on. The city is lucky to have decent to good cultural writing in the main daily newspaper and a plethora of alternative papers reporting on what's cool. As one of the most wired cities in the country, Portland also benefits from a burgeoning e-zine and e-newsletter network—the *buzz* gets around easily.

- One of Portland's most important characteristics is its informal civic culture. People, including newcomers, feel they can get involved and have impact—in politics, community development, planning, and in the cultural scene. Access and participation are easy and welcomed. Coffee houses and cafes—the meeting places of creatives—are ubiquitous. New organizations, coalitions, and movements—from political action committees to environmental coalitions, social justice organizations, and cultural entities—are constantly springing up.

SOURCE: Bulick, B. (with Coletta, C. Jackson, C., Taylor, A., & Wolff, S.). (2003). *Cultural development in creative communities.* New York: Americans for the Arts. Reprinted with permission.

Culture and Place

Cultural capital represents a form of capital that occurs in both community of place and community of interest. In terms of place-based concepts, culture, in the form of physical manifestations, can be recognizable—historic buildings and districts, museums, public art, and archaeological sites. These buildings and sites are obvious places where community members and visitors can recognize culture. Communities can do more to turn themselves into creative places from a physical-space perspective. They can promote arts through adaptive reuse of buildings, develop cultural empowerment zones, promote mixed-use development with a focus of encouraging the arts, and encourage a diverse mix of restaurants (Bulick, 2003).

Phillips (2004) provided a useful typology of arts-based community development programs:

1. Arts-based incubators—These facilities provide share services and assistance for arts businesses. The primary goal of these incubators is to help arts businesses at an early stage. Eventually, the businesses mature to a point where they can leave the incubator.

2. Arts cooperatives—Under this form of organization, artisans typically establish a nonprofit organization to market their products. Arts cooperatives hope to gain advantage in scale by promoting arts-based development as a collective. In several cases, this means establishing a retail outlet that is owned collectively or sharing costs of advertising and sales expenses.

3. Comprehensive approaches—In many communities, arts-based development becomes a central element of their economic development strategy. These approaches tend to build on community participation and planning in the art-based strategy.

Another approach is to link art-based development with a smart growth planning effort. Smart growth attempts to restore vitality and a sense of place through higher density and mixed-use developments or centers, transit accessible and walkable neighborhoods, and the preservation of open space and environmental areas.

A growing number of localities promote the arts within special districts. Los Angeles, Chicago, and Charlotte have established special arts districts that operate similar to a business improvement district. A special district is a form of local government created by a local community to focus on a particular area, such as a downtown area, or a specific service, such as storm water processing. These districts sometimes have taxing authority on property. A business improvement district (BID) is one type of special district that has grown in use across the United States. A BID generally has specific boundaries, often focuses on a downtown or commercial area, and focuses on revitalizing and maintaining these specific areas. One example is from the northern part of Charlotte, North Carolina. The area, now known as Noda, had once been the heart of the city's textile industry. By 1975, all of the area's mills had closed. A decade later two artists moved into the area and started to revitalize buildings. A neighborhood association now acts to maintain and develop the area.

CASE STUDY 12.3 WORCESTER ARTS DISTRICT

In the mid-1990s, the concept of an arts district in Worcester, Massachusetts, surfaced. ARTSWorcester, an advocacy organization supporting contemporary artists in the city, hosted a city council candidates forum on the arts, in which candidates discussed the need for artists to share space (Community Partners Consultants, Inc., 2001).

> Following this forum, officials started to undertake a process to establish an arts district that could support artists and ultimately economic development. In its first move in 1999, the city council adopted an arts district zone overlay for part of the main south area of the city. The city then established a task force. This group served the city manager in an advisory and a guidance capacity as the arts district took shape.
>
> SOURCES: City of Worcester (2006); Community Partners Consultants, Inc. (2001).

Several recent studies have attempted to measure the direct economic impact of arts and culture. In 2001, the Craft Organization Directors Association estimated that the direct economic impact of sales from handmade crafts was approximately $14 billion. It is estimated that the nonprofit arts industry generates approximately $134 billion in economic activity (Americans for the Arts, 2003).

The arts have other effects that are not considered frequently in economic impact studies. Arts districts make important contributions by transforming abandoned buildings and vacant lots into more productive venues. Many incubators (discussed earlier) have made good use of vacant office buildings to create space for the arts. Also, many local arts projects pay special attention to the needs of youth. These programs empower youth by providing new ways for them to express themselves and to become active in the community.

Community celebrations attract tourist dollars, which helps generate economic development. These celebrations, however, also recognize and build on local resources and assets. In the case of Bayfield, Wisconsin, the annual apple festival brings 60,000 visitors to a county with only 16,000 people. The festival highlights the unusual ecological zone along Lake Superior, where fruit orchards are a vital part of the identity of the community. Bayfield has gone so far as to establish a program to purchase development rights to protect this agricultural sector. These community celebrations, however, go beyond the impact to the local economy; they also contribute to the sense of community. Celebrations create public space and recognize a community's legacy, and they build social capital by increasing the interaction and trust among residents.

Government and CBOs in Cultural Capital

Cultural capital faces many of the same obstacles that other forms of community capital encounter. Most consumers lack sufficient information on the quality, availability, and cost of the arts. Conversely, artists may lack adequate knowledge of consumer desires and preferences for quality and authenticity. Some form of governmental or social intervention is necessary to help address the limitations of markets in promoting cultural capital.

Government can play an important role in funding cultural activities in communities. The **National Endowment for the Arts (NEA)** is the primary federal agency for assisting communities and local organizations with many kinds of arts programs. The NEA was established in 1965 and since then has awarded more than 111,000 grants to arts organizations and artists (National Endowment for the Arts, 2000). When the law establishing the National Foundation on the Arts and the Humanities was passed, the new agency's initial budget was set at $2.5 million. In the 2006 federal budget, the agency was appropriated about $124 million.

At the local level, the country's first local arts agencies were established in 1948 and 1949 at Quincy, Illinois, and Winston-Salem, North Carolina. According to the NEA, state and jurisdictional arts agencies have grown from 5 to 56, and local arts organizations from 400 to 4,000 from 1965 to 2000.

Local governments can affect their jurisdictions in many different ways. One way is through a comprehensive plan within which they can include an element addressing cultural resources. Box 12.3 lists questions that a community can consider during the planning process. Other organizations can use these questions as well as they go through a strategic process of including cultural capital in their programming.

BOX 12.3 CULTURAL RESOURCES

Cultural resources include historic buildings and structures as well as ancient and historic archeological sites.

Questions the Cultural Resources Section Should Address

Another way to develop the comprehensive plan's cultural resource section is to pose questions that the plan should answer. Communities should ask the following questions as part of the planning process:

- Which cultural resources are most important to the community?
- What are the current threats to the community's cultural resources?
- How should the community respond to these threats?
- What has the community done previously to protect and promote its cultural resources?
- What is the community doing currently to protect and promote its cultural resources?
- What future actions should the community take to protect and promote its cultural resources?
- When and how does the community want to implement its priorities?

SOURCE: Bernstein (2002).

In many cases, local officials do not consider the arts as a core function of government. Nonprofit organizations, in fact, are the major sponsors of the arts in most communities. Nonprofits at the national level provide much of the funding for the arts, and local nonprofit organizations are frequently sponsors and organizers of events and activities. Since the early 1990s, federal funding for the arts has declined by almost 50%. Since its inception in 1965, NEA's funding has grown considerably; however, since the 1990s it has declined precipitously. Although state and local public funding has increased during this period, it has not replaced most of the funds lost. Most of the nonprofits are involved in the performing arts, but an increasing number of nonprofit organizations are involved in other arts activities.

Phillips (2004) provided several recommendations for local governments and local organizations considering arts-based development:

- It is critical to build public participation into any effort to build support for the arts.
- Look for physical assets (e.g., vacant buildings and facilities) that are underutilized.
- Make an effort to link art-based development with other community development efforts.
- Collaboration across arts-based businesses improves the likelihood of success.
- Recognize the varied needs of arts-based businesses and use a flexible approach. (pp. 119–120)

Summary and Conclusions

Local culture is frequently an overlooked asset in community development. In a global economy, local culture makes places different and distinctive. Cultural capital should not only include "high culture" but also involve the cultural assets of poor communities. Florida's (2002) argument about the role of the creative class in local economies has sparked renewed interest in the role of arts and culture in economic growth and development. Most of the attention to these issues has focused on building arts centers, museums, and concert halls. This effort misses the point of Florida's analysis. It is the distinctiveness and the diversity of cities that attract the creative class and ultimately generate economic growth. Communities that build on their unique attributes and assets offer the greatest potential for development.

In this chapter, we focused much of our discussion of cultural capital on the arts, but we could have just as easily discussed music, architecture, or other forms of cultural capital. Cultural capital is often more difficult to identify than other forms of community capital. It is often the taken-for-granted aspect of community life. The strength of the asset-building approach is that it encourages people to think more positively about what their community has to offer to residents and others.

KEY CONCEPTS

Arts	Culture
Arts apprenticeship	National Endowment
Creative class	for the Arts (NEA)
Creative economy	Public art
Creative industries	Special districts

QUESTIONS

1. What is the creative class and how does it influence local economic growth and development?

2. What is a special district and how can it be used to promote the arts in communities?

3. Differentiate between embodied, objectified, and institutionalized cultural capital.

EXERCISES

1. Find out what is happening in your community in terms of the arts and culture. How many organizations in your community focus on the arts? What do they do? Can these organizations identify the effects of their programs on the community?

2. Talk with some business leaders in your community about arts and culture. Do these leaders provide financial support for the arts and culture in the local community? What benefits, if any, do they see in supporting the arts and culture?

3. Identify some community celebrations in your region. Talk with the organizers and find out how the celebrations are supported financially. How many people attend the celebrations? Can you estimate the impact of these celebrations on the local community?

REFERENCES

Americans for the Arts. (2002). *Arts and economic prosperity: The economic impact of nonprofit arts organizations and their audiences.* New York: Author.

Americans for the Arts. (2003). *Building creative economies: The arts, entrepreneurship and sustainable development.* New York: Author.

Bernstein, R. A. (2002). *A guide to smart growth and cultural resource planning.* Madison: Wisconsin Historical Society, Division of Historic Preservation.

Bourdieu, P. (1986). The forms of capital. In J. C. Richardson (Ed.), *Handbook of theory and research for the sociology of education* (pp. 241–258). New York: Greenwood.

Bulick, B. (with Coletta, C., Jackson, C., Taylor, A., & Wolff, S.). (2003). *Cultural development in creative communities.* New York: Americans for the Arts.

City of Worcester. (2006). *Worcester: Creating a home for the arts.* Worcester, MA: Author.

Community Partners Consultants, Inc. (2001). *Master plan for the Worcester Arts District, City of Worcester, MA.* Retrieved May 24, 2010, from http://www.worcestermass.org/arts-culture-entertainment/arts-culture/worcester-arts-district

Fernandez, L., Garg, N., & LaMore, R. L. (2005). *The dollars and sense of cultural economic development: Summary report of Michigan's cultural capacity.* Lansing: Michigan State University.

Florida, R. (2002). *The rise of the creative class.* New York: Basic Books.

Kotkin, J. (2005). Uncool cities. *Prospect Magazine, 115.* Retrieved March 24, 2007, from http://www.prospect-magazine.co.uk/vis_index.php?select_issue=510

Manchester Craftsmen Guild. (2006). *MCG youth.* Pittsburgh, PA: Author.

National Endowment for the Arts. (2000). *A brief chronology of federal support for the arts, 1965–2000.* Washington, DC: Author.

Phillips, R. (2004). Artful business: Using the arts for community economic development. *Community Development Journal, 39,* 112–121.

Whitt, J. A. (1987). Mozart in the metropolis: The arts coalition and the urban growth machine. *Urban Affairs Quarterly, 23,* 15–36.

Whitt, J. A., & Lammers, J. (1991). The art of growth: Ties between development organizations and the performing arts. *Urban Affairs Quarterly, 26,* 376–393.

ADDITIONAL READINGS AND RESOURCES

Readings

Americans for the Arts. (2005). *Creative industries 2005: The state report.* New York: Author.

Florida, R. (2003). Cities and the creative class. *City and Community, 2,* 3–19.

Gendron, R. (1996). Arts and craft: Implementing an arts-based development strategy in a "controlled growth" county. *Sociological Perspectives, 39,* 539–555.

Gibson, C., & Kong, L. (2005). Cultural economy: A critical review. *Progress in Human Geography, 29,* 541–561.

Kearns, G., & Philo, C. (1993). *Selling places: The city as cultural capital, past and present.* Oxford, UK: Pergamon Press.

National Endowment for the Arts. (2003). *2002 survey of public participation.* Washington, DC: Author.

Regional Technology Strategies. (2005). *The art of economic development: Community colleges for creative economics.* Carrboro, NC: Author.

Singer, M. (2000). Culture works: Cultural resources as economic development tools. *Public Management, 8,* 11–16.

Williams, L. (2004). Culture and community development: Towards new conceptualizations and practice. *Community Development Journal, 39,* 345–359.

Websites

Americans for the Arts—www.artsusa.org. This organization calls itself "the nation's leading nonprofit organization for advancing the arts in America."

Center for the Study of Art and Community—www.artandcommunity.com. This center is "an association of creative leaders from business, government and the arts who have succeeded in building bridges between the arts and a wide range of community, public and private sector interests." This center provides "expert guidance for developing artistic, educational, funding, community development and political collaborations."

Community Arts Network—www.communityarts.net. This site provides news and information about community-based art.

CoolCities.com—http://coolcities.com/main.html. Interesting site that provides information on initiatives to promote innovation, diversity, and talent in Michigan cities.

Creative Class—http://www.creativeclass.com/. Richard Florida's website, which provides some interesting background information on his theories and research.

Culture Shapes Community—www.cultureshapescommunity.org. This project is funded by the Ford Foundation and focuses on neighborhood-based arts and cultural organizations. It provides excellent resources on mobilizing arts and cultural resources for community development.

Institute for Community Development and the Arts—www.artsusa.org/information_resources/research_information/institute_community_development/default.asp. This site provides research-based information on the role of the arts in community development.

The Project for Public Spaces (PPS)—www.pps.org. This organization aims to create and sustain public spaces to build communities. PPS provides technical assistance, training, research, and other services to community clients.

Videos

Downside UP (2003), written, produced, and directed by Nancy Kelly and distributed by New Day Films. *Downside UP* examines the effects of America's largest museum of contemporary art, the Massachusetts Museum of Contemporary Art, on the working-class town of North Adams, Massachusetts. Available from New Day Films, 190 Route 17M, P.O. Box 1084, Harriman, NY 10926; phone: (888) 367–9154; fax: (845) 774–2945.

13

Food, Energy, and Community

The central assumption of the asset-based development approach is that community resources can be transformed and mobilized to better serve local needs and enhance the quality life of residents. This chapter focuses on community development efforts to reduce dependencies on external resources by promoting local sustainability. We focus on two key movements: local food systems and renewable energy. Both of these examples represent attempts to use local assets to build a more sustainable future. In both cases, communities may not have enough local resources to satisfy the demand by residents, but they can move toward increased sustainability by making better use of these assets.

What are the connections between food and energy? In both cases, national (and international) systems have emerged to deliver these important resources to communities. Fruit and vegetables travel around the globe to meet the demand for food. Several studies estimate that fresh food travels an average of 1,500 miles. Many people today refer to the "food odometer" as a way of capturing this process. Similarly, fuel (e.g., coal, natural gas, and petroleum) is transported around the globe. Efforts to create more sustainable communities have recognized the inefficiencies in these systems and have proposed more localized and regional systems to meet our needs for food and energy.

In both the case of food and energy, local efforts to promote sustainability involve creating markets for local producers. In some instances, this might involve linking producers directly with consumers and businesses. It may involve helping local entrepreneurs identify opportunities and providing them with the information they need to take advantage of those opportunities.

In the following, we briefly describe some of the community development efforts to promote sustainability in food and energy systems. We assess some of the opportunities and challenges that communities face in these efforts.

BOX 13.1 RENEWABLE ENERGY FACTS

- About 9% of U.S. electricity was generated from renewable sources in 2008.
- The majority of renewable resources are used for electricity.
- Biomass is the largest source of renewable energy in the United States.
- The United States has the largest share in the world of nuclear electricity generated.

SOURCE: Energy Kids, U.S. Energy Information Administration (http://tonto.eia.doe.gov/kids/index.cfm).

Local Food Systems and Community

There is growing criticism of the global food system (Pollan, 2007). Concerns with the food system include its effects on the environment, health/nutrition, and corporate control. Large-scale agriculture relies heavily on chemical inputs, such as fertilizer, pesticides, herbicides, and growth hormones. These chemicals have the potential of contaminating our water supply and endangering the health of farm workers and consumers. There is growing concern that our food system contributes to the high rates of obesity. Several factors are important here, including the high fat and sugar content in fast food. The increased concentration and centralization of the food system in the hands of a few corporations has implications for the cost of food, as well as the prices farmers receive for their commodities. Corporate control also contributes to the increasing size and declining number of farms and ranches.

The local food movement offers new opportunities to support small- and medium-size farms, reduce the environmental footprint of agriculture, and promote good nutrition among consumers. Regional producers, especially small farms, can bypass the agribusiness sector by selling products directly to consumers. Local foods are often equated with organic agriculture, which means that producers do not use the chemicals that that may be hazardous to farm workers and consumers. Local food systems also create stronger connections between producers and consumers. It also is argued that small-scale producers will use more environmentally friendly farming practices.

Interest in local food systems has skyrocketed in recent years, primarily because consumers are demanding higher quality products and are more concerned with the environmental consequences of transporting food across the globe. Locavores are defined as people who eat primarily food grown or raised in their region. Although the definition of *local* may vary, most locavores limit themselves to products from a 100- to 200-mile radius. Barbara Kingsolver's (2007) book, *Animal, Vegetable, Miracle,* popularized the concept of locavore. The local food movement has established a wide variety of institutions that link consumers with producers in their region.

Types of Local Food Systems

Below, we describe some of the most common types of local food systems that are being created by communities. These are general models, and there is actually a lot of variation in how they operate on the ground. In addition, producers and processors may participate in multiple local food systems. So, a farmer may sell produce at a farmers market, as well as participate in a farm-school program.

Community-Supported Agriculture (CSA)

Community-supported agriculture (CSA) was first established in the 1960s in Switzerland and Japan. Today, there are more than 1,000 CSAs in the United States, with the largest concentrations in the Midwest and Northeast. CSA farms tend to be located on the urban-rural fringe where they have better access to urban consumers. Most CSA operations use organic farming techniques. CSA farms tend to be relatively small, but the net return per acre is much higher than it is for conventional farms.

CSAs offer an innovative strategy for linking consumers directly with producers and thereby avoid the middleman. Typically, consumers receive a box of food each week (or biweekly) from their CSA farm. Consumers purchase shares in a farmer's crops each year. In purchasing shares, consumers bear some of the risk of the producer. If the farmer has a good crop, the consumer benefits by receiving more produce. If the crop fails, the consumers receive less in their weekly box. This system potentially benefits both producers and consumers. Producers receive a guaranteed income that reduces most of the market risk that small farmers face. Consumers avoid the costs added on by wholesalers/retailers in the food system because the food goes directly from the farm to the consumer. There are often other noneconomic benefits for consumers as well. Most CSA farms provide on-farm activities to educate consumers about their food. In addition, many consumers prefer the reassurance that their purchases help local businesses.

One of the criticisms of CSAs, as well as some of the other local food systems, is that they are oriented toward wealthy consumers and are largely inaccessible to poor people. The cost of CSA membership varies widely, but it is considerable (as much as $800–$1,000 per year) in some cases. There are a few efforts to address this problem. In some localities, health care providers will cover some of the costs of CSA membership. These health care providers assume that by encouraging households to purchase fresh vegetables, costs of health care will decline. In other regions, consortiums or associations of CSAs have worked together to help subsidize CSA memberships for low-income residents.

CSAs offer new opportunities for urban families to get directly connected with the farmers who produce their food. These programs provide some security for farmers, as well as healthy options for households. Community-based organizations can help CSAs address the needs of the poor, as well as make stronger linkages to neighborhoods. In addition, community-based organizations can help diversify CSA farms by connecting them with other local food systems that have been established.

Farm-to-School Programs

Farm-to-school programs connect schools and local farms with the objectives of serving healthy meals in school cafeterias, providing health and nutrition education, and supporting local small farmers. These programs help children understand where their food comes from and how their food choices affect their bodies, the environment, and their communities at large. There are now more than 2,000 farm-to-school programs in 40 states and 8,000 schools. Most of these programs are in K–12 programs, but there is growing interest in colleges and universities as well.

In farm-to-school programs, schools directly purchase food for lunches and snacks. Students are exposed to foods that they may have not tried at home. Educational programs about nutrition and health often accompany the meals. Farmers frequently interact with students in the classroom, providing information on agriculture in the region.

Farm-to-school programs face some difficult obstacles in many places. One of the typical problems is that it is difficult for small farms to match the demands of large school districts. Small farms have a limited capacity, which is why many school districts turn to food services to supply them. One strategy for addressing this issue is to create farmer associations or coalitions that can pool together their supply to adequately meet the needs of local institutions. Another possibility is to use websites that identify producers in the region. School districts may be able to purchase enough supplies by working with numerous farms.

Another obstacle is processing. Many school districts have a limited capacity to process food; much of it comes to them prepared or requires very little preparation. Small farms are often challenged in gaining access to processing facilities. Several options have emerged for small farms in this situation. In many cases, community kitchens have been built that allow farmers and retail establishments to process food for sale (see Case Study 13.1). These kitchens provide essential facilities for processing, as well as meet the health standards of local, state, and federal policies. Another approach is to build separate facilities through cooperatives.

Transportation can also be an obstacle for small farms, especially those that are not located close to schools. Cooperative arrangements may also work in these situations, as groups of farmers share the costs of transportation to get their products to schools.

The farm-to-school model offers lessons for other efforts to promote institutional buying of local foods. Hospitals, prisons, and colleges provide unique opportunities to support a local food system. The challenges of supply and processing are key obstacles. Obviously, it is more difficult to implement these programs during the winter in many regions. Innovative strategies, such as hoop houses, provide year-round opportunities for local growers.

Community-based organizations can play an important role in promoting farm-to-school programs. First, there is a need to link growers with schools to build these markets. Second, community-based organizations can help address some of the bottlenecks by helping coordinate processing facilities. This can be accomplished through developing cooperatives, locating facilities in the community, and promoting new facilities such as community kitchens.

CASE STUDY 13.1 CLINCH-POWELL COMMUNITY KITCHENS

In Hancock County, Tennessee, the community established a facility and services for food product businesses in the region. The facility provides equipment, a processing area, an office area, and storage facilities for businesses. Entrepreneurs can take advantage of free food safety training, product testing, and nutrition analysis. In addition, business services include market analysis, business counseling, and counseling in packaging and label development. The kitchen charges a nominal rate for renting the facilities. Farmers have been using the facilities to make strawberry jam, apple butter, marinade, and a variety of other products.

SOURCE: Clinch-Powell Community Kitchens (http://www.clinchkitchens.org/).

Community Gardens

A **community garden** is a plot of land where neighborhoods can come together to grow food and build community. The American Community Gardens Association (ACGA, n.d.) estimates that the number of community garden programs has grown from less than 20 in the early 1970s to more than 550 programs today. Community gardens have many goals, including building community, enhancing environmental quality, improving health, and developing the urban landscape of a community.

Community gardens differ from the other local food systems in that consumers are actually involved in growing their own food. Many community gardening programs offer technical assistance, training, and outreach to local neighborhoods. These programs have been proven to be very effective in some of the poorest neighborhoods in urban areas. They offer opportunities for residents to improve their nutrition and health, supplement their income with local food, and promote a sense of community. Community gardens are an especially effective strategy for many urban neighborhoods that have a lot of vacant land available. Many local and state offices are willing to share open space with neighborhood gardeners. Locating community gardens on school grounds can be an effective method for providing educational programs on local foods. Finally, universities have been providing plots for community gardens as a way for students to gain experience with organic farming techniques.

Community-based organizations often play a key role in identifying property for community gardens, obtaining support for poor residents (e.g., obtaining tools, seeds, and equipment), and providing information and training. In many cases, community gardens can provide surplus products to food pantries.

One of the central obstacles in developing community gardens is gaining access to available land. Although there is a considerable amount of vacant property in most inner cities, the owners may not support these activities. Most cities are primarily interested in increasing their tax rolls, which means they are trying to develop every available property. Yet, they recognize and appreciate the unique potential of community garden programs.

Farmers Markets

A **farmers market** provides farmers, growers, or producers from a defined local area with an opportunity to sell their own produce directly to the public. All products sold should have been grown, reared, caught, brewed, pickled, baked, smoked, or processed by the stallholder. Farmers markets have grown rapidly over the past 20 years, with several thousand existing now across the country. Most producers participating in farmers markets tend to be relatively small and use these markets to supplement their farm income. The majority of farmers markets (82%) are self-sustaining; that is, they cover all costs through profits from the market. Many of the markets are fairly selective and only include producers if they meet certain standards.

In addition to directly linking producers and consumers, farmers markets may play several other functions. Farmers markets are often a central cultural attraction in many cities. In Madison, Wisconsin, for example, approximately 20,000 people attend the farmers market on Saturdays in the summer at the capital square. Farmers markets also serve as kind of an incubator for entrepreneurs. Growers who participate learn how to market their products in different ways, as well as develop networks and social ties that enable them to pursue new products or ventures.

Like some of the other local food systems, farmers markets are often criticized for serving primarily an upper-middle-class clientele. Some farmers markets have addressed this criticism by developing programs that focus directly on the poor. More than half of the farmers markets now accept food stamps. About one-fourth of the farmers markets are involved in gleaning programs that direct food to needy populations.

A rapidly growing version of the farmers market is the farmers auction. Growers bring their products to a central location, much like a regular market, and restaurants and institutional buyers come to participate in an auction for these products. Auctions provide new markets for farmers, as well as make the local market more visible for both producers and consumers. It also helps overcome some of the barriers to meeting the demand for local foods by regional institutions.

Community-based organizations can significantly enhance the effectiveness of farmers markets. Training and support for local growers can improve their products and sales. Promoting networks among participants can enhance the learning that may occur in markets. Finally, community-based organizations can link farmers and growers with other market opportunities in the region.

Culinary Tourism

Culinary tourism is most often defined as pursuit of unique and memorable eating and drinking experiences. An example of a culinary tourism project would be a restaurant or an eatery connected with an orchard, farm, or ranch that has a unique ambiance, an interesting tasting room at a winery, cooking classes with a local product, or food festivals.

According to the Travel Industry Association (2007), 27 million travelers, or 17% of American leisure travelers, engaged in culinary or wine-related activities between 2003 and 2006. Culinary tourists have a significant impact on regional economies and spend about $1,000 per trip. Projected growth in culinary travel brings opportunities for economic development to rural America, along with challenges for farmers, ranchers, restaurateurs, and communities seeking to maintain their rural character and agrarian authenticity.

Culinary tourism has most often been associated with the wine industry. Several regions in the United States promote trails featuring regional wineries and, increasingly, breweries. Rather than marketing a specific locality, the entire region is promoted. Local breweries and wineries may offer tours and festivals. Restaurants may provide cooking classes on how to prepare regional foods. Retail establishments sell raw and processed local foods and beverages. Local farmers may sponsor on-farm visits and tours as well as participate in direct marketing opportunities such as farmer's stands and U-pick operations. Tourists are increasingly looking for authentic experiences that take them "back to nature" (Bessiere, 1998). Experiencing local cuisine and regional culture is one way to meet this demand.

Interest in culinary tourism is growing among consumers and restaurateurs who cater to these consumers. However, there are still significant barriers to deepening the linkages of culinary tourism. These include quality of delivery and service, the cost disconnect, and creating linkages. Most retail establishments and restaurants are concerned with the inconsistency and quality of delivery. Farmers and ranchers are concerned that the prices in these local markets are too low. And finally, culinary tourism may require greater coordination across the community, including farmers, retail establishments, and restaurants. There is greater need for key institutional actors to ensure that these local markets can continue to function.

Overall, there is growing consumer demand for locally grown food. There are, however, several common obstacles to building these systems. The most common issue facing communities is how to improve the match between the demand for and supply of local food. Local institutions, retail establishments and consumers have very little information on the supply of local products. Similarly, farmers, ranchers, and processors generally lack information on the demand for their products. To improve the match, communities need more transparent markets and intermediaries that can facilitate these linkages. In some cases, communities have developed websites that provide information on the supply of and demand for local products. Although technology can help promote local food systems, there is still a need for facilitators who can help build networks. These networks can help aggregate the supply of local food, as well as address some of the obstacles local farmers may face in processing their products.

A second common strategy for dealing with the obstacles of matching supply of and demand for local food is to promote greater collaboration among producers. This may take the form of legal cooperatives or informal networks. To meet the demand for local food, producers need to aggregate their supply. Collaboration may also address some of the concerns with transportation and processing.

Finally, the local food movement continues to be criticized for serving primarily wealthy consumers. If it is supporting local farms and ranches, this may not necessarily be a problem. Many communities, however, have sought to expand the reach of the local food system to the poor through innovative strategies.

CASE STUDY 13.2 KINGDOM SO DELICIOUS

Door County is located in northeast Wisconsin (the finger-like peninsula protruding into Lake Michigan). It has been a tourist destination for decades, especially for residents from the Chicago area who are attracted to the area for its classic farmscapes, abundant water and outdoor activities, and rich culinary traditions. Door County is known for its cherries, apples, whitefish, and maple syrup, and these foods are tied to cultural traditions, especially the fish boil (a culinary tradition in the Great Lakes states that consists of large chunks of fish boiled with potatoes in a cast iron kettle). Local foods are often featured in restaurants, retail establishments, and roadside stands. Door County and its cultural traditions received national attention in William Ellis's 1969 *National Geographic* article, "Wisconsin's Door Peninsula 'A Kingdom So Delicious,'" which sang the praises of Door County's history and tourism industry. Even in 1969, tourism was a $100 million a year business in Door County. In 2005, Door County developed a promotional campaign titled *A Kingdom So Delicious*. *Kingdom So Delicious* promotes regional foods by creating "packages" for participating lodging establishments, dining establishments, and other sources of entertainment (e.g., theater and art galleries). A hefty program of events serves as an incentive for area restaurants to feature local foods in their dishes and for art and theater venues to feature area history and culture-themed events. Food and beverage producers are encouraged to become involved by partnering with an art venue to offer combined art and cuisine events.

SOURCE: Green and Dougherty (2008).

Energy and Local Sustainability

Several factors are driving the growing interest in developing renewable energy sources. Climate change is forcing communities to consider alternatives to fossil fuel energy sources. Reducing carbon emissions is becoming a critical feature of policy debates. Many sources suggest that we will soon be at the tipping point for the supply of oil and that the demand will rapidly outstrip the supply, which means that the price of oil will skyrocket. Some strategies, such as ethanol, have already created unintended consequences, such as the rising cost of food in both developing and developed countries. So, the search is on for renewable fuels that will provide communities with a sustainable future. These developments will form the basis of a new clean energy economy.

Although much of the discussion about creating markets for clean energy has focused on state and federal policies, some of the most innovative programs are occurring at the local level. In this section, we focus on community development strategies for promoting renewable energy markets at the local level.

At the heart of the discussions about a clean energy economy is potential for developing alternatives to fossil fuels. This transition to renewable energy will have enormous consequences for our economy. There will be both winners and losers in this shift to clean energy. Regions heavily dependent on coal and oil will experience the largest decline in jobs, while regions developing renewable energy sources will see more sustainable development. In the aggregate, the research suggests that this transformation will create more jobs than those lost and will put communities on a more sustainable path. In the following, we discuss some of the issues involved in developing local sources of renewable energy.

Biofuels

Probably the most discussed form of renewable energy over the past few years has been biofuels. Biofuels include a wide range of renewable resources that can be converted into fuel. Corn ethanol is the most used biofuel in the United States. Technological advancements are making it possible to use other crops (e.g., beets), wood products, switchgrass, and other sources to make fuel. Most local strategies involve capturing biomass that is treated as a waste product or is a co-product of another production process (such as municipal trash, crop residues, or wood pulp residues). Other sources include waste vegetable oil, sugar cane, and palm oil.

The use of biomass has several advantages for community development. All biomass tends to be local. It is usually not very dense and is costly to move, which means that processing will also likely occur locally. It also suggests that biofuel operations are likely to be small and tend to be more locally owned operations.

This first generation of biofuels has sparked a huge backlash. Many of the studies that have looked at the efficiency of using biofuels suggest that they may take as much energy to produce as is gained. An example would be the production of ethanol. To consider how efficient ethanol is, we need to consider all of the fossil fuel that is required to produce it (e.g., fertilizer for the corn, transportation, and processing). Environmentalists have been concerned with some of the potential impacts of ethanol. Expansion of the corn ethanol industry led to increased corn production, many times on fields that were taken out of conservation. The concern was that increased corn production could lead to more soil erosion. As the corn ethanol industry grew rapidly, there were concerns that the high price of corn was contributing to the rapid increases in food prices. This had especially negative consequences for the poor and developing countries that rely heavily on food imports.

Biofuel production facilities are most likely to be located in rural areas. Many of these facilities are either cooperatives or community owned. (However, in many cases, these facilities are owned by large corporations.) In the case of corn ethanol, farmers see these facilities as a way to add value to their commodities and benefit the local economy. They also create new markets for farmers. This places farmers/owners in somewhat of a contradictory position. As prices rise, farmers benefit, but the biofuel facility must pay higher prices. If prices drop, the owners of the facility benefit while farmers receive less for their crops. Technological advances in biofuels will reshape the opportunities for communities to find new opportunities.

Wind

Wind energy is a tiny but rapidly growing alternative energy source in the United States. Wind power could account for about 20% of the U.S. electricity supply by 2030. Some estimates suggest that wind could provide as much as 15 times the existing world demand for energy. The technology for wind energy, however, is much more developed in Europe. Wind farms are being planned in many regions of the United States. The Great Plains has the greatest potential for the development of wind energy but is much less developed than other areas.

In addition to providing a new energy source, wind could also be a major contributor to job creation. Supplying wind turbine components has the greatest potential. Many existing manufacturing firms across the country could be quickly converted to producing these components. In addition, the jobs created in this sector would likely be middle-income jobs that require training.

One of the chief obstacles to the development of wind energy in local communities is the existing transmission system (grid). Most wind farms will be located in fairly isolated, rural areas. Although some of this energy may be used locally, much of it will be transmitted to urban areas. Existing lines lose much of the electricity, which makes the system very inefficient.

In many communities, there is strong opposition to wind energy. Much of the opposition is related to aesthetic concerns. In Massachusetts, there is considerable opposition to a plan to build a wind farm off Cape Cod. The plan would build turbines in the ocean, which many feel will obstruct the view. In other communities, there are concerns with the environment. Some research suggests that large wind turbines will kill bats and birds in the region.

There is a huge potential for wind energy on a community scale. One of the most successful recent examples of community-based energy development is the community wind project in Wilmar, Minnesota (The Minnesota Project, 2009). Although it faced several obstacles, the project had strong leadership and effectively solicited participation from the community-at-large. Siting these projects can be difficult, and developers often have to jump through numerous state and local hoops.

Solar

Solar energy has long been considered a potential alternative energy source. Solar energy systems produce electricity from sunlight through a photovoltaic process. Approximately one-quarter million households in the United States use some form of photovoltaic technology. Up to this point, technology and cost have been major obstacles to increased use of solar energy. Solar energy was not very efficient because it would require a multitude of panels to meet the needs of a household. And the cost of installing solar panels would take decades to recover the cost. Today, however, the technology has improved, and the cost considerations are making this alternative a realistic opportunity.

Approximately half of the states in the United States offer some form of rebate for adopting solar technology. Many communities are encouraging solar energy by providing tax incentives for households and businesses, as well as adopting solar energy for government facilities and buildings.

What role can community-based organizations (CBOs) play in promoting the adoption of solar technologies? One useful model is the case of Massachusetts Energy Consumer's Alliance in Boston. The Alliance was originally formed in the 1980s to cut home oil heating costs through bulk purchases. In 2000, the Alliance initiated the Solar Boston Initiative with a variety of area nonprofit organizations. The purpose of this initiative is to provide a link between the solar energy industry and consumers to reduce costs of installation of solar energy technology.

Energy Efficiency

Energy efficiency is seen as a powerful strategy to grow green-collar jobs because of the potential demand for energy audits and retrofits that exists in neighborhoods, schools, and businesses across the entire United States. The jobs related to energy efficiency are often concentrated in traditional building trades and construction industries. The jobs related to green buildings include not only green construction jobs but also sustainability analysts, urban planners specializing in brownfield redevelopment, and other development professionals with experience in green design.

Communities can drive green-collar job creation tied to efficiency and green building by crafting policies to improve their own facilities. Schools, government facilities, hospitals, and prisons are likely targets for retrofitting. Local policies can provide incentives for businesses and households to become more energy efficient. Energy efficiency will have the greatest impact on job creation in the local economy as many firms will be involved in manufacturing and installing equipment.

Local efforts to promote energy self-sufficiency face some common challenges. First, to maximize the benefits and to develop a more sustainable economy, it is important to attempt to promote local ownership. Local ownership improves the likelihood that the business will remain in the community and benefit local residents. Second, it is important to work back in the value chain. So, for example, in the case of wind energy, it would be beneficial to have regional businesses producing components for wind turbines. Other businesses may focus on installing or servicing turbines. This strategy helps ensure that the community maximizes the benefits to these investments and promotes greater sustainability.

Summary and Conclusions

Growth in local food systems and renewable energy reflects a growing interest in creating more sustainable communities. Dependence on external organizations and institutions for these key resources makes communities more vulnerable and limits the potential for developing these key local assets. One of the keys to promoting more sustainable communities will be establishing markets for local foods and energy. While federal and state policies can play a role in facilitating these markets, there is a need for local incentives and mandates as well.

To achieve these goals, we need to go beyond just establishing the incentives and mandates. Community-based organizations can play a critical role in making these markets more transparent by linking local businesses to the demand for local food and renewable energy. By making these connections, these efforts ensure that the community benefits to the fullest extent from these programs.

KEY CONCEPTS

Biofuels

Community gardens

Community-supported
   agriculture (CSA)

Culinary tourism

Farmers markets

Farm-to-school programs

Locavores

Solar energy

Wind power

QUESTIONS

1. What is the environmental impact of local foods (i.e., carbon footprint)?

2. What is the primary criticism of our food system? How do local food systems counteract some of these problems?

3. What are some of the typical obstacles that communities face in establishing a local food system?

4. Discuss how community-based organizations can facilitate the development of renewable energy systems.

EXERCISES

1. *Commodity chain analysis.* Students identify several food items at a local grocery store. The goal of the exercise is to identify how many miles the food traveled on the road to the grocery store. Most processed items can be traced to the processor. Fresh fruits and vegetables may be traced to the producers. The grocer may be able to help identify the wholesale source for students. Students can summarize their findings and estimate how much energy is used in transporting the products to the store.

2. *Solar energy conversion.* Students calculate how much it would cost to install solar panels in their home to meet all of their electricity needs. They will need to obtain their electricity bills for the entire year and estimate the demand in order to estimate how many solar panels they will need. On the basis of the demand, students should calculate the total cost of installing solar panels for their home and how long it will take before this investment would pay for itself.

3. *Renewable energy.* Have students evaluate the renewable energy sources being used by a local utility company. What percentage of electricity is produced from renewable energy sources? What and where are the renewable energy sources? What are the plans for increasing renewable energy sources in the local utility? Does the utility company offer any incentives for households and businesses to use renewable energy? If so, what are the programs?

REFERENCES

American Community Gardens Association. (n.d.). http://www.communitygarden.org/

Bessiere, J. (1998). Local development and heritage: Traditional food and cuisine as tourist attractions in rural areas. *Sociologia Ruralis, 38,* 21–34.

Green, G. P., & Dougherty, M. (2008). Localizing linkages for food and tourism: Culinary tourism as a community development strategy. *Community Development, 38,* 148–158.

Kingsolver, B. (2007). *Animal, vegetable, miracle: A year of food life.* New York: Harper.

The Minnesota Project. (2009). *Lessons and concepts for advancing community wind.* St. Paul, MN: Author. Retrieved February 19, 2010, from http://www.mnproject.org/pdf/TMP_Advancing-Community-Wind_Dec09.pdf

Pollan, M. (2007). *The omnivore's dilemma: A natural history of four meals.* New York: Penguin.

Travel Industry Association. (2007). *Comprehensive culinary travel survey provides insights on food and wine travelers.* Retrieved June 30, 2008, from http://www.tia.org/pressmedia/pressrec.asp?Item=750

ADDITIONAL READINGS AND RESOURCES

Readings

Demuth, S. (1993). *Community supported agriculture (CSA): An annotated bibliography and resource guide.* Washington, DC: U.S. Department of Agriculture, Alternative Farming Systems Information Center (AFSIC). http://www.nal.usda.gov/afsic/pubs/csa/csadef.shtml

Feenstra, G. W. (1997). Local food systems and sustainable communities. *American Journal of Alternative Agriculture, 12,* 28–36.

Geller, H. (2002). *Energy revolution: Policies for a sustainable future.* Washington, DC: Island Press.

Goldstein, D. B. (2007). *Saving energy, growing jobs: How environmental protection promotes economic growth, profitability, innovation, and competition.* Berkeley, CA: Bay Tree Press.

Heller, M. C., & Keoleian, G. A. (2000). *Life cycle-based sustainability indicators for assessment of the U.S. food system.* Ann Arbor: Center for Sustainable Systems, University of Michigan. http://css.snre.umich.edu/css_doc/CSS00–04.pdf

Hinrichs, C. C. (2003). The practice and politics of food system localization. *Journal of Rural Studies, 19,* 33–45.

Kingsolver, B., Hopp, S. L., & Kingsolver, C. (2007). *Animal, vegetable, miracle: A year of food life.* New York: HarperCollins.

LaSalle, T., Hepperly, P., & Diop, A. (2008). *The organic green revolution.* Kutztown, PA: Rodale Institute. http://www.rodaleinstitute.org/files/GreenRevUP.pdf

Nestle, M. (2002). *Food politics: How the food industry influences nutrition and health.* Berkeley: University of California Press.

Pirog, R., & Benjamin, A. (2003). *Checking the food odometer: Comparing food miles for local versus conventional produce sales in Iowa institutions.* Ames, IA: Leopold Center for Sustainable Agriculture. http://www.leopold.iastate.edu/pubs/staff/files/food_trave1072103.pdf

Pollan, M. (2007). *The omnivore's dilemma: A natural history of four meals.* New York: Penguin.

Pollan, M. (2008). *In defense of food: An eater's manifesto.* New York: Penguin.

Schlosser, E. (2001). *Fast food nation: The dark side of the all-American meal.* New York: Harper Perennial.

Waters, A. L., & Heron, K. (2008). *Slow food nations come to the table: The slow food way of living.* New York: Rodale, Inc.

Winne, M. (2009). *Closing the food gap: Resetting the table in the land of plenty.* Boston: Beacon.

Winter, M. (2003). Embeddedness, the new food economy and defensive localism. *Journal of Rural Studies, 19,* 23–32.

Websites

Apollo Alliance—http://apolloalliance.org/. This organization is working with cities across the United States to develop a more sustainable future. The alliance involves labor, environmental, and community groups in an effort to build a clean energy revolution.

Community Food Enterprise—http://www.communityfoodenterprise.org/. This is an excellent source for examining innovative community food enterprises. The website is supported by the Wallace Center of Winrock International.

Community Renewable Energy (Ltd) (CORE)—http://corecoop.net/. This organization is a social enterprise that focuses on helping communities develop systems that provide more sustainable energy futures.

Food Environment Atlas—http://maps.ers.usda.gov/FoodAtlas/foodenv5.aspx. This website provides a spatial view of a community's ability to access healthy food and its success in doing so.

Leopold Center for Sustainable Agriculture—http://www.leopold.iastate.edu/research/marketing_files/food/food.htm. The Leopold Center is a key resource for sustainable agriculture and food system research.

Local Energy—http://www.localenergy.org/. This nonprofit organization has numerous programs that help communities develop local, renewable energy sources. The website contains resources for local communities interested in these topics.

Slow Food USA—http://www.slowfoodusa.org. This website provides information on several programs that connect the food system to local communities and the environment. It includes information on food policy, sustainability, and various local food systems.

State and Local Energy Efficiency Programs—http://www.business.gov/expand/green-business/energy-efficiency/state-local/. This website includes a directory of various local, state, and regional programs to help businesses, consumers, and communities become more energy efficient.

USDA Official Farmers Market Directory—http://www.ams.usda.gov/farmersmarkets/map.htm. The USDA website provides basic information on farmers markets, as well as a directory of the more than 4,800 farmers markets in the United States.

Videos

Food, Inc. (2008), directed by Robert Kenner and coproduced by Robert Kenner and Eric Schlosser. Available from Magnolia Pictures, 49 W. 27th Street, 7th Floor, New York, NY 10001. http://www.foodincmovie.com.

The Future of Food (2004), directed by Deborah Koons Garcia and produced by Catherine Lynn Butler. Available from Lily Films, P.O. Box 895, Mill Valley, CA 94942. http://www.thefutureof-food.com.

Growing Local, Eating Local (2007), produced and directed by Bill McKibben, John Siceloff, and David Brancaccio. http://www.pbs.org/now/shows/344/. Available from PBS at http://www.shoppbs.org/product/index.jsp?productId=2899763&cp=&sr=1&kw=growing+local&origkw=Growing+Local&parentPage=search.

King Corn (2007), directed by Aaron Woolf and produced by Aaron Woolf, Ian Cheney, and Curt Ellis. Available from Bullfrog Films, P.O. Box 149, Oley, PA 19547; phone: (800) 543–3764. http://www.kingcorn.net.

The 11th Hour (2007), produced and directed by Nadia Conners and Leila Conners Peterson. http://11thhouraction.com/. Available from Amazon.com: http://www.amazon.com/dp/B00005JPXA?tag=11thhouracti-20&camp=14573&creative=327641&linkCode=as1&creativeASIN=B00005JPXA&adid=0E7HHXAHNP1HPJRPGX47&

14

Natural Disasters and Climate Change

The Role of Community Assets

In the past several years, the world has seen major natural disasters. In 2004, the Indian Ocean tsunami, created from a massive earthquake on the ocean floor, killed tens of thousands of people along coastlines in 11 countries (National Geographic News, 2004). In 2005, Hurricane Katrina devastated New Orleans in addition to parts of the Gulf Coast. In 2010, a large earthquake struck Haiti, near the capital city of Port-au-Prince, killing more than a hundred thousand people. Smaller natural disasters occur throughout the world regularly. In the United States, tornadoes consistently tear through communities. Greensburg, Kansas, was largely destroyed after a large tornado and has since vowed to rebuild (see Case Study 14.1). Sixty-four tornados tore across Oklahoma in May 2010, creating destruction along their paths. Extensive flooding occurred in parts of Iowa in 2008 with large parts of downtown Cedar Rapids under water. In 2010, Nashville experienced flooding of its downtown.

When natural disasters strike, they hit communities or an area along a river, on a coastline, near a volcano, within a short distance from an earthquake's epicenter, or in the corridor of a severe storm. Rarely do natural disasters devastate an entire country. Thus, most natural disasters are local and have an immediate impact on specific places.

The purpose of this chapter is to discuss natural hazards in terms of risk and vulnerability of human populations in specific places to those hazards. We focus on natural hazards and disasters, acknowledging that other types of hazards and disasters exist—industrial, terror related, wars, and disease. We will discuss both proactive community responses to natural hazards and reactive community responses to disasters. Finally, this chapter addresses climate change, how it will increase risk and vulnerability associated with particular natural hazards, and how communities are responding to anticipated changes.

CASE STUDY 14.1 RECOVERING
FROM DISASTER: THE CASE OF GREENSBURG, KANSAS

On May 4, 2007, a large, powerful tornado destroyed most of the community of Greensburg, Kansas. The tornado, classified as an EF-5, was 1.7 miles wide and had winds of about 205 miles per hour. Eleven people died as a result.

Greensburg is in southwest Kansas, slightly over 100 miles west of Wichita, which is the largest community in Kansas. The population in 2000 was 1,574. The current estimate is about 900 people. The city is about 2 square miles. The town was established in the late 1800s due to oil and gas production. Also, a rail line and a station were built during the same period. The community was known for the largest hand-dug well in the United States. It was originally dug in the late 1800s as rail for two lines was built and for the growing community. The tornado destroyed the Big Well Museum.

That night after the meeting and in the days following the tornado, assessments began to indicate the extent of the damage to the city and to people's lives. Ninety percent of the community's buildings were destroyed or severely damaged; all but two buildings in the downtown area survived. The county hospital was destroyed as well.

City leadership started to meet days after the storm to discuss whether to even come back to rebuild. In these discussions, the leadership realized that no one wanted to abandon their community despite the fact that the tornado had physically destroyed it. The community still had a strong commitment to Greensburg and was not willing to leave it. In the initial discussion days after the tornado, the community's leadership decided the community should rebuild in a sustainable way. One week after the storm, 500 people came to a community meeting that was held under a large tent. Considering that most homes were destroyed, most people were staying outside of town and needed to make the effort to find out about the meeting and drive upwards of a few hours to attend. At that first meeting, the mayor at the time announced that Greensburg would build back bigger, stronger, and greener. While many people wanted to move quickly, the leadership wanted to take time to plan. They saw that they would be making decisions that could last 100 years or more, so they didn't want to rush rebuilding. In addition, many people were not comfortable with the notion of building green. They didn't understand what it meant for them. However, with this announcement of rebuilding in a sustainable way, Greensburg garnered not only media attention but interest from state and federal officials.

Personnel from the Federal Emergency Management Agency (FEMA) arrived in Greensburg, many of whom had been dealing with the aftermath of Hurricane Katrina in New Orleans. FEMA and Greensburg leadership started to work on a long-range plan for recovery. For 12 weeks of intensive work and hundreds of meetings in tents, FEMA produced in August 2007 a long-term community recovery plan. The remaining part of this case study discusses the various forms of capital within Greensburg for a community development analysis. The key feature that was destroyed in Greensburg was its physical capital. With only about 10% of the buildings remaining, many of which were damaged, most people had no place to stay in the community. In addition, government buildings, the hospital, the Big Well Museum, and the downtown business district were gone. However, with a plan in place and a vow to rebuild, Greensburg in 3 years is well on its way to recovery. Below is a list of some, but not all, accomplishments:

- A business incubator was built—Sun Chips Business Incubator with the City of Greensburg and others, including federal funds, private-sector funds (including Sun Chips), and support from Leonardo DiCaprio. The incubator filled quickly, and three businesses are graduating.
- The Greensburg Wind Farm quietly started operating in March 2008, its 10 turbines supplying enough clean, renewable energy to meet the electrical needs of 4,000 households. Not only is every home and business in Greensburg running on energy harnessed from the wind, but they produce additional electricity to be sold on the grid.
- A new city hall was built, in part using reclaimed bricks from a destroyed building.
- 5.4.7 Arts Center was built and opened as a LEED Platinum building. That building opened in time for the first anniversary of the tornado.
- Kiowa County United is a nonprofit organization that raised more than $1 million to help construct a retail mall.
- Greensburg, Greentown, a new nonprofit started after the tornado, has a project on creating green homes. The "Chain of Eco-Homes Project" has a goal of constructing 12 model homes so that residents and visitors can experience a green home.
- In the Downtown Streetscape project, 303 LED streetlights have been installed.
- Kiowa County Memorial Hospital is the first LEED Platinum critical care facility in the United States.
- A new school will open in the fall of 2010 for all preschool through 12th-grade students. It has 96 geothermal wells to heat and cool the building.

One of the key reasons Greensburg was able to rebuild was the social capital in the community. Although the community is smaller now than before the storm, this group of 900 people, including children and youth, are committed to rebuilding it. With few places to stay, many people were willing to attend numerous meetings to help think through how to rebuild Greensburg. Youth also participated because they wanted to, in addition to having their opinions and thoughts valued in the planning process. Without a love of their community and the relationships among people in the community, it would have been difficult for Greensburg to rebuild as quickly and stick with the sustainable vision. Another critical element of Greensburg's recovery is its political capital. At the time of the disaster, Greensburg had trusted and visionary leadership. The mayor and others were ready and willing to step in to lead the community through a very difficult and challenging time. Without local leadership, it's possible that the efforts at rebuilding would not have been as successful.

SOURCES: "The World's Largest Hand-Dug Well" (n.d.), Federal Emergency Management Agency (2007), and Greensburg GreenTown (n.d.).

What Are Natural Disasters?

There are many definitions of natural disasters. This definition is from the United Nations Department of Humanitarian Affairs (UNDHA, 1992): "A serious disruption of the functioning of society, causing widespread human, material or environmental losses which exceed the ability of affected society to cope using only its own resources" (p. 27). This definition underscores a disaster's suddenness; the widespread disruption to a community, including all the forms of capital discussed in this book; and its potential overwhelming nature to recover.

BOX 14.1 TYPES OF NATURAL DISASTERS

Climactic

- Large-scale storms

  - Tropical cyclones
  - Extra-tropical cyclones
  - Snowstorms, blizzards, and freezing rain
  - Storm surges
  - Dust storms

- Localized storms

  - Thunderstorms, lightning, and hail
  - Tornadoes

- Drought
- Flooding

  - Flash floods
  - High-magnitude, regional floods

- Fires
- Oceanic

  - Waves
  - Sea ice
  - Sea level rise
  - Beach erosion

- Geological

  - Earthquakes
  - Volcanoes
  - Tsunamis
  - Land instability

SOURCE: Bryant (2005).

There are several types of natural disasters created from natural hazards. A **natural hazard** is defined as "a threatening event or the probability of occurrence of a potentially damaging phenomenon within a given time period and area" (UNDHA, 1992, p. 44). Box 14.1 lists the various types of natural disasters. Figure 14.1 shows the number of natural disasters reported from 1900 to 2009. Over that period, storms accounted for 59% of the natural disasters in the United States, including hurricanes and tornadoes. The next highest type of natural disaster is floods with 20% of the total. From 1990 to 1999, 258 natural disasters occurred in the United States, of which 166 were storms, and from 2000 to 2009, there 243 natural disasters, of which 129 were storms. On a worldwide scale, the International Red Cross and Red Crescent "indicate that there is an increase in the intensity and frequency of disasters. . . . For the period 1994–1998, reported disasters averaged 428 per year. That figure jumped to 707 during the period 1999–2003" (Prasad et al., 2009, p. 4).

The World Bank recently conducted a study of global disaster risk hot spots and found that "on the order of 25 million square kilometers (km²) (about 19 percent of the Earth's land area) and 3.4 billion people (more than half of the world's population) are relatively highly exposed to at least

FIGURE 14.1   Number and Percentage of Natural Disasters From 1900–2009 in the United States

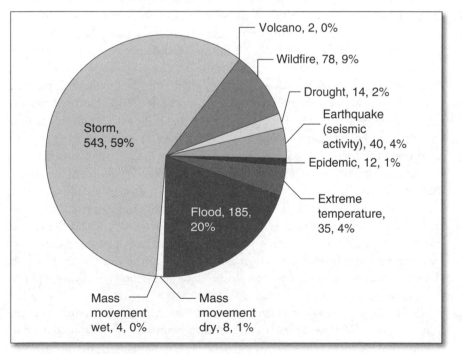

SOURCE: EM-DAT (2010).

one hazard" (Dilley, Chen, & Deichmann, 2005, p. 2). Natural disasters have high costs in both human life and overall damage to buildings, infrastructure, and the fabric of community life. Figure 14.2 shows the increasing costs of the damage wrought by natural disasters over two time periods. From 1990 to 1999, 50% of damages were incurred from wildfires and 27% by storms. Ninety percent of the damages occurred from storms in the 2000–2009 period, largely wrought by hurricanes. More than 4.7 million people were affected by natural disasters between 1990 and 1999, in which about 3,600 people died. The affected figure increased substantially between 2000 and 2009, with more than 20.8 million people affected by natural disasters, including 4,300 deaths. Although the latter period affected many more people than the earlier period, as a percentage, the deaths due to natural disasters were lower (EM-DAT, 2010). Natural disasters occur regularly although not predictably; they have high costs in terms of their effect on people and damages to infrastructure, buildings, and other systems. With this impact from natural disasters, the next section turns to why they occur.

What Creates Natural Disasters?

Natural disasters can be thought about in terms of risk. Risk is the degree to which a population is exposed to a natural hazard and the degree of vulnerability of that population. Let's think through an example. Santa Cruz, California, is located near the ocean on the north side of Monterey Bay. The San Lorenzo River flows out of the Santa Cruz Mountains and through the city on its way to the ocean. The mountainous terrain is in part covered with redwood forest. In addition, earthquake faults are nearby. There are potentially multiple natural hazards in the community: wildfire, landslides, tsunamis/tidal waves, earthquakes, and flooding. Different areas of that region are more exposed to one or more hazards depending on where one lives. If a resident lives close to or up into the foothills surrounded by forest, he or she is more exposed to the risk of a wildfire than the resident who lives a couple of blocks from the ocean. Both residents, however, are exposed to the risk of an earthquake. Another aspect to natural hazards is the vulnerability of populations to a particular hazard. Vulnerability is defined as the degree of loss (from 0% to 100%) resulting from a potentially damaging phenomenon. For example, one house may have an earthquake-resistant design and another house next door may not. The residents in one will be more vulnerable to an earthquake, although both are exposed to that particular hazard.

Rapid climate change is occurring because of the human-produced greenhouse gasses (GHGs) added to the atmosphere. The largest increases in GHGs have occurred since 1945, but GHGs have increased since the start of the industrial revolution. In the absence of policy actions, projections suggest that GHG emissions will increase by another 50% by 2025 (Energy Information Administration, 2003; International Energy Agency, 2004).

FIGURE 14.2   Damages (in U.S. Dollars) in the United States 1990–2009

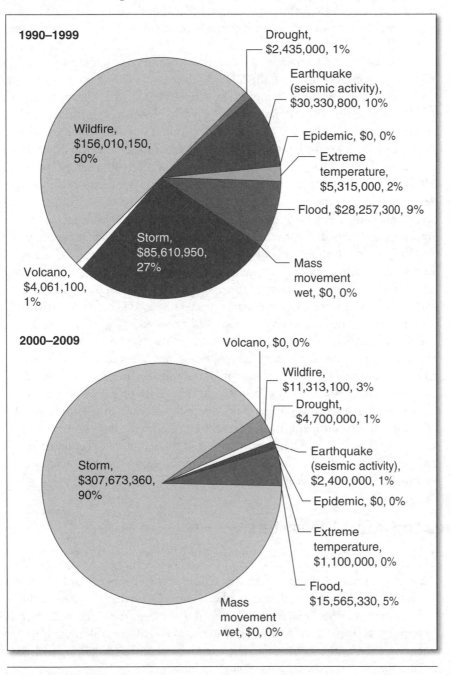

SOURCE: EM-DAT (2010).

GHG emissions come from almost every human activity. Energy consumption, primarily in the form of coal, oil, and natural gas, accounts for about 60% of total emissions. The industrial sector, taken as a whole, comprises about 21% of total GHG emissions. This includes both direct emissions (due to fossil fuel combustion) and indirect emissions (due to electricity consumption and industrial processes). Land use change/deforestation (18%) and agriculture (14%) are other major contributors to global GHG emissions, even though they consume relatively small amounts of energy (Haines et al., 2009).

A relatively small number of countries produce the majority of global GHG emissions. As of 2000, the United States was the largest emitter, with 21% of global emissions, followed by China (15%), the European Union (14%), Russia (6%), and India (6%) (World Resources Institute, 2005). Emissions growth rates are highest in developing countries such as China, where emissions grew about 50% from 1990 to 2002 (Haines et al., 2009).

Rapid climate change is expected to disrupt current weather patterns. Hurricane seasons may become longer, and the hurricanes may become more severe with higher winds. Some places may become drier, others wetter, some hotter, others cooler. Although communities, businesses, and residents can act to mitigate the effects of climate change, adaptation to climate change is necessary.

One way of dealing with the risks associated with **climate change** is to include those additional risks in an emergency management plan. If increased precipitation is a risk, managing those risks associated with particular natural hazards (flooding, for example) starts to make sense. Table 14.1 provides a way to understand the potential impacts of climate change. The table lists a number of sectors, such as water resources, recreation and infrastructure, the potential impacts, and a variety of adaptation measures to contend with the impacts. Although it does not quantify the impacts or risks, communities need to prepare residents, businesses, and others about the heightened need to prepare for natural disasters. Something else to note in the table are the direct impacts to different forms of community capital—environmental capital, physical capital, and human capital—and the indirect impact on financial capital. This discussion leads us to the next section, which focuses on responding to natural disasters.

Responses to Natural Disasters

Hazard mitigation is a responsibility of several federal agencies. Hazard mitigation is defined as the long-term reduction of the effects of natural hazard events. The U.S. Geological Survey, the National Oceanic and Atmospheric Administration, the U.S. Army Corps of Engineers, and the U.S. Forest Service are charged with managing a specific type of natural hazard. Other agencies, such as the Centers for Disease Control and Prevention, deal with other types of hazards, such as biological hazards.

Contending with natural hazards and climate involves two general strategies: **mitigation,** which can be divided into two types: one focused on climate change and the other on disaster management. Climate change mitigation refers to slowing and reversing the trend of warming by decreasing human-produced greenhouse gas emissions. Disaster management mitigation is the

(text continues on p. 299)

TABLE 14.1   A Sample of Sectors, Potential Climate Change Impacts, and Adaptation Measures

Sector	Impacts	Adaptation Measures
Hydrology and water resources	• Shift in the timing of spring snowmelt to earlier in the spring • Increased risk of drought • Increased risk of flooding • Increased competition for water • Warmer water temperature in lakes and rivers • Changes in water quality (variable by parameter)	• Expand the implementation of sustainable urban drainage systems, including permeable pavements, green roofs, stormwater retention ponds, constructed wetlands, and swales • Create natural ecosystem buffers for vulnerable water bodies and low-lying areas • Expand capacity of storm sewers, overland flow routes to manage extreme weather events • Flood-proof buildings in vulnerable locations • Educate the public on the need for proper grading to drain water away from their homes • Conduct water quantity audits every few years • Encourage mulching, drought-tolerant plants, and drip irrigation for drought-affected areas
Agriculture/forestry	• Changes in crop yields (varies by crop) • Potential ability to "double crop" • Increased risk of heat stress • Increased demand for irrigation water due to longer and warmer growing season • Increased risk of pest outbreaks and weeds	• Change planting dates • Plant different varieties or crop species • Develop and promote alternative crops • Develop new drought- and heat-resistant varieties • Encourage more use of intercropping • Use sustainable fertilizer and tillage practices (improving soil drainage, no-till, etc.) • Use improved crop residue and weed management • Use more water harvesting techniques • Encourage better pest and disease control for crops • Implement new or water-efficient irrigation systems

(Continued)

TABLE 14.1 (Continued)

Sector	Impacts	Adaptation Measures
		• Reduce water leakage, soil moisture conservation, and mulching • Improve livestock management (provide housing and shade, change to heat-tolerant breeds, change in stocking rate, alter grazing and rotation of pasture) • Encourage the use of agro-forestry practices
Biodiversity, aquatic ecosystems and forests (including parks and urban forests)	• Increase in growth and productivity in the near term where soil moisture is adequate and fire risk is low • Shift in the distribution and range of species • Increased risk of insect outbreaks • Increased risk of forest fires • Increased competition from invasive species • Shift in the distribution and range of species • Loss of species not able to adapt to changes • Increased competition from invasive species • Loss of habitat • Shifts in species range and distribution • Increased competition from invasive species • Increased stress on coldwater species in lakes and rivers	• Protect existing ecosystems (parks, tree stands, waterways, ponds, lakes, ravines, wetlands, etc.) and develop connected greenway system to allow natural species migration • Create and preserve green spaces in low-lying areas for flood management • Increase shoreline buffers to protect against increased runoff from more intense storms • Enhance conditions for street tree survival and growth (increase space for roots, control soil compaction, increase watering and maintenance, plant appropriate species) • Monitor and control pests and invasive species that can expand with warmer winters
Recreation	• Increased opportunities for warm-season activities • Reduced opportunities for cold-season recreation due to decreased snowpack and/or reduced snow or ice quality • Increased reliance on snow making at ski areas	• Consider extension of services and marketing for a longer summer season • Manage tourism growth in areas that will benefit from climate change and in areas that will be hurt. For example, make sure that facilities are sufficient to

Sector	Impacts	Adaptation Measures
	• Shifts in tourism dollars within a community from one recreation sector to another or from communities losing recreational opportunities to communities gaining opportunities	take advantage of longer, warmer summers while helping communities that are hurt by losses is winter sports • Create policy initiatives that offset economic dislocation in areas and populations especially hard hit by the negative effects of lost tourism through climate change
Energy	• Reduced heating demand during winter months • Increased cooling demand during summer months	• Expand conservation and demand-side management to reduce peak loads during heat waves that make transmission systems vulnerable to blackouts • Increase tree planting (particularly where they shade pavement or buildings) and maintenance of green roofs and high-albedo surfaces to reduce urban heat and unsustainable energy demand for air conditioning • Implement weatherization programs to reduce building loads, especially for low-income individuals • Expand distributed energy systems to reduce vulnerability to transmission interruptions from storms and high winds
Transportation	• Fewer travel disruptions and lower maintenance and infrastructure costs associated with snow and ice • More travel disruptions associated with landslides, road washouts, and flooding • Increased road surface damage due to higher temperatures	• Evaluate the vulnerability of port facilities and associated infrastructure due to changes in water level and increased wave activity • Assess and retrofit vulnerable transportation infrastructure systems such as culverts, tunnels, bridges, subway entrances, roads near waterways, etc.

(Continued)

TABLE 14.1 (Continued)

Sector	Impacts	Adaptation Measures
		• Ensure critical components such as switch gear or substations are above flood levels • Encourage less purchasing and use of road salt • Encourage more resurfacing and other road maintenance
Infrastructure	• Need for new or upgraded flood control and erosion control structures • More frequent landslides, road washouts, and flooding • Increased demands on stormwater management systems with the potential for more combined stormwater and sewer overflows	• Take account of the increased risks of flooding, heat waves, intense storms, wind speed, and other climate change effects in building development standards • In areas with flooding potential, retrofit ground-floor spaces for flood-compatible uses such as car parking • Plan for moving uses out of the floodplain • Design buildings for improved natural ventilation • Ensure roof systems and cladding materials can cope with higher wind speeds
Business	• Price volatility in energy and raw product markets due to more extreme weather events • Increased insurance premiums due to more extreme weather events • Fewer shipping disruptions due to snow and ice • Impacts on business infrastructure located in floodplains	• Conduct long- and short-term jobs analysis to identify which sectors/occupations will be positively/negatively affected, with an eye toward job creation opportunities • Retool education and job training programs for new workforce to take advantage of green economy growth • Promote activities that will promote climate change adaptation and the responsible use of state resources through education and outreach
Health	• More heat-related stress, particularly among the elderly, the poor, and other vulnerable populations • Fewer extreme cold-related health risks	• Conduct public education on climate-related health threats (vector-borne diseases, heat, air pollution, floods and storms) and prevention

Sector	Impacts	Adaptation Measures
	• Increase in vector-borne illnesses (e.g., West Nile virus) • Reduced summer air quality in urban areas due to increased production of ground-level ozone	• Interventions to reduce heat island effects, including street tree planting, green roofs, high albedo roof and road surfaces • Interventions to reduce air pollution, including emissions reduction measures and air quality warning systems • Interventions to prevent impacts from expansion of vector-borne diseases • Interventions to reduce health and security impacts from extreme weather events
Emergency response	• Increased demand on emergency response services related to extreme weather events (e.g., heat, flooding, storms)	• Assess the vulnerabilities and adaptive capacities of different regions, communities, and population groups • Provide extreme cold weather and extreme heat announcements via news media • Increase active intervention by public health and volunteer agencies (e.g., street patrols to locate and care for homeless people) • Increase the availability and accessibility of heated and air-conditioned public buildings, drop-in centers, and shelters • Develop new guidelines for managing long-term care facilities

SOURCE: Adapted from Haines et al. (2009).

"structural and non-structural measure undertaken to limit the adverse impact of natural hazards, environmental degradation, and technological hazards" (Prasad et al., 2009, p. 19). Communities can identify climate change mitigation measures that reduce GHG emissions and mitigate the effects of particular natural hazards such as the risk of flooding. Another general strategy to deal with natural hazards and climate change is adaptation. Adaptation measures focus on minimizing negative impacts and maximizing positive impacts (see Table 14.1).

Another important strategy to contend with hazards and the risk of climate change is to establish a set of **"no-regrets" policies**. "No-regrets policies and actions are those that make good sense to implement whether or not the consequences of climate change turn out to be as projected. These endeavors thus discount the uncertainty generated by climate change projections and predictions by supporting adaptation and mitigation strategies along with hazard-specific response capacity to building" (Prasad et al., 2009, p. 10).

Randolph (2004) has proposed four mitigation strategies to deal with natural hazards:

1. Avoid the impact (move away altogether). To this strategy we could add: don't move there at all. Two obvious areas to avoid are floodplains and along coast lines—beachfronts and dunelands. For the most part, federal, state, and local government agencies do not ban development completely from these areas.

2. Lessen the impact by modifying location on site (move away to a lesser impact area). This strategy implies locating a building as far from the hazard as possible given constraints on that site/property.

3. Lessen the impact by modifying design (applying engineering and design features). This strategy can involve building and construction projects, such as levees, floodways, and other structures along rivers. This occurs in places where the developed area has existed for many years. Many cities in the Northeast and Midwest, including along the Mississippi, have levees to deal with high water. Sometimes these systems fail, as we have seen in New Orleans.

4. Offset the impact (compensate for the impact by monetary relief, reconstruction, or re-creation). Floods along the Mississippi River in 1993 resulted in the buyout of many landowners to move away from the river, including homes, businesses, and farmland. The federal government manages the national Flood Insurance Program, which allows any resident within a participating community to buy flood insurance. Communities within the program must establish and enforce floodplain ordinances (Galloway, 2004).

In addition to the strategies discussed above, the process of **emergency management** is used by governments and community organizations to prepare for and respond to natural disasters. Emergency management is a process used by governments and businesses to think through the risk of natural and other hazards and how to respond if a natural or other type of disaster occurs. The emergency management process involves four phases: mitigation, preparedness, response, and recovery. Mitigation includes efforts to identify hazards and takes measures to minimize the effects of disasters from that hazard. This phase occurs before a disaster and is focused on long-term measures for reducing or eliminating risk. **Preparedness** involves emergency managers (fire and police, for example) developing an action plan so that when a disaster occurs, the response is coordinated and focused. These plans include several components: communication, maintenance and training for emergency services, warning methods, emergency shelters and evacuation plans, and disaster supplies and equipment. The response phase involves mobilizing emergency services and first responders.

In the response phase and depending on the severity of the disaster, humanitarian aid is needed. This type of aid provides immediate assistance to victims of an emergency. Humanitarian aid is usually a short-term response to provide clean water, food, shelter, clothing, health care, and other basics for human comfort and care. Humanitarian aid is often needed in countries that are unable to respond adequately to the situations confronting them. Haiti, in the days and months after the January earthquake, needed massive amounts of humanitarian aid. A similar humanitarian effort occurred after the tsunami in 2004.

The final phase is recovery. The recovery phase focuses on the short- to long-term efforts to recover rather than attending to the immediate needs either during or right after a disaster. After immediate disaster recovery, the effort is still on relief efforts, but for fewer and fewer people as food access and availability are eased, water shortages and infrastructure in addition to wastewater are dealt with, and housing provision begins. The long-term response is creating a strategy to rebuild. Rebuilding ideally mitigates the situation that originally created the disaster. One way to think about this recovery is restoring a community back to its original state. As the case study of Greensburg demonstrates, however, it is not necessary for everything to look like it once did. Although restoring physical capital to a community is critical, community buildings, homes, and other structures can look different. In the end, it's a community's social capital in particular, as well as capital in all its forms, that brings a community back from the brink of destruction. Table 14.2 focuses on all the forms of capital we have discussed in this book. Although the table is incomplete, its purpose is to show how natural disasters affect forms of community capital in different ways and degrees. It also shows that in a recovery phase, different forms of community capital have relationships among and between each other, and the strength or weakness of one can affect the whole—the entire community. Sometimes, it takes a natural disaster or some other shock to see how all the parts are interrelated. Responding to natural disasters involves many phases and organizations. The next section focuses on the role of community-based organizations in response to natural disasters.

———————— The Role of Community-Based Organizations

The Disaster Mitigation Act of 2000 requires local and tribal governments to submit action plans to reduce their long-term risk. The federal government provides some financial assistance for these efforts (Flint & Brennan, 2006). A popular approach to developing plans to reduce the risks of disasters is called the community emergency response team (CERT) (Brennan & Flint, 2007). The CERT program is part of Citizen Corps, which is a component of the Federal Emergency Management Agency (FEMA). The CERT program trains citizens

TABLE 14.2   Forms of Community Capital and Role in Recovery From a Natural Disaster

Capital	Role
Physical	Often destroyed or damaged; majority of funds and attention occur here.
Environmental/natural	Often destroyed or damaged; efforts to clean up waterways, replant wetlands, re-sand beaches
Financial	Short-term loss, especially if people who have the means to evacuate leave; connects with social capital
Political	Corruption can happen; strong versus weak leadership; loss of institutional memory; can find new leadership from disaster
Social	Often destroyed or damaged; in New Orleans after Hurricane Katrina, people evacuated and many rebuilt their lives elsewhere; old ties were destroyed and may not be renewed in place; in Greensburg, social ties were strong and important. Many people returned to rebuild purposely.
Cultural	Not destroyed unless too many people leave; tempting to return to status quo when the situation to reduce risk and vulnerability may be to rethink values; more physical forms of culture may have been destroyed and damaged but can be rebuilt.
Human	Many people in a natural disaster are injured and killed. Families in the aftermath of a disaster need to deal with loss and/or physical and mental health issues. Employers need to deal with loss as well in addition to rebuilding and reopening.

to prepare for and respond to disasters. Hundreds of CERTs have been set up all across the United States (Flint & Brennan, 2006). CERTs train volunteers in communities to respond to natural disasters. This type of organization is one type of community-based organization (CBO) with an identified goal of responding to disasters.

Other CBOs can play a variety of roles before, during, and after a natural disaster strikes a community. One of the key roles that CBOs play is disaster relief or humanitarian aid. Often, however, these organizations are not community based in the sense that we have talked about throughout this book. Often these organizations are international in scope and can bring lots of resources to bear on a given situation. The Red Cross and Red Crescent Societies, agencies within the United Nations, and other organizations such as CARE and Oxfam work in many developing countries around the world. In the United States, many organizations aid in humanitarian and relief efforts, such as the American Red Cross.

Despite the fact that many organizations assist in disaster relief in the United States, many people assume that local, state, and federal government take the lead. This was one of the major criticisms of the federal government in the aftermath of Hurricane Katrina. It appeared that neither the federal government nor any other organization was coordinating rescue and relief efforts adequately. Lacho, Bradley, and Cusack (2006) found that community-based organizations provided valuable services to their communities prior to Katrina. "In 2004, there were 2,324 nonprofits in the New Orleans MSA. . . . Some 9.7 percent of employed persons in New Orleans worked for nonprofits" (p. 66). Lacho et al. believe that New Orleans will be rebuilt by local people through nonprofit organizations and associations.

One example of this kind of rebuilding is through the Mary Queen of Viet Nam Community Development Corporation, Inc. (MQVN CDC). It is focused on the eastern part of New Orleans and takes a holistic approach to community by working on issues pertaining to health care, the environment, agriculture, education, housing, social services, economic development, and the arts. After Hurricane Katrina, MQVN CDC stepped in to provide emergency relief assistance to more than 3,000 Vietnamese Americans, including developing a trailer site with almost 200 homes. After the initial recovery efforts, MQVN CDC engaged "nearly 1,000 community members in identifying community needs and articulating priorities for neighborhood rebuilding processes" (http://www.mqvncdc.org/index.php).

Another community-based organization was formed only days after Hurricane Katrina to coordinate local and national philanthropic efforts in the short- and long-term recovery efforts along the Gulf Coast of Louisiana. The Louisiana Disaster Recovery Foundation (LDRF) has helped more than 2,500 families return to their homes in hurricane-affected areas. In addition, LDRF supports revitalizing the nonprofit sector in Louisiana.

The Hope Community Development Agency (HCDA) started through the efforts of one man 2 days after Hurricane Katrina. HCDA began supporting and coordinating relief and recovery efforts in the Biloxi area and then focused on affordable housing, economic development, community organizing, and relationship building. HCDA has changed many people's lives due to its efforts. These examples illustrate the types of work community-based organizations have engaged in after a particularly devastating natural disaster. This is an area needing documentation and research to show the role of community-based organizations to prepare for, react to, and recover from natural disasters. One interesting part of these examples is that two of the three examples were organized in the days after Hurricane Katrina. This shows the critical roles that CBOs play in recovery efforts and the unexpected opportunities to create CBOs where none existed previously.

Summary and Conclusions

Natural disasters can occur almost anywhere, and climate change may exacerbate disasters related to weather. Analyzing the risks associated with natural hazards and the vulnerabilities associated with those hazards is critical in preparing for and mitigating natural disasters. CBOs have an important role to play, whether it is a more formal role like the CERTs or the more traditional role of a community development corporation. CBOs need to prepare not only their own offices and staff for a natural disaster but their clients as well.

Much of the focus in the literature on climate change and natural disasters has focused on responses by national governments. For several reasons, we have argued that there is a need to a have an appropriate action plan at the local level as well. The ability to respond to these challenges will often depend on the capacity of communities to understand the threats and to effectively prepare to lessen the potential impact. Research has demonstrated that natural disasters can tear the fabric of communities (Erikson, 1976). Conversely, the capacity of communities to prepare for natural disasters will ultimately influence the ability to mitigate these disasters.

KEY CONCEPTS

Adaptation	Natural hazard
Climate change	"No-regrets" policy
Emergency management	Preparedness
	Response
Mitigation	Risk
Natural disaster	Vulnerability

QUESTIONS

1. Define a natural hazard and a natural disaster.

2. Describe the four mitigation strategies to dealing with natural disasters.

3. What is climate change, and what is affecting it?

4. What are some of the key impacts of climate change on communities?

5. Describe some adaption measures in response to climate change.

EXERCISES

1. Identify the kinds of natural hazards in your community and an emergency management plan. Interview a few small business owners and residents to see if they know about the hazards and their inherent risks and what they would do in case of a natural disaster.

2. Does your local government have a climate change action plan? Talk to officials within the local government and businesses about what prompted the plan. If there is no plan, ask them their views on climate change and the risks they see or do not see associated with it.

3. Identify a community in your region that has experienced a natural disaster (e.g., flood, tornado, hurricane, drought) in recent years. What have been the economic and social effects of this event? How prepared was the community for this disaster? What have they done since the event to reduce their risk to more disasters?

REFERENCES

Brennan, M. A., & Flint, C. G. (2007). Uncovering the hidden dimensions of rural disaster mitigation: Capacity building through community emergency response teams. *Southern Rural Sociology, 22,* 111–126.

Bryant, E. (2005). *Natural hazards* (2nd ed.). Cambridge, UK: Cambridge University Press.

Dilley, M., Chen, R., & Deichmann, U. (2005). *Natural disaster hotspots: A global risk analysis.* Washington, DC: The World Bank.

EM-DAT. (2010). *The OFDA/CRED International Disaster Database.* Université catholique de Louvain—Brussels—Belgium. Retrieved May 18, 2010, from www.emdat.net

Energy Information Administration. (2003). *International energy outlook 2003.* Washington, DC: Author.

Erikson, K. T. (1976). *Everything in its path: Destruction of community in the Buffalo Creek flood.* New York: Simon & Schuster.

Federal Emergency Management Agency (FEMA). (2007). *Long-term community recovery plan, Greensburg and Kiowa County, Kansas, August 2007.* Retrieved May 28, 2010, from http://greens burgks.org/recovery-planning/long-term-community-recovery-plan/GB_LTCR_PLAN_Final_ HiRes.070815.pdf

Flint, C., & Brennan, M. (2006). Community emergency response teams: From disaster responders to community builders. *Rural Realities, 1*(3), 1–9.

Galloway, G. (2004). *Integrated flood management, case study, USA: Flood management— Mississippi River.* The Associated Programme on Flood Management. Retrieved May 24, 2010, from www.apfm.info/pdf/case_studies/cs_usa_mississippi.pdf

Greensburg GreenTown. (n.d.). Retrieved May 28, 2010, from http://www.greensburggreentown.org/

Haines, A., Markham, L., McFarlane, D., Miskowiak, D., Olson, E., Roberts, R., et al. (2009). *Wisconsin land use megatrends: Climate change.* Stevens Point: Center for Land Use Education, University of Wisconsin–Extension/University of Wisconsin Stevens Point.

International Energy Agency. (2004). *World energy outlook 2004.* Paris: OECD/IEA.

Lacho, K. J., Bradley, D. B., & Cusack, M. (2006). Business nonprofits: Helping small businesses in New Orleans survive Katrina. *The Entrepreneurial Executive, 11,* 55–68.

National Geographic News. (2004). *The deadliest tsunami in history?* Retrieved May 12, 2010, from: http://news.nationalgeographic.com/news/2004/12/1227_041226_tsunami.html

Prasad, N., Ranghieri, F., Shah, F., Trohanis, Z., Kessler, E., & Sinha, R. (2009). *Climate resilient cities: A primer on reducing vulnerabilities to disasters.* Washington, DC: The International Bank for Reconstruction and Development/The World Bank.

Randolph, J. (2004). *Environmental land use planning and management.* Washington, DC: Island Press.

United Nations Department of Humanitarian Affairs (UNDHA). (1992). *International agreed glossary of basic terms related to disaster management.* Retrieved June 10, 2010, from http://wwww.reliefweb .int/rw/lib.nsf/db900SID/LGEL-5EQNZV?OpenDocument

World Resources Institute. (2005). *Navigating the numbers: Greenhouse gas data and international climate policy.* Retrieved June 10, 2010, from http://pdf.wri.org/navigating_numbers.pdf

The world's largest hand-dug well. (n.d.). Retrieved May 27, 2010, from http://www.bigwell.org/ bigwell.html

ADDITIONAL READINGS AND RESOURCES

Additional Readings

Abbott, P. L. (2008). *Natural disasters.* New York: McGraw-Hill.

Alexander, D. (1993). *Natural disasters.* New York: Routledge Taylor & Francis Group.

Merriman, P. A., & Browitt, C. W. A. (1993). *Natural disasters: Protecting vulnerable communities.* New York: Thomas Telford.

Mileti, D. (1999). *Disasters by design: A reassessment of natural hazards in the United States.* Washington, DC: National Academy Press.

Natural Hazards Center. (2006). *Holistic disaster recovery: Ideas for building sustainability after a natural disaster.* Retrieved January 26, 2010, from http://www.colorado.edu/hazards/publications/ holistic/holistic2006.html

Pan American Health Organization. (2000). *Natural disasters: Protecting the public's health.* Washington, DC: World Health Organization.

Pelling, M. (2003). *The vulnerability of cities: Natural disasters and social resilience.* Washington, DC: Earthscan Publications Ltd.

Steinglass, P., & Gerrity, E. (2006). Natural disasters and post-traumatic stress disorder short-term versus long-term recovery in two disaster-affected communities. *Journal of Applied Social Psychology, 20,* 1746–1765.

Wijkman, A., & Timberlake, L. (1984). *Natural disasters: Acts of God or act of man?* Washington, DC: Earthscan.

Websites

CDC—Emergency Preparedness and Response— http://www.bt.cdc.gov/. Provides users with credible, reliable health information on data and statistics, diseases and conditions, emergencies and disasters, environmental health, healthy living, injury, violence and safety, life stages and populations, travelers' health, workplace safety and health, and more. Lists most recent outbreaks and incidents at www.bt.cdc.gov/recentincidents.asp.

Community Capacity and Wildfire—http://www.uoregon.edu/~cwch/programs/CCE/wildfire.html. Focuses on building capacity in rural and underserved communities to address wildfire protection, increasing awareness about the relationships between wildfire and rural poverty, and providing resources for community efforts in fire and forest restoration. This program also examines broader relationships between natural disaster mitigation and social vulnerability.

Disaster Assistance.gov—Access to Disaster Help and Resources—www.disasterhelp.gov .DisasterAssistance.gov is a secure, user-friendly U.S. government web portal that consolidates disaster assistance information in one place.

Federal Emergency Management Agency—www.fema.gov. FEMA's mission is to support our citizens and first responders to ensure that as a nation, we work together to build, sustain, and improve our capability to prepare for, protect against, respond to, recover from, and mitigate all hazards.

NASA Earth Observatory—http://earthobservatory.nasa.gov/NaturalHazards. The Earth Observatory's mission is to share with the public the images, stories, and discoveries about climate and the environment that emerge from NASA research, including its satellite missions, in-the-field research, and climate models. Great images and information about past natural hazards.

National Geographic Natural Disasters—http://environment.nationalgeographic.com/environment/natural-disasters. Learn how rock, wind, ice, snow, raging storms, and Earth's inner fire have transformed the planet and life on it. Watch video from inside a tornado, create your own hurricane, and see photos of tsunami devastation. Awesome pictures.

National Hazards Center—www.colorado.edu/hazards/. The center collects and shares research and experience related to preparedness for, response to, recovery from, and mitigation of disasters, emphasizing the link between hazards mitigation and sustainability to both producers and users of research and knowledge on extreme events.

Natural Hazards.org—www.naturalhazards.org. At this site, you will find the what, where, when, and how of every major natural hazard on our planet.

United Nations Development Programme—Crisis Prevention and Recovery—www.undp.org/cpr/we_do/integrating_risk.shtml. The Bureau for Crisis Prevention and Recovery (BCPR) works around the world to restore the quality of life for men, women, and children who have been devastated by natural disaster or violent conflict. The bureau provides a bridge between the humanitarian agencies that handle immediate needs and the long-term development phase following recovery. Interactive Disaster Risk Map on the main page lists each month and shows the dangers to each country around the world.

USGS—Natural Hazards Gateway—www.usgs.gov/hazards. This series educates citizens, emergency managers, and lawmakers on seven natural hazards facing the nation—earthquakes, floods, hurricanes, landslides, tsunamis, volcanoes, and wildfires—and shows how USGS science helps mitigate disasters and build resilient communities.

Videos

National Geographic—Forces of Nature (2004), from National Geographic and Graphic Films, follows scientists on pulse-pounding quests to discover how natural disasters are triggered. http://www.nationalgeographic.com/forcesofnature/film/index.html.

NOVA: Fire Wars (2005). Every year, armed with the best technology, thousands of firefighters battle the blazes, but despite all their efforts, we are not winning the fire wars. Can we win them? Should we fight all fires? Ecologists claim that fire is a necessary and revitalizing element of healthy ecosystems. What would happen if we did eliminate all wildfires? http://www.shoppbs.org/product/index.jsp?productId=3245097&cp=&sr=1&kw=fire+wars&origkw=fire+wars&parentPage=search. For other Nova productions: http://www.pbs.org/wgbh/nova/archive/int_disa.html.

A Village Called Versailles (2010) is a feature documentary about Versailles, an isolated community in eastern New Orleans that has been settled by Vietnamese refugees since the late 1970s. In the aftermath of Hurricane Katrina, Versailles residents impressively rise to the challenges by returning and rebuilding before any other flooded neighborhood in New Orleans, only to have their homes threatened by a new government-imposed toxic landfill just two miles away. New Day Films, 190 Route 17M P.O. Box 1084, Harriman, NY 10926; phone: (888) 367–9154. http://www.newday.com/films/avillagecalledversailles.html.

When the Levees Broke—A Requiem in Four Acts (2006). Director Spike Lee's documentary is a harrowing, vivid documentation of the lives of the people affected by Hurricane Katrina in New Orleans. An HBO Production; runtime: 256 minutes.

15

The Future of Community Development

The field of community development faces numerous obstacles. Edward Blakely (1989) has argued that among the most important issues are the uncoupling of production from place, community consciousness, and community institutions. The production process is tied less to place and is now evolving into a global production process that is increasingly mobile. As a result, large corporations are less committed to places and workers. The effects of globalization on community development, however, may be somewhat overstated. Place still matters. Most businesses are not very mobile. In most cases, they are tied to their suppliers and customers in the region. Only a small percentage of businesses actually move each year. It is the threat of capital mobility that often affects local residents and policy makers. Ironically, globalization increases the significance of place in many regions because of the importance of producer services and other inputs that are required by multinational firms (Sassen, 2006). The growth of the service sector may dampen the effects of globalization because these firms are unlikely to be as mobile as a garment or automobile factory.

As we have suggested in earlier chapters, people are not as influenced today by territorial consciousness but are more likely to participate in organizations that are national and international in scope. This process has been taking place for decades but may have been exacerbated in recent years by technological change (e.g., the Internet) and globalization of the economy and culture. These developments may make it more difficult for communities to act on their local problems. Many people feel alienated and incapacitated because they have come to believe that they cannot effect change at the local level. In addition, individuals are more likely to maintain social contacts and ties outside of their local community. Also, because people now live, work, and consume in different places, their allegiance to a specific place becomes much more diffuse. Other developments, such as school choice, also contribute to these problems because the quality of local schools becomes less important to individuals. All of these changes make the connection between individual well-being and the conditions of a local place much harder to make for most residents.

We argued in Chapter 1 that although residents do not have social relationships exclusively with people in their neighborhoods, this does not mean that they cannot be motivated to act on local issues. Residents are especially likely to respond to threats to their neighborhood, such as a zoning, environmental, or school issues. These are essentially local issues. Several factors influence local attachment: length of residence, homeownership, and children increase participation and concern with local issues. Community development, however, stresses the importance of building the capacity of residents to address the issues affecting their quality of life.

Putnam (2000) has argued persuasively that there has been an erosion of civic society over the past 50 years. Much of his evidence for this claim is based on a systematic decline in the number of people belonging to and participating in local organizations. The decline of social capital has important implications for community development efforts. If local residents lack social and organizational ties, it is more difficult to mobilize residents to address local problems and raise their consciousness about issues affecting the collective good. Putnam's thesis, however, may be directed more toward middle-class communities rather than low-income neighborhoods. The problem in poor neighborhoods is the loss of middle-class residents who were the major supporters of local organizations and institutions (Wilson, 1987). Most low-income residents remain tied to local institutions and have fewer contacts outside their neighborhood. Putnam's point, however, is well taken, and the decline in civic organizations certainly has had negative effects on community development. At the same time, there is a wide variety of other sources of social capital available in poor and minority communities. Residents in poor and minority communities are more likely to rely on neighbors and kin to meet their material and emotional needs (Green, Hammer, & Tigges, 2000). Thus, there appears to be a wide basis for social contacts and ties within these neighborhoods. The problem may be that residents in these neighborhoods are less likely to have social relationships with individuals outside these neighborhoods who could provide assistance and support.

Overall, many societal trends seem to be working against community development. Society is becoming more mobile and individuals are less oriented toward local institutions than they used to be. At the same time, several forces are pushing for more community-based strategies for addressing local problems. In most countries, there is a marked trend toward decentralization of authority and decision making due to pressures to limit the size of national governments and fiscal constraints on the public sector. Decentralization has obviously placed much more stress on local communities, and it does not necessarily equip them with the tools to manage the problems they face.

As we discussed in Chapter 11, most local officials are often influenced by large corporations and development interests. Although there are differing opinions about how difficult it is to overcome these interests, there is agreement that a pro-growth regime dominates in most communities. These policies are not influenced by material (financial) interests alone; unions, community-based organizations (CBOs), and other progressive organizations often adopt pro-growth sentiments. This structure places a great deal of emphasis on community organization and institutionalization to counter the powerful interests associated with the growth machine.

Although critics are right to be concerned about the effects of global trends and capital mobility, as well as the influence of local development interests, we are convinced that these obstacles are not insurmountable. The asset-based development approach suggests that there are available resources in most communities that can be used to help build these areas. That there continue to be major social and economic problems in many communities is not necessarily an indictment of the failure of the community development movement but rather is a result of the failed national and state policies that have addressed these concerns.

Fulfilling the Promise of Community-Based Development

The community development field has become institutionalized in the past 50 years. Most local leaders and government officials today recognize the importance of engaging residents in the decisions that affect their locality. Federal, state, and local governments have formalized public participation efforts. Most programs require some form of public participation. You may question whether local residents actually have control over local decision making, but residents are asked for their input on almost all local matters. At a minimum, most public officials acknowledge that public participation affects the implementation of programs. When local residents have some input into the process, they are more likely to support these programs. Most public officials, however, still want to control the process, and they rely heavily on technical experts, rather than local knowledge, for the most important advice.

Similarly, the idea of place-based development is firmly entrenched in federal and state policy, largely because politicians see it as directly affecting their constituencies. Most policy makers recognize that economic development, even within a metropolitan area or rural region, may not affect neighborhoods or communities evenly within these areas. We have argued that markets and government programs have a limited capacity to address these problems, especially in poor and minority neighborhoods. CBOs have several advantages in carrying out place-based strategies of development.

Even some of the community-based development institutions, such as microenterprise loan funds, are now promoted by federal agencies (e.g., the Small Business Administration). Community development corporations (CDCs) are considered the key organizational mechanism for providing affordable housing in most cities and some rural areas. Although they can receive some federal funding, these institutions are not able to obtain enough funding to address the needs of low-income and poor neighborhoods. As these institutions become part of the mainstream, there is a danger they will lose their local orientation and become more standardized across communities.

Although the community development field is well established, most practitioners and policy analysts recognize that community development programs have not come close to addressing the breadth and depth of social and economic problems that exist in most communities CDCs have been able to produce only a small fraction of the affordable housing needed in most communities. Successful economic development efforts have not generated enough jobs to replace those that have been lost to technological advancements, economic restructuring, and the globalization. Although CBOs have been able to provide job training to underserved populations and help job searchers make connections with employers, the level of human capital in most inner cities and underdeveloped rural areas continues to lag behind other regions. New financial organizations have emerged to address the needs of poor and minority communities, but these too have only scratched the surface of the credit needs. Although many issues are at play here, one of the common problems that CBOs face is lack of resources. That is not to say that more financial resources alone will solve the problems. In fact, there are many instances where CBOs are faced with too many resources and no good plan for effectively allocating these resources. Providing stronger infrastructure that supports CBOs, however, could make them much more effective. We do not believe that the model of community-based development is the problem; it is the countervailing policies and actions at the state and federal levels that make it difficult for communities to address their problems.

In many instances, community-based development efforts are struggling to overcome the powerful influence of policies that undermine their activities. Probably the best illustration is in the area of economic development. Although there has been continuing federal and state support for CDC activity in the area of economic development, transportation programs have facilitated the flight of the middle class out of the city, leaving areas with concentrated poverty and little hope for investment. Government programs also have promoted the flight out to the suburbs by subsidizing home loans. Businesses have followed the migration out to the suburbs and have been provided incentives that often include federal tax breaks. The result has been the loss of job opportunities for low-skilled workers in the inner city. Community-based development, at least to this point, has not been able to overcome these forces. Community-oriented policies are needed that recognize the links between state and federal programs and the differential effect on places throughout the United States. Community-based development would have a much greater chance of success with these types of policies. The challenge here is to find innovative ways of promoting community-based development that ensures localities have the capacity and control they need.

There also is concern expressed by some critics that the community development field has become too institutionalized—it has lost its ability to challenge the existing power structure. Many of the successful community development efforts of the 1960s were built on community organizing efforts. CDCs were established as direct result of these efforts to mobilize communities. Today, most CDCs depend on the federal government and foundations for financial assistance. CDCs may be reluctant to challenge the political structure too much and may be less likely to get involved in mobilizing residents. Instead, they turn to providing technical assistance.

Although there may be some basis for this criticism, it is not necessarily an indictment of community-based development efforts. Clearly, organizations need to guard against becoming too bureaucratized and technical. Separating the functions of community organizing from development will not help solve these dilemmas. The issues are embedded in the larger economy and society. Organizations need resources. Their goals are often shaped by their resource needs. These problems exist for CBOs as well as any other type of organization in a capitalist society. What these CBOs need is more support from the federal and state governments, and foundations, so they can once again focus on community needs.

To overcome some of these limitations, federal and state governments need to make a long-term commitment to community development. Given the federal and state government deficits, it is unlikely that additional resources will be available for the short term. Instead, it may make more sense to decentralize many government programs to localities. With additional authority, community-based organizations need to be more accountable and demonstrate they are using resources in a fair and efficient manner. This may mean that CBOs will need to improve their accountability by demonstrating the outcomes and impacts of their programs. Many community development practitioners will resist the pressures to "show results" because they believe their objective is to build community capacity and it takes too long to see the ultimate outcomes of their activity. Although it is difficult to measure the long-term impacts of many community development activities, practitioners need to design programs more carefully so that a good evaluation can be conducted. This may mean that practitioners will need to collect baseline data on conditions, monitor progress, and plan for how to eventually assess the impacts of their programs.

Local Versus External Initiation of Community Development

One of the recurring issues in the community development field has concerned the appropriate role for external organizations and institutions in promoting development. On one hand, there is plenty of evidence that external support through foundations and intermediary institutions can influence the success of community development projects. External organizations can provide financial resources, information, technical assistance, and contacts with other communities or organizations. Intermediary organizations in community development have demonstrated their success in producing affordable housing. This model also has been used to a more limited extent in the support of human capital (training) and financial capital (lending) at the local level.

On the other hand, there is growing concern that CBOs often lose control to external organizations and institutions (Rubin, 2000). CBOs must rely on these organizations for financial assistance, the focus of the project may be changed, and the project may not be directed at the needs of local residents. Funding organizations and institutions have their own objectives, which may not be consistent with those of local residents. Assistance may have strings attached that require localities to fulfill requirements that have nothing to do with building community capacity.

The evidence from many case studies suggests that community development programs are less likely to be very successful if they are initiated outside, rather than self-initiated in, the community. Even cities that attempt to generate grassroots efforts within neighborhoods often face obstacles. One project by a major city to create a grassroots effort occurred in Atlanta, Georgia, where former President Jimmy Carter attempted to build capacity in more than 20 neighborhoods in Atlanta. Corporations in the region provided financial support for the project. Yet most of the evaluations suggest the effort had a minimal impact because it was never able to generate the neighborhood support for the project that was so badly needed. This example suggests that external organizations can at best play a supportive role and are limited in their ability to generate grassroots efforts.

The dilemma facing CBOs, then, is that they need institutional support from these external organizations, but they also need to maintain control over their activities. There is a delicate balance to maintain here, and there will always be external pressures to set the agenda. Community organizations need to formalize a planning process to avoid having their issues framed by outside institutions and organizations. They need to develop the capacity to resist these pressures. Well-organized communities are much more likely to shape the agenda than those who are looking for outside organizations and institutions to set the agenda.

An Agenda for Promoting Community Development in America

Fundamental changes have occurred in the social, political, and economic systems in which communities are embedded. How should practitioners respond to these changes? What types of policies help promote community-based solutions to the problems of inner cities and underdeveloped rural areas? One temptation is to long for the return to the sense of community that existed in America in the 1950s. The emphasis on participation in local organizations, a strong sense of neighborliness, and local institutions that primarily serve local residents is very appealing. Reconstructing community along these lines, however, may be impossible and not necessarily desirable. Communities in the 1950s also were characterized by a lack of individual freedom and choice and limited roles for women and minorities. Decision making in communities was not necessarily more democratic, either. Technological, economic, and social changes probably make it impossible to return to this world anyway.

Community development in the future needs to acknowledge the everchanging nature of communities. We need to recognize the important role that technology plays today and find ways of using it to promote collective interests. New technology may help promote greater interaction on local issues as well as encourage greater social interaction. Below, we have identified some key recommendations that are drawn from our review of the community development field today. This is not an exhaustive list, but it does represent some of the important issues that practitioners and residents need to consider in the community development process.

Build on Successes

So what is to be done? First, build on the successes of intermediary organizations, such as the Local Support Initiatives Corporations, in areas other than housing. Similar types of organizations could be established for lending programs, training programs, conservation programs, and other areas of economic development (e.g., small business incubators, food cooperatives). The Clinton administration initially planned to support hundreds of community development banks that were built on the model of the South Shore Bank in Chicago. This type of program is an ideal model of how community-based development can be promoted by the federal government and foundations. Another excellent example is community foundations. This model can be easily replicated with institutional support as well as lateral learning across communities. Many of these programs demonstrate concrete outcomes for communities. In an era when there is increased demand for accountability, these successful programs should be able to gain additional support from both the public and the private sectors.

These intermediaries, however, need to recognize the importance of community control. Intermediaries can play an important role, but they are secondary to the activities and goals of grassroots organizations. This is a delicate balance, and both community organizations and intermediaries must negotiate a relationship that will be beneficial to local residents.

Create Spaces for Meaningful Participation

Second, it may be difficult to reconstruct the sense of community that society once had, but it may be possible to create spaces for community visioning and planning. These opportunities, frequently called search conferences or visioning sessions, permit local residents to identify their common values and develop a vision of what they would like their community to look like in the future. Too often communities are simply responding to local crises and do not act in a proactive way to shape themselves. Search conferences or visioning sessions are excellent opportunities for bringing together diverse interests in the community and discussing the major issues they face. Many of these programs are currently sponsored by universities and some state governments.

This type of activity may be criticized because it lacks focus or does not address specific issues or problems. Given the loss of voluntary organizations and local institutions in most communities, new opportunities for social interaction are needed. Schools are still valuable institutions to provide opportunities for participation. Neighborhood associations also continue to be viable organizations in many settings. Promoting greater participation will help build the capacity of communities and build trust among residents.

There is a need to reconsider public participation efforts practiced by federal, state, and local governments. Most of these efforts do not provide local residents with any decision-making authority. The emphasis that the federal government places on community-based decision making is often a thinly veiled attempt to gain local support for decisions that are made elsewhere. These efforts could provide real opportunities for local residents to participate fully in the decision making that affects their community. There may be a role for CBOs to facilitate these processes in the future. Most agencies do not have adequate resources to fully engage the public and they do not have personnel who are trained in public participation methods. Community-based organizations have more access to and experience working with local residents on substantive issues.

Provide Training for CBOs

Third, we need to provide more professional development opportunities for community development practitioners. Many practitioners feel they do not have the background or training necessary to address their community's needs. Several training programs for nonprofit organizations exist, but fewer opportunities are available for training of professions in other types of CBOs. CBOs rely heavily on volunteers who have essentially no opportunity for training. Training could be provided at a regional level and linked to the intermediary organizations discussed earlier. Rather than just focus on technical information, the organizations could help develop the process skills that community organizers need.

Colleges and universities are logical institutions to provide some technical support to community-based organizations. They have faculty who can provide training on a wide variety of substantive issues, as well as process skills. Students can provide support and training for many technical issues, such as web design, computer skills, and finance and accounting.

Form Regional CBO Consortiums/Networks

Fourth, communities are no longer self-contained entities where residents live, work, and consume in the same place. In most cases, community development efforts are influenced by regional factors. Efforts to create new jobs in an urban neighborhood may be influenced by the health of the economy in the region. Planning for development can be influenced by the actions of other neighborhoods. Thus, it is important for community development practitioners to consider how their programs are influenced by and, in turn, are shaping other communities. One of the best means of accomplishing this goal is to form consortiums of neighborhood and community development organizations that can work together on issues of common interest. These consortiums will have greater influence with local governments and foundations as well.

Regional development and planning organizations are the logical entities to help organize these networks. They may be able to bring together CBOs across a metropolitan area or rural region through their existing networks and associations. They also often have access to resources that may be helpful in establishing these networks.

Improve Diversity in Local Decision Making

Political, social, and economic changes in America in the past 50 years have shaped the civic capacity of most communities. Suburbanization has contributed to the segregation of communities along class and racial lines. Political boundaries often are drawn to reduce diversity in municipalities as well. As a result, most residents do not have to confront the difficult issues in their region or incorporate different perspectives from minority groups.

Several examples might help illustrate this point. Many communities do not have to grapple with issues of affordable housing. Because of the high level of income segregation, wealthier communities can simply ignore the issue because it is someone else's problem (although they are often indirectly influencing access to affordable housing through their zoning practices). In a similar manner, suburban residents seldom have to deal directly with concentrated poverty, nor do they have to interact with the poor.

This segregation undermines the democratic process and ultimately deters civic involvement of residents in local decision making. If there are no controversial issues facing the community, there is less reason to participate. There is a tradeoff to be made here. Residents can address concerns by increasing the size of municipalities, which increases the likelihood that diverse interests will be considered in the decision-making process. Increasing the size of municipalities, however, decreases civic participation (Oliver, 2001). Oliver (2001) made the following suggestion:

> Political fragmentation and social segregation sharply limit the role of local government as a socializing agent for the conflicts that come from its internal social divisions. Through exclusionary zoning and tax policies, many suburban municipalities effectively curtail the types of conflicts that arise and the agenda of local politics. High levels of racial and economic segregation also prevent many class and racial issues from being contested within municipal boundaries and force their resolution at the state or federal level. (p. 203)

Oliver's (2001) solution is a rather radical one. He advocates reorganizing all municipalities so their populations fall between 50,000 and 100,000, which will allow them to approximate the level of diversity in a metropolitan area. This solution keeps municipalities at a scale that encourages participation and generates enough diversity to regenerate local politics. Large-scale structural change would offer new challenges, and opportunities, for civic participation.

Strengthen University-Community Partnerships

Many college campuses across the U.S. and Europe have developed formal programs to promote stronger partnerships with local communities. Many of these programs focus on service-learning, community-based research, and internships (see Case Study 15.1). The goals of these programs are to increase access to university resources and improve community relations. For students, these programs offer real-world experiences where they can apply the ideas they learn in the classroom. Universities benefit through improved partnerships with the communities that surround them. And community-based organizations potentially gain improved access to the resources available at the university.

One of the central challenges in developing strong university-community partnerships is ensuring that all partners are benefitting from the arrangement. Do students have an opportunity to develop skills and experiences that build on coursework? Many times, service-learning programs fail to integrate coursework with the service project. The community organization may benefit through the volunteer activity, but students do not see the connection with their courses. Service-learning activities need to be tightly linked to specific skills and material in coursework.

Do community organizations actually benefit from campus-community partnerships? There is some evidence suggesting that service-learning programs often fail to meet the needs of community organizations (Stoecker & Tryon, 2009). One of the perennial problems is that academic schedules often conflict with the timetables for community organizations. Some service-learning programs attempt to deal with this problem by requiring a full-year commitment by students or by encouraging students to make a large enough commitment to the activity to ensure that the needs of the organization are being met.

Campus-community programs require a major commitment by faculty to help students make these linkages. In many instances, the reward structures at universities do not support this type of engagement. Most faculty are rewarded for publications and grants, not service to local organizations. Substantial changes are needed in the reward system to encourage faculty to become more engaged in these programs.

CASE STUDY 15.1 CENTER FOR COMMUNITY ENGAGEMENT AND SERVICE-LEARNING (UNIVERSITY OF DENVER)

The University of Denver has developed a broad set of programs to enhance community engagement. Through its Public Achievement (PA) program, university students work with high school students in the city to build citizenship skills. The Community Scholars program has used several programs to create a "Guide to Denver" for homeless individuals and service providers catering to displaced and homeless persons. The Community Leadership Corps includes a program to train community organizers on social justice issues. The summer internship places students in community organizations to prepare them for public work. The university offers a wide variety of service-learning courses that are coordinated through the Center for Community Engagement and Service-Learning.

SOURCE: http://www.du.edu/engage/index.htm

Summary and Conclusions

The field of community development has undergone dramatic changes in the past 50 years. Originally conceived of as community organizing around social service delivery, the field has evolved into areas such as economic development, planning, housing, and natural resources. As a result, community development has become more professional and dependent on external resources. These changes have produced both benefits and costs for communities and practitioners. Local organizations now need to know how to "play the game" and to develop the necessary expertise. Local residents may become frustrated when dealing with external organizations, such as foundations, and the need to become more knowledgeable about the issues affecting their communities. Yet access to resources and information may ultimately improve the success of these community development efforts. The challenge is to keep the development efforts accountable to residents and based on their visions of what their community should look like in the future.

To accomplish these objectives will require political and institutional changes that enhance community capacity. Federal and state policies need to recognize, respect, and enhance community assets. Rather than seeing policies as the solutions to the problems, policies should be viewed as tools that build the capacity of communities to address their own problems. This does not mean we support a reduced role of federal and state policies in community development. Instead, we see state and federal governments playing a critical role in promoting what Clavel, Pitt, and Yin (1997) referred to as the community option. These policies not only promote decentralized authority and responsibility but also consider development of community capacity as an important element of long-term strategies to development.

At the same time, there is a need for federal and state policies to provide incentives for greater community cooperation across regions. One strategy is community-based regionalism. This approach combines neighborhood mobilization with metropolitan and regional strategies (Morin & Hanley, 2004).

Another important trend in the field of community development has been the growing fragmentation of community developers. Professional community developers tend to work increasingly in very specialized areas, such as youth, natural resources, downtown revitalization, economic development, and others.

We remain optimistic about the future of community development. Community-based development will never be able to counter the strong effects of global markets and federal government policies, but they have proven they can make important social, economic, and political contributions. In the end, it may be community development's influence on democracy that has the most lasting impact. By promoting public participation and capacity building, community development programs can potentially generate larger structural changes in global markets and federal policy.

KEY CONCEPTS

Community-based research

Community option

Intermediaries

Service-learning

University-community
   partnerships

QUESTIONS

1. What are the benefits and costs of involving external organizations in community development programs? How can external organizations support local grassroots efforts?

2. What are the primary obstacles that community-based development projects face?

3. Discuss the major dilemmas that community development organizations must manage with external organizations and institutions.

4. What are some of the major obstacles in establishing university-community partnerships to promote development?

EXERCISES

1. Talk with a local community development practitioner and ask him or her to identify the major obstacles faced in the field. What solutions would be most helpful in the practitioner's efforts to revitalize the community?

2. Talk with a city or county government official who is responsible for community development activities. Ask the official to identify specific efforts he or she is making to increase the capacity of neighborhood organizations and groups. What type of relationship does the official see as most beneficial?

3. Identify a community-based organization that has developed a partnership with a local university, such as a service-learning initiative or a community-based research project. Interview the staff from the community-based organization. How did the partnership get established and how is it maintained? Has the partnership been able to adequately meet the needs of the community? How could the university more effectively meet the needs of communities?

REFERENCES

Blakely, E. J. (1989). Theoretical approaches for a global community. In J. A. Christenson & J. W. Robinson, Jr. (Eds.), *Community development in perspective* (pp. 307–336). Ames: Iowa State University Press.

Clavel, P., Pitt, J., & Yin, J. (1997). The community option in urban policy. *Urban Affairs Review, 32*, 435–458.

Green, G. P., Hammer, R., & Tigges, L. M. (2000). Someone to count on: Social resources. In D. L. Sjoquist (Ed.), *The Atlanta paradox: Race, opportunity, and inequality in a new Southern city* (pp. 244–263). New York: Russell Sage Foundation.

Morin, R., & Hanley, J. (2004). Community economic development in a context of globalization and metropolitization: A comparison of four North American cities. *International Journal of Urban Regional Research, 28*, 369–383.

Oliver, J. E. (2001). *Democracy in suburbia.* Princeton, NJ: Princeton University Press.

Putnam, R. D. (2000). *Bowling alone: The collapse and revival of American community.* New York: Simon & Schuster.

Rubin, H. J. (2000). *Renewing hope within neighborhoods of despair: The community-based development model.* Albany: State University of New York Press.

Sassen, S. (2006). *Cities in a world economy.* Thousand Oaks, CA: Pine Forge Press.

Stoecker, R., & Tryon, E.A. (2009). *The unheard voices: Community organizations and service learning.* Philadelphia: Temple University Press.

Wilson, W. J. (1987). *The truly disadvantaged: The inner city, the underclass, and public policy.* Chicago: University of Chicago Press.

RECOMMENDED READINGS

Alperovitz, G., Dubb, S., & Howard, T. (2008). The next wave: Building university engagement for the 21st century. *The Good Society, 17,* 69–75.

Boyer, E. L. (1990). *Scholarship reconsidered: Priorities of the professoriate.* Princeton, NJ: The Carnegie Foundation for the Advancement of Teaching.

Bridger, J. C., & Alter, T. R. (2006). The engaged university, community development, and public scholarship. *Journal of Higher Education Outreach and Engagement, 11,* 163–178.

Bringle, R. G., & Hatcher, J. A. (2002). Campus-community partnerships: The terms of engagement. *Journal of Social Issues, 58,* 503–516.

Brown, M. J. (2007). *Building powerful community organizations.* Arlington, MA: Long Haul Press.

Homan, M. S. (2010). *Promoting community change: Making it happen in the real world.* Belmont, CA: Brooks/Cole.

Jacoby, B. (2003). *Building partnerships for service-learning.* San Francisco, CA: Jossey-Bass.

Kendall, J. C. (1990). *Combining service and learning: A resource book for community and public service* (Vols. 1–2). Raleigh, N.C: National Society for Internships and Experiential Education.

Peters, S. J., Jordan, N. R., Adamek, M., & Alter, T. R. (2005). *Engaging campus and community: The practice of public scholarship in the state and land-grant university system.* Dayton, OH: Kettering Foundation Press.

Robinson, J., & Green, G. P. (Eds.). (2010). *Introduction to community development: Theory, practice, & service-learning.* Thousand Oaks, CA: Sage.

Vernon, A., & Ward, K. (1999). Campus and community partnerships: Assessing impact and strengthening connections. *Michigan Journal of Community Service Learning, 6,* 30–37.

Williamson, T., Imbroscio, D., & Alperovitz, G. (2002). *Making a place for community: Local democracy in a global era.* New York: Routledge.

Index

About the Authors _____

Gary Paul Green is a Professor in the Department of Community and Environmental Sociology at the University of Wisconsin–Madison and a community development specialist at the University of Wisconsin–Extension. His research, teaching, and outreach focus on community, workforce, and economic development issues. He is author of *Finance Capital and Uneven Development* and *Workforce Development Networks in Rural Areas: Building the High Road* and a coeditor of *Amenities and Rural Development: Theory, Methods and Public Policy, Introduction to Community Development: Theory, Practice & Service-Learning,* and *Mobilizing Communities: Asset Building as a Community Development Strategy.* He has worked as an adviser on community development issues in New Zealand, South Korea, Uganda, and Ukraine.

Anna Haines is an Associate Professor in the College of Natural Resources at the University of Wisconsin–Stevens Point and the director of the Center for Land Use Education at the University of Wisconsin–Extension. She received her PhD from the University of Wisconsin–Madison in the Department of Urban and Regional Planning. Her research and teaching focus is on land use planning, urban and regional planning, and community and economic development. She has served in the U.S. Peace Corps as an urban planner in Kenya and has worked as a consultant for the World Bank.